PARA
Family Guides

MAUI
AND LANA'I

Making the Most of Your Family Vacation

by Greg & Christie Stilson

P PRIMA PUBLISHING
PO Box 1260 STI
Rocklin, CA 95677
PRIMA

In affiliation with Paradise Publications

MAUI and Lana'i, A Paradise Family Guide
Copyright © 1992 Paradise Publications, Portland, Oregon

First Edition: Dec 1984   Fourth Edition: May 1990
Second Edition: May 1986   Fifth Edition: Oct 1992
Third Edition: May 1988

Illustrations: Janora Bayot
Maps: Greg Stilson, Janora Bayot
Layout & Typesetting: Paradise Publications
Cover Design: The Dunlavey Studio
Cover Photograph: Merritt, 1988, Lahina Harbor, Maui, Hawai'i

Published By Prima Publishing, Rocklin, California

Library of Congress Catologing-in-Publication Data

Stilson, Greg H.
    Maui and Lana'i, making the most of your family vacation/Greg & Christie Stilson.
        p.   cm. -- (Paradise Family Guide)
    Includes indexes.
    ISBN 1-55958-234-0 : $12.95
    1. Maui (Hawai'i)--Guidebooks. 2. Lana'i (Hawai'i)--Guidebooks.
    3. Family recreation -- Hawai'i -- Maui -- Lana'i.
    I. Stilson, Christie. II. Title. III. Series.
    DU628.M3S76   1992
    919.69'2044--dc20   92-23769
                                                         CIP

92 93 94 95 RRD 10 9 8 7 6 5 4 3 2 1
Printed in the United States of America

WARNING-DISCLAIMER
Prima Publishing in affiliation with Paradise Publications has designed this book to provide information in regard to the subject matter covered. It is sold with the understanding that the publishers and authors are not liable for the misconception or misuse of information provided. Every effort has been made to make this book as complete and as accurate as possible. The purpose of this book is to educate. The author, Prima Publishing and Paradise Publications shall have neither liability nor responsibility to any person or entity with respect to any loss, damage, or injury caused or alleged to be caused directly or indirectly by the information contained in this book. They shall also not be liable for price changes, or for the completeness or accuracy of the contents of this book.

HOW TO ORDER
Quantity discounts are available from the publisher, Prima Publishing, PO Box 1260 STI, Rocklin, CA 95677; telephone (916) 786-0449. On your letterhead include information concerning the intended use of the books and the number of books you wish to purchase.

"Maui No Ka Oi"

(Maui is the Best)

Dedicated to Maren and Jeffrey, two terrific travelers.

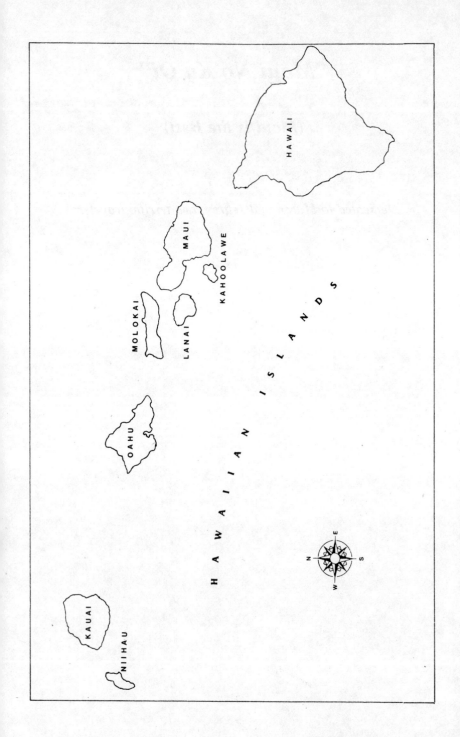

TABLE OF CONTENTS

VII. THE ISLAND OF LANA'I

VIII. RECOMMENDED READING

IX. INDEX

X. READER RESPONSE - ORDERING INFORMATION

BREADFRUIT

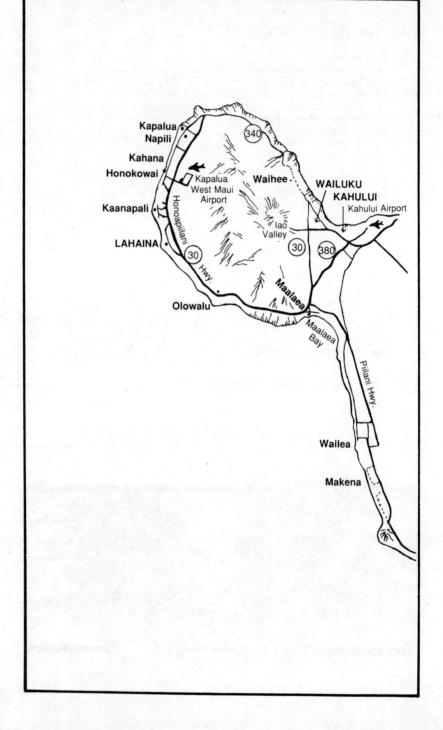

MAUI

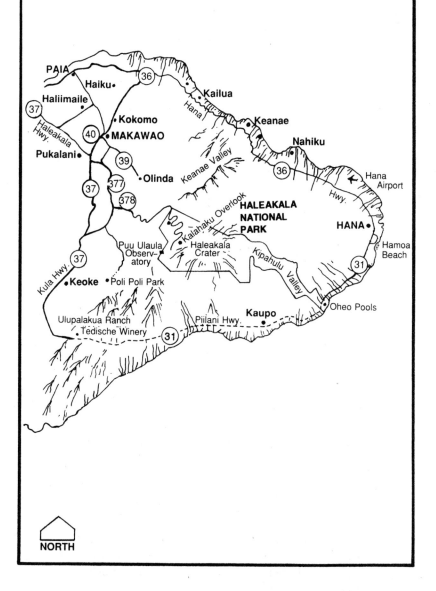

NORTH

E'Ike Mai

I luna la, i luna
Na manu o ka lewa

I lalo la, i lalo
Na pua o ka honua

I uka la, i uka
Na ulu la 'au

I kai la, i kai
Na i'a o ka moana

Ha'ina mai ka puana
A he nani ke ao ne

Behold

Above, above
all birds in air

below, below
all earth's flowers

inland, inland
all forest trees

seaward, seaward
all ocean fish

sing out and say
again the refrain

Behold this lovely world

Excerpt from *The Echo of Our Song, Chants & Poems of the Hawaiians.* Translated and Edited by Mary K. Pukui and Alfons L. Korn. Reprinted with permission from the University of Hawaii Press.

INTRODUCTION

Congratulations on choosing Maui as the site of your vacation. You will soon see why it has the deserved slogan, *Maui No Ka Oi* (Maui is the Best). The sun and lush tropicalness, and some of the finest accommodations, blend sublimely together to create a perfect holiday paradise - a place both magical and beautiful.

Our personal perspective is that of the visitor. We continue to travel frequently to the island to update our information, discover new things, rediscover old things, make wonderful new friends, and to thoroughly enjoy the tropical energy and seductive charm of Maui. While first-time visitors will delight in the diversity of activities that Maui has to offer, those making a return visit can enjoy discovering new sights and adventures on this magnificent island.

The chapters on accommodations and sights, restaurants, and beaches are conveniently divided into areas with similar characteristics and indexes are provided for each chapter. This allows a better feel for, and access to, the information on the area in which you are staying, and greater confidence in exploring other areas. Remember that except for Hana, most of the areas are only a short drive and worth a day of sightseeing, beach exploring, or a meal at a fine restaurant.

Maui can be relatively inexpensive, or extravagantly expensive, depending on your preference in lodgings, activities, and eating arrangements. Therefore, we have endeavored to give complete and detailed information covering the full range of budgets. The opinions expressed are based on our personal experiences, and while the positive is emphasized, it is your right to know, in certain cases, our bad experiences. To aid in your selections, a *BEST BET* summary is included at the beginning of the General Information Chapter. Also refer to individual chapters for additional best bets and check for ★'s which identify one of our special recommendations.

Our guide is as accurate as possible at the time of publication, however, changes seem extremely rapid for an island operating on "Maui Time." Ownerships, managements, names, and menus do change frequently, as do prices. For the latest information on the island, Paradise Publications has available *THE MAUI UPDATE*, a quarterly newsletter. We invite you to receive a complimentary issue or to order a yearly subscription; see ORDERING INFORMATION at the back of this guide.

If your itinerary includes visits to the other islands, the Paradise Family Guide Series includes *Kaua'i, A Paradise Family Guide* by Don and Bea Donohugh, and *Hawai'i: The Big Island, A Paradise Family Guide* by John Penisten. These essential travel accessories not only contain information on all the condos, hotels, restaurants, along with specific recreational activity information, but also inside information that most visitors never receive, shared by an author who knows and loves the islands. Each of these titles also feature update newsletters. See ORDERING INFORMATION.

As this guide features pen and ink sketches, a couple of recommendations for picture books might be helpful. An inexpensive, 48-page, full-color photographic book *Maui The Romantic Island*, highlights the most memorable sights and gives you a good feel for the island. It is available through Paradise Publications; see ORDERING INFORMATION. A magnificent coffee table size publication, *Maui, On My Mind*, by Rita Ariyoshi contains outstanding photographs that depict the island at its best. The book is available at local island gift and book stores and at mainland travel bookstores.

We are confident that as you explore these islands, you too will be charmed by their magic. Keep in mind the expressive words used by Mark Twain nearly 100 years ago when he visited and fell in love with Hawaii.

> *"No alien land in all the world has any deep strong charm for me but that one, no other land could so longingly and so beseechingly haunt me, sleeping and waking, through half a lifetime, as that one has done. Other things leave me, but it abides; other things change, but it remains the same. For me its balmy airs are always blowing, its summer seas flashing in the sun; the pulsing of its surfbeat is in my ear; I can see its garlanded crags, its leaping cascades, its plumy palms drowsing by the shore, its remote summits floating like islands above the cloud wrack; I can feel the spirit of its woodland solitudes, I can hear the splash of its brooks; in my nostrils still lives the breath of flowers..."*

Although the islands have changed greatly during the century since his visits, there remains much to fall in love with. The physical beauty and seductiveness of the land remains despite what may seem rampant commercialism, and the true aloha spirit does survive.

Aloha,

Greg and Christie

Greg and Christie Stilson

GENERAL INFORMATION

OUR PERSONAL BESTS

BEST FOOD SPLURGE: Sunday brunch at the Prince Court (Maui Prince Resort in Makena), champagne Sunday brunch at Raffles' (Stouffer Wailea Beach Resort), or champagne Sunday brunch at the Sound of the Falls (Westin Maui at Kaanapali). A fabulous meal at the Lodge at Koele or a sumptuous seafood buffet at the Garden Restaurant at Kapalua. Dinner at the Grand Hyatt's Grand Dining Room or Prince Court at the Maui Prince Resort in Makena.

BEST SUNSET AND COCKTAILS: West Maui - Kapalua Bay Lounge; South Maui - Maui Prince Resort, Molokini Lounge.

BEST SUNSET DINING VIEW: The Plantation House Restaurant at Kapalua.

BEST DAILY BREAKFAST BUFFET: Swan Court at the Hyatt Regency.

BEST SALAD BAR: Royal Ocean Terrace.

BEST SALADS: Gado Gado and Chinese Chicken Salad at Avalon restaurant in Lahaina.

BEST AMBIANCE: Gerard's restaurant in Lahaina.

BEST DINING VIEW: The Plantation Restaurant at Kapalua.

BEST DINNER VALUES: Early bird specials are offered at a number of island restaurants. There are generally more specials offered during the summer months and the price may also reflect the time of year. Some of the better early bird offerings are at the Marriott's Moana Terrace at Kaanapali, Chuck's or Island Fish House in Kihei, and the Orient Express in Napili.

BEST FAMILY DINING VALUES: Koho Bar and Grill in Napili and Kahului. All you can eat at Perry's Smorgy in Kihei.

BEST PIZZA: Shaka Sandwich and Pizza in Kihei.

MOST LAVISH RESTAURANT ATMOSPHERE: The Sound of the Falls at the Westin and The Grand Dining Room at the Grand Hyatt Wailea Resort.

MOST OUTRAGEOUS DESSERTS; The Lahaina Provision Company's Choco-holic Bar at the Hyatt Regency Maui and the artistic mastery served in dessert form at the Grand Hyatt Wailea's Grand Dining Room.

BEST SHOPPING: Affordable and fun - Kahului Swap Meet each Saturday, and one in Kihei too!; Touristy - Lahaina waterfront; Practical - Kaahumanu Shopping Center in Kahului; Extravagant - Any of the gift shops at the fine resorts on Maui; Odds 'n Ends - Long's Drug Store, Kahului, Lahaina and Kihei.

BEST HOTEL VALUE: Entertainment book coupon discounts with half price at several Maui hotels and condominiums. The Entertainment book is printed in most major cities around the country and contains coupons for dining and activities in that area. In addition, they carry discounts for accommodations in other regions of the U.S., including Hawai'i. The books are published and sold only once a year and are usually sold by non-profit organizations as fund-raisers. Check your phone book under Entertainment, Inc. There is also a Hawai'i edition which carries coupons for dining and attractions, largely for O'ahu, but the outer islands are included as well. For information contact Entertainment Publications at their Honolulu office at 737-3252 or write them at 4211 Waialae Ave., Honolulu, HI 96816. There is a fee for these books (about $40.)

BEST NEW DISCOUNT BOOK: In the summer of 1992, Paradise Television network inaugurated a new Destination Maui program. The concept is similar to the Entertainment book. Members receive a card and a restaurant and activity review guide and are eligible for discounts at a variety of restaurants and for a number of activities. The current issue we examined included 43 restaurants and a dozen air, land and sea activities. The $30 membership fee is good for 30 days. Discounts range from 10-20% in the edition we viewed. In their review guide they include list of the top twenty island restaurants, as rated by local residents. For more information call (808) 661-1111.

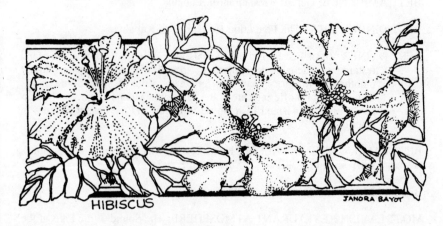

HIBISCUS

JANORA BAYOT

MOST SPECTACULAR RESORT GROUNDS: Hyatt Regency at Kaanapali and the Grand Hyatt in Wailea.

BEST MAUI GET AWAY FROM IT ALL RESORT: Hotel Hana Maui in Hana, Maui, and the Lodge at Koele or Manele Bay Resort on Lana'i.

ALOHA WEAR: The traditional tourist garb is available in greatest supply at the 17,000 square foot Hilo Hattie's factory in the new Lahaina Center at the Kaanapali end of Lahaina. The muumuu factory at the Maui Mall in Kahului has a good selection as do the stores in the Kaahumanu Shopping Center, also in Kahului. Gentlemen might be especially interested in Kula Bay. On Lahainaluna just off Front St. in Lahaina, this shop takes classic aloha shirt styles of the 1930s, 40s and 50s, updates the colors, and uses an all cotton fabric for easy care and comfort.

BEST EXCURSIONS: Most spectacular - a helicopter tour.
Most unusual - a bike trip down Haleakala.
Best adventure on foot - a personalized hike with guide Ken Schmitt.
Best sailing - a day-long snorkel and picnic to Lana'i with the congenial crew of the Trilogy.

BEST BEACHES: Beautiful and safe - Kapalua Bay and Ulua Beach. Unspoiled - Oneloa (Makena) and Mokuleia (Slaughterhouse) Beaches. For kids try Puunoa Beach near Lahaina.

BEST RECREATION AND TOURS: See beginning of Recreation & Tours Chapter for ideas!

BEST BODY SURFING: Slaughterhouse in winter (only for experienced and strong swimmers).

BEST SURFING: Honolua Bay in winter (for experienced surfers).

BEST SNORKELING: North end - Honolua Bay in summer. Kapalua area - Kapalua Bay and Namalu Bay. Kaanapali - Black Rock at the Sheraton. Olowalu at Mile Marker 14. Wailea - Ulua Beach. Makena - Ahihi Kinau Natural Reserve. Island of Lana'i - Hulopoe Beach Park. And Molokini Crater.

BEST WINDSURFING: Hookipa Beach Park (for experienced windsurfers).

BEST FLOWERS: For best flower values visit the Kahului Swap Meet (for making your own arrangements). Leis are sometimes available here also. Check Ooka's grocery in Wailuku for fresh flowers and leis.

BEST NIGHT SPOTS: Lively evenings are available at Spats at the Hyatt and the incredible new Tsunami lounge at the Grand Hyatt Wailea. J.J.'s at 505 Front Street has varying entertainment. More nightlife information is listed at the conclusion of the restaurant chapter.

BEST TAKE-HOME FOOD PRODUCTS: Paradise Fruit in the Rainbow Mall, Kihei.

BEST SEAFOOD: Maalaea Waterfront Restaurant.

MOST UNUSUAL VISUAL ADVENTURE: The Omni-Experience Theater in Lahaina.

UNUSUAL GIFT IDEAS: For the green thumb, be sure to try Dan's Green House on Prison Street in Lahaina for a Fuku-Bonsai planted on a lava rock. They are specially sprayed and sealed for either shipping or carrying home. Perfumes made from all-island products are a "scent-sational" gift from the original Waikiki Fragrance Factory at the Cannery in Lahaina. Chocolate Chips of Maui, "the ultimate munchie," is a combination of rich dark chocolate or milk chocolate and the original "Kitchen Cook'd" Maui potato chip. Try them frozen or use them as a scoop for ice cream. Check at Long's Drug store for these.

BEST T-SHIRTS: Our favorites are Crazy Shirts, more expensive than the run of the mill variety, but excellent quality and great designs. There is a crazy shirt outlet at most malls and several in Lahaina.

A huge selection of inexpensive shirsts are available at the T-Shirt Factory near the Kahului Airport. Sizes range from infants to XL adults and, with plenty to choose from, it is easy to mix and match styles and sizes. The Kihei Swap Meet and the Kahului Swap Meet have an assortment of inexpensive shirts as well.

BEST FREE STUFF: A walk through Lahaina Galleries on Friday nights which are "art night" and feature special attractions. Free snorkeling, scuba and windsurfing instruction clinic at Ocean Activities Center at Stouffers (879-9969). Free introductory scuba instruction offered poolside at many of the major resorts including Kapalua. A self-guided tour of the Grand Hyatt Wailea, Hyatt Regency Maui or Westin Maui Resorts. The Maui Zoo in Wailuku. All the public beaches with their free parking. Canoe races held at Honokaoo Park. Halloween Parade in Lahaina. Free shuttle bus between Lahaina and Whaler's Village shops.

There are a number of free Hawaiian shows and musical entertainment around Maui. The times and days change, so please check. The Hula show at the Kapalua Shops (currently Thursday mornings) is complimentary and a free hula show at Whaler's Village is performed by the Royal Lahaina Resort luau performers (currently on Tuesdays at 3 p.m., Saturdays at 12:30 p.m. and includes free poi sampling!) Lahaina's keiki (children ages 5 - 16) perform the hula on Sundays at 1 p.m. at the Lahaina Cannery. Wailea Shopping Village features Hawaiian entertainment at no charge each Tuesday at 1:30 pm. Phone 871-6230. A string trio entertain evenings in the courtyard at the Maui Prince Resort. The Makawao Parade held Fourth of July weekend. Fourth of July festivies at Kaanapali Beach. Sand Castle Contest in Kihei (November).

16

The Whaler's Village Whaling Museum at Kaanapali is free to the public. In Lahaina at the Crazy Shirts shop located on the Kaanapali end of town is a interesting display of Whaling memorabilia and a big cannon sits out behind the shop. Inside the Hobie Sports store at the Cannery shopping center is a great display of old surfing long boards.

Weekly whale lectures by Kayaker Richard Roshon are featured at the Kapalua Bay Hotel on Wednesday evenings from 6-7 pm. Roshon gains his expertise from spending much of his time paddling his one-man, 18 1/2-foot ocean kayak inter-island to live with and study the Pacific humpback whales and life at sea. Without the disturbance of an engine, Roshon is able to examine and photograph sea life in the most natural way. His presentations, entitled "The Sea & Its Species," focus on the relationship of man and the sea, with an emphasis on the humpback whale. If you're not on Maui during whale season, check with the hotel. One summer they had Roshon also giving his interesting weekly talk about Maui's many other marine animals. Thanks Kapalua! For additional information while on Maui call the hotel at 669-5656.

BEST GIFT FOR FRIENDS TRAVELING TO MAUI:

A copy of *MAUI, A PARADISE FAMILY GUIDE* and a subscription to the quarterly *MAUI UPDATE* newsletter!

HISTORY

Far beneath the warm waters of the Pacific Ocean is the Pacific Plate, which moves constantly in a northwest direction. Each Hawaiian island was formed as it passed over a hot vent in this plate. Kaua'i, the oldest of the major islands in the Hawai'i chain was formed first and has since moved away from the plume, the source of the lava, and is no longer growing. Some of the older islands even farther to the northwest have been gradually reduced to sandbars and atolls. The Big Island is the youngest in the chain and is continuing to grow. A new island called Lo'ihi (which means prolonged in time), southeast of the Big Island is growing and expected to emerge from the oceanic depths in about a million years.

It was explosions of hot lava from two volcanos that created the island of Maui. Mauna Kahalawai (Ma-ow-na Ka-HA-la-why) is the oldest, creating the westerly section with the highest point (elevation 5,788 ft.) known as Pu'u Kukui (Poo'oo koo-KOO-ee). The great Haleakala (HAH-leh-AH-kuh-LAH), now the world's largest dormant volcano, created the southeastern portion of the island. (The last eruption on Maui took place about 1789 and flowed over to the Makena area.) A valley connects these two volcanic peaks, hence the source of Maui's nick-name, "The Valley Isle."

The first Hawaiians came from the Marquesa and Society Islands in the central Pacific. (Findings suggest that their ancestors came from the western Pacific, perhaps as far as Madagascar). The Polynesians left the Marquesas about the 8th

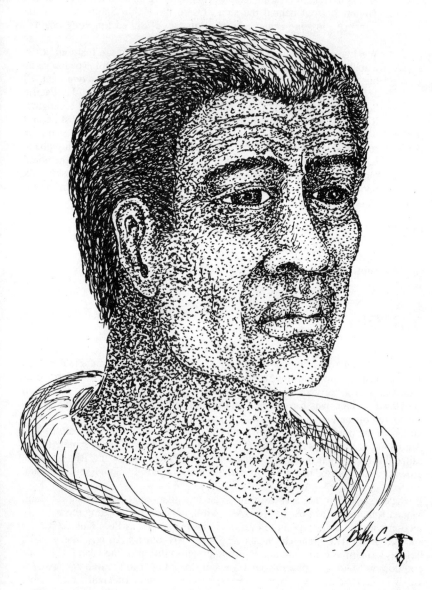

King Kamehameha the First

century and were followed by natives from the Society Islands sometime between the 11th and 14th centuries. The Hawaiian population may well have been as high as 300,000 by the 1700's, spread throughout the chain of islands. Fish and poi were diet basics, supplemented by various fruits and occasionally meat from chickens, pigs and even dogs.

Four principal gods formed the basis of their religion until the missionaries arrived. The stone foundations of Heiaus, the ancient religious temples, can still be visited on Maui.

The islands were left undisturbed by western influence until the 1778 arrival of James Cook. He first spotted and visited Kaua'i and O'ahu and is believed to have arrived at Maui on November 25 or 26, 1778. He was later killed in a brawl on the Big Island of Hawai'i.

The major islands had a history of independent rule, with open warfare at times. On Maui, Kahului and Hana were both sites of combat between the Maui islanders and the warriors from neighboring islands.

Kamehameha the First was born on the Big Island of Hawai'i about 1758. He was the nephew of Kalaiopi, who ruled the Big Island. Following the King's death, Kalaiopi's son came to power, only to be subsequently defeated by Kamehameha in 1794. The great chieftain Kahekili was Kamehameha's greatest rival. He ruled not only Maui, but Lana'i and Moloka'i, and also had kinship with the governing royalty of O'ahu and Kaua'i. King Kahekili died in 1794 leaving control of the island to his son. It was a bloody battle (more like a massacre since Kamehameha used western technology, strategy, and two English advisors) in the Iao Valley which resulted in the defeat of Kahekili's son, Kalanikupule, in 1795. Kamehameha united all the islands and made Lahaina the capital of Hawai'i in 1802. It remained the capital until the 1840's when Honolulu became the center for government affairs. Lahaina was a popular resort for Hawaiian royalty who favored the beaches in the area. Kaahumanu, the favorite wife of Kamehameha was born in Hana, Maui, and spent much of her time there. (Quiet Hana was another popular spot for vacationing royalty.)

Liholiho, the heir of Kamehameha the Great, ruled as Kamehameha II from 1819 to 1824. Liholiho was not a strong ruler so Kaahumanu proclaimed herself prime minister during his reign. She ended many of the kapus of the old religion thus creating a fortuitous vacuum which the soon to arrive missionaries would fill. These New England missionaries and their families arrived in Lahaina in the spring of 1823 at the invitation of Queen Keopuolani. They brought drastic changes to the island with the education of the natives both spiritually and scholastically. The first high school and printing press west of the Rockies was established at Lahainaluna. Built just outside of Lahaina, it now houses a museum, and is open to the public.

Liholiho and his wife were the first Hawaiian royalty to visit the United States. When their travels continued to Europe, they succumbed to the measles while in London. Liholiho was succeeded by Kauikeaouli (the youngest son of Kamehameha the Great), who ruled under the title of Kamehameha the III from 1824 to 1854.

Beginning in 1819 and continuing for nearly 40 years, whaling ships became a frequent sight, anchored in the waters off Lahaina. The whalers hunted their prey north and south of the islands, off the Japanese coast and in the Arctic. Fifty ships were sometimes anchored off Lahaina, and during the peak year of whaling, over 400 ships visited Lahaina with an additional 167 in Honolulu's harbor. Allowing 25 to 30 seamen per ship you can quickly see the enormous number of sailors who flooded the area. While missionaries brought their Christian beliefs, the whaling men lived under their own belief that there was "No God West of the Horn." This presented a tremendous conflict between the sailors and missionaries, with the islanders caught right in the middle.

After months at sea, sailors arrived in Lahaina anxious for the grog shops and native women. It was the missionaries who put the island girls in muu-muus and set up guidelines that forbid them to visit the ships in the harbor. In 1832, a coral fort was erected near the Lahaina harbor following an incident with the unhappy crew of one vessel. The story goes that a captain, disgruntled when he was detained in Lahaina for enticing "base women," ordered his crew to fire shots at the homes of some Lahaina area missionaries. Although the fort was demolished in 1854, remnants of the coral were re-excavated and a corner of the old fort reconstructed. It is located harborside by the Banyan Tree.

An interesting fact is reported in the 1846 Lahaina census. The count included 3,445 Hawaiians, 112 foreigners, 600 seamen, 155 adobe houses, 822 grass houses, 59 stone and wooden houses, as well as 528 dogs!

A combination of things brought the downfall of the whaling industry. The onset of the Civil War depleted men and ships, (one Confederate warship reportedly set 24 whaling vessels ablaze) and the growth of the petroleum industry lessened the need for whale oil. Lastly, the Arctic freezes of 1871 and 1876 resulted in many ships being crushed by the ice. Lahaina, however, continues to maintain the charm and history of those bygone whaling days.

The whaling era strengthened Hawaii's ties with the United States economically and the presence of the missionaries further strengthened this bond. The last monarch was Liliuokalani, who ruled from 1891 to 1893. Hawai'i became a territory of the United States in 1900 and achieved statehood in 1959.

Sugar cane brought by the first Hawaiians was developed into a major industry on Maui. Two sons of missionaries, Henry P. Baldwin and Samuel T. Alexander played notable roles, and their construction of a water pipeline to irrigate the arid central isthmus of Maui thus securing the future of the sugar industry and other agricultural development on the island.

Pineapple, another major agricultural industry, has played an important role in the history of Maui. Historians believe that pineapple may have originated in Brazil and was introduced to the modern world by Christopher Columbus on return from his second visit to the Americas. When it arrived in the islands is uncertain, but Don Francisco de Paula y Marin writes, in his diary on January 21, 1813 that "This day I planted pineapples and an orange tree." The first successful report of pineapple agriculture in Hawai'i is attributed to Captain James Kidwell, an English horticulturist. He brought the smooth cayenne variety of pineapple from

21

Jamaica and began successfully raising and harvesting the fruit on Oʻahu in 1886. Since the fresh fruits perished too quickly to reach the mainland, Captain Kidwell also began the first cannery, called Hawaiian Fruit and Packing Company, which operated until 1892 when it was sold to Pearl City Fruit Company. James Dole, a young Harvard graduate arrived on Oʻahu from Boston in 1899, and by 1901 had established what has today become known as the Dole Pineapple Company.

Grove Ranch and Haleakala Ranch Company both began pineapple cultivation on Maui in 1906. Baldwin Packers began as Honolua Ranch and was owned by Henry Baldwin started in 1912. The Grove Ranch hired David T. Fleming as company manager and began with several acres in Haiku which soon increased to 450 acres. W. A. Clark succeeded Fleming as Grove Ranch manager and while the acreage increased, for some unknown reason the pineapples failed. For ten years the fields were leased to Japanese growers who were successful. During these early years Haleakala Ranch Company continued to expand their acreage and to successfully produce pineapples. J. Walter Cameron arrived from Honolulu to become manager of Haleakala Ranch Company in about 1925.

In 1929 the ranch division was divided from the pineapple division and the company became Haleakala Pineapple Company. In 1932 the Haleakala Pineapple Company and Grove Ranch merged forming Maui Pineapple Company Limited and thirty years later in 1962, Baldwin Packers merged with Maui Pineapple Company to form what we know today as Maui Land and Pineapple. Maui Land and Pineapple continues to raise pineapples as well as develop land into the fine resort area known as Kapalua. The company owns 29,800 acres of land and uses 7,300 acres for company operations while employing approximately 1,800 people on a year-round or seasonal basis. While competition from abroad, particularly Thailand, has been fierce, Maui Land and Pineapple has chosen to maintain their market by supplying a quality product. Maui Land and Pineapple Company is the only 100% Hawaiian producer of canned pineapple in the world.

It was about 100 years ago that the first Macadamia Nut trees arrived from Australia. They were intended to be an ornamental tree, since they had nuts that were extremely difficult to crack. It was not until the 1950's that the development of the trees began to take a commercial course. Today, some sugarcane fields are being converted to Macadamia. It is a slow process, taking seven years for the grafted root (they do not grow from seed) to become a producing tree. However, beware of their hazards, 1/2 ounce of nuts contains 100 calories!

The Kula area of Maui has become the center for many delicious fruits and vegetables as well as the unusual Protea flower, a native of South Africa. Wineries are also making a comeback with the opening of the Tedeschi Winery a few years ago. They first began producing an unusual pineapple wine. In 1984, they introduced a champagne, and in 1985, a red table wine. Be sure to also sample the very sweet Kula onions (these are not the same as "Maui onions" that can be grown anywhere in Maui County) raised in this area and are available for shipping home. Coffee is currently being tested for commercial feasibility in Upcountry.

MAUI'S NAMES AND PLACES

Haiku (HAH-ee-KOO) abrupt break
Haleakala (HAH-leh-AH-kuh-LAH) house of the sun

Hali'imaile (HAH-LEE-'ee-MAH-ee-leh) maile vines spread
Hana (HAH-nuh) rainy land

Honoapiilani (HOH-noh-AH-PEE-'ee-LAH-nee) bays of Pi'ilani
Honolua (HOH-noh-LOO-uh) double bay

Iao (EE-AH-oh) cloud supreme
Kaanapali (KAH-AH-nuh-PAH-lee) land divided by cliffs

Kahana (Kuh-HAH-nuh) meaning unknown, of Tahitian origin
Kaho'olawe (kuh-Ho-'oh-LAH-veah) taking away by currents

Kahului (Kah-hoo-LOO-ee) winning
Kapalua (KAH-puh-LOO-uh) two borders

Kaupo (KAH-oo-POH) night landing
Ke'anae (keh-'uh-NAH-eh) the mullet

Keawakapu (Keh-AH-vuh-KAH-poo) sacred harbor
Kihei (KEE-HEH-ee) shoulder cape

Lahaina (LAH-HAH-ee-NAH) unmerciful sun
Lana'i (LAH-NAH-ee) meaning lost

Maalaea (MAH-'uh-LAH-eh-uh) area of red dirt
Makawao (mah-kah-wah-oh) forest beginning

Makena (Mah-KEH-nuh) abundance
Napili (NAH-PEE-lee) pili grass

Olowalu (oh-loh-wah-loo) many hills
Paia (PAH-EE-uh) noisy

Pukalani (poo-kah-lah-nee) sky opening
Ulupalakua (OO-loo-PAH-luh-KOO-uh) ripe breadfruit

Waianapanapa (WAH-ee-AH-NAH-puh-NAH-puh) glistening water
Wailea (WAH-ee-LEH-uh) water Lea (Lea was the canoe maker's goddess)

Wailua (WAH-ee-LOO-uh) two waters
Wailuku (WAH-ee-LOO-KOO) water of slaughter

HAWAIIAN WORDS - MEANINGS

alii (ah-lee-ee) chief
aloha (ah-loh-hah) greetings

hale (Hah-lay) house
hana (HAHA-nah) work

Heiau (heh-ee-ah-oo) temple
kai (kye) ocean

kahuna (kah-HOO-nah) teacher, priest
Kamaaina (Kah-mah-ai-nuh) native born

kane (kah-nay) man
kapu (kah-poo) keep out

keiki (kayee-kee) child
lanai (lah-nah-ee) porch or patio

lomi lomi (loh-mee-LOH-mee) to rub or massage
luau (loo-ah-oo) feast

makai (mah-kah-ee) toward the ocean
mauka (mah-oo-kah) toward the mountain

mauna (MAU-nah) mountain
mele (MAY-leh) Hawaiian song or chant

menehune (may-nay-hoo-nee) Hawaiian dwarf or elf
moana (moh-ah-nah) ocean

nani (NAH-nee) beautiful
ono (oh-no) delicious

pali (PAH-lee) cliff, precipice
paniolo (pah-nee-ou-loh) Hawaiian cowboy

pau (pow) finished
pua (POO-ah) flower

puka (POO-ka) a hole
pupus (poo-poos) appetizers

wahine (wah-hee-nay) woman
wiki wiki (wee-kee wee-kee) hurry

WHAT TO PACK

When traveling to paradise, you won't need too much. Comfortable shoes are important for all the sightseeing. Sandals are the norm for footwear. Dress is casual for dining. Many restaurants require men to wear sport shirts with collars, but only one or two require a tie. Clothes should be lightweight and easy care. Cotton and cotton blends are more comfortable for the tropical climate than polyesters. Shorts and bathing suits are the dress code here! A lightweight jacket with a hood or sweater is advisable for evenings and the occasional rain showers. The only need for warmer clothes is if your plans should include hiking or camping in Haleakala Crater. While it may start out warm and sunny, the weather can change very quickly in Upcountry. Even during the daytime, a sweater or light jacket is a good idea when touring upcountry. (The cooler weather here is evidenced on the roofs of the homes where chimney stacks can be spotted.) Tennis shoes or hiking shoes are a good idea for the rougher volcanic terrain of Haleakala or hiking elsewhere as well. Sunscreens are a must. A camera, of course, needs to be tucked in. Many visitors are taking their memories home on video tape, and VHS rental units are available around the island. Binoculars are an option and may be well used if you are traveling between December and April when the whales arrive for their winter vacation. Special needs for traveling with children are discussed in the next section. Anything that you need can probably be purchased once you arrive. Don't forget to leave some extra space in those suitcases for goodies that you will want to take back home!

TRAVELING WITH CHILDREN

Traveling with children can be an exhausting experience for parents and children alike, especially when the trip is as long as the one to Maui. There are an increasing number of direct flights to Maui out of Seattle, San Francisco, Los Angeles, Chicago and Dallas, which saves stopping over in Honolulu. These flights are very popular and fill up well in advance. Packing a child's goody bag for the long flight is a must. A few new activity books or toys that can be pulled out enroute can be sanity saving. Snacks (boxes of juice are a favorite with our children) can tide over the little ones at the airport or on the plane while awaiting your food/drink service. A thermos with a drinking spout works well and is handy for use during vacations. A change of clothes and a swim suit for the little ones can be tucked in your carry-on bag. (Suitcases have been known to be lost or delayed.) Another handy addition is a small nightlight as unfamiliar accommodations can be somewhat confusing for little ones during the bedtime hours.

Young children may have difficulty clearing their ears when landing. Many don't realize that cabins are pressurized to approximately the 6,000 foot level during flight. To help relieve the pressure of descent, have infants nurse or drink from a bottle, and older children may benefit from chewing gum. If this is a concern of yours, consult with your pediatrician about the use of a decongestant prior to descent.

CAR SEATS: By law, children under 4 must travel in child safety seats. While most rental agencies do have car seats for rent, you need to request them well in advance as they have a limited number. The one, and only, car seat we have rented had seen better days, and its design was only marginal for child safety. Prices run about $20- $25 per week or $4-$5 per day. You may wish to bring your own with you. Several styles are permitted by the airlines for use in flight, or it may be checked as a piece of baggage.

BABYSITTING: Most hotels have some form of babysitting service which runs about $8 an hour. *Babysit Services of Maui* is an independent company that will send the sitter to your hotel or condominium. Their rates are $8 per hour with a three hour minimum. $1.00 additional for each child in the family and $2.50 an hour for each additional child from another family. Contact Tony at 661-0558. We have used several of their people and found them all to be efficient and caring.

Another agency is *Kihei Keiki Babysitting Service* which charges $8 for one child, $9 for two and $1 per hour for each additional child. They provide island-wide service. Contact Carla Gandy or Kerri DeBeers 879-2522 or 669-3812. With any of these agencies, or through your hotel, at least a 24 hour notice is requested. We suggest phoning them *as soon* as you have set up your plans. At certain times of the year, with the limited number of sitters available, it can be nearly impossible to get one. If you can plan out your entire vacation babysitting needs, it might also be possible to schedule the same sitter for each occasion.

Check with your condo office as they sometimes have numbers of local sitters. As you can easily figure from the above rates, spending much time away from your children can be costly. Consider the feasibility of bringing your own sitter, it may actually be less expensive, and certainly much more convenient. This has worked well for us on numerous occasions. We have also tried contacting the Maui high schools, and even advertised in the local papers, with no success.

CRIBS: Most condos and hotels offer cribs for a rental fee that may vary from $2 to $10 per night. Companies such as Maui Rent (877-5827) charge $6 a day, $30 a week, and $42 for two weeks. For an extended stay you might consider purchasing one of the wonderful folding cribs that pack up conveniently. We tried the Fisher-Price version that weighs 20 pounds and fits into a small duffle bag. It checked easily as luggage and is very portable for car travel as well. We have heard recommendations about other types including the Snugli's carrier bed and diaper bag combo that zips easily to form a compact shoulder carryall, and the Houdini full-size playpen by Kantwent which weighs only 16 pounds and folds into a 8x8x42 inch space. Each of the units may be purchased for less than the cost of a ten-day rental fee. If you don't want to pack along a stroller, Fun Rentals (661-3053) in Lahaina rents them for $7 a day, $32 a week.

EMERGENCIES: There are several clinics around the island which take emergencies or walk-in patients. Your condominium or hotel desk can provide you with suggestions, or check the phone book. Kaiser Permanente Medical Care Facilities are located in Wailuku (243-6000) and in Lahaina (661-7400). See the section on Helpful Information for additional numbers.

BEACHES - POOLS: Among the best beaches for fairly young children are the Lahaina and Puunoa beaches in Lahaina, where the water is shallow and calm. Kapalua Bay is also well protected and has fairly gentle wave action. Remember to have children well supervised and wearing floatation devices, for even the calmest beaches can have a surprise wave. Several of the island's beaches offer lifeguards, among these are the Kamaole I, II, and III beaches in Kihei. Kamaole III Park also has large open areas and playground equipment. In the Maalaea area, follow the road down past the condominiums to the public access for the beach area. A short walk down the kiawe lined beach, to the small rock jetty with the large pipe, you'll discover a seawater pool on either side that is well protected and ideal for the younger child. Another precaution on the beach that is easily neglected is the application of a good sunscreen and reapply after swimming.

A number of complexes have small shallow pools designed with the young ones in mind. These include the Marriott, Kaanapali Alii, Sands of Kahana and the Kahana Sunset. We recommend taking a life jacket or water wings (floaties).

Packing a small inflatable pool for use on your lanai or courtyard may provide a cool and safe retreat for your little one. Typically Maui resorts and hotels DO NOT offer lifeguard services.

ENTERTAINMENT: Currently there two theaters in Kahului. The Wharf Shopping Center in Lahaina has a tri-cinema with first run movies and a $3 early admission. There are a number of video stores which rent movies and equipment. See the listing under Best Bets for other free things to do with kids!

There is a free Polynesian show at the Wailea Shopping Village on Tuesdays 1:30 - 3:30. Also, a free hula show is held at the Kapalua Shopping Center, currently on Thursday mornings, we suggest you call to verify all times and days! The Wailea Village Shopping Center has a free weekly hula show. The Whalers Village and Royal Lahaina Resort have a twice weekly hula show that is free. Held on Tuesdays at 3 p.m. and Saturdays at 12:30 p.m. at the center stage of the village. Audience participation is encouraged to learn the hula and fresh poi is available for sampling! The Napili Kai Beach Club's Sea House Restaurant has for years been involved with local performers. They currently offer a Friday evening dinner show where children perform Hawaiian songs and dances. The Napili Kai Foundation Dinner Show costs $25 for adults and $20 for children.

Maui Academy of Performing Arts, formerly the Maui Youth Theater, having lost its performance hall in Puuene, will be on the move for the next couple of years until it relocates to the Kahului Performing Arts Center, currently under construction. To find out where and when performances are scheduled, call 244-8760.

The 112 acre *Maui Tropical Plantation* has become one of the top visitor attractions in the state. We find it "touristy," but an interesting stop anyway. Surrounding the visitor center are acres planted in sugar cane, macadamia, guava, mango, banana, papaya, pineapple, passion fruit, star fruit, and coffee in addition to an array of flowers. There are also displays of the State's agricultural history throughout the grounds. Admission to the plantation market and restaurant are free, but there is a charge for the tram which takes visitors amid the working plantation.

The *Maui Zoo*, located in Kahului, has free admission and while only a limited number of animals make their home here, it's a great stop off. Bring along a picnic lunch! For more information see WHERE TO STAY - WHAT TO SEE, Wailuku & Kahului.

Theatre Theatre Maui is a new community and youth oriented theater organization in West Maui. The productions will be held at the Corner of Dickenson and Wainee St. (formerly the Muumuu Factory store) in Dickenson Square. For more information contact them at RR 1, Box 379 #401, Maalaea, HI 96793 or call Dona Wade, Lois Kelly or Derek Nakagawa at 242-0877 or 875-4449.

In the Lahaina-Kaanapali area, the colorful *Sugar Cane Train* runs a course several times a day along Honoapiilani Highway from Kaanapali to Lahaina. Transportation can be purchased alone or in combination with one of several excursions in Lahaina. After arrival in Lahaina, you will board a red, double decker bus for the short drive to the Lahaina Harbor. (See Land Tours for additional details). There is time for a stroll or a visit to the missionary homes before returning to the train for the trip home or combine your train excursion with a trip to the Omni-Theater.

The Whaling Museum at Whaler's Village Shopping Center in Kaanapali is a most informative stop. Also see the Best Bets information in the front of the book for additional suggestions! The annual Keiki Fishing Tournament is held sometime during July each year in Kaanapali. The large pond in the golf course is stocked with fish for the event.

The local bookstores offer a wealth of wonderful Hawaiian books for children. A young snorkeler might enjoy *Hawaiian Reef Fishes*, a coloring book by Lori Randall featuring forty reef fish with background information on each. The *Hawaiian Animal Life* coloring book by Sean McKeown has more than just pictures to color. The text presents interesting factual information designed to stimulate each child with a fundamental knowledge of Hawaii's birds, reptiles, amphibians and mammals. A number of colorful Hawaiian folk tales may be a perfect choice to take home for your children to enjoy, or as a gift.

SUGAR TRAIN

Many restaurants offer a Keiki (children's) menu. There are also an assortment of Burger King's and McDonald's on the island. *Paradise Fruits* at the Rainbow Mall in Kihei has terrific yogurt shakes and healthy snacks or sandwiches along with a good selection of fresh fruits and vegetables. Inexpensive hamburgers and sandwiches are also available at the Azeka's Market take-out counter.

Flashlights can turn the balmy Hawaiian evenings into adventures! One of the most friendly island residents is the Bufo (Boof-oh). In 1932 this frog was brought from Puerto Rico to assist with insect control in the cane fields. Today this large toad still emerges at night to feed or mate and seems to be easier to spot during the winter months, especially after rain showers. While they can be found around most condominiums, Kawiliki Park (the area behind the Luana Kai, Laule'a and several other condominium complexes with access from Waipulani Road off South Kihei Road) seems to be an especially popular gathering spot. We suggest you don't touch them, however. We also enjoy searching for beach crabs and the African snails which have shells that may grow to a hefty five inches.

The other Hawaiian creature that cannot go without mention is the gekko. They are finding their way into the suitcases of many an island visitor, in the form of tee-shirts, sunvisors and jewelry. This small lizard is a relative of the chameleon and grows to a length of three or four inches. They dine on roaches, termites, mosquitos, ants, moths and other pesky insects. While there are nearly 800 species of geckos found in warm climates around the world, there are only about five varieties found in Hawaii. The house gecko is the most commonly found, with tiny rows of spines that circle its tail, while the mourning gecko has a smooth, satiny skin and along the middle of its back it sports pale stripes and pairs of dark spots. The mourning gecko species is parthenogenic. That means that there are only females which produce fertile eggs, no need for a mate!

The stump-toed variety is distinguished by its thick flattened tail. The tree gecko enjoys the solitude of the forests, and the fox gecko, with a long snout and spines along its tail, prefers to hide around rocks or tree trunks. The first geckos may have reached Hawai'i with early voyagers from Polynesia, but the house gecko may have arrived as recently as the 1940s, along with military shipments to Hawaii. Geckos are most easily spotted at night when they seem to enjoy the warm lights outside your door. We have heard they each establish little territories where they live and breed so you will no doubt see them around the same area each night. They are very shy and will scurry off quickly. Sometimes you may find one living in your hotel or condo. They're friendly and beneficial animals and are said to bring good luck, so make them welcome.

If you headquarter your stay near the Papakea Resort in Honokowai, you might take an adventurous nighttime reef walk. If an evening low tide does not conflict with your children's bedtime, put on some old tennis shoes and grab a flashlight. (Flashlights that are waterproof or at least water resistant are recommended.) The reef comes right into shore at the southern end of Papakea where you can walk out onto it like a broad living sidewalk. Try and pick a night when the low tide is from 9 - 11 pm (tide information is available in the Maui News or call the recorded weather report) and when the sea is calm. Searching the shallow water will reveal sea wonders such as fish and eels that are out feeding. Some people looked at us strangely as we pursued this new recreation, but our little ones thought it an outstanding activity. Shoes are a must as the coral is very sharp. Afterwards, be sure to thoroughly clean your shoes promptly with fresh water or they will become horribly musty smelling.

Check with your resort concierge for additional youth activities. During the summer months, Christmas holidays and Easter, many of the resort hotels offer partial or full day activities for children. Rates range from free to $35 per day.

Following are a few of the programs offered by some Maui resorts. Please be sure to check with the resort to see the current status and prices for their children's programs. Be sure to call for current schedules, availability and prices.

Here are a few programs offered by Maui resorts and hotels:

The Maui Inter-Continental in Wailea offers the "Keiki's Club Gecko Program" for children age 5 and older. Cost is $35 per day and includes lunch, snacks and T-shirt. Activities include Hawaiian arts & crafts, and off-property tours. Children's menus available in restaurants. Seasonal family package plans available. Contact resort for details.

The Four Seasons Wailea features "Kids for all Seasons," a complimentary program for youths age 5 - 12 years with year round supervised activities from 9 a.m. until 5 p.m. Activities include Hawaiian songs, lei-making, hula, arts & crafts, beach games. Keiki menus available in all restaurants. Family package plans available.

Grand Hyatt Wailea Resort & Spa is one of the newest properties in Wailea with an incredible 20,000 sq. foot space devoted to their youthful guests. The day camp (9 a.m.- 4:30 p.m.) is $35 including lunch, nite camp 4 - 10 p.m. includes dinner for $25. The camp area provides a computer center, soda fountain, swimming pool, video room, arts & crafts center, movie theater for children ages 6 months to 15 years. Activities include nutrition and fitness courses. Program is available year round. Children's menus available in restaurants. Special family plan information available by contacting Hyatt Vacations at 1-800-772-0011.

Kea Lani Hotel offers "Keiki Lani" (Heavenly Kids) for youths aged 4 to 11 years of age. Offered year round Monday thru Saturday from 9 a.m. until 3 p.m. includes lunch. Activities range from face painting to sailing, picnics to hula and off-property excursions. Children's menus available in the restaurant. Family package plans available.

Stouffer Wailea Beach Resort provides "Camp Wailea" for kids 5 - 12 years. Price is $35 and includes T-shirt, admission to attractions, lunch, two snacks and craft supplies. Offered Monday, Tuesday, Thursday and Saturday from 9 a.m. - 3 p.m. Available Easter, summer thru Labor Day and Christmas vacations. Family Plans available.

Wailea Resort Company offers Junior tennis clinics and golf lessons during various weeks in the summer months, as well as tennis camps. Contact the Wailea Tennis Club or Wailea Golf Course Clubhouse for details.

Kihei Kamaole Sands offers a summer only program for kids ages 5 - 12 years. The program is 9 a.m. - noon and 1 p.m. until 3:30 p.m. Mon.-Friday. Kamp Kamaole is offered free to children of guests registered at the Aston Kamaole Sands. Each child receives a complimentary T-shirt.

Kaanapali Shores Resort announced in 1992 that it would begin a year round program for children ages 3 - 8 years. Camp Kaanapali will be offered from 9 a.m. - 2 p.m. Monday thru Friday. A $10 initial registration will include a camp T-shirt. Optional, at a nominal fee, are lunch at $6, excursions and other special activities.

Embassy Suites at Kaanapali offers a program that runs $35 a day for one child, $65 for two children ages 5 - 12 years. Hours are 8:30 - 3:30. The program currently operates Monday thru Friday year-round and takes a maximum of 15 children.

Kapalua Bay Resort offers Camp Kapalua which includes a T-shirt, excursions, arts and crafts and much more. Available seasonally.

TRAVEL TIPS FOR THE PHYSICALLY IMPAIRED

Make your travel plans well in advance and inform hotels and airlines when making your reservations that you are handicapped. Most facilities will be happy to accommodate. Bring along your medical records in the event of an emergency. It is recommended that you bring your own wheelchair and notify the airlines in advance that you will be transporting it. There are no battery rentals available on Maui. Other medical equipment rental information is listed below.

ARRIVAL AND DEPARTURE: On arrival at the Kahului airport terminal, you will find the building easily accessible for mobility impaired persons. Two parking areas are located in front of the main terminal for disabled persons. Restrooms with handicapped stalls (male and female) are also found in the main terminal. If you are unable to use the steps of the boarding ramps, you will need to be boarded with a special lift. Advance notification to the airlines is important.

TRANSPORTATION: There is no public transportation on Maui and taxi service can be spendy. The only two car rental companies providing hand controls are Avis and Hertz. See the Rental Car listing for phone numbers. They need some advance notice to install the equipment. The Maui Economic Opportunity Center operates a van with an electric lift for local residents, however, visitors can make arrangements with them by calling (808) 877-7651.

Aloha Wheelers is a new agency on Maui offering van rentals with hand controls and delivery and pick up of island visitors. Phone 1-800-456-1371 or (602) 878-3540. They are new to Maui, but have operations in Florida and the Southwestern U.S.

Hawaii Care Van Shuttle and Tour offers island-wide service in specially equipped vans. They offer airport transfers and island tours. Contact Armijo, Inc., 85 Alo Alo Place, Lahaina, HI 96761. Phone (808) 669-2300.

MEDICAL SERVICES AND EQUIPMENT: Maui Memorial Hospital is located in Wailuku (808-242-2036). There are also good clinics in all areas of the island. Check the local directory. Several agencies can assist in providing personal care attendants, companions, and nursing aides while on your visit. Maui Center for Independent Living (808-242-4966) provides personal care attendants, as does Aloha International Employment Service Health Care Registry (808-871-6373). Medical Personnel Pool (808-877-2676).

The following companies offer medical equipment rentals. Lahaina Pharmacy, Lahaina Shopping Center (808-661-3119) has wheelchairs, crutches, canes, and walkers with delivery by special arrangement. Maui Rent, 349 Hanakai, Kahului (808-877-5827) has walkers, wheelchairs, and shower chairs. It is again recommended that you contact them well in advance of your arrival.

ACCOMMODATIONS: Each of the major island hotels offer one or more handicapped rooms including bathroom entries of at least 29" to allow for wheelchairs. Due to the limited number of rooms, reservations should be made well in advance. Information on condominium accessibility is available from the Maui Commission of the Handicapped Office.

ACTIVITIES: None of the van tour companies currently offer wheelchair access. The Easter Seal Society of Hawai'i can provide information on recreational activities for the disabled traveler. Among the options are wheelchair tennis or basketball, bowling and swimming. Contact them in advance of your arrival at (808-877-4443). Wheelchair access to some of the tourist attractions may be limited. More information and phone numbers can be found in RECREATION AND TOURS.

Additional information can be obtained from the State Commission on Persons with Disabilities, c/o State Department of Health, 54 High St., Wailuku, Maui 96793 (808-243-5411), or the State Commission on Persons with Disabilities, 5 Waterfront Plaza, 500 Ala Moana Blvd. #210, Honolulu, Hawai'i 96813 (808-546-8121). Currently we are told that the publication on travel for persons with disabilities is entitled *Aloha Guide to Accessiblity, Part One and Two.* It can be picked up, free of charge, from the Maui or Honolulu office, or send $3 to cover shipping if you would like it mailed to you.

Over the Rainbow, Inc. is the only travel, tour and activity agency on Maui that specializes in assisting the disabled traveler. "Imagination is your limit" they report when it comes to the activities they offer. They can assist in making reservations at a condominium, hotel or home to fit the needs of the traveler, make airport arrangements including van accessible wheelchair lifts and arrange for personal care such as attendants, pharmacists, or interpreters. As for recreation, how about snorkeling, bowling, golf, horseback riding, luaus, tennis (disabled opponent available), tours, jet skiing, or ocean kayaking! Wedding and honeymoon arrangements, too. Write or call for their free brochure 186 Mehani Circle, Kihei, Maui, HI 96753. (808) 879-5521.

WEDDINGS - HONEYMOONS

If a Hawaiian wedding (or a renewal of vows) is in your dreams, Maui can make them all come true. While the requirements are simple, we have heard that some people have been given conflicting and confusing information. Here are a few tips, based on current requirements at time of publication, for making your wedding plans run more smoothly. The bride will need to have a rubella blood test and have the results certified by the lab and the physician. This can be done at home and brought with you although Hawai'i does not recognize blood tests from the states of Maine, Maryland, Minnesota, Missouri, Nevada, Oregon, South Carolina, Washington State, Puerto Rico, the US Virgin Islands and parts of Canada. In these states you will need to write for a Hawai'i premarital blood test form and have your state licensed laboratory use it in order for Hawai'i to recognize it. However, the test is not required if the female has had rubella immunization, has had rubella in the past, has had sterilization, is past menopause or has other reasons for inability to conceive. A health certificate attesting to one of these reasons for not having the test is required. On Maui the test can be done at the Maui Medical Group in Lahaina or the Maui Reference Lab in Wailuku. Both parties must be 18 years of age or have consent from both parents. Proof of age is required for anyone age 19 or under and evidence should be a certified copy of your birth certificate or baptismal record. A license must be purchased in person in the state of Hawaii. Call the Department of Health in Kahului (808-243-5313) for the name of a licensing agent in the area where you will be staying. The fee is currently $16. There is no waiting period once you have the license. Check with the Chamber of Commerce in Kahului for information regarding a pastor. Many island pastors are very flexible in meeting your needs, such as an outdoor location, etc.

For copies of current requirements and forms, write in advance to the State of Hawaii, Department of Health, Marriage License Section, 1250 Punchbowl St., Honolulu, Hi 96813. 808-586-4544. The Maui Visitors Bureau also can provide a copy of the requirements for weddings. Call them at 808-871-8691. Included in the information are some free public wedding locations at Hawai'i State and National Park. The Second Circuit Court is located at 2145 Main St. in Wailuku. Phone 808-244-2210.

Several independent companies are also available to handle all those important details. A basic package costs anywhere from $300 - $400. Although each company varies the package slightly, it will probably include assistance in choosing a location and getting your marriage license, a minister and a varying assortment of extras such as champagne, limited photography, cake, leis, and a bridal garter. Video taping, witnesses, or music are usually extra.

A Maui Wedding 808-879-2355, 1993 S. Kihei Rd., Suite 202, Kihei, Maui, HI 96753. Contact Jan Lyle.

A Wedding Made in Paradise 808-879-3444 or 1-800-657-7734 or FAX 808-874-1278, PO Box 986, Kihei, Maui, HI 96753. Contact Alicia Bay Laurel.

Aloha Weddings 808-244-8488 or 1-800-367-8047 ext. 540, P.O. Box 12091, Lahaina, Maui, HI 96761. Contact Cheryl Hutton.

Arthur's Limousine Service 808-871-5555, 1-800-345-4667 or FAX 808-877-3333, 296A Alamaha St., Kahului, Maui, HI 96732.

Beautiful Beginnings 808-667-7555, 505 Front St., Suite 226, Lahaina, Maui, HI 96761. Contact Sandy Moore or Sandy Barker.

John Pierre's Photographic Studio 808-667-7988, 129 Lahainaluna Rd., Lahaina, Maui, HI 96761.

Royal Hawaiian Weddings 1-800-657-7857 U.S. or 808-875-0625, P.O. Box 424, Puunene, HI 96784. Andrea Thomas and Janet Renner have been putting together the ceremonies for the most special occasions since 1977. Choose from dazzling beachside sunsets, spectacular Iao Valley, sleek yachts or remote helicopter landings. Name your dream.

Special Services and Accommodations 808-244-5811, 252A Awapuhi Place, Wailuku, Maui, HI 96793. Burt and Linda Freeland offer a range of wedding services. Their brochure itemizes each of the various charges. A non-denominational service begins at $125, higher rates for remote locations and holidays. Photograph packages $175-$375, video taping $260, wedding cakes $50 - $370.

Tropical Gardens of Maui 808-244-3085, RR 1, Box 500, Wailuku, Maui, HI 96793. They provide a garden area in the Iao Valley. They can provide tables, tents, buffet tables, chairs, and flowers. Furnish your own food.

Weddings the Maui Way 808-877-7711, 353 Hanamau St., Suite 21, Kahului, Maui, HI 96732. Contact Libby Valley or Richard Dickinson. Can provide Christian wedding services in Japanese.

Royal Hawaiian Cruises can provide a party coordinator for your wedding plans. Honeymoon packages are available from a number of Maui resorts. Prices vary depending on your length of stay and current air fares. Services might include your rental car, champagne, meals, sunset sails or sporting activities. Contact the complexes of your choosing for current honeymoon package rates.

SEASIDE CHAPEL, GRAND HYATT

Also, the social director of the major resorts can assist you with your wedding plans and there are a variety of locations on the grounds of these beautiful resorts to set the scene for your very special wedding. However, only the new Grand Hyatt Wailea has constructed a seaside wedding chapel on their grounds. The picturesque white chapel features stained-glass windows, designed by artist Yvonne Cheng, that depict a royal Hawaiian wedding. Woods of red oak, teak and cherry dominate the interior which is accented by three hand-crafted chandeliers from Murano, Italy. Outside the chapel is a flower-filled garden with brass-topped gazebos.

If you'd like to have your food catered, there are several companies on Maui. One including Clam Bake Hawaiian Style, 808-242-5095 and Tableside Chefs of Maui 808-875-0823. See restaurant section for more information.

ESPECIALLY FOR SENIORS

More and more businesses are beginning to offer special savings to seniors. RSVP book agency offers special rates for seniors who book their accommodations through them. They are listed in the Rental Agents section of our accommodations chapter. Whether it is a boating activity, an airline ticket or a condominium, be sure to ask about special senior rates. And be sure to travel with identification showing your birthdate.

A number of airlines have special discounts for seniors. Some also have a wonderful feature which provides a discount for the traveling companion, or even companions, (any age) of the senior.

Aloha Airlines, one of the two major inter-island carrier, offers those over 65 20% off regular fares, but no companion discount. *American Airlines* provides Senior Saver Coupon Books for those age 62 and over plus 10% discounts on regular tickets. NOTE! This applies to companions of any age. They also have a Deal of the Month club that might have some special rates.

America West features savings on some of their routes under their "Preferred Senior" plan and their "Senior Saver Pack." Make an inquiry! *Continental Airlines* gives 10% off for passengers 62 and over and also allows younger companions to benefit from the discount as well. Ask about their "Freedom Passport" program if you fly a lot, and their "Global Golden Traveler Passport."

Delta Air Lines gives passengers over age 62 discounts of 10% and includes the discount for their traveling companions of any age. They also offer "Young at Heart" coupons. *Hawaiian Airlines* gives 10% off all fares from the mainland (and inter-island) to those 65 and over, but no companion discounts.

Northwest Airlines provides 10% discounts for passengers over 62 and includes the discounts for flying companions of any age. Their "World Horizons Club" members also receive fare discounts in addition to discounts on hotels and rental cars. *United Air Lines* offers 10% off to those 62 and over, and to companions of any age. Their "Silver Wings Club" is for those 60 plus. Ask about the discounts Club members can receive on hotels, rental cars and travel packages.

HELPFUL INFORMATION

INFORMATION BOOTHS: Booths located at the shopping areas can provide helpful information and lots of brochures! Brochure displays are everywhere.

MAUI VISITORS BUREAU: (808-871-8691), 250 Alamaha, Suite N16, Kahului, Maui, HI 96732

TELEVISION: KBPC Cable Television, Channel 7, is designed especially with tourists in mind. Information is provided on recreation, real estate, shopping, restaurants and other points of interest.

RADIO: Our favorite, KPOA 93.5 FM plays great old and new Hawaiian music, with a daily jazz program 8 pm to 1 am Tune in and catch the local disk jockeys "talking story"! KKUA 90.7 has Hawai'i Public Radio and classical music. KDLX 94.3 has country music, KAOI on either 95.1 (or Upcountry 96.7) has contemporary rock, KMVI 98.3 has Maui's rock, KNUI 99.9 (or upcountry 99.3) light rock/Hawaiian and KLHI 101 is adult contemporary. On the AM dial KMVI is at 550 with island music, KNUI 900 oldies and Hawaiian music and KAOI 1110 with contemporary rock.

PERIODICALS: Maui Star, Art to Onions, This Week Maui, Maui Gold, Rent A Car Drive Guide, Maui Island Guide, The Kaanapali Beach Guide, The Kihei/Wailea Beach Guide, The Makena Beach Guide, Lahaina Historical Guide, Real Estate Maui Style, The Maui Island Guide, Gold Coast News and A Taste of Maui are all free publications available almost everywhere. Most of these free publications offer lots of advertising, however, they do have coupons which will give you discounts on everything from meals to sporting activities to clothing. It may save you a bit to search through these before making your purchases.

There are also a number of newspaper style publications which offer helpful and interesting information. *The Bulletin* - This is primarily a T.V. guide which is published newspaper style and available at no charge. It does have features on some local events and is very popular among the residents. You may have a little more trouble locating a copy of this one. *Maui Beach Press* - This free newspaper format weekly has informative local stories, maps, entertainment, and restaurant information. *Gold Coast News* - A free newspaper publication listing some interesting feature articles about Kihei's sunny south shores.

Lahaina News - A small weekly newspaper. It contains a television guide and local news and lots of advertisements. Fee charged. *Maui News* - This is the local Maui newspaper, published Monday thru Friday, and is available for 35 cents. A good source of local information. *The Maui Press* - A weekly paper, charge 50 cents. Lots of good local information geared more for the island resident than visitor, but if you want insight into what is happening on Maui, check this out! It does have a very complete calendar of events on the back page and Dona Early does a great review column.

SUN SAFETY: The sunshine is stronger in Hawai'i than on the mainland, so a few basic guidelines will ensure that you return home with a tan, not a burn. Use a good lotion with a sunscreen, and reapply after swimming and don't forget the lips! Moisturize after a day in the sun. Wear a hat to protect your face. Exercise self-control and stay out a limited time the first few days, remembering that a gradual tan will last longer. It is best to avoid being out between the hours of noon and three when it is the hottest. Be cautious of overcast days when it is very easy to become burned unknowingly. Don't forget that the ocean acts as a reflector and time spent in it equals time spent on the beach.

FOR YOUR PROTECTION: Do not leave valuables in your car, even in your trunk. Many rental car companies urge you to not lock your car as vandals cause extensive and expensive damage breaking the locks. Many companies also warn not to drive on certain roads (Ulupalakua to Hana and the unpaved portion of Hwy. 34) unless you are willing to accept liability for all damages.

HELPFUL PHONE NUMBERS:

> EMERGENCY: Police - Ambulance - Fire 911
> NON-EMERGENCY POLICE:
> > Lahaina 661-4441
> > Hana 248-8311
> > Wailuku 244-6400
> Poison Control 1-800-362-3585
> Helpline (suicide & crisis center) 244-7407
> Red Cross 244-0051
> Consumer Protection 243-5387
> Visitor Complaint Hotline 871-7947
> Directory Assistance:
> > Local . . . . (1) 411
> > Inter-island 1-555-1212
> > Mainland . . . . 1-(area code)-555-1212
> Customs 877-6013
> Hospital (Maui Memorial):
> > Information 242-2036
> > Emergency 242-2343
> Camping Permits:
> > State Parks 243-5354
> > County Parks 243-7389
> Maui Visitors Bureau 871-8691
> Time of Day 242-0212
> Information - County of Maui 243-7866
> Complaint Office
> > - County of Maui . . . . 243-7587 or 243-7866
> Haleakala National Park Information 572-7749
> Haleakala Park Headquarters 572-9306
> Haleakala Weather 871-5054
> Ohe'o Headquarters 248-8251
> Carthaginian 661-8527
> Weather:
> > Maui 877-5111
> > Marine (also tides, sunrises, sunsets) 877-3477
> > Recreational Area 871-5054

COSTS PER HOUR: Did you ever wonder what something was costing in relation to the time spent. This is what we came up with based on approximate lengths of time with average prices.

$300/hr	Parasail (based on $50 for a 10 min. ride)
$133.00	Maui helicopter tour (1 1/2 hour trip)
$ 75.00	Sailboat charter (usually 4 - 8 hrs.)
$ 60.00	Rolls Royce limousine service
$ 50.00	Fishing boat charter (8 hrs.)
$ 47.00	Round trip coach airfare LA to Maui (11 hrs.)
$ 43.00	Dinner for two at a top restaurant (2 hrs.)
$ 21.40	18 holes of golf at a resort course ($75 greens fee - 3 1/2 hrs of play)
$ 20.00	Horseback rides (up to $25 per hr.)
$ 17.50	Introductory scuba dive (3 hrs.)
$ 16.50	Molokini snorkel trip (4 hrs. - $66)
$ 15.00	Lana'i snorkel/sail/tour (8 hrs.)
$ 13.75	Haleakala bike trip (8 hrs. - $110)
$ 11.85	Deep sea fishing - Shared boat (8 hrs.)
$ 9.38	Hotel room ($225/day)
$ 7.00	Diver certification course (36 hrs.)
$ 6.20	Haleakala sunrise van tour (6 hrs.)
$ 6.00	Hana van tour (10 hrs.)
$ 5.00	Moderate condominium ($120/day)
$ 1.25	Rental car ($30/day)

GETTING THERE

The best air prices can generally be arranged through a reputable travel agent who can often secure air or air with car packages at good prices by volume purchasing. Prices can vary considerably, so comparison shopping is a wise idea.

The major American carriers that fly from the mainland to The Honolulu International Airport on O'ahu, Hawai'i are:

AMERICAN AIRLINES - 1-800-433-7300, Los Angeles 213-935-6045, Honolulu 808-523-9376. Direct flights to Maui from San Francisco and Los Angeles.

AMERICAN WEST AIRLINES - 1-800-247-5692; offers service to Honolulu through its major mainland hubs of Las Vegas and Phoenix with connecting service to over 60 cities nationwide.

CANADIAN AIR LINES INTERNATIONAL - Eighteen weekly flights from Vancouver to and from Honolulu. Then connecting inter-island carriers to Maui.

CONTINENTAL - 1-800-525-0280; in Honolulu, 808-836-7730. Currently flights only to Honolulu with connecting service to Maui, no direct Maui flights.

DELTA AIR LINES - 1-800-221-1212. They fly out of Atlanta, stopping in Los Angeles, then direct flights to Maui.

HAWAIIAN AIRLINES - 1-800-367-5320; in Honolulu, 808-537-5100. Based on acquaintances, friends, and our own experiences, Hawaiian Airs lower fares must be tempered by the increased risk of flight changes, delays, cancellations, and reroutings which occur all too frequently.

NORTHWEST AIRLINES - 1-800-225-2525; in Honolulu, 808-955-2255. No direct Maui flights.

TWA - 1-800-321-2000; in Honolulu, 808-241-6522.

UNITED AIRLINES - United has more flights to Hawai'i from more U.S. cities than any other airline. They have no central 800 number, but do have one for each area in the United States. See your telephone directory. Their Honolulu number is 808-547-2211. They have a number of direct flights to Maui from Los Angeles, Denver, Chicago, Philadelphia and San Francisco. On Maui, phone 242-7911.

The direct flights available on United, Delta, and American Airlines save time and energy by avoiding the otherwise necessary stopover on O'ahu. Travel agents schedule at least an hour and a half between arrival on O'ahu and departure for Maui to account for any delays, baggage transfers, and the time required to reach the inter-island terminal. If you do arrive early, check with the inter-island carrier. Very often you can get an earlier flight which will arrive on Maui in time to get your car, and maybe some groceries, before returning to pick up your luggage when it arrives on your scheduled flight. Alert! We were foiled by this terrific plan when we hopped onto an earlier flight only to find that it was a prop-jet and the flight was enough longer that we arrived at the same time we would have on our scheduled jet! Oh well!

The inter-island carriers that operate between Honolulu and Maui are:

ALOHA AIRLINES - They fly only jets - mostly 737s. 1-800-367-5250 U.S., 1-800-663-9471 Canada, 1-800-663-9396 Alberta and B.C. Their Honolulu number is 808-836-1111, on Maui 808-244-9071. This airline tends to have more respect for its schedule than the others. They fly 1,200 flights weekly with their fleet of 15 Boeing 737s. Also weekly charter service to Christmas Island and long range charters upon request.

ALOHA ISLAND AIR - (formerly Princeville) Their fleet consists of 8 - 18 passenger twin engine deHavilland Dash 6 Twin Otters (turbo-prop) aircraft. They service the Kahului, Hana and Kapalua West Maui Airports on Maui as well as all other islands. From Hawai'i the toll free number is 1-800-652-6541 or 1-800-323-3343 U.S., locally (808-877-5755). Charters available.

HAWAIIAN AIRLINES - The Honolulu number is 808-537-5100, in Maui 808-244-9111. Toll free 1-800-367-5320 U.S., 1-800-882-8811 Hawaii, 1-800-663-6296 Alberta, 1-800-663-2074 Canada B.C. They fly DC-9s, and deHavilland Dash 7s. They service both the Kahului and Kapalua West Maui Airports. A recent press release notes that Hawaiian has added two new MD-80 jet aircraft with more to be added during the summer of 1990 to "assure Hawaiian's inter-island passengers of an on-time and reliable schedule."

UNITED - (See phone numbers above) Wide body DC-10s are now making 21 weekly flights between Lihue, Kona and Maui, to and from Honolulu.

Most visitors arrive at the Kahului Airport, via direct or inter-island flights. The Kahului Airport is currently undergoing some major and much needed expansion. Improvements in the parking area are also underway. A new rental car center has already opened.

From the airport it is only a 20-30 minute drive to the Kihei-Wailea-Makena areas, but a 45 to 60 minute drive to the Kaanapali/Kapalua areas. If your destination is West Maui from O'ahu, Kaua'i, or Hawai'i, it might be more convenient to fly into the new *Kapalua West Maui Airport*. However, the airport is serviced only by a few airlines. Restrictions allow only prop-jets to land here which means the flight is lower, slower, and louder, but more scenic.

In addition to inter-island commuter flights, there are two boats which shuttle between islands. *The Expedition* (661-3756) departs from Lahaina to the island of Lana'i four times daily, cost is $50 round trip adults, $40 children. *The Maui Princess* travels between Lahaina, Maui and Kaunakakai on Moloka'i once each day. $50 adults, $25 children. The *Maui Princess* (661-8397) also offers cruise drive, golf, mule ride and overnight excursions.

One luxurious way to see the islands is aboard one of the *American Hawaii Cruises* ships, the *Independence* or *Constitution*. These comfortable 700-foot (800 passenger) ships provide adequate accommodations and friendly service during the seven day sail around the islands. They come into port at each of the major islands for a day of touring. Also available are three and four day trips combined with land accommodations, which are especially convenient for honeymooners who often arrive Sundays. Another option is to extend your stay on land following a seven day cruise. About half the crew are from Hawaii. For additional information write American Hawai'i Cruises and Land Vacations, 550 Kierny St., San Francisco, CA 94108. Phone 1-800-765-7000 from the U.S. (415) 392-9400 in San Francisco) or from Canada phone collect (415) 392-9400.

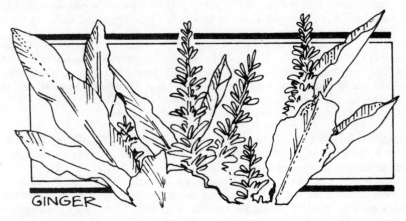

GINGER

GETTING AROUND

FROM THE AIRPORT: After arriving, there are several options. Taxi cabs, because of the distances between areas, can be very costly (i.e., $40 from Kahului to Kaanapali). There are several bus/limo services available also. Arthur's Limousine Service currently quotes a $125 plus tax fee to most resorts from the Kahului airport. The limited around-the-island public transportation that did exist has been terminated at this time with no plans to reinstate it. There are some local area shuttles. The best option may be a rental car unless your resort provides transportation.

Trans Hawaiian 1-800-533-8765 U.S., 1-800-654-2282 inter-island, 808-877-7308, provides the Kahului Airport with service to Lahaina and Kaanapali. Baggage is charged per piece. The shuttle currently departs every hour from 7 am until 6 pm. Check in by baggage claim area #3. (Call to verify current schedules and price). Service from Kahului to Kaanapali/Kapalua is $13. ***Akina Bus Service Ltd.*** offers shuttle service from the Kahului Airport to the Kihei area every hour on the hour from 8 am until 4 pm $9.50. (879-2828)

Travel in style with one of the following limousine services. Rates are $60 per hour plus tax with a minimum of 1 1/2 - 2 hours. ***Arthur's Limousine Service*** 1-800-345-4667 or 808-871-5555. Arthur's offers several limosines including a super-stretch Lincoln limousine with VCR, two TV's, 3 bars, and 2 sunroofs. Also a stretch Cadillac, Lincoln Continentals, Lincoln Town cars and a stretch van. ***Silver Cloud Limousine Service*** (669-8580), Alii Cab 808-667-7800. These companies offer a variety of limousines and Lincoln Town cars for transportation or island tours with service to the Kahului or Kapalua-West Maui airports. Also available with some companies are chauffers as drivers for your own car.

LOCAL TRANSPORTATION: If you don't choose a rental car, you will find limited public transportation. There is a free shuttle between Whalers Village and Kahana which runs between 9:30 a.m. and 10 p.m. They have pick ups at the Sands of Kahana, Hale Mahina, Papakea, Kaanapali Shores, Embassy Suites, and Maui Kai. Kapalua has a shuttle running 6:15 am to midnight between the condos and the hotel. Call the front desk to request it. Most van tours offer pickup at your hotel or condo.

RENTAL CARS AND TRUCKS: It has been said that Maui has more rental cars per mile of road than anywhere in the nation. This is not surprising when you realize that Maui has virtually no mass transit, a population of 85,000 (1990 figures for Island of Maui), and over two million visitors per year. Recently, shuttles have been initiated to help eleviate this problem. A choice of more than 30 car rental companies offer luxury or economy and new or used models. Some are local island operators, others are nation-wide chains, but all are very competitive. The rates may vary between high and low season and the best values are during price wars, or super summer discount specials.

Given the status of public transportation on Maui, a rental car is still the best bet and sometimes only way to get around the island and, for your dollar, a very good buy. Prices for compacts range from $13.95 to $20.95/day, mid-size from $20.95 to $34.95, vans from $45.95, and jeeps from $30. The least expensive choice is a late-model compact, with stick shift and no air conditioning. Often these cars are only 2 - 3 years old and in very good condition. Also available from specialty car rental agencies are a variety of luxury cars. A Porsche or Mercedes will run $200 plus per day. Currently there are no companies which rent camping equipment. Vans are available from a number of agencies, but camping in them is not allowed.

Many of the rental companies have booths near the main terminal building at the Kahului Airport. There is also a large courtesy phone board in the main terminal (not at the United terminal). This free phone is for those rental agencies not having an airport booth, or for regular shuttle service, so that you can call for a pick up. A pay phone is available in the United terminal. A few agencies will take your flight information when your car reservation is made and will meet you and your luggage at the airport with your car.

The policies of all the rental car agencies are basically the same. Most require a minimum age of 21 to 25 and a maximum age of 70. All feature unlimited mileage with you buying the gas ($1.50 - $1.60 per gallon). Be sure to fill up before you return your car, the rental companies charge about $2.25 per gallon to do it for you. A few require a deposit or major credit card to hold your reservation. Insurance is an option you may wish, which can run an additional $5 - $10 a day. A few agencies will require insurance for those under age 25. Add to the rental price a 4% sales tax. Most of the car rental agencies strongly encourage you to take the additional insurance coverage. Hawai'i is a no-fault state and without the insurance, you are required to take care of all the damages before leaving the island. We suggest you check with your own insurance company before you leave to verify exactly what your policy covers.

A few of Maui's roadways are rough and rugged. The rental agencies recommend that cars not traverse these areas (shown on the map they distribute) and that if these roads are attempted, you are responsible for any damage.

As a starting point, we would suggest you call Tropical Rent-A-Car as one possible choice. They have competitive prices and we have always been pleased with their service.

ORCHIDS

42

RENTAL CAR LISTING:

ADVENTURES
RENT A JEEP
877-6626

ALAMO
RENT A CAR
1-800-327-9633
Kahului 877-3466
Lahaina 661-7187

ANDRES
RENT A CAR
Kahului 877-5378

ARTHUR'S
LIMOUSINE SERVICE
1-800-345-4667
Lahaina 661-5466

ATLAS U DRIVE
1-800-367-5238
Kahului 871-2860

AVIS
1-800-331-1212
Kahului 871-7575
Kaanapali 661-4588
Kihei 879-1905

BUDGET
1-800-527-0700
Kaanapali 661-8721
Wailea 879-9150
Kahului 871-8811

CHARTON U DRIVE
Kahului 877-7836

DOLLAR
RENT A CAR
1-800-367-7006
Kahului 877-2731
Kaanapali 667-2651
Interisland
1-800-342-7398

HERTZ
1-800-654-8200
Kahului 877-5167
Interisland
1-800-654-3131
Kaanapali 661-3195

ISLAND AUTO
LEASING
Kahului 877-0031

KIHEI RENT A CAR
Kihei 879-7257

KLUNKERS
USED CARS
Kahului 877-3197

MAUI RENT A JEEP
Kahului 877-6626

NATIONAL
1-800-227-7368
Kahului 871-8851
Kaanapali 667-9737

RAINBOW
Lahaina 661-8734

SEARS RENT A CAR
contracts with Budget
1-800-451-3600
Kahului 877-0916

SUNSHINE
RENT A CAR
1-800-367-5140
Kahului 871-6222

SURF RENT A CAR
(flat beds, pick-ups)
Wailuku 244-5544

THRIFTY
1-800-367-2277
Kahului 871-7596
Kaanapali 667-9541
Interisland
1-800-342-1540

TROPICAL
RENT A CAR
Kahului 877-0002
Kaanapali 661-0061
Interisland & mainland
US 1-800-678-6000

UNITED TRUCK
RENTAL
Kahului 871-9458

VIP CAR RENTAL
1-800-367-6080
Kahului 877-2054

WORD OF MOUTH
RENT A CAR
Kahului 877-2436

GROCERY SHOPPING

Grocery store prices may be one of the biggest surprises of your trip. While there are some locally grown foods and dairies, most of the products must be flown or shipped to the islands. The local folks can shop the advertisements and use the coupons, but it isn't so easy when traveling. To give you an idea of what to expect at the supermarket, here are some grocery store prices. Bread $1.65 and up, bananas .99 /lb., chicken $1.29 /lb., hamburger $1.49 - $2.99 /lb., mayonnaise $1.69 - 2.15, Starkist Tuna $1.33, disposable diapers 12-24 count size $4.99 - $6.99, 32 oz. ketchup $2.49, 2% milk $1.72 half gallon.

The three major grocery stores in Kahului are Foodland, Safeway (accepts Visa or Mastercard), and Star Market. In Lahaina you can choose between Foodland or Nagasako at the Lahaina Shopping Center, or the Safeway at the Cannery Shopping Center. In Kihei the major markets are Foodland, Azeka's, and Star Market. These larger stores offer the same variety as your hometown store and the prices are better than at the small grocery outlets. In Hana there is Hasegawa's and the Hana Ranch Store. Long's Drug Stores carry some food items.

A few of the more unusual or specialty markets include: *Paradise Fruits* ★, located at the Rainbow Mall in Kihei (open 24 hours), offers a variety of fresh fruits and vegetables which are also available for shipment home. *Azeka's Market* (879-0611) at Azeka's Place in Kihei can provide you with those world famous Azeka (Kalbi) ribs for cooking. *The Farmers' Market* is a group of people who bring produce down from the Kula area. They set up roadside shopping, and you can't find it fresher. Their locations seem to change each time we visit. Just look for the green sandwich board signs that are set up roadside.

Take Home Maui (661-8067) is located just off Front Street in Lahaina and offers a selection of fruits and vegetables for shipment home. *Fresh Island Fish* (244-9633 or 242-6532) is located near the dock at Maalaea Harbor, open Mon.-Sat. 10 - 5. They offer a wonderful selection of fresh island fish and a cafe, open 10 am - 8 am (see restaurants). The *Nagasako Fish Market* on Lower Main Street in Wailuku. They have what may be the most diverse selection of fresh seafood from reef fish to live clams and crabs.

Local grocery shopping is a little more adventuresome. The largest local stores are in Wailuku and Kahului. In addition to the regular food staples they often have deli sections which feature local favorites and plate lunches. *Takamiya's* at 359 N. Market St. in Wailuku has a huge deli section with perhaps more than 50 cooked foods and salads as well as very fresh meats. *Ah Fook's* at the older Kahului Mall has a smaller deli section with plate lunches running about $3. *Ooka's* is the largest of the three. The packed parking lot and crowded aisles prove its popularity and low prices. Besides the usual sundry items, they have a fascinating and unusual array of foods. How about a tasty fresh pig ear ($1.29 lb.), pig blood ($1.99 lb.), tripe ($3.99), calf hoof or tongue too. In the seafood isle check out the Opihi ($25 lb.), cuttlefish ($13 lb.), Tobikko (Flying Fish Roe, $14.29 lb.), lomi salmon ($3.78 lb.) and whole or filets of fresh island fish like whole catfish ($3.99 lb.) or Onaga ($5.95 lb. is a great price!).

ANNUAL MAUI EVENTS

JANUARY/FEBRUARY
- Chinese New Year celebration at Ming Yuen Restaurant. A gourmet 10 course dinner is offered on several different evenings. 871-7787

FEBRUARY
- Marine/Art Expo runs two months at the Stouffer Resort in Wailea
- Chinese New Year champagne brunch at the Maui Inter-Continental Resort

MARCH
- Annual Maui Marathon from Wailuku to Lahaina, sponsored by the Valley Isle Road Runners
- Annual Kukini Run along the Kahakuloa Valley Trail
- The 26th is Prince Kuhio Day, a state holiday.
- Held February or March, the LPGA Women's Kemper Open at the Kaanapali Golf Course

APRIL
- The Na Mele O Maui Festival celebrates Hawai'i's music heritage throughout the Kaanapali Resort
- David Malo Day at Lahainaluna High School includes Hawaiian entertainment

MAY
- May Lei Day celebration in Wailea (check with the Inter-Continental Hotel for their events)
- Seabury Hall in Makawao sponsors their annual craft fair the Saturday prior to Mother's Day
- Statewide Hula Competition and Annual Lei Festival
- Annual Hard Rock Cafe World Cup of Windsurfing at Hookipa Beach Park

JUNE
- Kapalua Music Festival - a week of Hawaiian and classical music
- Obon Season (late June through August) - Bon Odori festivals are held at the many Buddhist temples around the island. They are announced in the local newspapers and the public is invited.
- King Kamehameha Day Celebration
- Maui Upcountry Fair
- Art Night Celebration & Art in the Park. A Friday/Saturday event that begins with a Friday eve street party with food, entertainment and art followed by juried arts and crafts fair under the Banyan Tree on Saturday

JULY
- Annual 4th of July Rodeo & Parade in Makawao
- Canoe races at Hookipa State Park
- Maui Jaycees Carnival at Kahului Fairground
- Annual Sausa Cup races in Lahaina, sponsored by the Lahaina Yacht Club
- Victoria to Maui Yacht Race

GENERAL INFORMATION
Annual Events

- Kapalua Wine Symposium and Chefs Festival. A great one day event featuring goodies from the best chefs in the best restaurants from all the islands.
- Keiki Fishing Tournament at Kaanapali
- Maui Onion Festival at Whaler's Village Shopping Center

AUGUST
- Run to the Sun Marathon, a grueling trek from sea level up to the 10,000 foot level of Haleakala Crater
- The 21st is Admissions Day, a state holiday

SEPTEMBER
- Maui County Rodeo in Makawao
- Aloha Week Festival
- Labor Day Fishing Tournament
- Wailea Speed Crossing, a windsurfing regatta across the seven mile stretch of Pacific to Molokini and back. Sponsored by the Maui Inter-Continental
- "Taste of Lahaina" Food Festival at Lahaina Center. Proceeds from the festival will be donated to the Make-A-Wish Foundation to grant wishes for Maui children with terminal or life threatening illnesses.

OCTOBER
- Maui County Fair at the Kahului Fairgrounds
- Open Pro-Am Golf Championship
- Parade and Halloween festivities in Lahaina
- Lahaina Coolers Historic Fun Run. A 5K run/walk with Lahaina's history with entertainment and re-enactments at each landmark. In connection with the Aloha Festival

NOVEMBER
- Kapalua International Championship of Golf
- Queen Kaahumanu Festival at the Maui High School
- Sand Castle contest, check for current beach location in Kihei, usually held Thanksgiving weekend
- Thanksgiving weekend Santa arrives at Kaahumanu Mall
- Thanksgiving, La Hoomaikai, luau celebration at Maui Inter-Continental

DECEMBER
- Kapalua/Betsy Nagelsen Pro-Am Tennis Invitational
- Christmas House at Hui Noeau, near Makawao, is a non-profit organization featuring pottery, wreaths, and other artwork.
- Santa arrives by canoe at the Maui Inter-Continental Resort in Wailea

For the exact dates of many of these events, write to the Hawai'i Visitors Bureau, 2270 Kalakaua Avenue #801, Honolulu, Hawai'i 96815, and request the Hawai'i Special Events Calendar. The calendar also gives non-annual information and the contact person for each event. Check the local papers for dates of additional events.

WEATHER

When thinking of Hawaii, and especially Maui, one visualizes bright sunny days cooled by refreshing trade winds, and this is the weather at least 300 days a year. What about the other 65 days? Most aren't really bad - just not perfect. Although there are only two seasons, summer and winter, temperatures remain quite constant. Following are the average daily highs and lows for each month and the general weather conditions.

January	80/64	May	84/67	September	87/70
Feb.	79/64	June	86/69	October	86/69
March	80/64	July	86/70	November	83/68
April	82/66	Aug.	87/71	December	80/66

Winter: Mid October thru April, 70 - 80 degree days, 60 - 70 degree nights. Tradewinds are more erratic, vigorous to none. Kona winds are more frequent causing wide-spread cloudiness, rain showers, mugginess and even an occasional thunderstorm. 11 hours of daylight.

Summer: May thru mid October, 80 degree days, 70 - 80 degree nights. Tradewinds are more consistent keeping the temperatures tolerable, however, when the trades stop, the weather becomes hot and sticky. Kona winds are less frequent. 13 hours of daylight.

Summer type wear is suitable all year round. However, a warm sweater or lightweight jacket is a good idea for evenings and trips such as to Haleakala.

If you are interested in the types of weather you may encounter, or are confused by some of the terms you hear, read on. For further reference consult *Weather in Hawaiian Waters*, by Paul Haraguchi, 99 pages, available at island bookstores.

POINSETTIA

TRADE WINDS: Trade winds are an almost constant wind blowing from the northeast through the east and are caused by the Pacific anti-cyclone, a high pressure area. This high pressure area is well developed and remains semi-stationary in the summer causing the trades to remain steady over 90% of the time. Interruptions are much more frequent in the winter when they blow only 40 to 60% of the time. The major resort areas of South and West Maui are situated in the lee of the West Maui Mountains and Haleakala respectively. Here they are sheltered from the trades and the tremendous amount of rain (400 plus inches per year) they bring to the mountains.

KONA WINDS: The Kona Wind is a stormy, rain-bearing wind blowing from the southwest, or basically from the opposite direction of the trades. It brings high and rough surf to the resort side of the island - great for surfing and boogie-boarding, bad for snorkeling. These conditions are caused by low pressure areas northwest of the islands. Kona winds strong enough to cause property damage have occurred only twice since 1970. Lighter nondamaging Kona winds are much more common, occurring usually two to five times almost every winter (November thru April).

KONA WEATHER: Windless, hot and humid weather is referred to as Kona weather. The interruption of the normal trade wind pattern brings this on. The trades are replaced by light and variable winds and, although this may occur any time of the year, it is most noticeable during the summer when the weather is generally hotter and more humid, with fewer localized breezes.

KONA LOW: A Kona low is a slow-moving, meandering, extensive low pressure area which forms near the islands. This causes continuous rain with thunderstorms over an extensive area and lasts for several days. November through May is the most usual time for these to occur.

HURRICANES: Hawai'i is not free of hurricanes. However, most of the threatening tropical cyclones have weakened before reaching the islands, or have passed harmlessly to the west. Their effects are usually minimal causing only high surf on the eastern and southern shores of some of the islands. At least 21 hurricanes or tropical storms have passed within 300 miles of the islands in the last 33 years, but most did little or no damage. Only Hurricane Dot of 1959 and Hurricane Iwa of 1982 caused extensive damage. In both cases, the island of Kaua'i was hit hardest, with lesser damage to southeast O'ahu and very little damage to Maui.

TSUNAMI: A tsunami is an ocean wave produced by an undersea earthquake, volcanic eruption, or land slide. Tsunamis are usually generated along the coasts of South America, the Aleutian Islands, the Kamchatka Peninsula, or Japan and travel through the ocean at 400 to 500 miles an hour. It takes at least 4 1/2 hours for a tsunami to reach the Hawaiian Islands. A 24-hour Tsunami Warning System has been established in Hawai'i since 1946. When the possibility exists of a tsunami reaching Hawaiian waters, the public will be informed by the sound of the attention alert signal sirens. This particular signal is a steady one minute siren, followed by one minute of silence, repeating as long as necessary. Immediately turn on a TV or radio; all stations will carry CIV-Alert emergency information and instructions with the arrival time of the first waves. Do not take chances -

false alarms are not issued. Move quickly out of low lying coastal areas that are subject to possible inundation.

The warning sirens are tested throughout the state on the first working Monday of every month at 11 am. The test lasts only a few minutes and CIV-Alert announces on all stations that the test is underway. Since 1813, there have been 112 tsunamis observed in Hawai'i with only 16 causing significant damage.

Tsunamis may also be generated by local volcanic earthquakes. In the last 100 years there have been only six, with the last one November 29, 1975, affecting the southeast coast of the island of Hawaii. The Hawaiian Civil Defense has placed earthquake sensors on all the islands and, if a violent local earthquake occurs, an urgent tsunami warning will be broadcast and the tsunami sirens will sound. A locally generated tsunami will reach the other islands very quickly, therefore, there may not be time for an attention alert signal to sound. Any violent earthquake that causes you to fall or hold onto something to prevent falling is an urgent warning, and you should immediately evacuate beaches and coastal low-lying areas.

For additional information on warnings and procedures in the event of a hurricane, tsunami, earthquake or flash flood, read the civil defense section located in the forward section of the Maui phone book.

TIDES: The average tidal range is about two feet. Tide tables are available daily in the Maui News or by calling the marine weather number, 877-3477.

SUNRISE AND SUNSET: In Hawaii, day length and the altitude of the noon sun above the horizon do not vary as much throughout the year as at the temperate regions because of the island's low latitude within the sub-tropics. The longest day is 13 hours 26 minutes (sunrise 5:53 am, sunset 7:18 pm) at the end of June, and the shortest day is 10 hours 50 minutes (sunrise 7:09 am and sunset 6:01 pm at the end of December). Daylight for outdoor activities without artificial lighting lasts about 45 minutes past sunset.

LAYSAN ALBATROSS

WHERE TO STAY
WHAT TO SEE

INTRODUCTION

Maui has more than 16,000 hotel rooms and condominium units in vacation rental programs, with the bulk of the accommodations located in two areas. These are West Maui, a 10-mile stretch between Lahaina and Kapalua, and the South shore of East Maui, which is also about ten miles of coastline between Maalaea and Makena. On the northern side, there are four properties near the Kahului Airport, several complexes in Hana and one in upcountry. This chapter contains a list of essentially all of the condominiums that are in rental programs, as well as the island's hotels. Bed and Breakfast homes are sprinkled around the island.

HOW TO USE THIS CHAPTER: For ease in locating information, the properties are first indexed alphabetically following this introduction. In both South and West Maui, the condominiums have been divided into groups that are geographically distinct and are laid out (sequentially) as you would approach them arriving from the Kahului area. These areas also seem to offer similar price ranges, building style, and beachfronts. At the beginning of each section is a description of the area, sights to see, shopping information, best bets and a sequential listing of the complexes. For each complex, we have listed the local address and/or P.O. Box and the local and toll-free phone numbers. Often times the management at the property does reservations, other times not.

In many cases there are a variety of rental agents handling units in addition to the on-site management and we have listed an assortment of these. We suggest that when you determine which condo you are interested in that you call all of the agents. One agent, ***Gentle Island Holidays***, 1-800-544-6050 books many more properties than we had room to list. Be aware that while one agent may tell you they have no vacancy, another will have several. The prices we have listed are generally the lowest available (although some agents may offer lower rates but with the reduction of certain services such as maid service on check in only - that means your room is clean when you arrive - rather than daily maid service). At the end of the accommodations chapter is an alphabetical listing of rental agents and the properties they handle. Prices can vary, sometimes greatly, from one agent to another, so we suggest again that you contact them all.

Prices are listed to aid your selection and, while these were the most current available at press time, they are subject to change without notice. As island vacationers ourselves, we found it important to include this feature rather than just giving you broad categories such as budget or expensive. After all, one person's "expensive" may be "budget" to someone else!

For the sake of space, we have made use of several abbreviations. The size of the condominiums are identified as studio (S BR), one bedroom (1 BR), two bedroom (2 BR) and three bedroom (3 BR). The numbers in parenthesis refers to the number of people that can occupy the unit for the price listed and that there are enough beds for a maximum number of people to occupy this unit. The description will tell you how much it will be for additional persons over two, i.e. each additional person $6/night. Some facilities consider an infant as an extra person, others will allow children free up to a specified age. The abbreviations o.f., g.v., and o.v. refer to oceanfront, gardenview and oceanview units. The prices are listed with a slash dividing them. The first price listed is the high season rate, the second price is the low season rate. A few have a flat yearly rate so there will be only be a single price.

All listings are condominiums unless specified as a (Hotel). Condos are abundant, and the prices and facilities they offer can be quite varied. We have tried to indicate our own personal preferences by the use of a ★. We felt these were the best buys or special in some way. However, it is impossible for us to view all the units within a complex, and since condominiums are privately owned, each unit can vary in its furnishings and its condition.

WHERE TO STAY: As for choosing the area of the island in which to stay, we offer these suggestions. The Lahaina and Kaanapali areas offer the visitor the hub of the island's activities, but accommodations are a little more costly. The beaches are especially good at Kaanapali. The values and choice of condos are more extensive a little beyond Kaanapali in Honokowai, Kahana (Lower Honoapiilani Hwy. area) and further at Napili. However, there are fewer restaurants here and slightly cooler temperatures. Some of the condominiums in this area, while very adequate, may be a little overdue for redecorating. While many complexes are on nice beaches, many are also on rocky shores. Kapalua offers high class and high price condominium and hotel accommodations. Maalaea and Kihei are a half-hour drive from Lahaina and offer some attractive condo units at excellent prices and, although few are located on a beach, there are plenty of easily accessible public beach parks. Many Maui vacationers feel that Kihei offers better weather in the winter months. There are plenty of restaurants here and an even broader selection by driving the short distance to Wailuku. The Wailea and Makena areas are just beyond Kihei and are beautifully developed resort areas. Wailea is experiencing a recent boom in development with a number of plush resorts and condominiums in varying stages of construction. The beaches in this area are excellent for a variety of water activities, however, this area is significantly more expensive than the neighboring Kihei area. We suggest reading the introductory section to each area for additional information.

HOW TO SAVE MONEY: Maui has two "price" seasons. High or "in" season and low or "off" season. Low season is generally considered to be April 15 to December 1, and the rates are discounted at some places as much as 30%. Different resorts and condominiums may vary these dates by as much as two weeks and a few resorts are going to a flat, year round rate. Ironically, some of the best weather is during the fall when temperatures are cooler than summer and there is less rain than the spring months. (See GENERAL INFORMATION - weather for year round temperatures).

For longer than one week, a condo unit with a kitchen can result in significant savings on your food bill. While this will give you more space than a hotel room and at a lower price, you may give up some resort amenities (shops, restaurants, maid service, etc.) There are several large chain grocery stores around the island with fairly competitive prices, although most things at the store will run slightly higher than on the mainland. (See GENERAL INFORMATION - Shopping.)

Money can be saved by using the following tips when choosing a place to settle. First, it is less expensive to stay during the off or low season. Second, there are some areas that are much less expensive. Although Kahului has some motel units, we can't recommend this area as a place to headquarter your stay. The weather is wetter in winter, hotter in summer, generally windier than the other side of the island, and there are few good beaches. Two recently renovated old hotels in Wailuku now offer serviceable, basic and affordable accommodations for the budget minded, and they should especially appeal to the windsurfing community with nearby Hookipa Beach. There are some good deals in the Maalaea and Kihei areas, and the northern area above Lahaina has some older complexes that are reasonably good values. Third, some condo type units without kitchens are less expensive, but you must weigh the cost savings versus doing your own cooking. Fourth, there are some pleasant condo units either across the road from the beach or on a rocky, less attractive beach. This can represent a tremendous savings, and there are always good beaches a short walk or drive away. Fifth, hotel rooms or condos with garden or mountain views are less costly than oceanview or ocean-front rooms. We find the mountain view, especially in Kaanapali, to be, in fact, superior. Not only are the mountains gorgeous, but your room does not get the full day sunlight and stays cooler.

There is a growing trend to offer only limited maid service in the condominiums, perhaps only on check out or once a week. Additional maid service is usually available for an extra charge. Rooms without telephones or color televisions usually have lower prices, and a few condominiums do not have pools. A few words of caution, condominium units within one complex can differ greatly and, if a phone is important to you, ask! More complexes are adding phone service to their rooms, however, there are still some that have only a courtesy phone or a pay phone at the office. Some may also add 50 - 75 cents per in-room local call, others have no extra charge. Some units have washers and dryers in the rooms, while others do not.

Travel agents will be able to book your stay in the Maui hotels and also in most condominiums. If you prefer to make your own reservation, we have listed the various contacts for each condominium and endeavored to quote the best price generally available. Rates vary between rental agents, so check all those listed for a particular condominium. We have indicated toll free 800 numbers for the U.S. when available. For additional Canadian toll free numbers check the rental agent list at the end of this chapter. Look for an 808 area code preceding the non-toll free numbers. You might also check the classified ads in your local newspaper for owners offering their units, which may be a better bargain.

Although prices can jump (and have done so in recent years), most go up only 5-10% per year. Prices listed do not include sales tax.

GENERAL POLICIES: Condominium complexes require a deposit, usually equivalent to one or two nights stay, to secure your reservation and insure your room rate from price increases. Some charge higher deposits during winter or over Christmas holidays. Generally a 30 day notice of cancellation is needed to receive a full refund. Most require payment in full either 30 days prior to arrival or upon arrival, and many do not accept credit cards. The usual minimum condo stay is 3 nights with some requiring one week in winter. Christmas holidays may have steeper restrictions with minimum stays as long as two weeks, payments 90 days in advance and heavy cancellation penalties. It is not uncommon to book as much as two years in advance for the Christmas season. ALL CONDOMINIUMS HAVE KITCHENS, T.V.'S. AND POOLS UNLESS OTHERWISE SPECIFIED.

Monthly and oftentimes weekly discounts are available. Room rates quoted are generally for two. Additional persons run $8 - $15 per night per person with the exception of the high class resorts and hotels where it may run as much as $25 to $35 extra. Many complexes can arrange for crib rentals. (See GENERAL INFORMATION - Traveling with Children). We have tried to give the lowest rates generally available, which might not be through the hotel or condo office, so check with the offices as well as the rental agents. When contacting condominium complexes by mail, be sure to address your correspondence to the attention of the manager. The managers of several complexes do not handle any reservations and we have indicated to whom you should address reservation requests. If two addresses are given, use the P.O. Box or R.R. rather than street address.

BED AND BREAKFAST

An alternative to condominiums and hotels are the Bed and Breakfast organizations. They offer homes around the island, and some very reasonable rates. *Bed & Breakfast Hawaii* is among the best known. To become a member and receive their directory, which also includes the other islands, contact: Bed and Breakfast Hawaii, Directory of Homes, Box 449, Kapaa, Hawaii 96746. Another organization, *Bed and Breakfast Maui Style* can be reached at P.O. Box 886, Kihei, Maui 96753 (808-879-7865) or (808-879-2352). *Go Native Hawaii* also features bed and breakfast vacations, contact them at P.O. Box 13115, Lansing, MI 48901, phone (517-349-9598).

Here are just a few facilities on Maui:

Ahinahina Farm Bed and Breakfast, 120 Ahinahina Pl., Kula, Maui, HI 96790. (808) 878-6096 or 1-800-241-MAUI. Located in peaceful upcountry Maui overlooking the ocean, and West Maui mountains. A private setting, located minutes from Haleakala National Park and a short drive to North shore beaches. Rates $75-$90. Non-smoking accommodations, no children under age 12.

Ann & Bob Babson's B & B Vacation Rentals, 3371 Keha Drive, Kihei, Maui, HI 96753. (808) 874-1166 or toll free 11-800-824-6409. The Babson's offer four vacation rentals with panoramic oceanviews in Maui Meadows, located just above Wailea on the Southwest side of Maui. Maui Meadows is a quiet residential area with views of the Pacific Ocean. All their rentals include cable TV, telephone, and washer/dryer facilities. The main house is situated on a half acre and offers two bed and breakfast units $60-$70. They also offer a one-bedroom, one bath apartment on the ground floor of the home with a private outside entrance, a livingroom, dining room and kitchen combination with separate bedroom $70. The cottage offers 2 BR, 2 full baths and sleeps six with a sleeper sofa in the living room $95.

Kula B & B, P.O. Box 322, Kula, HI 96790. (808) 878-6736. Located in the cool upcountry region on the slopes of Haleakala. They offer private room, bath and deck with own entrance.

Nani Kahua B & B, 2825 Kauhale St., Kihei, Maui, HI 96753. (808) 874-0831. Private room with bath $45 - $60.

Old Lahaina House Bed & Breakfast, 407 Ilikahi St., Lahaina, HI 96761. (808) 667-4663. FAX (808) 667-5615. Hosts John and Sherry Barbier offer a home in the historic Lahaina area. Swimming pool, private, Hawaiian continental breakfast. Walking distance to Old Lahaina Town. Two suites each $95 per night with private baths and king beds. Two rooms at $50 per night each with twin beds and a shared bath.

Pualani Retreat, PO Box 1135, Makawao, Maui, HI 96768. (808) 5752-6773. Pualani, which means lovely flower. Two people, three night minimum $100. Described as a private spiritual Health & Rejuvenation Retreat. The five bedroom, three bath home offers panoramic views. You can enjoy swimming in their 50' lap pool or relaxing in their outdoor spa. The facility is available for workshops and seminars. Available at an extra charge are breakfast or other vegetarian meals, yoga instruction and massage.

Silver Cloud Upcountry Guest Ranch, Old Thompson Rd., RR Box 201, Kula, Maui, HI 96790. (808) 878-6101. FAX (808) 878-2132. SilverCloud Ranch was originally part of the Thompson Ranch, which had its beginnings on Maui in 1902. The nine-acre ranch is located at the 2,800 ft. elevation on the slopes of Haleakala. Owners Mike and Sara Gerry and done major renovations and now offer 12 rooms, suites and cottages, each with private bathrooms and most with private lanais and entrances. The King Kamehameha and Queen Emma suites are located in the main house with a private lanai and view of the lush upcountry. The Lahaina Cottage offers total privacy with a complete kitchen, clawfooted bathtub, woodburning stove surrounded by a lovely flower garden and lanai. The Paniolo Bunkhouse has studios that are furnished in Hawaiian motif. They offer kitchenettes and lanais. The Bunkhouse's Haleakala suite is a larger facility with a bedroom, separate living area, fireplace and complete kitchen. Room rates are $75 - $125 per night and includes breakfast and use of the main house and kitchen. No minimum stay, and discounts for seven nights or longer.

Tony's Place, 13 Kauala Rd., Lahaina, Maui, 96761. (808) 661-8040. Located at the corner of Kauala Rd. and Front Street. Basic lodging with kitchen privileges in a simply furnished home. Complimentary Kona Coffee each morning, continental breakfast $4.50. Tax included $50 single, $60 double.

Whaler's Way, 541 Kupuhulau Drive, Kihei, Maui, HI 96753. (808) 879-7984. Located in the foothills above Kihei, the home of Ken and Carol Svenson affords panoramic vistas of Kaho'olawe, Lana'i and the West Maui Mountains. Guest rooms are located on the garden level and each room is separate from the main living areas. There is also a separate guest cottage called Whale's Tail and decorated in a whale motif. It features a two bedroom cottage.

PRIVATE RESIDENCES

For a large family, a couple of families, or a group of frients, a vacation home rather tahn a condo, may be a more spacious and cost effective option. Homes are availabe in all areas of the island.

Here are a list of agents which handle home rentals.

Bello Realty-Maui Beach Homes, P.O. Box 1776, Kihei, Maui, HI 96753. (808-879-3328). 1-800-541-3060 U.S. & Canada. Condos and homes rented by the day, week or month. Specializing in the Kihei area.

Elite Holidays Unlimited, P.O. Box 10817, Lahaina, Maui, HI 96761. 1-800-448-9222 U.S. & Canada, (808-667-5527). Condos, family homes and luxury estates available for weekly and monthly rentals on Maui and other islands. Condos include The Whaler, Polo Beach, Kaanapali Plantation and Kapalua Bay and Golf Villas. Condo and car packages available.

Hana Bay Vacation Rentals, Stan Collins offers eight homes in the Hana area. Contact Hana Bay Vacation Rentals, P.O. Box 318, Hana, Maui, HI 96713. (808-248-7727)

Hawaiian Apartment Leasing Enterprise, 479 Ocean Ave., Suite B., Laguna Beach, CA 92651. 1-800-472-8449 California, 1-800-854-8843 U.S. except California, 1-800-824-8968. 150 plus homes and 90 condominium properties on all islands.

Hawaiian Island Reservations, P.O. Box 1863, Kailua, Hawaii 96734. Home rentals on a weekly basis.

Hawaiian Luxury Vacation Homes, 1-800-982-8778, 1-808-669-1737. Luxury homes with minimum one week stay, two weeks over Christmas. Maid service available.

Kihei Maui Vacations, 1-800-542-6284 US, 1-800-423-8733 ext. 4000 Canada (808-879-7581). In addition to condos they offer homes and cottages in the Kihei, Wailea and Makena areas.

Maui and All Islands, P.O. Box 1089, Aldergrove, BC V0X 1A0. 1-800-663-6962 from B. C. and Alberta. (604) 533-4190. Approximately 150 homes rented weekly, bi-weekly and monthly on Kaua'i and Maui.

Maui Condo and Home Rental, P.O. Box 1840, Kihei, Maui, Hi 96753. 1-800-822-3309 U.S., 1-800-822-4409 U.S. & Canada, (808-879-5445). Homes and condos rented daily, weekly and monthly in Kihei and Wailea areas.

Vacation Locations, Hawaii, 1-800-522-2757 or (808-874-0077). Rent homes on Maui or neighbor islands. Don't want to cook or clean? Select a home with daily maid service and a cook.

Windsurfing West, Ltd., P.O. Box 330104, Kahului, Maui, HI 96733. 1-800-367-8047 ext. 170 U.S. (808-572-5601). Private homes and cottages available for vacation rental.

LONG-TERM STAYS

Almost all condo complexes and rental agents offer the long term visitor moderate to substantial discounts for stays of one month or more. Private homes can also be booked through the agents listed above.

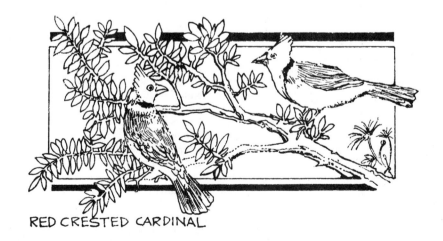

RED CRESTED CARDINAL

CONDOMINIUM & HOTEL INDEX

Old Lahaina Town

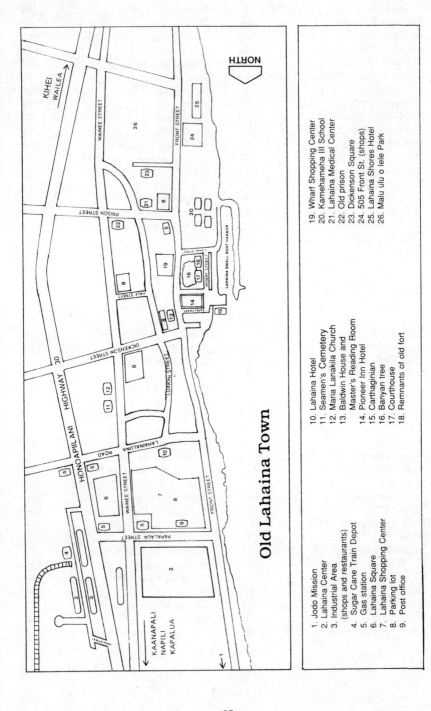

1. Jodo Mission
2. Lahaina Center
3. Industrial Area
   (shops and restaurants)
4. Sugar Cane Train Depot
5. Gas station
6. Lahaina Square
7. Lahaina Shopping Center
8. Parking lot
9. Post office

10. Lahaina Hotel
11. Seamen's Cemetery
12. Maria Lanakila Church
13. Baldwin House and
    Master's Reading Room
14. Pioneer Inn Hotel
15. Carthaginian
16. Banyan tree
17. Courthouse
18. Remnants of old fort

19. Wharf Shopping Center
20. Kamehameha III School
21. Lahaina Medical Center
22. Old prison
23. Dickenson Square
24. 505 Front St. (shops)
25. Lahaina Shores Hotel
26. Malu ulu o lele Park

LAHAINA

INTRODUCTION

As you leave the Kahului area on Hwy. 38, you plunge immediately into miles of sugar cane. The rugged and deeply carved valleys of the West Maui mountains are on the right, and on the left is the dormant volcano, Haleakala. Its broad base and seemingly gentle slopes belie its 11,000 foot height, and no hint of its enormous moon-like crater is discernible from below. On a clear day the mountains are so distinct and sharp edged they appear to have been cut out with giant scissors. The drive across the isthmus ends quickly as you pass Maalaea Harbor where the gently swaying sugar cane gives way to rugged sea cliffs and panoramic Pacific vistas. Across the bay is the South Maui coastline and in the distance the islands of Kaho'olawe and Lana'i. Construction of this road was to accommodate the new resort developments at Kaanapali that began in the 1960's. Traffic must have been far different on the old road which is still visible in places along the craggy cliffside. The tunnel, built in 1951, is the only one on Maui. Just beyond it are enormous metal chain blankets hanging along the rocky cliffs above the road. Termed a protective measure by some and an eyesore by others, they were installed in 1987.

As you descend from the cliffs the first glimpse of the tropical and undeveloped West Maui coastline is always a thrill. Stretching as far as the eye can see are sugar cane fields hugging the lower slopes of the mountains and a series of narrow, white sand beaches lined by kiawe trees and coconut palms. For several miles the constant stream of traffic is the only clue to the populated areas ahead. The first sign of civilization is Olowalu, a mere hamlet along the roadside and an unusual location for one of the island's best restaurants, Chez Paul. Public beaches continue to line the highway and the unobstructed view of the ocean may reward the observant with a whale sighting during the December to April humpback season.

A few homes to the left and the monolithic smoke stack of the Pioneer Mill announce your arrival to Lahaina, the now bustling tourist center of Maui. It has maintained the aura of more than a century ago when it was the whaling capitol of the world. Located about a 45 minute drive from the Kahului Airport (depending on traffic), this coastal port is noted for its Front Street, which is a several block strip of shops and restaurants along the waterfront. The Lahaina Harbor is filled with boats of varying shapes and sizes, eager to take the visitor afloat for a variety of sea excursions.

The oldest accommodation on the island, Pioneer Inn, is located here. Still popular among many a visitor, it offers a nostalgic and rustic atmosphere, and very reasonable prices. Other accommodations include a luxuriously expensive condominium complex and two charming new country inns. Although several complexes are located oceanfront, the beaches in Lahaina are fronted by a close-in reef which prohibits swimming. Only Puamana has a beach suitable for swimming. If you want to be in the midst of the action on Maui, you might want to investigate staying in this area.

61

WHAT TO DO AND SEE

There is much to see and do in busy Lahaina town. The word Lahaina means "merciless sun," and it does tend to become quite warm, especially in the afternoon with little relief from the tropical trade winds. Parking can be somewhat irksome. Several all day lots are located near the corner of Wainee and Dickenson (only a couple blocks off Front Street) and charge $5 for all day. One nearer to Front Street charges $7 per day. The inexpensive lots fill up early in the day. The Lahaina Shopping Center has a three hour (free) parking area, but it is always very crowded. The new Lahaina Center, across the street from the Lahaina Shopping Center has pay parking, validated with purchase from one of the stores. If you don't mind a short walk, parking is available across the road from the Lahaina Shores Village. (See the Lahaina map for locations of other parking areas). On-street parking is very limited and if you are fortunate enough to find a spot, many are only for one hour. BEWARE, the police here are quite prompt and efficient at towing.

Now that you have arrived, let's get started. Historical memorabilia abounds in Lahaina. The historical landmarks have all been identified by numbered markers. A free pamphlet is available at the historical sites in Lahaina (Baldwin House, Carthaginian, Masters Reading Room, and Wo Hing Temple) for your own self-guided tour. You may be able to purchase admission at a package price. Check at the Wo Hing Temple, Carthaginian or Baldwin House for more information on this option. The following is a brief discussion of the most interesting sites.

The Banyan Tree is very easy to spot at the south end of Lahaina adjacent to Pioneer Inn on Front Street. Planted on April 24, 1873 by Sheriff William Owen Smith, it was to commemorate the 50th anniversary of Lahaina's first Protestant Christian Mission.

The stone ruins of ***the old fort*** can be found harborside near the Banyan Tree. The fort was constructed in the 1830's to protect the missionaries homes from the whaling ships and the occasional cannon ball that would be shot off when the sailors were aroused. The fort was later torn down and the coral blocks reused elsewhere. A few blocks have been excavated and the corner of the fort was rebuilt as a landmark in 1964. On the corner near the Pioneer Inn is a plaque marking the site of the 1987 Lahaina Reunion Time Capsule, which contains newspapers, photos and other memorabilia.

Pioneer Inn, built in 1901, is the distinguished green and white structure just north of the Banyan Tree. It was a haven for inter-island travelers during the early days of the 20th century. Having survived the dry years of prohibition, it added a new wing in 1966 along with a center garden and pool area. Two restaurants operate here (one of our favorite haunts for breakfast) and accommodations are available in the original and the newer structure. The history of Pioneer Inn is an interesting one and is discussed under the accommodation information which follows. (See RESTAURANTS - Lahaina and WHERE TO STAY - Lahaina for additional information).

The **Lahaina Courthouse** was built in 1859, at a cost of $7,000, from wood and stone taken from the palace of Kamehameha II. You'll find it near the Lahaina Harbor. The Lahaina Restoration and Preservation Foundation anticipates in the future to begin renovations to restore and convert it into a museum featuring Lahaina's plantation era, and the importance of the reign of Kamehameha III on the Hawaiian Islands. The first floor would also house an information center.

In front of Pioneer Inn is the **Lahaina Harbor.** You can stroll down and see the boats and visit stalls where a wide variety of water sports and tours can be arranged. (See RECREATION AND TOURS) *The Carthaginian,* anchored just outside the harbor, is a replica of a 19th century square rigger, typical of the ships that brought the first missionaries and whalers to these shores. The first *Carthaginian* sank on Easter Sunday, April 2, 1972. It had been built in 1921 in Denmark as a schooner and the 130 foot vessel had sailed the world as a cargo ship. She was purchased by Tucker Thompson and sailed to Hawai'i in 1964. Her original name was *Wandia,* but was rechristened *Carthaginian* in Honolulu with a bottle of passion fruit juice. The ship was used in the South Pacific for a time and later was restored to resemble a whaling vessel for the movie version of Michner's "Hawai'i." The Lahaina Restoration Foundation worked to acquire the *Carthaginian* for $75,000. The ship found a home at the Lahaina wharf, becoming an exhibit of the whaling era. On June 20, 1971 it was discovered by the ship's skipper, Don Bell, that the vessel was sinking. The ship was pumped and a large hole was patched, the cause seeming to be dry rot. It was decided the following year to tow her to Honolulu for repairs in dry dock, however 150 yards from dock she became lodged on the reef and valiant efforts to save her were not successful. An immediate search began for a replacement and it was found in the Danish port of Soby. The ship was a 97 foot steel hulled freighter that had originally been a schooner, but had been demasted. The ship called *Komet* had been built in the shipyards in Germany in 1920. It was available for sale and purchased for $20,500. An all Lahaina crew sailed via the Panama Canal and arrived in Hawai'i in September 1973. Volunteers set to work transforming the ship to the proud vessel it is today and it was christened *Brig Carthaginian* on April 26, 1980. Today the ship features video movies and recorded songs of humpback whales and an authentic 19th century whale boat. All items are on display below deck. The ship is open daily from 9 to 4:30. Admission $3 adults and children free.

CARTHAGINIAN

Whale watching is always an exciting pastime in Lahaina. The whales usually arrive in November and December to breed and calve in the warm waters off Maui for several months. There is also a number to call to report any sightings you make. WHALE WATCH HOTLINE at 879-8860. Numerous whale watching excursions are available. (See RECREATION AND TOURS.)

Adjacent to the Carthaginian is the oldest Pacific lighthouse. "It was on this site in 1840 that King Kamehameha III ordered a nine foot wooden tower built as an aid to navigation for the whaling ships. It was equipped with whale oil lamps kept burning at night by a Hawaiian caretaker who was paid $20 a year." In 1866 it increased to 26 feet in size and was again rebuilt in 1905. The present structure of concrete was dedicated in 1916. (Information from an engraved plaque placed on the lighthouse by the Lahaina Restoration Foundation.)

The Hauola Stone or Healing Rock can be found near the Lahaina Harbor. Look for the cluster of rocks marked with a visitors bureau warrior sign. The rock, resembling a chair, was believed to have healing properties which could be obtained by merely sitting in it with feet dangling in the surf. Here you will also find remnants of the **Brick Palace** of Kamehameha the Great. Vandals destroyed the display which once showed examples of the original mud bricks.

The Baldwin House is across Front Street from Pioneer Inn. Built during 1834-1835, it housed the Reverend Dwight Baldwin and his family from 1837 to 1871. Tours of the home, furnished as it was in days gone by, are given every 15 minutes between the hours of 9:30 and 4:30. Adults are $2, no charge for children. The empty lot adjacent was once the home of Reverend William Richards, and a target of attack by cannon balls from angry sailors during the heyday of whaling. On the other side of the Baldwin Home is the Master's Reading Room. Built in 1833, it is the oldest structure on Maui. Its original purpose was to provide a place of leisure for visiting sea captains. It is not open to the public at this time.

The Old Prison (Hale Paahao) on Prison Street just off Wainee, is only a short trek from Front Street. Upon entry you'll notice the large gate house which The Lahaina Restoration Foundation reconstructed to its original state in 1988.

BALDWIN HOUSE

Nearby is a 60 year old Royal Palm, and in the courtyard an enormous 150 year old breadfruit tree. The cell block was built in 1852 to house the unruly sailors from the whaling vessels and to replace the old fort. (It was reconstructed in 1959.) In 1854 coral walls (the blocks taken from the old fort) were constructed. The jail was used until the 1920's when it was relocated to the basement of the Lahaina Court House next to the Harbor. While you're at Hale Paahao be sure to say hello to the jail's only tenant, George. He is a wax replica of a sailor who is reported to have had a few too many brews at Uncle Henry's Front Street Beer House in the 1850's, then missed his ship's curfew and was tossed into jail by Sheriff William O. Smith. George will briefly converse with you by means of a taped recording. The grounds are open to the public daily, no charge.

Construction of the **Waiola Church** began in 1828 on what was then called the Wainee Church. Made of stone and large enough to accommodate 3,000 people, the church unfortunately did not survive the destructive forces of nature and man. The current structure dates from only 1953. In the neighboring cemetery you will find tombs of several notable members of Hawaiian royalty, including Queen Keopuolani, wife of Kamehameha the Great and mother of Kamehameha II and III. The church is located on Wainee and Shaw Streets. The **Maria Lanakila Church** is on the corner of Wainee and Dickenson. Built in 1928, it is a replica of the 1858 church. Next door is the Seamen's Cemetery.

Hawaiian Experience Omni Theatre ★ at 824 Front Street occupies what was once the site of the old Queen's Theatre. The seating for 150 persons is such that everyone gets an unobstructed view of the 180 degree screen which curves up and to the sides of the auditorium. The history of the islands is narrated as the viewer is thrilled to a bird's eye view of the remote Hawaiian leeward islands of Tern, Nihoa and Necker. Travel through the jungles and volcanoes of the major islands as well as the underwater world of the Pacific. The adults in our group found the show realistic enough to cause an occasional "seasick" sensation (especially the bike ride down Haleakala), but the kids were riveted and motionless for the 40 minute show. The film, "Hawaii: Island of the Gods," is an informative as well as entertaining show and the air-conditioned comfort is a pleasant break from the warm sidewalk shopping in Lahaina. The show is offered hourly from 10 am - 10 pm. $5.95 adults, children ages 4 - 12 $3.95, under 4 are free. Phone 661-8314.

The Wo Hing Temple on Front Street opened following restoration in late 1984. Built in 1912, it now houses a museum which features the influence of the Chinese population on Maui. Hours are 9 am - 9 pm with a $1 admission donation. The adjacent cook house has become a miniature theatre which features movies filmed by Thomas Edison during his trips to Hawaii in 1898 and 1906.

A small, but interesting **Whaling Museum** is located in the Crazy Shirts shop on Front Street. No admission is charged.

Follow Front Street towards Kaanapali to find **The Seamen's Hospital**. This structure was once a hideaway for King Kamehameha III and a gaming house for sailors of Old Lahaina. Now it houses The Paradise Television Network, a local television station.

Hale Pa'i is on the campus of Lahainaluna school. Founded in 1831, Lahainaluna is the oldest school and printing press west of the Rockies. You will find it located just outside of Lahaina at the top of Lahainaluna Road. Open weekdays 10 - 4. No charge. Donations welcomed.

The Lahaina Jodo Mission is located on the Kaanapali side of Lahaina, on Ala Moana Street near the Mala Wharf. The great Buddha commemorated the 100th anniversary of the Japanese immigration to the islands which was celebrated at the mission in 1968. The grounds are open to the public, but not the buildings. The public is welcome to attend their summer O'Bon festivals, usually in late June and early July. Check the papers for dates and times.

WHERE TO SHOP

Shopping is a prime fascination in Lahaina and it is such a major business that it breeds volatility. Shops change frequently, sometimes seemingly overnight, with a definite "trendiness" to their merchandise. It was a few years back that visitors could view artisans creating scrimshaw in numerous stores. The next few years saw the transformation to T-shirt stores. There still are plenty, but the clothing stores are diminishing in numbers. The theme now is art, art, art, with galleries springing up on every corner. It's a wonderful opportunity to view the fine work of the many local artists with no admission charge! Original oils, watercolors, acrylics, carvings and pottery are on display, as well as fine quality lithographs.

Reliable sources tell us that 16 shops closed their doors during the first half of 1991. Some have just retired, but others may have been affected by a very slow winter visitor season. A few of the old timers that have recently left are Gems and Jade and Claire the Ring Lady. There are several interesting new additions. Environmental awareness has arrived at the *Endangered Species Store* at 707 Front St. It's filled with tee-shirts, collectibles, books and toys that all focus on endangered wildlife worldwide. Next door is an fun store with a novel idea that certainly makes this shop memorable from the many others that line Front Street. Step through the door of *The Gecko Store* and take a look at what is under your feet! We'll let you be surprised!

JODO MISSION

Here are some shops that are unusual, or favorites of ours:

Lahaina Galleries at 728 Front Street, plus galleries in Kaanapali and Kapalua. Begun in 1976, their art falls in the $500 - $30,000 (and up) range. The works by local artists are the most popular.

The Foundation Galleries, 143 Lahainaluna Rd., 661-4399 is a gallery exhibiting work of more than 30 artists. The foundation's policy is "Art for Conservation," whereby art buyers are asked to deduct 10% from the purchase price and write a check directly to the conservation society of their choice.

New galleries are opening constantly. Some of the larger ones are the Dolphin Gallery, Sunset Galleries (two locations in Lahaina), The Dyansen Gallery, The Larry Dotson Gallery, and The Hansen Gallery. A number of "retired" movie and television stars have turned artist and you'll see the work of Tony Curtis, Red Skelton, Anthony Quinn and Buddy Epsen. Originals, numbered lithographs and poster prints by popular Hawaiian artists Peggy Hopper, Diana Hansen and others can be found in many shops as well. The best representation of local artists may be found at the Lahaina Gallery, The Village Gallery and in the Old Jail in the courthouse basement, which is operated by the Lahaina Arts Society. Located on 143 Lahainaluna Rd., just off Front Street in Lahaina, is a new art gallery. Not just any gallery, Foundation Gallery operates with a different twist. They seek to preserve the beauty of the plant as well as provide the beauty of art. With this in mind, president/general manager Paulette Feeney nad partner, marine life sculptor Randy Puckett ask the art buyers to contribute 10 percent of the purchase price of the art to a conservation society of their choice. Thus a check for 90% goes to the gallery for the art work selection and 10% to a good cause.

Friday night in Lahaina is ART NIGHT! Participating galleries feature a special event between 6 and 9 pm that might include guest artists and refreshments.

You will find the rebirth of the aloha shirt at *Kula Bay*, Lahaina Market Place, on Front Street near Lahainaluna Road (667-5852). They've taken original patterns from the 1930's, and 40's, updated and subdued the colors, and then recreated them on comfortable all cotton fabric. Stop by and Erik will be delighted to show you their 100% cotton, made in the U.S.A., slacks, shorts and shirts. Many of the shirts have coconut buttons! They are also available in solid colors.

Island Sandals is tucked away in a niche of the Wharf Shopping Center near the postal center at 658 Front Street, Space #125, Lahaina, Maui, Hi 96761, (661-5110). Michael Mahnensmith is the proprietor and creator of custom-made sandals. He learned his craft in Santa Monica from David Webb who was making sandals for the Greek and Roman movies of the late 50's and early 60's. He rediscovered his sandal design from the sandals used 3,000 years ago by the desert warriors of Ethiopia. He developed the idea while living in Catalina in the 1960's and copyrighted it in 1978. The sandals are all leather, which is porous and keeps the feet cool and dry, with the exception of a non-skid synthetic heel. They feature a single strap which laces around the big toe, then over and under the foot, and around the heel, providing comfort and good arch support. As the sandal breaks in, the strap stretches and you simply adjust the entire strap to maintain proper fit (which makes them feel more like a shoe than a sandal). They are clever and functional. His sandals have been copied by others, but never duplicated. So beware of other sandals which appear the same, but don't offer the fit, comfort or function of Michael's! The charge is $85 for the right shoe and the left shoe is free. Charges may be slightly higher for men's sandals over size 13. Anyone who gets shoes from Island Sandals becomes an agent and is authorized to trace foot prints of others. Commissions are automatic when your sales reach the "high range." (However, you must like coconuts and bananas.) Michael stresses the importance of good footwear while on Maui, so stop in upon your arrival, or they can be ordered by sending a tracing of your foot and big toe (or by having an "authorized agent" do so) along with $85 to Island Sandals. Michael can also assist with leather repair of your shoes, purses, bags, or suitcases.

Seegerpeople at the Wharf has an interesting photographic twist. Located in the lower level corner, they have on display hundreds of samples of their work. After a photographic sitting that lasts about half an hour with a dozen poses, selections are made. The prints are first adhered to a heavy plastic board, then to white plastic, after which the photographs are cut out closely around the head and body.

This results in miniature people that can be creatively arranged and mounted on stands. They're not cheap, but they sure are fun. We enjoyed just looking at all their samples! A sitting, three mounted poses, and the stand runs about $100.

Shell Hansson describes his shop as a fossil remainder. According to Hansson, the *Mad Hatter*, located on the street level of the Wharf Center, is the only place in the world still producing custom-made straw hats. While he specializes in straw, you can find just about any kind of hat or cap and in any price range. At any one time there are 4,000 - 5,000 hats on display with 20,000 - 30,000 hats in stock. The Mad Hatter is one of the original Wharf tenants, opening his shop in 1973, however, he recently reduced the size of his store. Notable purchasers include Red Skelton, Vincent Price, Charlton Heston and Buddy Epsen, to name only a few. Stop in and try on his motto, "If you have the head - I have the hat."

For the collector of just about anything the *Coral Tree* at the Wharf Shopping Center needs to be penciled in on your Lahaina itinerary. The buyer, Pat Adams, has collected items from around the world and they fill shelves from the floor to ceiling of this small shop. (She adds jokingly that the smallness of the shop is because in Lahaina space is rented by the square inch per minute.) Turtles, frogs, trunk-up elephants (trunk-down elephants are bad luck) and cats are the most popular collectibles. However, if pigs or dogs or zebra are your hobby then you'll find them here! You won't find things made out of just coral either, there is black jet from England, amber from the Dominican Republic, turquoise pieces made by the Zumi Indians or bone and alabaster from Indonesia. The collector of jewelry will find this an intriguing stop as well.

A three screen movie theater was added in 1989 to the second level of the *Wharf Cinema Center* and has a seating capacity of 330 people (current special matinee prices are currently $3). The *Fun Factory* is located in the lower level with video games and prize oriented games. The shopping center has also introduced "Aloha Friday" - a free show each Friday at 6:30 pm.

Dickenson Square (On Dickenson St. off Front St.) bears a strong resemblance to Pioneer Inn. A yogurt shop, hairdresser, quick stop market, Lahaina Coolers restaurant and Nautilus Center are located here.

505 Front Street is a short walk past the Banyan Tree. Originally developed to be a shopping center, then unsuccessfully converted into condominiums, it has now been restored into busy shops and restaurants. The Old Lahaina Luau is held on the beachfront and restaurants include Bettino's, J. J.'s Restaurant and above it is a nightspot, Studio 505 and the Old Lahaina Cafe. Shops change here faster than we can keep track. Village Pizzeria or Juicy's Sandwich and Juice Bar offer a respite for the hungry shopper!

Dan's Green House at 133 Prison Street (661-8412) has a variety of beautiful tropical birds for sale as well as an array of plants for shipping home. Their specialty is the Fuku-Bonsai "Lava Rock" plants. These bonsai are well packaged to tolerate the trip home.

The newest shopping complex in West Maui is the *Lahaina Center*; not to be confused with the adjoining and older, more established Lahaina Shopping Center. This new center has kept the low level, pioneer type architecture and has a paid parking area. *Hilo Hatties* has relocated here with a 17,000 square foot location. Hatties is famous around the islands for its aloha wear. The *Hard Rock Cafe* is a major attraction. Several other eateries include Munchies, Chili's and Red Lobster. Woolworth's is a disappointed, not very large and not nearly as fun as the Kahului location. Liberty House is another disappointment for us. Not nearly as large as the former Kaanapali location. No toy section, no books, all sections reduced in size. An interesting art gallery is located near the Hard Rock Cafe and more stores are opening all the time.

An area slightly removed from Lahaina's Front Street is termed the industrial area. Follow Honoapiilani Road and turn by the Pizza Hut. *The Sugar Cane Train* main depot is here. This nostalgic railroad will transport you between Kaanapali and Lahaina. One way for adults is $4.25, and children $2.00, round trip for adults runs $6.50 and children $3.25. "Babes in arms are free." Special package options include train trips combined with lunch in Lahaina, a visit to the Baldwin House and the Carthaginian, or a trip in the glass bottom boat, the Lin Wai. Make your plans early as space is limited and sometimes the return trips are booked. The red double decker bus stops at the Wharf Shopping Center and in front of Pioneer Inn to transport you to the Sugar Cane Depot. (See Land tours for additional information.) Also in the industrial area, *The Bakery* is a personal favorite for some really fine pastries and breads. *MGM, Maui Gold Manufacturing* (661-8981) not only does standard repairs, but designs outstanding jewelry pieces. They can design something to your specifications, or choose a piece from one of their many photograph books. A limited number of pieces are ready made for sale as well. *J.R.'s Music Shop* (661-0801), on the back side of The Bakery building, has a large selection of Hawaiian tapes and records as well as just about any other type of music.

Just on the Kaanapali side of Lahaina, a drive of less than a mile, is *The Cannery Shopping Center* which opened in 1987. The original structure, built in 1920, was used as a pineapple cannery until its closure in 1963, and this new facility was built to resemble its predecessor. It's easy to spot as you leave Lahaina heading for Kaanapali. A large parking area makes for convenient access. This enclosed air conditioned mall is anchored by Safeway and Longs Drug Store. Within the mall are several fast food eateries, Marie Callendar's restaurant, Walden's bookstore, Sir Wilfred's coffee house, jewelry, clothing and sporting goods stores. The surf board display at *Hobie Sports* is very interesting.

BE FOREWARNED!!! If you have the time, do a lot of window shopping before you buy. Prices can vary significantly on some items from one store to another.

ACCOMMODATIONS - LAHAINA

Puamana	Plantation Inn
Lahaina Shores Beach Resort	Lahaina Hotel
Pioneer Inn	Lahaina Roads
Maui Islander Hotel	Puunoa

BEST BETS: *Puamana* - A nice residential type area of two-plex and four-plex units, some oceanfront.
Lahaina Shores - A moderately priced colonial style high rise right on the beach and within walking distance of Lahaina shops.
Plantation Inn and *Lahaina Hotel* are both tastefully done with all the elegance of bygone days.

PUAMANA ★
P.O. Box 515, Lahaina, Maui, HI 96761. (808-667-2551) 1-800-628-6731. Agents: Klahani Investments 1-800-669-MAUI U.S. and Canada. 228 units in a series of duplexes and four-plexes in a garden setting. This large oceanside complex resembles a residential community much more than a vacation resort. The variation in price reflects location in the complex, oceanfront to gardenview. Limited maid service. $300 deposit, wkly/mnthly discounts, 3-night minimum.
1 BR (4) $120-175 / $ 95-150
2 BR (6) $155-250 / $135-200
3 BR (6) $300-350

LAHAINA SHORES BEACH RESORT ★
475 Front Street, Lahaina, Maui, HI 96761. (808-661-4835 Hotel only, no reservations). Agents: Classic Resorts 1-800-628-6699, Rainbow Reservations 1-800-367-6092.

200 oceanfront units in this 7-story building of Victorian style offer air conditioning, lanais, full kitchens, daily maid service, and laundry facilities on each floor. The beach here is fair and the water calm due to offshore reefs, but shallow with coral. Lahaina town is only a short walk away, plus this complex neighbors the Lahaina Shores Village which offers several restaurants and a small grocery store. Car/condo packages also available.

SBR(3)	*mtn.v.-o.v.*	*$115-135 /$ 95-105*	*Extra persons, $10 per day*
1BR(4)	*o.v.-o.f.*	*$140-170 /$120-140*	*Children under 12, no charge*
Penthouse	*mtn.v.-o.f.*	*$180-225 /$150-190*	

PIONEER INN (Hotel)

658 Wharf St., P.O. Box 243, Lahaina, Maui, HI 96764. 1-800-457-5457, FAX 1-808-667-5708, (808-661-3636). If you want rustic, this is it, and the prices can't be beat. The original building was constructed in 1901 as accommodations for inter-island travelers. George Freeland a robust 300 pound, 6 ft. 5 inch English-man, had relocated to Vancouver, Canada and become a Royal Canadian Mountie. He was sent to Hawai'i in 1900 to capture a suspect, but failing to do so, chose to make Maui his home. He formed the Pioneer Hotel Co., Ltd and sold $50 shares of stock. In October of 1901 he constructed the hotel, similar to the plantation house of the Maunalei Sugar Company on Lana'i for a total cost of $6,000. (Note: On Lana'i we heard a report that the Maunalei Plantation House was transported to Maui and became Pioneer Inn, but this was not accurate. Apparently the Honolulu Star-Bulletin printed an article to this effect. G. Alan Freeland, son of Pioneer Inn's founder George Freeland spoke with Lawrence Gay, the owner of most of Lana'i at the turn of the century, and was told that when the construction of Pioneer Hotel was completed, the similar-designed building on the island of Lana'i was still standing.) Soon George Freeland opened the Pioneer saloon, the Pioneer Grange, the Pioneer Wholesale Liquor Company and in 1913 the Pioneer Theater. The Pioneer Theater ran silent movies to packed crowds and had stage shows and plays in the theater as well. He died on July 25, 1925, survived by his wife, a Hawaiian woman named, three sons and four daughters. His eldest son George Alan Freeland ran the business until the early 1960's. In the late 1960's the inn was expanded and at that time the theater was torn down. A complete history of the Pioneer Inn is available along with their brochure. A guest in 1901 would have been required to adhere to the following bizarre "house rules:"

> "You must pay you rent in advance. You must not let you room go one day back. Women is not allow in you room. If you wet or burn you bed you going out. You are not allow to gamble in you room. You are not allow to give you bed to you freand. If you freand stay overnight you must see the mgr. You must leave you room at 11 am so the women can clean you

PIONEER INN

room. Only on Sunday you can sleep all day. You are not allow in the down stears in the seating room or in the dinering room or in the kitchen when you are drunk. You are not allow to drink on the front porch. You must use a shirt when you come to the seating room. If you cant keep this rules please dont take the room."

With such a colorful history, Pioneer Inn remains a nostalgic Lahaina landmark. Many of the units in the old building have shared baths and the furnishings are spartan. Don't let the "new" in new wing give you ideas of grandeur. This Mauka wing was added in 1966 and is only a little more modern, with each having a private bath, air conditioning, and lanais. Here you are in the hub of activity in Lahaina and sounds of the music downstairs will lull you to sleep.
Original building: Rooms - shared bath (1-2) $30, private bath (1-2) $35-42
Mauka wing: Superior $70, Deluxe $80, third person $10, child under 10 $5

MAUI ISLANDER HOTEL
660 Wainee Street, Lahaina, Maui, HI 96761. (808) 667-9766. 372 rooms include hotel rooms w/ refrigerators. Studio and 1 BR suites w/ kitchens. Located in the heart of Lahaina town, less than a 5 minute walk to the sea wall, yet far enough away to be peaceful. The back of the building borders the Honoapiilani Hwy., so there may be more traffic noise in those units - request the front units. Daily maid service, air conditioning, laundry facilities, tennis courts, pool. Group rates available. Two night deposit. Room and car packages available.
Room with refrigerator - no kitchen (2) $95/83
Studio (3) $107/95, 1 BR (4) $119/107, 2 BR (6) $170/158

PLANTATION INN ★
174 Lahainaluna Rd., Lahaina, Maui, HI 96761 (808-667-9225) 1-800-433-6815, FAX 1-808-667-9293. It's wonderful to see this kind of development in Lahaina. This new 18 room building has all the charm of an old inn, while all the benefits of modernization. Filled with antiques, unique decor, hardwood floors, and stained glass, they also offer air conditioning, refrigerators and even VCR's. Located a block from the ocean in the heart of Lahaina, it also has a 12 foot deep tiled pool, and a spa. An added bonus is the outstanding Gerard's Restaurant, which provides guests with discounts for breakfast and dinner. Some suites include kitchens and jacuzzis. Honeymoon and packages available.
Standard $99, Deluxe $125, Superior $145, Suites $175

LAHAINA HOTEL ★ (Hotel)
127 Lahainaluna Rd., Lahaina, Maui, HI 96761. (808-661-0577), FAX (808) 667-9480, 1-800-669-3444. Rick Ralston, who also owns Crazy Shirts, undertook renovations at this ideally situated location and the transformation was dramatic. Gone are the $25 a night "rustic" units. The fully air conditioned hotel will have 13 rooms for single or double occupancy only.

The hotel has been restored exactly as if it were sent into a time warp between 1860 and 1900. No details have been overlooked from the authentic antiques to the ceiling moldings. All the furnishings have come from Rick Ralston's personal collection so each room is different. The headboard/footboards are intricately carved as are the highboy dressers. Each room is unique with lush wallpaper in

deep greens, burgundy, blues and golds and offers a small, but adequate private bathroom. Ten of the rooms are standard and three are larger parlour suites. Each has its own lanai complete with rocking chairs. Manager Ken Eisley emphasizes that this is a service oriented hotel with 24 hour desk service. Adjacent is the new David Paul's Lahaina Grill. Parking $7 per day. Honeymoon packages.
Std. rooms with full size bed, m.v. $89, harbor view $99 - $129
Parlour suites with queen and king $129

LAHAINA ROADS

1403 Front St., Lahaina, Maui, HI 96761. (808-661-3166) 1-800-624-8203. 42 oceanview units, covered parking and elevator to upper levels. Microwaves, washer/dryer, cable TV. Maid service available for extra charge. A very unpretentious, non-resort looking property. Additional person $10/night, 3-night minimum, two nights deposit, deposit forfeited on cancellation if unit not re-rented. Weekly and monthly discounts.
1 BR (2,max 4) $100/80, 2 BR (4,max 6) $130/110, Penthouse (4) $210/160

PUUNOA BEACH ESTATES

45 Kai Pali Place, Lahaina, Maui, HI 96761. Agents: Classic Resorts (808-667-1400) 1-800-642-MAUI. Amenities include full size swimming pool, jacuzzi, his and hers sauna, and paddle tennis courts. Units include laundry rooms, lanais, master bath with jacuzzi, full bar and daily maid service. These luxury units are located on Puunoa Beach in a residential area just north of Lahaina. Beautiful and spacious air-conditioned units, convenient to restaurants and shops. The beachfront has a coral reef which makes for calm conditions for children, but swimming or snorkeling are poor due to the shallowness and coral. A full size rental car is included. Three night minimum.
2 BR 2 bath o.f. (4) $580/550, 2 BR with loft (6) $695/580
3 BR o.f $730/605, 3 BR with loft (8) $800/665

KAANAPALI

INTRODUCTION

The drive through Lahaina is quick (unless it's rush hour). All that is really visible are a couple gas stations, the old mill, a few nondescript commercial buildings, and a Pizza Hut. Old Lahaina and the waterfront cannot be seen as they are a couple of large blocks off to the left. The large shopping center on the left is the Cannery, described above. As you leave Lahaina, the vista opens with a view of the Hyatt Regency and the beginning of the Kaanapali Beach Resort a mile off in the distance. The resort is beautifully framed by the West Maui mountains on the right, the peaks of Moloka'i appearing to be another part of Maui in the background, the island of Lana'i off to the left, and of course, the ocean. The name Kaanapali means "rolling cliffs" or "land divided by cliffs" and refers to the wide, open ridges that stretch up behind the resort toward Pu'u Kukui, West Maui's highest peak. The beaches and plush resorts here are what many come to Hawaii to find.

WHERE TO STAY - WHAT TO SEE
Kaanapali

Kaanapali is an Amfac Development that began in the early 1960's with the first hotels, the Royal Lahaina and the Sheraton, opening in late 1962 and early 1963 respectively. The Kaanapali Resort, 500 acres along three miles of prime beachfront, is reputed to be the first large-scale planned resort in the world. There are six beachfront hotels and seven condominiums which total more than 5,000 rooms and units, two golf courses, 37 tennis courts, and a shopping village.

Now that the Kaanapali Airport has been closed, there are another 700 acres available for development. Construction has been awaiting the road improvements in the Kaanapali to Lahaina area. The resort boasts the most convention space of any of the neighboring islands, with the Marriott, Westin Maui and the Hyatt Regency being popular locations. All the hotels are located beachfront, although some of the condos are situated above the beach in the golf course area. All are priced in the luxury range. The wide avenues and the spaciousness of the resort's lush green and manicured grounds are most impressive. No on-street parking and careful planning has successfully given this resort a feeling of spaciousness. Nestled between a pristine white sand beach and scenic golf courses with a mountain range beyond, this may be the ideal spot for your vacation.

This may be paradise, but traffic congestion between Kaanapali and Lahaina may have reminded you more of L.A. in the past few years. Non-synchronized traffic lights, roads designed for 20 years ago, and greatly increased traffic, caused the three mile transit through Lahaina to Kaanapali (or Kaanapali to Lahaina) to consume over an hour during the afternoon rush (most other times there was only light traffic). Of deep concern to the government, residents and business interests alike, this situation was eased considerably with the recent completion of all four lanes from Kaanapali to Lahaina. The major bottleneck is now at the first Kaanapali entrance where the four lanes end. Getting past this point in either direction can be difficult. Hopefully, the four lanes will extend up to at least Napili or Kahana in the near future.

WHAT TO DO AND SEE

The Hyatt Regency and ***The Westin Maui*** must be put at the top of everyone's list of things to see. Few hotels can boast that they need their own wildlife manager, but upon entry you'll see why they do. Without spoiling the surprises too much, just envision the Hyatt with palm trees growing through the lobby, peacocks strolling by, and parrots perched amid extraordinary pieces of oriental art. The lagoon and black swans are spectacular. The pool area occupies two acres and features two swim-through waterfalls and a cavern in the middle with a swim up bar. A swinging bridge is suspended over one of the two pools and a water slide offers added thrills for hotel guests. The newest project at Kaanapali is the Westin Maui. To appreciate this property, a little background may be necessary. The Maui Surf was the original hotel with the single curved building and a large expanse of lush green lawn and two pools. The transformation has been extraordinary. The pool areas are unsurpassed, with five swimming pools on various levels fed by waterfalls and connected by two slides. There are exotic birds afloat on the lagoons which greet you upon your arrival and glide gracefully by two of the hotel's restaurants. The oriental art collection surpasses even the Hyatt's.

Both resorts feature glamorous shopping arcades, with prices to match of course. Both developments were designed by the remarkable, champion hotel builder of Hawaii, Chris Hemmeter.

WHERE TO SHOP

Whaler's Village Shopping Center is located in the heart of Kaanapali. Some part or other of this center always seems to be under construction or renovation. It offers several small shops for grocery items, as well as a bounty of jewelry and clothing shops, and restaurants. A multi-level parking structure is adjacent to the mall and parking is $1 for the first two hours or fraction thereof, and 50 cents for each additional half hour, with a $10 maximum charge. Restaurants can provide validation. *"Hale Kohola"* (House of the Whale) is a museum located on the upper level. Admission is free, but donations are welcome. They recently expanded in size and have a wonderful exhibition the great whales with special emphasis on the Humpback Whale. Information Director Susan Bemrose gives lectures on topics from scrimshaw to the life of a sailor. Call for times at 661-5992. Private group lectures are also a possibility. Near the front of the complex is a complete whale skeleton displayed along with models and information on many different whales. Restaurants include The Rusty Harpoon, Leilani's, El Crab Catcher, and Chico's. The new 5,400 square foot food court on the lower level opened recently. Featuring a nautical architectural theme it features Chinese, Italian, and deli selections and indoor or outdoor seating.

Liberty House here closed and the area was been sub-divided into smaller retail shops. The center has a bountiful assortment of clothing stores, art galleries and jewelry stores. There is a Crazy Shirts outlet, The Sharper Image and a Walden's has a very good bookstore here with an excellent selection of Hawaiian literature. The mall is a pleasant place for an evening stroll and shop browsing, before or after dinner, followed by a seaside walk back to your accommodations on the paved beachfront sidewalk.

ACCOMMODATIONS - KAANAPALI

Hyatt Regency	Royal Lahaina Resort
Marriott	Maui Kaanapali Villas
Kaanapali Alii	Kaanapali Plantation
Westin Maui	International Colony Club
The Whaler	Maui Eldorado
Kaanapali Beach Hotel	Kaanapali Royal
Sheraton	

BEST BETS: *Hyatt Regency Maui* - An elegant and exotic setting with a wonderful selection of great restaurants. *Marriott* - Beautiful grounds with a nice pool area and attractively decorated rooms. *Westin Maui* - A gorgeous resort and a pool aficionados paradise. *Kaanapali Alii* - One of only three condominiums that are oceanfront. Luxurious, expensive and spacious. (Our choice to purchase a unit with future lottery winnings!). *Royal Lahaina Resort* - A beautiful property on sandy Kaanapali Beach. *The Whaler* - condominiums on the heart of Honokaoo Beach adjacent to the Whaler's Shopping Center.

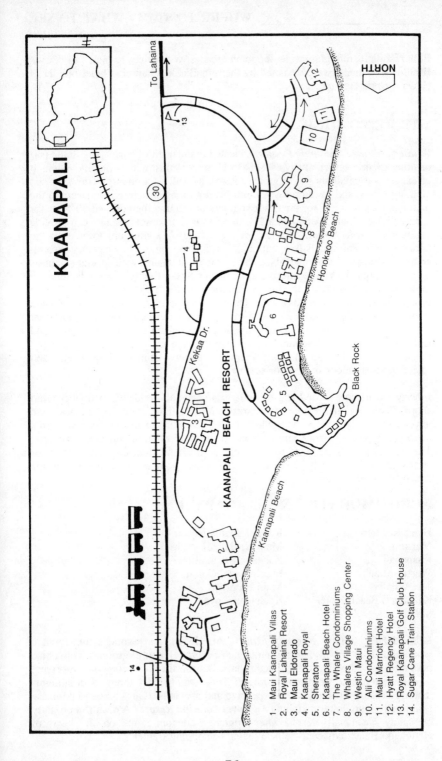

KAANAPALI

NORTH

To Lahaina

KAANAPALI BEACH RESORT

Kekaa Dr.

Kaanapali Beach

Honokaoo Beach

Black Rock

1. Maui Kaanapali Villas
2. Royal Lahaina Resort
3. Maui Eldorado
4. Kaanapali Royal
5. Sheraton
6. Kaanapali Beach Hotel
7. The Whaler Condominiums
8. Whalers Village Shopping Center
9. Westin Maui
10. Alii Condominiums
11. Maui Marriott Hotel
12. Hyatt Regency Hotel
13. Royal Kaanapali Golf Club House
14. Sugar Cane Train Station

76

HYATT REGENCY ★ (Hotel)
200 Nohea Kai Drive, Lahaina, Maui, HI 96761. (808-661-1234) 1-800-223-1234. This magnificent complex is located on 18 beachfront acres and offers 815 rooms and suites. The beach here is beautiful, but has a steep drop off. Adjoining Honokaoo Beach Park there is a gentler slope into deeper water. The pool area is an impressive feature, covering two acres and resembling a contemporary adventure that Robinson Crossway could only have dreamt. The pool is divided by a large cavern that can be reached on either side by swimming beneath a waterfall. Once inside there is a swim up bar! One side of the pool is spanned by a large swinging rope bridge. Stand on the bridge and enjoy viewing guests whizzing into the water via the long waterslide.

Penquins, jewel-toned koi, parrots, peacocks and flamingos around the grounds require full time game keepers. The lobby is a blend of beautiful pieces of oriental art and paths that lead to the grounds. Originally there had been a huge tree, the focal point of the lobby, however, it quite unexpectedly toppled over one night. Part of the base remains and has become a popular parrot walk. The birds are apparently so at home here that one exotic pair surprisingly gave birth, a rarity for this species in captivity! Non-guests should definitely visit the Hyatt for a self guided tour of the grounds, the art, the elegant shops and for an opportunity to enjoy one of this resort's fine restaurants. It's worth coming here just to look around! Restaurants include Swan Court, Lahaina Provision Company, The Pavilion and Spats.
Terrace rooms $240/230, golf/mtn.v. $300/280, o.f. $315-330 / 345-360
Suites: Ocean $600, Deluxe $900, Regency $1,400, Presidential $3,000

The Regency Club consists of certain floors that feature special services, including continental breakfast, evening cocktails and appetizers, and complimentary health club access. Room rates are based on single/double occupancy (for additional persons 13 years or older $25 charge per night/Regency Club level $45 charge per night.) 3 adults or 2 adults 2 children maximum per room.
Regency Club (mtn.v.) $410/380, (o.f.) $430/410

MARRIOTT ★ (Hotel)
100 Nohea Kai Drive, Lahaina, Maui, HI 96761. (800-228-9290) 1-808-667-1200. This 720 room complex has a large, open lobby in the middle featuring an array of fine shops. Although not as exotic as its neighbor the Hyatt, this is still a very attractive, upscale property. The pool area is large and a keiki (children's) wading pool is a welcome addition for families. On site restaurants are Nikko's Steak House, Lokelani's, Moana Terrace and the Kau Kau Bar. The 1992 rates are called "Everything Under The Sun Club" with amenities including lei greeting, free beach rentals of snorkel sets, boogie boards or soft floats, free tennis, free parking, and discounts at the Ocean Activities Center and some of their restaurants, some shops and the luau. Additional persons add $25. For Modified American Plan (MAP) breakfast and dinner add $64 per person, Full American Plan (FAP) for all three meals is $86 per person. Every Sunday their lobby offers a Comedy Club. Tickets currently $12 per person, over 21 only. Thursday thru Saturday they feature Karaoke hosted by Barry Kim.
Mtn.-golf view $179, mtn.-o.v. $205, o.v. $230, deluxe o.v. $255

KAANAPALI ALII ★

50 Nohea Kai Dr., Lahaina, Maui, HI 96761. 1-800-367-6090. Agents: Classic Resorts 1-800-642-MAUI or FAX (808) 661-0147, Whaler's Realty 1-800-367-5632, Hawaiian Apt. Leasing 1-800-854-8843, 1-800-472-8449 CA, Hawaiiana Resorts 1-800-367-7040. This is the newest condo development in Kaanapali. All 264 units are very spacious and beautifully furnished, with air conditioning, microwaves, washer/dryer, and daily maid service. Other amenities include security entrances and covered parking. The 1-bedroom units have a den, which actually makes them equivalent to a 2-bedroom. Three lighted tennis courts, pool (also a children's pool), and exercise room. No restaurants on the property, but shops and restaurants are within easy walking distance. A very elegant, high-class and quiet property with a very cordial staff and concierge department. They charge for local phone calls from room, as do most hotels. 3-night min., extra person $15/night

1 BR (2) g.v. $225/195, g.v. dlx. $250/205, o.v. $295/245
2 BR (4) g.v. $280/250, g.v. dlx. $300/270, o.v. $375/310, o.f. $450/410

WESTIN MAUI ★ (Hotel)

2365 Kaanapali Parkway, Lahaina, Maui, Hi 96761. (808-667-2525). Westin Central Reservations 1-800-228-3000. Under the direction of Chris Hemmeter, champion hotel builder in Hawaii, this new resort offers 762 deluxe rooms, including 28 suites. The Westin Maui has an ocean tower of 11 stories with 556 guest rooms and a beach tower with 206 guest rooms and suites. Guest rooms are provided for those with disabilities as well as non-smoking floors. The rooms have been designed in comfortable hues of muted peach and beige. The top two floors of the new tower, house the Royal Beach Club, which offers guests complimentary continental breakfast buffet, afternoon cocktails, evening cocktails and hors d'oeuvres, and a guest relations coordinator. Complimentary shuttle service to the Royal Lahaina Tennis Ranch, the largest tennis facility on Kaanapali with 11 tennis courts and 6 courts lit for night play. Complimentary shuttle service is also available to the Royal Kaanapali Golf Courses. Conference and banquet facilities are available as well as an array of gift, art, and fashion shops. The focal point of this resort is the 55,000 square foot aquatic playground, complete with meandering streams, 15 - 20 foot waterfalls, and a 25,000 square foot pool area featuring five free-form pools, two waterslides and a swim-up jacuzzi hidden away in a grotto. The pool areas are spacious and well arranged. Eight restaurants and lounges overlook the ocean, waterfalls and pools. The hotel exercise room includes complete exercise and weight rooms, with sauna and whirlpool. Tour the grounds with a guide to learn more about the Westin's family of birds and their tropical surroundings. This resort's 2.5 million art collection could put a museum to shame and each piece was carefully selected and placed personally by Chris Hemmeter. Numerous nooks with comfortable chairs and art work provide intimate conversation areas. Parents may appreciate the resort's Camp Keiki which offers activities and care for children during vacation periods.

Rates are based on single or double occupancy. Third person add $25, to Royal Beach Club add $45 (maximum 3 persons to a room). Family Plan offers no extra charge for children 18 or under sharing the same room as parents. A 25% discount is available for additional rooms occupied. Complimentary valet parking.
Standard $195, garden view $235, golf-mtn. view $265, oceanview $300
Deluxe ocean view $330, Royal Beach Club $375, Suites $500-$1,600

THE WHALER ★

2481 Kaanapali Parkway, Lahaina, Maui, Hi 96761. (808-661-4861) Managed by Village Resorts 1-800-367-7052. Agents: Whaler's Realty 1-800-367-5632, Kaanapali Vacations 1-800-822-4252, Hawaiian Apt. Leasing 1-800-854-8843 (U.S. except California), 1-800-472-8449 Calif., RSVP 1-800-663-1118.

Choice location in the heart of Kaanapali next to the Whaler's Village Shopping Center and on an excellent beach front. A large pool area is beachfront and they provide an excellent children's program during the summer. Underground parking. $200 deposit, 2-night minimum except over holidays, balance on check-in. 2-week refund notice.

S BR 1 bath (2) o.v. $185/170, g.v. $170/155   Cribs $12/night
1 BR 1 bath (4) o.v. $245/230, g.v. $210/200   Rollaway beds $15/night
1 BR 2 bath (4) o.v. $260/250, g.v. $220/210, o.f. $310/295
2 BR 2 bath (6) o.v. $345/330, o.f. $415/390

KAANAPALI BEACH HOTEL (Hotel)

2525 Kaanapali Pkwy, Lahaina, Maui, HI 96761 (808-661-0011) 1-800-367-5170.

This property is expected to close for construction in late 1992 or early 1993 and will be closed for a full year. 430 units located on Kaanapali beach near Black Rock and Whaler's Village Shops. Air conditioning. Tennis available at nearby Royal Lahaina. Try their whale-shaped swimming pool! Restaurants on site include the Kaanapali Beach Hotel Koffee Shop and the Tiki Terrace Restaurant. A great location, but not a "posh" resort. Some freshening up would do wonders for this comfortable hotel, but then it would also be reflected in the prices!

A good value and, this is Maui's most Hawaiian hotel where the staff are actually instructed in Hawaiiana. *Std. $135, courtyard $145, partial o.v. $155, o.v.$165, o.f. $175. Suites $185 - $525. Crib no charge. Roll-away bed $15 per night, additional person $20 per night. Children under 17 free when sharing room with parents using existing bedding. Compact deluxe rental car with air conditioning and unlimited mileage available during certain times of the year.*

PARROTS

SHERATON HOTEL (Hotel)

2605 Kaanapali Parkway. (808-661-0031) 1-800-325-3535. This 494 unit hotel winds around the side of Black Rock and was one of the first completed in Kaanapali. There are also six-unit cottages on the grounds. The hotel is continuing updating and renovations of the rooms. The beachfront here is excellent for snorkeling and everyone comes here to enjoy the nearly tame fish. The only problem is finding a place to park if you're not staying here. The complex features a variety of shops. Restaurants include The Discovery Room and Black Rock Terrace. They continue to feature the dramatic cliff dive nightly.
Molokai Wing $129, Valueline $144, Standard $170, g.v. $205, partial o.v. $240, o.v. $260, o.f. $300, o.v. suites from $400   Extra adults $25/night

ROYAL LAHAINA RESORT ★

2780 Kekaa Drive, Lahaina, Maui, HI 96761. (808-661-3611) 1-800-44-ROYAL. 540 units located on excellent Kaanapali Beach just north of Black Rock. Located on 27 tropical acres, all cottage suites have kitchens and are situated around the lush, spacious grounds. A mini-mall is conveniently located on the property. Ten tennis courts, three swimming pools. Restaurants on the property include Royal Ocean Terrace, which features a very good Sunday Brunch, Moby Dick's and Chopsticks Restaurant. Nightly luaus in the luau gardens. Children under 17 sharing parents room in existing beds are free. Three swimming pools.
Std. $150/120, superior $175/145, dlx. $200/170, dlx. o.f. $225/195
garden cottage $160-210/130-210, oceanfront cottages $235-275/235-275
1 & 2 BR oceanfront cottages $375 - $1,000   No low season discounts for
Suites 1 BR o.f. $500; 2 BR o.f. $725   suites or o.f. cottages

MAUI KAANAPALI VILLAS

2805 Honoapiilani Hwy., Lahaina, Maui, 96761 (808-667-7791). Agents: Aston 1-800-221-2558, Whaler's Realty 1-800-367-5632, Hawaiian Apt. Leasing 1-800-854-8843 (U.S. except Calif.), 1-800-472-8449 Calif., Kaanapali Vacation Rentals 1-800-822-4252, 1-800-423-8733 ext. 515 Canada, RSVP 1-800-663-1118.

Located on fabulous, sandy Kaanapali Beach, this was once a part of the Royal Lahaina Resort, and before that the Hilton, prior to being converted into condos.
Room with refrigerator (2) $119/99
Studio with kitchen (2) $155-179/$124-149
1 BR with kitchen (4) $180-215/$150-185
2 BR 2 Bth w/kitchen (6) $220/190   Extra person $10

KAANAPALI PLANTATION

150 Puukolii Rd., (PO Box 845) Lahaina, Maui, HI 96761. No rental units available at this time from on-site management. Mostly long term rentals, or rentals through individual owners. 62-unit one, two and three bedroom units in a garden setting situated on a hillside with golf course and ocean views. Washer/dryers. No air conditioning, only ceiling fans.

INTERNATIONAL COLONY CLUB

2750 Kalapu Dr., Lahaina, Maui, HI 96761 (808-661-4070) 1-800-526-6284. 44 low-rise single family cottages on 10 lush acres. Full kitchens, lanais, most have washer/dryers, but coin-op laundry also on premises. Maid service provided on stays of seven days or more. Two heated swimming pools. This property is located across Honoapiilani Highway and up the road from the Kaanapali resorts. It is a bit of a walk to the beach. 4-day minimum April - Dec. 15, 7 day minimum Dec. 16 - March. Deposit equal to 2 nights plus 9.43% tax is refundable with 2 week notice prior to check-in, some restrictions for high season. NO CREDIT CARDS.

1 BR (2) $115, 2 BR (2) $125, 3 BR (3) $145   Extra persons over age 6, $10/nite

MAUI ELDORADO
2661 Kekaa Drive, Lahaina, Maui, Hi 96761. (808-661-0021) 1-800-367-2967, Canada 1-800-663-1118. Agents: Hawaiian Apt. Leasing 1-800-472-8449 CA, 1-800-854-8843 U.S. except CA, Kaanapali Vacations 1-800-822-4252, 1-800-667-9559, Marc Resorts 1-800-535-0085.

204 air conditioned units located on golf course. Private lanais with free HBO and Disney cable TV. Daily maid service. Daily newspaper. Three pools. Free shuttle to cabana on nearby beachfront. Variation in rates reflect location.

S BR (1-2) g.v. $135, o.v. $150	*Extra persons $15*
1 BR (1-4) g.v. $160, o.v. $180	*5-day minimum, weekly/monthly discounts.*
2 BR (1-6) g.v. $210, o.v. $240	*Rollaways $15 and cribs $5 day*

KAANAPALI ROYAL ★
2560 Kekaa Dr., Lahaina, Maui, HI 96761. (808-661-8687) Agents: Hawaiiana Resorts 1-800-367-7040, Whaler's Realty 1-800-367-5632, Hawaiian Apt. Leasing 1-800-472-8449 CA, 1-800-854-8843 U.S. except CA, RSVP 1-800-663-1118.

These very spacious condos, 1,600 - 2,000 sq. ft., offer air conditioning and lanais and are situated on the 16th fairway of the Kaanapali golf course overlooking the Kaanapali resort and Pacific Ocean. Daily maid service. Washer/dryers. Note that while all units have two bedrooms, they may be rented as a one bedroom based on space availability. One bedroom reservations may be wait listed outside of 30 days of arrival. No minimum stay except over Christmas holiday. One night deposit.

1 BR (2,max 4) garden or golf view $165/150, o.v. or dlxe golf view $185/165
2 BR (2,max 6) garden or golf view $190/175, o.v. or dlxe golf view $220/195

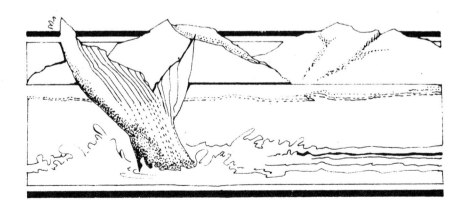

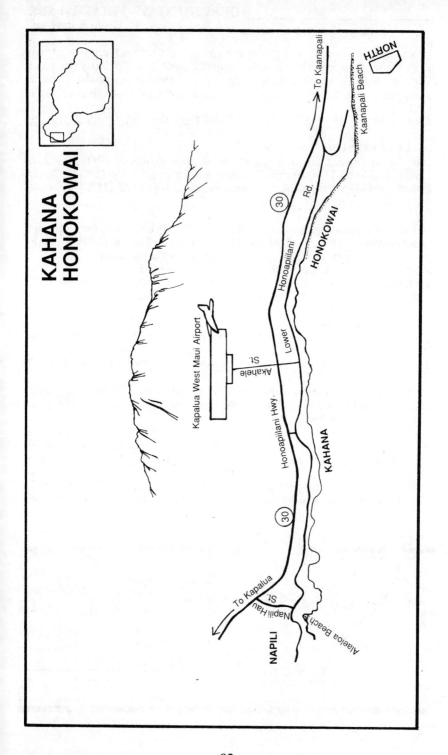

KAHANA
HONOKOWAI

NORTH

To Kaanapali

Kaanapali Beach

Rd.

30

Honoapiilani

HONOKOWAI

Kapalua West Maui Airport

Akahele St.

Lower

KAHANA

Honoapiilani Hwy.

30

To Kapalua

Napili Hau St.

Alaeloa Beach

NAPILI

82

HONOKOWAI

INTRODUCTION

As you leave the Kaanapali Resort there is a stretch of yet undeveloped beachfront on the left still planted with sugar cane. This was the site of the old Kaanapali Airport. Resorts will be stretched along this beach within the next few years. Ahead, four large condo complexes signal the beginning of Honokowai, which stretches north along Lower Honoapiilani Highway. Accommodations are a mix of high and low rise, some new, however, most are older. The beachfront is narrow and many complexes have retaining walls. A close-in reef fronts the beach and comes into shore at Papakea and at Honokowai Park. Between the reef and beach is generally shallow water unsuitable for swimming or other water activities. The only wide beach and break in the reef for swimming and snorkeling is at the Kaanapali Shores and Embassy Suites. In late 1987, several condominiums made a major investment in saving the beachfront by building a seawall beneath the sand to prevent winter erosion. A number of the condominiums are perched on rocky bluffs with no sandy beach.

Many people return year after year to this quiet area, away from the bustle of Lahaina and Kaanapali and where prices are in the moderate range. A couple of small grocery stores are nearby. For dining out there is the Beach Club restaurant at the Kaanapali Shores and The Embassy Suites offers three restaurant choices. Just a short walk up the road is one of our Best Bets for great food. Fat Boy's features enormous, juicy hamburgers and great affordable plate lunches. Feed the family and have change left over.

The condominiums are individually owned for the most part, and the quality and care of each (or lack of) is reflected by the owner. Perhaps it is the shape of the sloping ridges of Pu'u Kukui that cause this area to be slightly cooler and cloudier with more frequent rain showers in the afternoon than at neighboring Kaanapali.

ACCOMMODATIONS - HONOKOWAI

Mahana Resort	Hale Kai	Hale Ono Loa
Maui Kai	Pikake	Lokelani
Embassy Suites Hotel	Hale Maui	Hale Mahina
Kaanapali Shores	Apt. Hotel	Beach Resort
Papakea	Nohonani	Hoyochi Nikko
Maui Sands	Kulankane	Kuleana
Paki Maui	Makani Sands	Polynesian Shores
Honokowai East	Kaleialoha	Mahinahina Beach
Maui Parkshores	Hale Royale	Mahina Surf
Honokowai Rsrt. Apts.	Hono Koa	Noelani

BEST BETS: Kaanapali Shores - A high-rise surrounded by lovely grounds on the best beach in the area. **Papakea** - A low rise complex with attractive grounds and pool. **Embassy Suites Hotel** - A mix between a condo and a hotel, spacious rooms and breakfast is included, a good sandy beach.

MAHANA
110 Kaanapali Shores Place, Lahaina, Maui, HI 96761. (808-661-8751) Agents: Aston 1-800-922-7866, Whaler's Realty 1-800-367-5632, RSVP 1-800-663-1118, Hawaiian Apt. Leasing 1-800-854-8843 in U.S. except CA, 1-800-472-8449 CA.

All units oceanfront. Two twelve-story towers with two tennis courts, heated pool, central air conditioning, saunas, elevators, small pool area. Located on narrow beachfront with offshore coral reef precluding swimming and snorkeling. A better swimming area is 100 yards up the beach. This is a rather drab looking condominium on the outside, the pool sits out on a slab of cement without much in the way of atmosphere. They have been experiencing trouble with beach erosion as have the other properties along this stretch of Honokowai.

S BR 1 bath (1-2) $159/139   3-night minimum
1 BR 1 bath (1-4) $185/165
2 BR 2 bath (1-6) $230/210

MAUI KAI
106 Kaanapali Shores Pl., Lahaina, Maui, Hi 96761. (808-661-0002) 1-800-367-5635. Agents: Blue Sky Tours 1-800-678-2787, Condo Network 1-800-321-2525, Paradise Resorts 1-800-367-2644, Kumulani 1-800-367-2954.

A single ten-story building with 79 units. 2-night deposit, 2-night minimum. Units offer central air conditioning, private lanais, full equipped kitchens. Property amenities include swimming pool, jacuzzi, laundry facilities, free parking. 5th person in room $10 per night. No charge children under 2. Built in 1970, it is one of the older properties. Weekly/monthly discounts.

Studio (1-3) $110/90, 1 BR (1-4) $130/115, 2 BR (1-4) $180/160

EMBASSY SUITES RESORT ★
104 Kaanapali Shores Place, Lahaina, Maui, HI 96761. (808-661-2000). 1-800-462-6284 U.S., 1-800-458-5848 Canada. On 7 1/2 acres this pink pyramid structure with a three-story blue waterfall cascading down the side can't be missed. A new concept in resorts on Maui, it blends the best of condo and resort living together. The pool area is large and tropical with plenty of room for lounge chairs. For the past few years this beach has suffered from erosion problems, but seems to have somewhat stabilized since the neighboring Kaanapali Shores conducted some extensive erosion control measures. The lobby is open air. (When it opened they discovered there was a little too much breeze and glass walls were installed to keep the wind from whistling in too briskly!) Glass enclosed elevators whisk you up with a view!

Each one bedroom suite is a spacious 840 sq. ft, two bedroom suites are 1,200 sq. ft. Each features lanais with ocean or terrace views. Master bedrooms are equipped with a remote control 29" television and an large adjoining master bath with soaking tub. The living room, decorated in comfortable hues of blue and beige contains a massive 35" television, stereo receiver, VCR player and cassette player. Living rooms have a sofa that makes into a double bed. A dining area with a small kitchenette is equipped with a microwave, small refrigerator and sink. Toaster ovens, hot plates and ironing equipment available upon request. One phone in the living room and another in the bedroom have two lines which connect to a personal answering machine for your own recorded message.

Their two presidential suites are 2,100 sq. ft. and offer two bedrooms, two full baths and a larger kitchen. One features an Oriental theme, the other is decorated with a contemporary California flare. Made-to-order breakfasts are served in their Oihana restaurant. The Maui Rose offers more formal dining and the Lokahi Terrace features a prime rib buffet. Children's program is $35 per day, $30 for each additional child. Cost of lunch and activities included. Ages 5 - 12 years.
1 BR terrace view $195, mtn.v. $225, o.v. $255, o.f. $275-325
2 BR mtn.v. $390, o.v. $450, Presidential Suite $1,000

KAANAPALI SHORES ★
100 Kaanapali Shores Place, Lahaina, Maui, Hi 96761, (808-667-2211). Agents: Aston 1-800-922-7866, Whaler's Realty 1-800-367-5632, RSVP Reservations 1-800-663-1118.

463 units, all offer telephones, free tennis, daily maid service, and air conditioning. Nicely landscaped grounds and a wide beach with an area of coral reef cleared for swimming and snorkeling. This and the Embassy Suites are the only resorts on north Kaanapali Beach that offers a good swimming area. Putting green, jacuzzi and the Beach Club Restaurant are all located in the pool area. In 1992 they announced that they would begin to offer their childrens program, Camp Kaanapali year-round at this property, but we suggest you verify. Costs for the 9 a.m. - 2 p.m. Mon.-Fri. program is $10 for initial registration, which includes t-shirt and optional at a nominal fee are lunch at $6 per day, excursions and other special activities designed for kids three to eight years.
S BR (1-4) g.v. $159/129, o.v. $179/149   *7-night minimum over*
1 BR (1-4) g.v. $189/159, o.v. $209/179   *the christmas holidays*
2 BR (1-6) g.v. $249/209, o.v. $279/249, o.f. $375/350

PAPAKEA ★
3543 L. Honoapiilani, Lahaina, Maui, HI 96761. (808-669-4848) 1-800-367-5637. Agents: Maui Resort Management 1-800-367-5037. Whaler's Realty 1-800-367-5632, Rainbow Reservations 1-800-367-6092, RSVP 1-800-663-1118, Hawaiian Apt. Leasing 1-800-472-8449 CA, 1-800-854-8843 U.S. except CA., Maui Network 1-800-367-5221, More Hawaii for Less 1-800-967-6687.

364 units in five four-story buildings. Two pools, two jacuzzi's, two saunas, tennis courts, putting green, washer/dryers, and BBQ area. A seawall was installed in an effort to prevent further beach erosion. The shallow water is great for children due to a protective reef 10-30 yards offshore, but poor for swimming or snorkeling. A better beach is down in front of the Kaanapali Shores. One of the nicer grounds for a condominium complex with lush landscaping and pool areas. A comfortable, and quiet property that we recommend especially for families. No smoking units available. Crib or roll-away $6/day. Christmas holiday 14-day minimum with no refunds after October 1. 7-day refund notice, 2 night deposit. Cribs $12/night.
S BR (2) partial o.v. $134/119, o.f. $144/129   *Wkly/monthly discounts*
1 BR (4) partial o.v. $154/139, o.f. $174/159
2 BR (6) partial o.v. $189/174, o.f. $219/204

MAUI SANDS
3559 L. Honoapiilani, Lahaina, Maui, HI 96761. (808-669-4811) Maui Resort Management 1-800-367-5037. Agent: Rainbow Reservations 1-800-367-6092.

All 76 units have air conditioning and kitchens. Limited maid service. Microwaves, coin-op laundry facility, rollaway & cribs available $9 night. A very friendly atmosphere where old friends have been gathering each year since it was built in the mid-sixties. A large central laundry facility is available and a large pool area with barbecues. Large boulders line the beach. A good family facility.
1 BR (2,max 4) std. $ 80/68, g.v. $105/ 85, o.f. $135/115 - Extra persons $9/nite
2 BR (2,max 6) std. $100/81, g.v. $130/108, o.f. $160/135 - 15% monthly discount

PAKI MAUI
3615 L. Honoapiilani, Lahaina, Maui, HI 96761. (808-669-8235) Agents: Marc Resorts Group, 1-800-535-0085. This complex surrounds a garden and waterfall. No air conditioning. With Marc rentals, suite rates include complimentary European breakfast and sunset Manager's cocktail reception daily. Daily maid service.
S BR (1-2) o.f. $139/119   *2-nite deposit*
1 BR (1-4) g.v. $139/119, o.f. $159/139   *cribs $5/nite*
2 BR (1-6) o.f. $199-219 / $179-199   *children under 2 free*

HONOKOWAI EAST
3660 L. Honoapiilani Hwy., Lahaina, Maui, HI 96761 (808-669-8355) 51 units, mostly studios, in a 4-story building. Long term property.

MAUI PARK
3626 L. Honoapiilani Hwy., Lahaina, Maui, HI 96761. (808-669-6622) Agents: Aston 1-800-922-7866, RSVP Reservations 1-800-663-1118, Maui Condominiums 1-800-663-6962. Located across the road from Honokowai Beach Park which lacks a sandy shoreline. A quiet area of West Maui with nearby grocery store. All units have complete kitchen. Coin-op laundry facility. Originally built as residential apartments they offer phones, and daily maid service. Because of its original intention, this property does resemble a residential area more than a vacation resort. All units are garden view. Cribs $6, rollaways $10.
S BR (1-2) $89/79, 1 BR (1-4) $109/99, 2 BR (6) $149/139

HONOKOWAI PALMS RESORT
3666 L. Honoapiilani, Lahaina, Maui, HI 96761. (808-669-6130) 1-800-843-1633. Agent: Klahani Investments 1-800-669-0795, 30 units across road from Honokowai Beachfront Park. Built of cement blocks this property lacks a great deal of ambience as a vacation retreat. Perhaps for the real budget conscious it would be suitable, but it is a very basic, functional complex. Deposit $200 or 25% of first 28 days. Cancellations must be made 30 days prior to arrival. NO CREDIT CARDS through property, however, Klahani will take visa or mastercard.
1 BR (2,max 4) $60/65   *Extra person $6/nite*
2 BR (2,max 6) $75/70   *Wkly/monthly discounts*

HALE KAI
3691 L. Honoapiilani Hwy., Lahaina, Maui, HI 96761. (808-669-6333) 1-800-446-7307 U.S. and Canada. FAX (808) 669-7474. 40 units in a two-story building. The units do have lanais, kitchens, and a pool, but the beach is somewhat rocky. A simple and quiet property. 3-night minimum except Christmas. $250 refundable with 45 day notice. NO CREDIT CARDS. Minimum 3 nights. 10% monthly discounts - additional discounts may be given at individual owner's discretion.
1 BR (2) $90 & up, 2 BR (4) $120 & up - Extra persons over 3 years $10/night

PIKAKE

3701 L. Honoapiilani, Lahaina, Maui, HI 96761. (808-669-6086) 1-800-446-3054. A low-rise, two-story, Polynesian style building with only twelve apartments completed in 1966. Private lanais open to the green lawn or balconies, with a beach protected by sea wall. Central laundry area. Light housekeeping provided after two week's stay. 3-night deposit, 3-night minimum, Extra persons $10/night. NO CREDIT CARDS. *1 BR (2,max 4) $84/77, 2 BR (4,max 6) $110/99*

HALE MAUI APARTMENT HOTEL

P.O. Box 516, Lahaina, Maui, HI 96761. (808-669-6312). Limited maid service. Coin-operated washer/dryer. BBQ. Weekly and monthly discounts. 3-day minimum, 7-day during Christmas. NO CREDIT CARDS.
1 BR (2, max 5) $65-85   Extra persons $8/night

NOHONANI

3723 L. Honoapiilani, Lahaina, Maui, HI 96761. (808-669-8208) 1-800-822-7368. Office open 9 am - 5 pm Mon. - Sat. Two 4-story buildings containing 22 two-bedroom units and 5 one-bedroom units. All units are oceanfront. Complex has large pool, telephones, and is one block to grocery store. Maid service on checkout. Extra persons $15/night. $200 deposit with 60-day refund notice, 4-day minimum stay. Weekly/monthly discounts. NO CREDIT CARDS.
1 BR (1-2) $102-106 / $92-102, 2 BR (1-4) $125/110

KULAKANE

3741 L. Honoapiilani (P.O. Box 5236), Lahaina, Maui, HI 96761. (808-669-6119) 1-800-367-6088. 42 oceanfront units with fully equipped kitchen, laundry facilities on premise. Lanais overlook ocean but no sandy beach. $10 extra person. 3 night minimum low season, 5 night high season. $150 deposit. 10% monthly discounts. *1 BR 1 bath (1-2) $90-95, 2 BR 2 bath (1-4) $135*

MAKANI SANDS

3765 L. Honoapiilani Hwy., Lahaina, Maui, HI 96761. (808-669-8223). 30 units in a four-story building. Dishwashers, washer/dryers, elevator. Oceanfront with small sandy beach. Weekly maid service. Deposits vary, weekly/monthly discounts, 3-night minimum, extra persons $10/night.
1 BR (2) $85, 2 BR (4) $120, 3 BR (6) $140

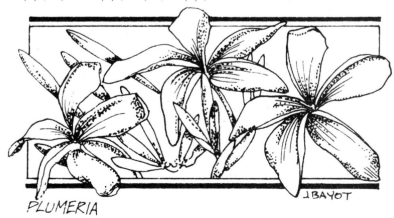

PLUMERIA   JBAYOT

KALEIALOHA
3785 L. Honoapiilani, Lahaina, Maui, HI 96761. (808-669-8197) 1-800-222-8688. 67 units in a 4-story building. 3-night minimum. Deposit equal to three nights stay, $7.50 extra persons over age 2. Refundable if cancelled 45 days prior to arrival. Washer/dryers. Weekly discounts. 3 night minimum. Credit cards accepted. *Studio (1-2) mtn.v. $75, 1 BR (1-4) o.v. superior $85, deluxe $95*

HALE ROYALE
3788 L. Honoapiilani, Lahaina, Maui, HI 96761. (808-669-5230). No short term rental units available at this time.

HONO KOA
3801 L. Honoapiilani, Lahaina, Maui, HI 96761. (808-669-0979) 1-800-225-7215. Agent: Ironwood Resorts 1-800-745-7666. 28 units in one four-story building. Washer/dryer, dishwasher, microwave, BBQ. Pool with jacuzzi. No minimum stay. Advance deposit of one or two nights, refunded with 72 day cancellation notice except high season. $10 extra person, children 6 and under free. Limited maid service. *2 BR 2 bath (1-4, max 6) g.v. 150, o.v. $175, o.f. $200*

HALE ONO LOA ★
3823 L. Honoapiilani, Lahaina, Maui, HI 96761. (808-669-6362) Agents: More Hawaii 1-800-967-6687 U.S. & Canada, Klahani 1-800-669-MAUI (U.S. & Canada), Maui Accommodations 1-800-252-MAUI (U.S.) 67 oceanfront and oceanview units. Maid service extra charge. Beachfront is rocky. The units we toured were roomy and nicely furnished with spacious lanais. The grounds and pool area were pleasant and well groomed. A good choice for a quiet retreat. Grocery store nearby.
1 BR 1 bath (4) g.v. $85(535/wk) / $75(475/wk), o.v. $95(600/wk) / $85(535/wk)
2 BR 2 bath (6) g.v. $150(840/wk), o.v. 160(920), o.f. $170(1,000/wk)

LOKELANI
3833 L. Honoapiilani, Lahaina, Maui, HI 96761. (808-669-8110) 1-800-367-2976. Agents: Rainbow Reservations 1-800-367-6092. Three 3-story 12 unit buildings with beachfront or oceanviews. The 1-BR units are on beach level with lanai, 2-BR units are townhouses with bedrooms upstairs and lanais on both levels. Units feature washer/dryers and dishwashers. Weekly discount, 3-night minimum low season, 7-night high season, extra persons $8, $25 cancellation fee. Three night deposit, balance due two weeks prior to arrival.
1 BR (1-2) $90-105 / 80-95, 2 BR (townhouses) (1-4) $115-145 / 105-130

HALE MAHINA BEACH RESORT
3875 L. Honoapiilani, Lahaina, Maui, HI 96761. (808-669-8441) 1-800-367-8047 ext. 441. Agents: Maui Network 1-800-367-5221, Rainbow Reservations 1-800-367-6092, Kaanapali Vacation Rentals 1-800-822-4252, Klahani 1-800-669-MAUI (U.S. & Canada). Hale Mahina means "House of the Pale Moon" and offers 52 units in two, four-story buildings and one two-story building featuring lanais, ceiling fans, microwaves, washer/dryer. BBQ area, jacuzzi. Extra persons $10/-night. 3-day minimum, deposit within two weeks of reservations, balance on arrival. Klahani Resorts offers the seventh night free.
1 BR (1-2) $115/100, 2 BR (1-4) $135/120

HOYOCHI NIKKO

3901 L. Honoapiilani, Lahaina, Maui, HI 96761. (808-669-8343) Agents: Klahani 1-800-669-MAUI (U.S. & Canada). 18 one-bedroom oceanview units (on a rocky beachfront) in two-story building bearing an oriental motif. Underground parking, "Long Boy" twin beds, some with queens, half size washer/dryers in units. Maid service on check-out. $100-250 deposit with 30-day refund notice low season, 60-day high season. Prepayment required. NO CREDIT CARDS through property. Agent Klahani will take MC or Visa. *1 BR ($80-90) - extra persons $10/night*

KULEANA

3959 L. Honoapiilani, Lahaina, Maui, HI 96761. (808-669-8080) U.S. Mainland or Canada 1-800-367-5633. Agents: Kaanapali Vacation Rentals 1-800-822-4252. 118 1-bedroom units with queen size sofa bed in living room. Large pool with plenty of lounge chair room and tennis court. A short walk to sandy beaches. Weekly/monthly discounts. 3 night minimum stay. Extra persons $7.50. Children under 2 free. Cribs $4/night, rollaways $6. 3-night deposit refundable with 14 day notice. *1 BR o.v. $85/80, o.f. 95/90*

POLYNESIAN SHORES

3975 L. Honoapiilani, Lahaina, Maui, HI 96761. (808-669-6065) 1-800-433-6284, from Canada toll free 1-800-488-2179. 52 units on a rocky shore but nice grounds with deck overlooking the ocean. Color TV. Additional persons $10 each. 7th night free. 10% monthly discount. $300 deposit. 60 days cancellation notice for refund. $200 deposit, 3-day minimun, 10% discount for 29 days or more.
1 BR 1 bath (2) $105/95, 2 BR 2 bath (4) $135-145 / $125-135
3 BR 3 bath (6) $155/145

MAHINAHINA BEACH

4007 L. Honoapiilani, Lahaina, Maui, HI 96761. Units only through owners.

MAHINA SURF

4057 L. Honoapiilani, Lahaina, Maui, HI 96761 (808-669-6068) 1-800-367-6086, FAX (808) 669-4534. Agent: Klahani 1-800-669-MAUI (U.S. & Canada). 56 one-bedroom and one-bedroom with loft units. Dishwashers, maid service available at hourly charge. Located on rocky shore, the nearest sandy beach is a short drive to Kahana. Large lawn area around pool offers plenty of room for lounging. $300 deposit, 4-week refund notice.
1 BR 1 bath (2,max 4) $100/85   Extra persons $8/nite including children
2 BR 1 bath $115/100, 2 bath $120/105 Wkly/monthly discounts

NOELANI

4095 L. Honoapiilani, Lahaina, Maui, HI 96761. (808-669-8375) 1-800-367-6030. Agent: Condominium Connection 1-800-423-2976. 50 oceanfront units in one 4-story building and two 2-story structures. Kitchens with dishwashers and washer/dryers only in 1, 2, and 3-bedroom units. Three bedroom units feature a sunken livingroom as do the two bedroom units on the third floor. Complex has two pools and maid service mid-week. Located on a rocky shore, nearest sandy beach is short drive to Kahana. Weekly/monthly discounts. Extra person $7.50 day. 3 day minimum low season/7 day high season.
S BR 1 bath (1-2) $ 77, 1 BR 1 bath (1-2) $ 97   3-nite deposit
2 BR 2 bath (1-2) $130, 3 BR 3 bath (1-6) $155   2-wk refund notice

KAHANA

INTRODUCTION

To the north of Honokowai, and about seven miles north of Lahaina is a prominent island of high rise condos with a handful of two-story complexes strung along the coast in its lee. This is Kahana. The beach adjacent to the high rises is fairly wide, but tapers off quickly after this point. Several of the larger complexes offer very nice grounds and spacious living quarters with more resort type activities than in Honokowai. The prices are lower than Kaanapali, but higher than Honokowai. Several restaurants and quick-stop groceries are located nearby. Over the past year or so there has been a continuing problem with a green algae along the shoreline from Honokowai to Kapalua. The major problem, though, appears to be in the Kahana area where shoreline conditions, ocean currents and wind bring the algae into shore, frequently rendering the beaches here less than desirable places to play. The algae tends to accumulate in large blankets under water at the other beaches, like Napili and Kapalua, but doesn't tend to come onto shore. The most recent reports indicate that it is an algae bloom resulting from the runoff of chemicals such as nitrates. The state officials are, as yet, unable to pinpoint the source and indicate that it could be a combination of factors. Monitoring stations will be established in the waters around West Maui to track the situation. The county may find it necessary to institute controls on the amount of fertilizers used in the area.

WHERE TO SHOP

There are a few shops in the lower level of the Kahana Manor. The new Kahana Gateway has opened at the entrance to the Kahana area. Shops include gift and dive shops, a gas station and Whaler's General Store, beauty salon, children's fashion store, a laundry, McDonald's and Roy's Kahana Bar & Grill.

ACCOMMODATIONS - KAHANA

Kahana Beach Hotel	Valley Isle Resort	Kahana Reef
Kahana Villa	Royal Kahana	Kahana Outrigger
Kahana Falls	Hololani	Kahana Village
Sands of Kahana	Pohailaini/Maui Kalani	Kahana Sunset

BEST BETS: *Sands of Kahana* - Spacious units on a nice white sand beach. ***Kahana Sunset*** - Low rise condos surrounding a secluded cove and beach.

KAHANA BEACH HOTEL
4221 L. Honoapiilani, Lahaina, Maui, HI 96761. (808-669-8611) Agent: Pleasant Hawaiian Holidays (package tours) 1-800-242-9244. All units offer oceanview. The studios sleep up to four and have kitchenettes. The 1 BR units have kitchens, 2 lanais, living room with queen-size sofa bed, bedroom with 2 queen beds, 2 full-size baths, dressing room, and will accommodate 7. Coin-op laundry on premises. Nice, white sandy beach fronting complex.

KAHANA VILLA

4242 L. Honoapiilani, Lahaina, Maui, HI 96761. (808-669-5613) Agents: Marc Resorts Group 1-800-535-0085, Hawaiian Apt. Leasing 1-800-854-8843 (1-800-472-8449 CA), RSVP 1-800-663-1118. Across the road from the beach. Units have microwaves, washer/dryers, telephones. Daily maid service. Sauna, tennis courts, store, restaurants. Cribs $5, rollaway $15.

1 BR 1 bath g.v. (1-4) $129/109, o.v. $149/129, o.v. superior $169/149
2 BR 1 bath g.v. (1-6) $169/149, o.v. $189/169, o.v. superior $209/189

KAHANA FALLS

4260 Lower Honoapiilani Hwy, Lahaina, Maui, HI 96761. 1-800-531-9054, (808) 669-0420. FAX (808) 669-0518. This property opened in March 1991 and offers 36 2-bedroom 2-bath (which can convert to a studio plus one bedroom unit) and 24 1-bedroom units (which can be divided to form a hotel room and one bedroom unit). The units are furnished with washer and dryer (except hotel unit), cable television, air conditioning, telephones, whirlpool tub, VCR player. Children's pool, five waterfalls, sand-bottom swimming pool, on-site activities, fitness center. This is a vacation ownership resort, meaning people can purchase time shares. However, they currently are also operating as a hotel/condo. Children under 12 free. Rollaway or crib $8. Deposit. Check out time 9 a.m., check in 4 p.m.

1 BR 2 bath (1-4) $120, Hotel unit with 1 bath (1-2) $60
2 BR 2 bath (1-4) $160, Studio with 1 bath $90

SANDS OF KAHANA ★

4299 L. Honoapiilani, Lahaina, Maui, HI 96761. (808-669-0400) Agents: Hawaiian Apt. Leasing 1-800-854-8843 (1-800-472-8449 CA), RSVP 1-800-663-1118, Whaler's Realty 1-800-367-5632.

96 units on Kahana Beach. Underground parking. If you're looking to be a little away from the hustle of Lahaina/Kaanapali, with quarters large enough for a big family, and luxuries such as microwaves and full-size washer/dryers then this may be just what you seek. Located on a sandy beachfront and only a couple miles from Kaanapali, it is also less than a mile from the West Maui Airport. Four 8-story buildings surround a central restaurant (The Kahana Terrace) and a dual pool area.

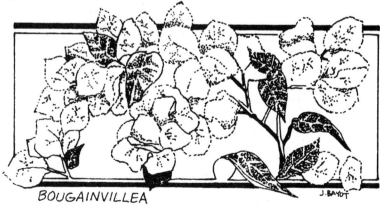

BOUGAINVILLEA

J. BAYOT

Sands of Kahana is family oriented from the size of their rooms to their children's playground and summer programs. Spacious one, two and three bedroom units have enormous kitchens and beautifully appointed living rooms. Plenty of room to spread out! Moloka'i is beautifully framed in the large picture windows of the oceanview units, or select among the slightly less expensive garden view units. Although an annoying green algae has been invading the beaches lately, which pretty well prohibited swimming, there was plenty of fun in the sun. The beachside volleyball court was filled each afternoon, and the large three foot deep children's pool was popular, as was another larger and deeper pool with jacuzzi, three tennis courts and a putting green.

Most complexes restrict the use of snorkel gear or flotation equipment in the pool, however, here it is allowed to the delight of the children. A small children's play area offers diversion while parents make use of several garden area charcoal barbecues. The summer children's program is very reasonable and invites children between the ages of 5 and 12 to participate in activities. Across the street is a small grocery store and several restaurants are within walking distance. Extra persons $10. Under age 18 free in existing space.

1 BR 1 bath o.v. (4) $205/170, o.f. $240/200, mtn.v. $185/155
2 BR 1 bath o.v. (6) $270/245, o.f. $310/280, mtn.v. $240/200
3 BR 2 bath o.v. (8) $320/290, o.f. $340/310, mtn.v. $310/280

VALLEY ISLE RESORT
4327 L. Honoapiilani, Lahaina, Maui, HI 96761. (808-669-5511) Agent: Rainbow Reservations 1-800-367-6092. Partial air conditioning. Telephones. Located on Kahana Beach. On site restaurant and grocery store. Prices are for stays of 1 to 3 days. Substantial discounts for 5 or more days (i.e. 5 day stay, low season studio is $65). Payment in full 30 days prior to arrival. Weekly maid service.

S BR 1 bath (2) o.f. $ 85/ 65   *Extra persons $10, under 3 free*
1 BR 1 bath (2) o.v. $ 90/ 75, o.f. $ 95-105 / $80-90
2 BR 2 bath (4) o.v. $115/100, o.f. $130/120

ROYAL KAHANA
4365 L. Honoapiilani, Lahaina, Maui, HI 96761. (808-669-5911) 1-800-447-7783, FAX (808) 669-5950. Agents: Hawaiiana Resorts 1-800-367-7040. 12 story high-rise complex built in 1975 with 236 oceanview units on Kahana Beach. Underground parking and air conditioning. Daily maid service. A nice pool area with sauna. Tennis courts. Units have full kitchens and microwaves. Nearby grocery stores, restaurants and shops. Rollaway/cribs $6/per day.

1 BR 1 bath (1-2) o.v. $124/97, Studio (1-3) o.v. $95/80   *2-nite deposit*
2 BR 2 bath (1-6) o.v.-o.f. $153-181 / $125-157   *15-day refund notice*

HOLOLANI
4401 L. Honoapiilani, Lahaina, Maui, HI 96761. (808-669-8021) 1-800-367-5032, 1-800-423-8733 ext. 318 Canada. Agent: Rainbow Reservations 1-800-367-6092. 27 oceanfront units on sandy, reef protected beach. Covered parking. Grocery store. 7-day/3-day minimum. $250 deposit, full payment 60/30 days prior to arrival. Children under 5 free. NO CREDIT CARDS. Extra persons $10/night.

1 and 2 BR 2 bath (2,max 6) $125-165 / $110-130

POHAILANI (MAUI KAILANI)

4435 L. Honoapiilani, Lahaina, Maui, HI 96761 (808-669-6994) FAX (808) 669-4046. Agent: Rainbow Reservations 1-800-367-6092. Maui Kailani is the rental portion of the Pohailani. The Maui Kailani offers a mixture of two-bedroom and studio apartments. The larger units are situated around eight park-like acres, while the studio units sit directly on the beach. Walking distance to restaurants and grocery stores. Swimming pool, tennis courts, laundry facilities. T.V. cable and T.V. rental are available for each unit, but cannot be requested prior to arrival. Full kitchens in both studio and two bedroom units. Twice weekly maid service. Extra person $5 day. Monthly rates available. Deposit varies.
S BR o.f. (2, max 3) $75, 2 BR g.v. (2, max 5) $75. Weekly rates $455 for either

KAHANA REEF ★

4471 L. Honoapiilani, Lahaina, Maui, HI 96761. (808-669-6491) 1-800-253-3773 FAX (808) 669-2192. 88 well-kept units. Limited number of oceanfront studios available. Laundry facilities on premises. 15% monthly discounts. Maid service daily except Sun. NO CREDIT CARDS. Room and car packages available. $200 deposit, extra persons $8/night. A good value. *1 BR 1 bath (2,max 5) o.v. $100/90*

KAHANA OUTRIGGER

4521 L. Honoapiilani, Lahaina, Maui, HI 96761. (808-669-6550) 1-800-852-4262. Agents: Rainbow Reservations 1-800-367-6092. Sixteen spacious 3-bedroom oceanview condo suites in low-rise complex on a narrow sandy beachfront. Units have microwaves and washer/dryers and are appointed with lots of Italian tile. These are rented as a vacation "home" and no on-property service provided.
3 BR 2 bath (6) $195/165, 3 BR 3 bath (6) $215/180

KAHANA VILLAGE ★

4531 L. Honoapiilani, Lahaina, Maui, HI 96761. (808-669-5111) 1-800-824-3065. Agents: Kumulani 1-800-367-2954, RSVP 1-800-663-1118. Attractive townhouse units. Second level units are 1,200 sq.ft.; ground level 3-bedroom units have 1,700 sq.ft. with a wet bar, sunken tub in master bath, Jenn-aire ranges, microwaves, lanais, and washer/dryers. Pool area jacuzzi. Nice but narrow beach offering good swimming. 5-day minimum. Bi-weekly maid service. NO CREDIT CARDS. $300 deposit, balance due prior to arrival. Monthly discounts. Additional person $20.
2 BR o.v. $170/140, o.f. $200/170, 3 BR o.v. $225/185, o.f. $250/210

KAHANA SUNSET ★

P.O. Box 10219, Lahaina, Maui, HI 96761. (808-669-8011) 1-800-669-1488, FAX (808) 669-9170. Agents: RSVP 1-800-663-1118, Whaler's Realty 1-800-367-5632.

Ninety units on a beautiful and secluded white sand beach. Units have very large lanais, telephones, and washer/dryers. Each unit has its own lanai, but they adjoin one another, adding to the friendly atmosphere of this complex. One of the very few resorts with a heated pool and heated children's pool, BBQ. You can drive up right to your door on most of the two bedroom units making unloading easy (and with a family heavy into suitcases that can be a real back saver.) Extra persons $8/night including infants, 10% monthly discounts. NO CREDIT CARDS if booked through office on property.
1 BR 1 bath (2) o.v. $150, 2 BR 2 bath (2) o.v. $185, o.f. $235

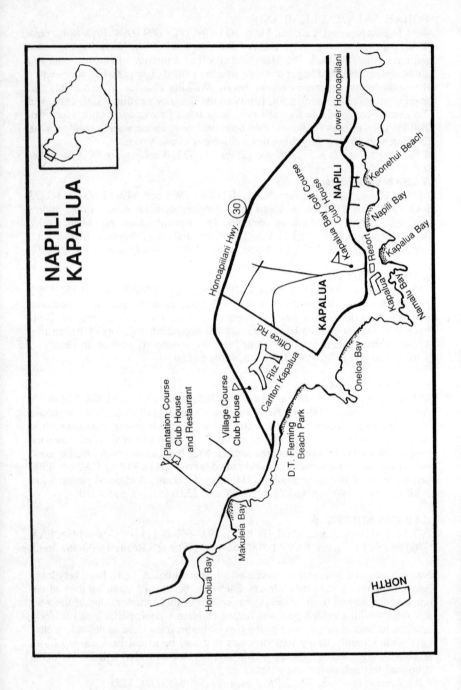

NAPILI
KAPALUA

Lower Honoapiilani
Keonehui Beach
Napili Bay
Kapalua Bay
Namalu Bay
Kapalua
NAPILI
Kapalua Bay Golf Course
Kapalua Bay Club House
Resort
KAPALUA
Honoapiilani Hwy. (30)
Office Rd.
Oneloa Bay
Ritz Carlton Kapalua
Village Course Club House
D.T. Fleming Beach Park
Plantation Course Club House and Restaurant
Makuleia Bay
Honolua Bay

NORTH

NAPILI

INTRODUCTION

This area's focal point is the beautiful Napili Bay with good swimming, snorkeling and boogie boarding, and it even has tide pools for children to explore. The condominium units here are low-rise, with prices mostly in the moderate range, and are clustered tightly around the bay. A number are located right on the beach, others a short walk away. The quality of the units vary considerably, but generally a better location on the bay and better facilities demands a higher price. The complexes are small, most under 50 units, and all but one has a pool. A small grocery store or two is within walking distance and, depending on your location, a couple of restaurants could be reached on foot. The Napili Plaza Shopping Center recently opened.

WHERE TO SHOP
The Napili Shopping area is in a new addition to the area. It includes Subway Sandwiches, West Maui Floral, Maui Pizza Fresh, First Hawaiian bank, Food Pantry and Koho Grill and Bar.

ACCOMMODATIONS - NAPILI

Honokeana Cove	Napili Bay
Napili Sands	Napili Sunset
Coconut Inn	Hale Napili
Napili Point	Napili Village Suites
Napili Shores	Mauian
Napili Surf	The Kahili
	Napili Kai Beach Club

BEST BETS: *Napili Sunset* - Centered right on the edge of Napili Bay, rooms are well kept. *Napili Kai Beach Club* - A quiet facility on the edge of Napili Bay. Large grounds and a restaurant are on site. Resort activities are offered.

HONOKEANA COVE
5255 L. Honoapiilani, Lahaina, Maui, HI 96761. (808-669-6441) 1-800-237-4948. 38 oceanview units on Honokeana Cove near Napili Bay. Attractive grounds. 3-night minimum, 3-night deposit (except Christmas). NO CREDIT CARDS.
1 BR 1 bath (2) $ 95, 1 BR 2 bath (2) $105
2 BR 2 bath (4,max 4) $135, 3 BR 2 bath (6,max 6) $155, Townhouse (4) $150
Wkly/monthly discounts, extra persons (all ages) $10-$15/nite

NAPILI SANDS
Hui Rd. "F," Lahaina, Maui, HI 96761. 44 studios and 88 one-bedroom units in 11 two-story buildings. One block to small grocery store and walking distance to bus stop and beach. Long term stays only.

COCONUT INN

Hui Rd. "F," P.O. Box 10517, Napili, Maui, HI 96761. (808-669-5712) 1-800-367-8006. 40 units in two-story retreat about 1/4 mile above Napili Bay. 5 studios, 30 one-bedroom units and 5 deluxe one-bedroom units. Built in 1975, renovated in 1989. Free shuttle to or from West Maui Airport. No oceanviews. Pool, spa, daily maid service. Attractive tropical grounds. Charge for local calls. Laundry facilities. Continental breakfast included. Extra persons $10/night. *Studio (2) $85/75, 1 BR (2) $95/85, deluxe with loft (2) $105/95*
Extra persons $10/night

NAPILI POINT

5295 L. Honoapiilani, Lahaina, Maui, HI 96761. (808-669-5611) 1-800-669-6252. Located on rocky beach, but next door to beautiful Napili Bay. Units have washer/dryer, direct dial phones, daily maid service. Two pools. In some suites the second bedroom is loft-style.
1 BR 1 bath (4) o.v. $164/134, o.f. $174-184 / $144-154
2 BR 2 bath (6) o.v. $195/170, o.f. $205-225 / $180-190

NAPILI SHORES

5315 L. Honoapiilani, Lahaina, Maui, HI 96761. (808-669-8061) FAX (808) 669-5047. Agents: Colony Resorts 1-800-367-6046, Hawaiian Apt. Leasing 1-800-854-8843, Rainbow Reservations 1-800-367-6092, RSVP 1-800-663-1118.

152 units on Napili Bay. Rooms offer lanais and the one-bedroom units have dishwashers. Laundry facilities on premises as well as two pools, hot tub, croquet, and BBQ area. Restaurant, cocktail lounge and grocery store on property. Extra persons $15/night, no minimum stay, daily maid service. Studios have one queen and one twin bed. Crib $8, rollaway $15/per day.
S BR (2,max 3) g.v. $150/135, o.v. $160/145, o.f. $175/160
1 BR (2,max 4) g.v. $170/155, o.v. $185/170

NAPILI SURF

50 Napili Place, Lahaina, Maui, HI 96761. (808) 669-8002. 1-800-541-0638. 53 units on Napili Bay. Two pools, BBQ, shuffleboard, lanais, daily maid service, and laundry facilities. Extra persons $15/night, 12% monthly discount, $300 deposit, 14-day refund notice, 5-night minimum except 10-day during Christmas, NO CREDIT CARDS.
S BR (2,max 3) g.v. $94, o.v. $114/104, 1 BR (2,max 5) $159/142

NAPILI BAY

33 Hui Drive, Lahaina Maui, HI 96761. (808-669-6044). Agents: Whalers Realty 1-800-367-5632, Hawaiian Apt. Leasing 1-800-854-8843 (1-800-472-8449 CA), Hawaiian Ensign (808) 661-3911.

This older complex on Napili Bay is neat, clean and affordably priced. Studio apartments offer 1 queen & 2 single beds, lanais, kitchens, daily maid service. Coin-op laundromat with public phones. Extra persons $8/night, children under 12 free. 3-night minimum, 2-night deposit, 7-day refund notice, weekly and monthly discounts. *Studio (2,max 4) g.v. $75-95, partial o.v. $100-125*

NAPILI SUNSET ★

46 Hui Rd., Lahaina, Maui, HI 96761. (808-669-8083) 1-800-447-9229 U.S. Mainland, 1-800-223-4611 Canada, FAX (808) 669-2730. Forty-one units located on Napili Bay. Daily maid service.These units have great oceanviews and are well maintained. A very friendly atmosphere. Kitchens have microwaves. Deposits vary. 15 day notice for full refund. 10% monthly discount. 3-day minimum.
Studio (2) g.v. $85, 1 BR 1 bath (2) o.f. $159, 2 BR 2 bath (4) o.f. $249

HALE NAPILI

65 Hui Rd., Napili, Maui, HI 96761. (808-669-6184) 1-800-245-2266. 18 units oceanfront on Napili Bay. Lanais. Daily maid service except Sunday. Laundry facilities on property. No pool. 3-night minimum. Extra persons $8/night, $150 deposit, 7-day refund notice, monthly discounts, NO CREDIT CARDS.
Studio (2) g.v. $75, o.f. $95, 1 BR (2) o.f. $120

NAPILI VILLAGE SUITES

5425 Honoapiilani, Lahaina, Maui, HI 96761. (808-669-6228) 1-800-336-2185 U.S. & Canada. All rooms have king or queen size beds, daily maid service. Free laundry facilities on premises. Located a short walk from Napili Bay. Extra persons $6/night, 3-night deposit. Deposits $200-$250, 14 day refund notice.
Studio (2) $89/79

MAUIAN

5441 Honoapiilani, Lahaina, Maui, Hi 96761. (808-669-6205) 1-800-367-5034. Studio apartments on Napili Bay. Kitchen plus microwave, one queen and two twin day beds. BBQ area. Two public phones on property, one courtesy reservations phone. Television only in recreation center. Daily maid service. 3-day minimum, 3-night deposit, 14-day refund notice. 5% two week, 12% monthly discounts. Rental crib $8/night. Extra person $9 night. The Maui is offering a flexible sliding scale room rate based upon the percentage of occupancy at the time the reservation is made. The rates can result in some very good values, so be sure and ask about it!
Studio garden $116/91, o.v. $124/100, o.f. $142/118

THE KAHILI

5500 Honoapiilani Hwy., Lahaina, HI 96761. (808) 669-5636. Agent: Marc Resorts Group 1-800-535-0085. Thirty units available for rentals. This property opened in the fall of 1990 na offers one and two bedroom units. Some with golf course view of Kapalua's 18th hole, others garden/pool view. Spa and pool, BBQ's, daily maid service. *1 BR 99/79; 2 BR 130/110*

NAPILI KAI BEACH CLUB ★

5900 Honoapiilani, Lahaina, Maui, HI 96761. (808-669-6271) 1-800-367-5030, Canada 1-800-263-8183. Units feature lanais, kitchenettes, telephones, and washer/dryer facilities. Complimentary tennis equipment, beach equipment, croquet, putters, and snorkel gear. Daily coffee and tea party in Beach Club. Sea House Restaurant located on grounds. 2 tennis courts, 4 pools, very large jacuzzi. The grounds are extensive and the area very quiet. A relaxed and friendly atmosphere, a great beach, and a wide variety of activities may tempt you to spend most of your time enjoying this very personable and complete resort. Approximately 30 new luxury units with an oriental motif have been added in

what used to be the large lawn area. 2-night deposit. 14-day refund notice. NO CREDIT CARDS.
S BR (2) luxury g.v. no kitchen $155, with kitchen $175, suites $290-435
S BR deluxe o.v. $80-195, suites $210-400, dlx. o.f. $195, suites $235-275
S BR luxury o.v. no kitchen $185, with kitchen $205, suites $350-505
S BR luxury o.f. $220-240, suites $275-450
Suites 2-4 persons, S BR 1-2 persons. Extra person $15. Package rates available.

KAPALUA

INTRODUCTION

The modern day history of Kapalua dates back to 1836 when the Baldwin family of New England settled on the island of Maui as missionaries. By the late 1800s, the property that is now Kapalua was part of Honolua Ranch, complete with Hereford herds, taro patches, fishing boats and fields of red coffee bean bushes. At the turn of the century, H.P. Baldwin (the great-grandfather of Colin Cameron) acquired the Honolua Ranch. D.T. Fleming, whose name today signifies one of Kapalua's three beaches, served as plantation manager. Kapalua became a bustling enclave in the island, with a working ranch that supplied pork and beef to the port of Lahaina.

In the years that followed, Kapalua's acres of grassy slopes were transformed into geometric patterns of silver-blue pineapple fields and the first crop of this fruit was harvested in 1914. Today Maui Land & Pineapple Company Inc. is ranked as the largest producer of private-label pineapple and pineapple juice in the world.

In the 1970's a new master plan for Kapalua began to take place when Colin Cameron chose 750 acres of his family's 23,000 acre pineapple plantation for the development of this up-scale resort. The result is the Kapalua Bay Hotel and Villas which opened in 1979 and the surrounding resort area which includes a residential community, golf courses, and the soon to be completed Ritz Carlton Kapalua resort.

The mood reflected at the Kapalua Bay Hotel is serene with their philosophy being quality of food and service in a resort setting offering the ultimate in privacy and luxury living. The grounds are spacious with manicured lawns and an oasis of waterfalls and gardens. Recent renovations have meant a new butterfly-shaped pool located nearer the beachfront. More than 400 condominium units are located in the Ridge, Golf and Bay Villas, of which about 125 are available for rent. There are now three 18-hole championship golf courses, a tennis garden, a shopping area with a myriad of boutiques and a deli/restaurant. There are several excellent restaurants in the area from which to choose. The Kapalua Garden restaurant is located in the hotel and the Bay Club Restaurant is situated on a scenic promontory nearby. The new Plantation Restaurant, located at Kapalua's Plantation Golf course club house, features fine dining and an unsurpassed panormaic ocean view. The new Ritz Carlton also offers several fine dining options. Kapalua Bay is a small cove of pristine white sand, nestled at the edge of a coconut palm grove. It has been named among the top beaches in the world. The protected bay offers good snorkeling and a safe swimming area for all ages.

WHERE TO STAY - WHAT TO SEE

WHAT TO SEE AND DO

Kapalua, "arms embracing the sea," is the most north-western development on Maui. The logo for Kapalua is the butterfly, and with a close look you can see the body of the butterfly is a pineapple. One might enjoy a stop at the elegant Kapalua Bay Hotel. The lobby bar is ideally situated for an evening refreshment, music, and sunset viewing. The resort has a small shopping mall located just outside the hotel. The resort grounds are attractive and spacious. The road beyond Kapalua is paved and in excellent condition, and offers some magnificent shoreline views. However, it finally turns to a rough dirt road and rental car agencies are not responsible should you choose this route. (A wash out has closed this section of the road for some time, check with the county to see if it is accessible.) After several miles the road returns to pavement before you arrive at Wailuku. Slaughterhouse Beach is only a couple of miles beyond Kapalua and you may find it interesting to watch the body surfers challenge the winter waves. Just beyond is Honolua Bay where winter swells make excellent board surfing conditions. A good viewing point is along the roadside on the cliffs beyond the bay. Continuing on, you may notice small piles of rocks. This is graffiti Maui style. They began appearing a few years ago and these mini-monuments have been sprouting up ever since. There are some wonderful hiking areas here as well. One terrain resembles a moonscape, while another is windswept peninsula with a symbolic rock circle formation. See RECREATION & TOURS "hiking" for more details. Kapalua is home to a number of outstanding annual events. The Kapalua Tennis Jr. Vet/Sr. Championship is held each May. In June both the Kapalua Music Festival and Kapalua Wine Symposium are held at the Kapalua Bay Hotel. There are two popular events for the tennis aficionado, the Kapalua Open Tennis Tournament is in September and the Kapalua Betsey Nagelson Tennis is held the end of November and/or the first part of December. The nationally televised Kapalua International is held in November and top PGA golfers will try their skills on the newest Kapalua course, The Plantation Course.

WHERE TO SHOP

The Kapalua Shopping Center, an entirely covered mall, offers a showcase of treasures. Here you will find *The Kapalua Shop* (669-4172) where everything from men's and women's resort wear to glassware display the Kapalua butterfly logo. The newest shop, *Kapalua Kids* features fashions for infants through boys and girls size 7 (669-0033). *The Market Cafe* (669-4888) has fresh pastries, wines, gourmet items to go, or enjoy breakfast, lunch, or dinner at their restaurant.

ACCOMMODATIONS - KAPALUA

Kapalua Bay Hotel & Villas   Ritz-Carlton
Kapalua Bay and Golf Villas   The Ridge
Ironwoods

BEST BETS: The Kapalua Bay Hotel & Villas - This resort offers quiet elegance, top service, great food with all the amenities. Any of the condominium units in this area would be excellent, however, they are not all located within easy walking distance of the beach. A shuttle service is available. The condominiums at Kapalua offer spacious living and complete kitchen facilities. The new Ritz Carlton is slated for a grand opening October 1992 and a formal grand opening in the spring of 1993.

Rental information for the Kapalua Villas is in three different sections, and there are a number of rental agents. The Kapalua Hotel handles rentals of these luxurious condominiums. Also see the listing below for "Kapalua Bay Villas" and "Ridge Villas" for other rental management companies.

KAPALUA BAY HOTEL & THE KAPALUA VILLAS ★
One Bay Drive, Kapalua, Maui, HI 96761. (808-669-0244) 1-800-367-8000. 194 hotel rooms plus villa condominiums. Rooms have service bars and refrigerators, no kitchens. All rooms have air conditioning with decor in warm neutral shades of taupe, rose and muted terra cotta. Five-star restaurants include The Bay Club and The Garden. A cafe is available in the Kapalua Shops, located adjacent to the hotel. Lovely grounds, excellent beach and breathtaking bay. The resort includes The Bay Course and The Village Course, two 18-hole championship golf courses designed by Arnold Palmer, and the newly opened Plantation Course. A tennis garden with 10-plexipave courts, 4 lighted for night play are available for guest use. The new pool is butterfly-shaped, located near the ocean. The expanse of lawn gives way to lush tropical foliage, waterfalls, pools and gardens. This is elegance on a more sophisticated scale than the glitter and glitz of the Kaanapali resorts. Children 14 or younger free if sharing room with parent. Extra persons $35 high season, $25 low season. Cribs available at no charge. 3-night's deposit high season, one low season. 14-day refund notice. Modified American Plan is available at $65 per person.
G.v. $215-250 / $185-205, o.v. $315-340 / $270-$295, o.f. $360-385
Parlor Suite $430-630 / $500-680, 1 BR suite $750-950, 2 BR suite $1,050-1,250

THE RITZ-CARLTON, KAPALUA ★
One Ritz Carlton Drive, Kapalua, Maui, HI 96761. (808) 669-6200. Below Honolua Store on D.T. Fleming Beach. Discovery of some ancient burial sites temporarily halted construction during 1989 on the newest Kapalua resort, the Ritz-Carlton. The 550 room oceanfront resort (opening as we go to press - October 1992) follows in the same quality and high standards set for all of Kapalua. A Hawaiian motif with a plantation feel features native stonework throughout hotel. Accommodations include 314 Kings, 170 doubles, 63 executive suites and 2 Ritz-Carlton suites. Twice daily made service, in-room terry robes, complimentary in-room safe, multilingual staff, babysitting, full service beauty salon. Ten tennis courts plus a 10,000 sq. ft., three level swimming pool are among the amenities. Restaurants include the Sunset Grill and Lounge with seating for 130 and a private 15-seat dining room. Cafe and Terrace includes indoor and outdoor dining and serves breakfast, lunch and dinner. The Pool Bar and Restaurant offers casual indoor-outdoor dining. The Library Lounge provides a quiet retreat complimented by a spectacular ocean view. The Beach Cabana offers cocktails on the beach and a Luau facility can accommodate 550 in an outdoor setting. Conference facilities provide over 30,000 square feet with a 15,750 sq. ft. ballroom.
Garden Mt. $285, partial o.v. $325, o.v. $400, o.f. $455, Ritz Carlton Club $495
1 BR executive suite $625, 1 BR executive Club Suite $750, 1 BR o.f. suite $900
Ritz Carlton Suite $2,800

KAPALUA BAY VILLAS ★

500 Office Road, Kapalua, Maui, HI 96761, Kapalua, Maui, HI 96761. (808) 669-8088, 1-800-545-0018 U.S. and Canada. AGENTS: Kapalua Vacation Rentals (808) 669-4144, 1-800-326-6775, Kapalua Hotel (808) 669-0244, 1-800-367-8000, Hawaiian Apt. Leasing 1-800-854-8843 (1-800-472-8449 in California, 1-800-824-8968 in Canada). Whaler's Realty handles golf villas only (808) 661-8777, 1-800-367-5632, Ridge Rentals handles only Ridge villas (808) 669-9696, 1-800-326-6284 in U.S. and Canada. Agents: Kapalua Hotel 1-800-367-8000, Whaler's Realty (golf villas only) 1-800-367-5632, Hawaiian Apt. Leasing 1-800-854-8843 (1-800-472-8449 CA). There are over 400 units in the villages and each is spacious and beautifully appointed. Wonderful units for several couples or a larger family. They feel much more like a home than a condominium. Units include kitchens, washer/dryers, and daily maid service. Several pools and tennis courts. Extra persons $35 per night. 3-night deposit high season, 2-night low season. The Kapalua Hotel which is among the rental agents which handles the property, currently has gone to a flat year round rate, no discounts for low season. However, Kapalua Villas (808) 545-0018 are the company we have dealt with and they do have discounts for low season. The following prices are a mix of the high and low prices we surveyed from several different agents for high season. Differences in prices are also reflected by location and view. A little calling may be worth your while. We'd suggest starting with a call to Kapalua Villas.
1 BR (4, max 6) fairway v. $175-275, o.v. $225-315, o.f. $250-375
2 BR (4, max 6) fairway v. $225-375, o.v. $250-415, o.f. $375-475

THE RIDGE ★

Agents: Ridge Rentals 1-800-326-6284 U.S. & Canada, Kapalua Hotel 1-800-367-8000, Kumulani 1-800-367-2954. Part of the Kapalua condominiums, these are also well appointed but slightly less expensive. With its location above the hotel in the golf course area it is quite a walk to the beach, however, a free on-call shuttle is available for transport to the hotel and beach. 5-day minimum, $100 deposit, 14-day notice of cancellation between 12/15 and 4/15, other dates 48 hours. Maid service only on check in. NO CREDIT CARDS.
1 BR 2 bath o.v. $165/90, 2 BR 2 bath o.v. $240/135 (prices-Ridge Rentals)

IRONWOODS

Beautiful and very expensive oceanview homes. Currently no rentals available.

THE RITZ-CARLTON   KAPALUA, MAUI

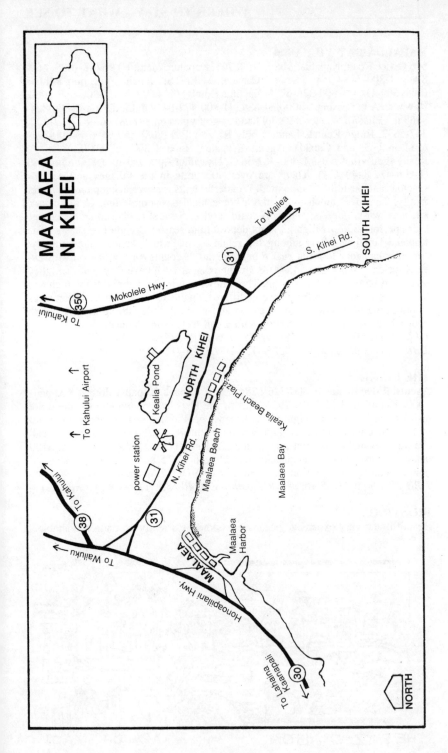

MAALAEA

INTRODUCTION

Maalaea to many is just a signpost enroute to Kaanapali, or a harbor for the departure of a tour boat. However, Maalaea (which means "area of red dirt") is the most affordable and centrally located area of the island. A short 10 minutes from Kahului, 30 minutes from Lahaina and 15 minutes from Wailea makes it easy to see all of the island while headquartered here. You can hop into the car for a beach trip in either direction. Even better is the mere six-mile jaunt to Kahului/Wailuku for some of Maui's best and most affordable eateries. This quiet and relaxing area is a popular living area for local residents. Seven of the ten condominium complexes are located on a sea wall on or near the harbor of Maalaea, while the other three are on one end of the three mile long Maalaea Bay beach. The two end complexes, Maalaea Mermaid and the Maalaea Yacht Marina are actually within the harbor.

The ocean and beach conditions are best just past the last condo, the Makani A Kai. There is less turbidity providing fair snorkeling at times, good swimming and even two small swimming areas protected by a reef. These are found on either side of the small rock jetty with the old pipe. This length of beach is owned by the government and is undeveloped, providing an excellent opportunity for beach walkers who can saunter all the way down to Kihei. The condominium complexes are small and low-rise with moderate prices and no resort activities. The vistas from many of the lanais are magnificent, with a view of the harbor activity and the entire eastern coastline from Kihei to Makena, including majestic Haleakala, as well as Molokini, Ka'aholawe and Lana'i. The view is especially pleasing at night and absolutely stunning when a full moon shimmers its light across the bay and through the palm trees with the lights of Upcountry, Kihei and Wailea as a backdrop. No other part of the island offers such a tranquil setting. Another plus are the almost constant trade winds which provide non-air conditioned cooling as opposed to the sometimes scorching stillness of the Lahaina area. Summer in Maalaea is time for surfing. Summer swells coming into the bay reportedly create the fastest right-breaking rideable waves in the world and are sometimes referred to as "the freight train." The local kids are out riding from dawn to dusk. Winter brings calmer seas with fair snorkeling over the offshore reef. The calm conditions, undisturbed by parasailing and jet-skiing, also entices the Humpback whales into the shallow waters close to shore.

Local eating options are limited. One nice restaurant, The Waterfront, at the Milowai condominiums is excellent! In addition to sandwiches at the Maalaea Mermaid market, a limited number of snacks are available at the Maalaea store. Casual seafood lunch and dinners are served Monday through Saturday at the Island Fish Market. Buzz's Wharf sits at the end of the Harbor and is open for lunch, dinner and cocktails.

Under development is the new Maalaea Fishing Village. Plans call for a shopping center about as large as the Lahaina Cannery. The two-story design is reported to incorporate a local Hawaiian theme with lots of small shops and vendors selling fresh produce and island crafts. Five or six restaurants are being figured into the preliminary reports. There is also mention that the Maui Historical Society is reportedly considering a museum and museum shop. It will be located across from the harbor near the old fishing shrine. All in all, Maalaea is a quiet and convenient choice. It is not for those seeking the hub of activity or convenient fine dining, but for the independent and quiet traveler. Undecided about where to stay? Maybe you should try Maalaea!

WHAT TO DO AND SEE

The Maalaea Harbor area is a scenic port from which a number of boats depart for snorkeling, fishing and whale watching. Also in this area is Buzz's Wharf Restaurant, open for dinner. Fresh Island Fish Company, a seafood market, open Monday thru Saturday 10 - 5.

ACCOMMODATIONS - MAALAEA

Maalaea Mermaid   Island Sands
Maalaea Yacht Marina   Maalaea Banyans
Milowai   Kana'I A Nalu
Maalaea Kai   Hono Kai
Lauloa   Makana A Kai

BEST BETS: *Kana'i A Nalu* - Attractive complex with all two-bedroom units on a sandy beachfront, affordably priced. ***Lauloa*** - Well designed units oceanfront on the seawall. ***Makani A Kai*** - Located on a sandy beachfront, two bedroom units are townhouse style.

MAALAEA MERMAID
No rental information available. Located within the Maalaea Seawall. Small market on the ground floor.

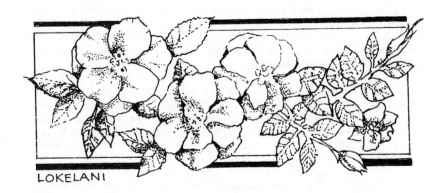

LOKELANI

MAALAEA YACHT MARINA

Hauoli St., Maalaea, Maui, HI 96793. (808-244-7012). Agents: Maalaea Bay Rentals 1-800-367-6084, Kihei Maui Vacations 1-800-542-6284, Hawaiian Apt. Leasing 1-800-854-8843 (1-800-472-8449 CA).

All units are oceanfront, a beach is nearby. The units we viewed were pleasant with a wonderful view of the boats from most units, and the added plus of having security elevators and stairways. Many of the units have no air conditioning and laundry facilities are located in a laundry room on each floor. A postage stamp size grassy area in front and a small, but adequate pool.
1 BR (2) $80/70, 2 BR (4) $90-110/80

MILOWAI

Hauoli St., Maalaea, Maui 96793. Agents: Kihei Maui Vacations 1-800-542-6284, Maalaea Bay Rentals 1-800-367-6084, Hawaiian Apt. Leasing 1-800-854-8843 (1-800-472-8449 CA).

One of the larger complexes in Maalaea with a restaurant on location, The Waterfront. This complex has a large pool area, with a BBQ along the seawall. The corner units are a very roomy 1,200 square feet with windows off the master bedrooms. Depending on condo location in the building, the views are of the Maalaea harbor or the open ocean. The one bedroom units have a lanai off the living room and a bedroom in the back. Washer/dryer. Weekly/monthly discounts.
1 BR (2) $80/70, 2 BR (4) $90-110/80

MAALAEA KAI

Hauoli St., Maalaea, Maui, HI 96793. (244-7012). Agents: Maalaea Bay Rentals 1-800-367-6084, Kihei Maui Vacations 1-800-542-6284. 70 oceanfront units. Laundry facilities, putting green, BBQ, and elevator to upper levels. Located on the harbor wall, the rooms were standard and quite satisfactory. Some do not have washer and dryers in the rooms. There is a pool area and large pleasant grounds in front along the harbor wall. A few blocks walk down to a sandy beach. Monthly discounts. *1 BR (2) $80/70, 2 BR (4) $90-110/80*

LAULOA ★

Hauoli Street,(RR 1 Box 383) Maalaea, Maui, HI 96793. (808-242-6575). Agent: Maalaea Bay Rentals 1-800-367-6084.

Forty-seven 2-bedroom, 2-bath units of 1,100 sq.ft. One of the Lauloa's best features is their floor plan. The living room and master bedroom are on the front of the building with a long connecting lanai and sliding glass patio doors which offer unobstructed ocean views. A sliding shoji screen separates the living room from the bedroom. Each morning from the bed you have but only to open your eyes to see the palm trees swaying and a panoramic ocean view. The second bedroom is in the back of the unit. These two bedroom units are spacious (only two bedroom units are currently available in the rental program) and are in fair to good condition (depending on the owner). Each has a washer/dryer in the unit. The pool area and grounds are along the seawall. With a stairway in the sea wall, there often are local fishermen throwing nets and lines into the ocean. $200 deposit. Maid service extra charge. Monthly discounts.
2 BR 2 bath (4) $110-120/85

ISLAND SANDS

Hauoli St., (RR 1, Box 391) Wailuku, Maui, HI 96793. Island Sands Resort Rentals 1-800-826-7816, (808) 244-0848, FAX (808) 244-5639.

Eighty-four units in a 6-story building. This is one of Maalaea's larger complexes located along the seawall. Offers a Maui shaped pool, a grassy lawn area, BBQ. Many of these units also have a lanai off the master bedroom, however the lanais have a concrete piece in the middle of each railing which somewhat limits the view while sitting or laying in bed. Washer/dryers, and air conditioning. Elevators. Extra person $7.50/night. Weekly and monthly discounts. 4-night minimum, $200 deposit with 15-day refund notice. Children under 3 free. NO CREDIT CARDS. *Studio (2) $75/55, 1 BR 1 Bath (2) $95/75, 2 BR 2 Bath (4) $110/90*

MAALAEA BANYANS

Hauoli St., (RR 1 Box 384) Maalaea, Maui, HI 96793. (808-242-5668). Agents: Maalaea Bay Rentals 1-800-367-6084, Oihana 1-800-367-5234, Real Hawaii 1-800-967-6687. Seventy-six oceanview units with lanai and washer/dryer. Weekly/monthly discounts. Oceanfront on rocky shore, short walk to beach. Pool area, jacuzzi, BBQ's. Extra persons $10/night. 7-night minimum. NO CREDIT CARDS.
1 BR (2) $80/70
2 BR (4) $90-110/80

KANA'I A NALU ★

Hauoli Street, Maalaea. Agents: Maalaea Bay Rentals 1-800-367-6084, Oihana 1-800-367-5234. 80 units with washer/dryers in four buildings with elevators. No maid service. This is the first of the three condominiums along a sandy beach-front. Its name means "parting of the sea, surf or wave." The complex is V-shaped with a pool area in the middle. Nicely landscaped grounds, a decent beach and only a short walk along the beach to the best swimming and playing area. Overall one of the best values in the Maalaea area. One of the places we keep coming back to! 5-day minimum, $200 deposit, 30-day refund notice. Weekly discounts. *2 BR (4) o.v. $110-135/$80-100, o.f. $130-165/$100-125*

HONO KAI

Hauoli St., Maalaea. (244-7012) Agent: Maalaea Bay Rentals 1-800-367-6084. Forty-six units located on the beach. Choice of garden view, oceanview or oceanfront. Laundry facilities, BBQ, pool. This is one of three properties managed by Maalaea Bay Rentals and according to the agent this property is the "chevrolet" model. This complex is on the beach and bears attention for the budget conscious traveler, but don't expect any frills.
1 BR $85-95/$60-75, 2 BR $77-88/$105-115, 3 BR $130/93

MAKANI A KAI

Hauoli St., Maalaea. Agent: Maalaea Bay Rentals 1-800-367-6084. These deluxe units are also on the beach and offer a choice of oceanfront or oceanview. Laundry room on property, pool, BBQ. This is the last property along the beach in Maalaea. Beyond this is a long stretch of sandy beach along undeveloped state land and about a four mile jaunt down to North Kihei. Great for you beach walkers! The two bedroom units are townhouse style. Unfortunately, these do not have in-room washer/dryers. In our opinion, a must for the traveling family!
1 BR $80-125 / $70-95, 2 BR $110-165 / $80-125   5-day minimum stay

NORTH KIHEI

INTRODUCTION

North Kihei is 15 minutes from the Kahului Airport and located at the entrance to South Kihei. The condominiums here stretch along a gentle sloping white sand beach. The small Kealia Shopping Center is located between the Kihei Sands and Nani Kai Hale. Another small shopping area is found at the Sugar Beach Condominiums. Several snack shop restaurants can be found along Kihei Road in this area. A little to the south down Kihei Road are additional restaurants, grocery stores and large shopping areas. Along with Maalaea, this is one of our favorite places to stay because of the good units, central, but quiet location, nice beach, cooling breezes and certainly some of the island's best vacation buys.

ACCOMMODATIONS - NORTH KIHEI

Kealia	Kihei Kai
Sugar Beach	Maalaea Surf
Kihei Sands	Kihei Beach Resort
Nani Kai Hale	

BEST BETS: *Kealia* and *Maalaea Surf.*

KEALIA ★
191 N. Kihei Rd., Kihei, Maui, HI 96753. (808-879-9159) 1-800-367-5222. Fifty-one air conditioned units with lanais, washer/dryers, and dishwashers. Maid service on request. The one bedroom units are a little small, but overall a good value. Well maintained and quiet resort with a wonderful sandy beach. Shops nearby. Extra person $10. 10% monthly discount. $125 deposit, $10 cancellation fee. 100% payment required 30 days prior to arrival. 7-day minimum winter, 4-day in summer. NO CREDIT CARDS. *Studio (2) $75/55, 1 BR (2) $90/75*

SUGAR BEACH RESORT
145 N. Kihei Rd. Kihei, Maui, HI 96753. (808-879-7765). Agents: Condo Rental HI 1-800-367-5242, The Ching Connection 879-7866 or 874-8891, Hawaiian Apt. Leasing 1-800-854-8843 (1-800-472-8449 CA), Maui Condos 1-800-663-6962 Canada, RSVP 1-800-663-1118, Rainbow Rentals 1-800-451-5366, More Hawaii 1-800-967-6687. 215 units in several six-story buildings with elevators. Air conditioning. Jacuzzi, putting green, gas BBQ grills. Sandwich shop and quick shop market on location. A fairly large property with a nice pool area and located on an excellent swimming beach. In previous editions we gave this a recommended rating, however, on a recent stay we found our particular unit to be long overdue for some major renovations and down deep cleaning. That is not to say that there aren't a number of excellently cared for units but this is one of many properties that is very popular and heavily rented leaving little time for remodeling and refurbishing. Apartment owners that don't make regular inspections are another part of the problem. This condo and others with similar discrepancies from unit to unit need management established criteria which would eliminate those units from the rental pool that are not up to certain standards. Extra persons $7.50/night, weekly discounts. *1 BR g.v. $95/75, o.f. $105/85, 2 BR o.v. $175/130*

KIHEI SANDS
115 N. Kihei Rd., Kihei, Maui, HI 96753. (808-879-2624) Thirty oceanfront air-conditioned units. Shops and restaurant nearby. 7-night minimum high season/3-day minimum low season, $100 deposit with $20 cancellation fee. Full payment on arrival. No maid service or room phone. Coin laundry area. Complete kitchens. NO CREDIT CARDS. Extra persons $6/night.
1 BR (2) $75- 95 / $60-75
2 BR (4) $90-115 / $70-90

NANI KAI HALE ★
73 N. Kihei Rd., Kihei, Maui, HI 96753. (808-879-9120) 1-800-367-6032. 46 units in a six-story building. Under building parking, laundry on each floor, elevator. No maid service, no room phones. Patio and BBQ's by beach. Lanais have ocean and mountain views. Prices based on 7-day/3-day minimum stay. $100 deposit. Monthly discounts. Children under 5 years no charge. Extra person $10 per night.
S BR w/o kitchen (2) $ 65/50,
1 BR 2 bath (2) o.v. $ 80/65, o.f. $125/ 90
2 BR 2 bath (2) o.v. $125/90, o.f. $150/130

KIHEI KAI
61 N. Kihei Rd., Kihei, Maui, HI 96753. (808-879-2357) 1-800-367-8047 ext. 248. Twenty-four units in a two-story beachfront building. Recreation area and laundry room. Units have air conditioning or ceiling fans. BBQ. On seven-mile stretch of sandy beach, near windsurfing, grocery stores. A very good value. Minimum 7-days winter, 4-days summer. $100 deposit ($200 deposit for 2 weeks or longer.) Full payment upon arrival. NO CREDIT CARDS. Extra persons $5/night. Weekly discounts.
1 BR (2,max 4) $75-90 / $60-75

KIHEI BEACH RESORT
36 S. Kihei Rd., Kihei, Maui, HI 96753. (808-879-2744) 1-800-367-6034. Agents: Maui Network 1-800-367-5221, Maui Condo & Home 1-800-822-4409, Maui Condo 1-800-663-6962 Canada. 54 beachfront units with oceanview, phones. Resort offers central air conditioning, recreation area, elevator, maid service. Extra person $9/night. 3-day deposit with 3-day refund notice low season, 30-day high season. Balance must be prepaid in full. Weekly and monthly discounts. NO CREDIT CARDS. *1 BR (2,max 4) $96/82, 2 BR (4,max 6) $133/113*

MAALAEA SURF ★
12 S. Kihei Rd., Kihei, Maui, HI 96753. (808-879-1267) 1-800-423-7953. Sixty oceanview units in 8 two-story oceanfront buildings. Units have air conditioning and microwaves. Daily maid service, except Sundays and holidays. Two pools, two tennis courts, shuffleboard. Laundry facilities in each building. Very attractive and quiet low rise complex on a great beach. In this price range, these spacious and attractive units, along with the beautiful grounds, are impressive and hard to beat. Extra persons $8/night. NO CREDIT CARDS. $200-300 deposit. High season balance due 30 days prior to arrival, low season on arrival. 60-day refund notice with $10 cancellation fee during high season, 30-day notice low season.
1 BR 1 bath (2,max 4) $145/125
2 BR 2 bath (4,max 6) $200/170

SOUTH KIHEI

INTRODUCTION

South Kihei began its growth after that of West Maui, but unfortunately with no planned system of development. The result is a six-mile stretch of coastline littered with more than 50 properties, nearly all condominiums, with some 2,400 units in rental programs. Few complexes are actually on a good beach, however, many are across Kihei Road from one of the Kamaole Beach Parks. A variety of beautiful beaches are just a few minutes drive away.

The drive from Maalaea to Kihei is but a few miles. There is a mix of sugar cane which blends into the mudflats of Maalaea on your left and a rather indistinguishable flatland on your right. The area on your right can best be seen from an aerial perspective. It is the enormous Kealia pond which was recently slated to become Hawai'i's second-largest national wildlife refuge. The federal government agreed to pay $6.9 million for ownership of the 437 acre pond and another 263 acres will be donated as a federal wildlife easement by Alexander & Baldwin. Among the endangered species currently making their home in the pond are the Hawaiian coot and Hawaiian stilt.

This section of East Maui has a much different feel than West Maui or Lahaina. There are no large resorts with exotically landscaped grounds, very few units on prime beachfront, and more competition among the complexes making this area a good value for your vacation dollar. (And a good location for extended stays.)

Kihei always seemed to operate at a quieter and more leisurely pace than that of Kaanapali and Lahaina, but the last couple of years has seen a significant upsurge of development, not of condos, but of shopping complexes. Even parts of South Kihei Rd. have been repaved and regular curbs installed. These changes indicate the increasing tourist activity along with a corresponding loss of Kihei's once laid-back charm. Restaurant selections remain more limited and many vacationers staying in condominiums utilize their kitchens. Most needs can be filled locally at one of several large grocery stores or the growing number of small shopping centers. Kahului, Wailuku, Wailea and Lahaina remain an easy drive for additional shopping and dining out.

WHAT TO DO AND SEE

The only historical landmark is a totem pole near the Maui Lu Resort which commemorates the site where Captain Vancouver landed.

WHERE TO SHOP

Every corner of Kihei is sprouting a new shopping mall. The complexes all seem to have quick markets, video stores and a T-shirt shop. The following are now complete.

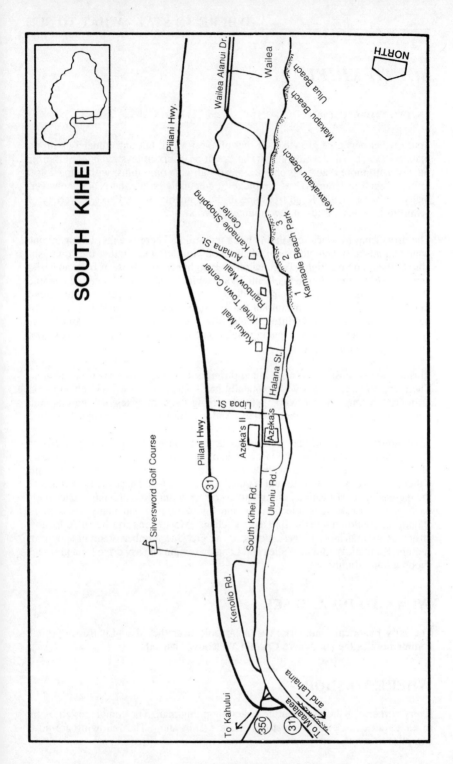

SOUTH KIHEI

Traveling down Kihei Road the first center is *Azeka's* and across the street the new *Azeka Place-Mauka.* At Azeka's market you can pick up Azeka's famous ribs to cook yourself. The *International House of Pancakes, Royal Thai Cuisine* and *Luigi's* are among the restaurants here. *Liberty House* relocated to a much larger facility in the new Azeka shopping mall and was joined by a new *Long's Drug Store.* You'll also find the *Silversword Bookstore,* a *Ben Franklin* and a tourist shops.

The *Lipoa Shopping Center* is a block down Lipoa Street and offers a medical center and pharmacy, a cycle and sport shop, *Sweet Cream's,* and *Henry's Bar and Grill.*

Just past the Kapulanikai condominiums, the *Kukui Mall,* at 1819 S. Kihei Rd., gets our vote for the most attractive mall. This large complex is done in a Spanish style of architecture with a wide assortment of shops. *Subway Sandwich* shop is a handy stop for lunch enroute to one of Wailea's fine beaches. For a cool treat there's *I Can't Believe It's Yogurt.* A new *Walden's* bookstore is a welcome addition for visitors and residents alike, with a great selection of books on just about any subject, also *Kihei Art Gallery,* and several clothing shops. There is also *Perry's Smorgy* an all-you-can-eat restaurant.

Just beyond is *The Kihei Town Center* which offers a selection of shops including sporting goods, novelty shops, pharmacy, grocery, and clothing. The only restaurant here is *Chuck's* and *McDonald's* on the corner.

The next few shopping areas run almost together. The *Dolphin Plaza,* 2395 S. Kihei Rd., across from Kamaole I Beach is one of the smaller new shopping centers. Here you'll find *The New York Deli, Pizza Fresh, Baskin Robbins Ice Cream,* the *Kihei Bakery* and a video store.

Between the Dolphin Plaza and Rainbow Mall is the *Kamaole Beach Center,* 2411 S. Kihei Rd. *The Sports Page Grill and Bar* is the focal point here with a yogurt place and pizza restaurant rounding out the center.

The Rainbow Mall is a small center also located on the mauka side (towards the mountain) of South Kihei Road offering an ice cream shop, *Chum's* restaurant which offers local style plate lunches and *Paradise Fruits.* Paradise Fruits relocated in 1992 and is no longer open 24 hours. It still offers fresh fruits and vegetables, (some organic), many of which are Maui grown. They also have a snack bar that features "healthy" sandwiches, burritos, espresso, and the islands best yogurt shakes and smoothies.

Kamaole Shopping Center is one of the larger new malls and offers several restaurant selections, including *Denny's,* the *Canton Chef* and *Erik's Seafood Broiler.*

The last shopping center in Kihei, across from Kamaole III Beach, is the *Nani Kai Center. La Bahia, Kihei Prime Rib* and *The Greek Bistro* restaurants make up this complex.

ACCOMMODATIONS - SOUTH KIHEI

Nona Lani	Kihei Garden	Kihei Alii Kai
Kihei Holiday	Hale Kai O Kihei	Royal Mauian
Wailana Sands	Maui Sun	Kamaole Nalu
Resort Isana	Waiohuli Beach	Hale Pau Hana
Pualani	Kihei Beachfront	Kihei Kai Nani
Sunseeker Resort	Kapulanikai	Kihei Akahi
Maui Lu Resort	Island Surf	Maui Banyan
Kihei Bay Vista	Kihei Park Shores	Haleakala Shores
Kihei Bay Surf	Shores of Maui	Maui Parkshore
Menehune Shores	Punahoa	Kamaole Sands
Kihei Resort	Kalama Terrace	Hale Kamaole
Koa Lagoon	Beach Club Apts.	Maui Kamaole
Koa Resort	Lihi Kai Cottages	Maui Hill
Kauhale Makai	Maui Vista	Kihei Surfside
Leinaala	Kamoa Views	Mana Kai Maui
Luana Kai	Kamaole One	Surf and Sand
Maui Schooner	Maui Coast Hotel	Hale Hui Kai
Maui Sunset	Kamaole Beach	
Leilani Kai	Royale	

BEST BETS: Maui Hill - Situated on a hillside across the road from the ocean, some units have excellent ocean views. The three-bedroom units here are roomy and a good value for large families. **Haleakala Shores** - Across from Kamaole III Beach Park. **Mana Kai Maui** - One of Kihei's larger resorts, and the only one right on a very good beach.

NONA LANI
455 S. Kihei Rd.,(P.O. Box 655) Kihei, Maui, HI 96753. (808-879-2497). Eight individual cottages with kitchens, queen bed plus 2 day beds, full bath with tub and shower, and lanais. Large grounds, public phone, two BBQ's, and laundry facilities. Located across the road from sandy beach. Weekly rates available. Extra person $7 night. $100 deposit, $50 non-refundable. No personal checks or credit cards. *1 BR (2) $65*

KIHEI HOLIDAY
483 S. Kihei Rd., Kihei, Maui, HI 96753. (808-879-9228) Agents: Kihei Maui Vacations 1-800-542-6284, Hawaiian Apt. Leasing 1-800-854-8843 (1-800-472-8449 CA), RSVP 1-800-662-1118. Units are across the street from the beach and have lanais with garden views. Pool area jacuzzi and BBQ's. $100 deposit, full payment 30 days prior to arrival. Maid service on request. NO CREDIT CARDS. *1 BR/ $90/75, 2 BR (4) $110/85*

WAILANA SANDS
25 Wailana Place, Kihei, Maui, HI 96753. Agent: Pali Kai 808-879-2026. 10 units, overlook courtyard and pool area, in a two-story structure. Quiet area on a dead end road. A one block walk to Kihei Beach. 4-day minimum, $100 deposit. NO CREDIT CARDS. *1 BR $65/45*

PUALANI TOWNHOUSES
15 Wailana Place, Kihei, Maui, HI. Agent: Kihei Maui Vacations 1-800-542-6284.
1 BR $85/70

RESORT ISANA
515 S. Kihei Road, Kihei, Maui, HI 96753 (808) 879-7800, 1-800-633-3833. One of Kihei's newest, these fifty one-bedroom units are decorated in muted beige and blues and are complete down to an electric rice cooker and china dishes. A spacious pool area is the focal point of the central courtyard. Located across the road from the beach. Washer/dryer, cable tv., maid service. Extra person $15.
1 BR (1-3) $110, 2BR (1-5) $140   Weekly and monthly rates available

SUNSEEKER RESORT
551 S. Kihei Rd. (P.O. Box 276) Kihei, Maui, HI 96753. (808-879-1261). Six units including studios with kitchenettes, one and two bedrooms with kitchens. Monthly discounts available. No room phones, no pool. Across street from beach. Popular area for windsurfing. Minimum stay in studio or 1 BR is 3 days and in two bedrooms 7 day. $150 deposit. NO CREDIT CARDS.
S BR $55/50, 1 BR $65/60, 2 BR (4) $90/85   Extra person $6

MAUI LU RESORT
575 S. Kihei Rd., Kihei, Maui, HI 96753. (808-879-5881) Agent: Aston 1-800-922-7866. 180 units on 26 acres. Cottages have full kitchens, fans, but no air conditioning. Hotel rooms have air conditioning, small refrigerator and hot water maker. Pool is shaped like the island of Maui. Many of the hotel rooms are set back from South Kihei Road and the oceanfront units are not on a sandy beachfront. One of the first resorts in the Kihei area and unusual with its spacious grounds. Extra persons $10, under 18 no charge.
Hotel rooms (2) $99-118/$79-$108, 1 & 2 BR cottages (1-3) $118/108

KIHEI BAY VISTA
679 S. Kihei Rd., Kihei, Maui, HI 96753. (879-75811), 1-800-367-7040 U.S., 1-800-423-8733 ext. 159 Canada. Agents: Hawaiian Apt. Leasing 1-800-854-8843 (1-800-472-8449 CA), Maui condos 1-800-663-6962 Canada. Built in 1989 this complex offers pool, spa, jacuzzi, putting green, air conditioning, washer/dryer, lanais and full kitchens. A short walk across the road to the Kamaole I Beach. Overlooking Kalepolepo Beach. *1 BR g.v. and o.v. units $95-110 / $85-100*

KIHEI BAY SURF
715 S. Kihei Rd. (Manager Apt. 110), Kihei, Maui, HI 96753. (808-879-7650) Agents: Kihei Maui Vac. 1-800-542-6284, Island Discount Rentals 1-808-879-1466, Hawaiian Apt. Leasing 1-800-854-8843. 118 studio units in 7 two-story buildings. Pool area jacuzzi, recreation area, gas BBQ's, laundry area, tennis. Across road from Kamaole I Beach. Phones. Weekly discounts. *Studios $70/60*

MENEHUNE SHORES
760 Kihei Rd., Kihei, Maui, HI 96753. (808-879-1508) Agents: Kihei Kona Rentals 1-808-879-5828, Kihei Maui Vacations 1-800-542-62824, RSVP 1-800-663-1118, Menehune Reservations 1-800-558-9117 U.S., Maui Network 1-808-572-9555. 115 units with dishwashers, washer/dryers and lanais in a 6-story building. Recreation room, roof gardens with whale-watching platform, and

shuffleboard. The ocean area in front of this condominium property is the last remnant of one of Maui's early fish ponds. These ponds, where fish were raised and harvested, were created by the early Hawaiians all around the islands. Extra persons $7/night, $150 deposit. Rates quoted are for seven-night stay. Slightly higher for 4-6 day stay. 4-day minimum.

1 BR 1 bath (2) $ 90/ 75, 1 BR 2 bath (2) $110/88.50
2 BR 2 bath (2) $120/100, 3 BR 2 bath (6) $150/140

KIHEI RESORT

777 S. Kihei Rd., Kihei, Maui, HI 96753. Agents: Kihei Maui Vacations 1-800-542-6284, RSVP 1-800-663-1118, Maui Condo 1-800-663-6962 Canada, Rainbow Rentals 1-800-451-5366, Hawaiian Apt. Leasing 1-800-854-8843. Sixty-four units, two-story building, located across the street from the ocean, BBQ's, pool area jacuzzi. NO CREDIT CARDS.

1 BR (2) $ 85/70   7-nite minimum, $100 deposit, 10-day refund notice
2 BR (4) $105/90   Extra persons $7/night, 10% monthly discount

KOA LAGOON

800 S. Kihei Rd., Kihei, Maui, HI 96753. (808-879-3002) 1-800-367-8030. 42 oceanview units in one 6-story building. Bar and ice-maker, washer/dryers. Pool area pavilion, BBQ's. Located on a small sandy beach that is often plagued by seaweed which washes ashore from the offshore coral reef. This stretch of Kihei is very popular with windsurfers. Extra person $10 additional. $250 deposit, full payment 30 days prior to arrival. 30-day cancellation notice. 14-day minimum stay during Christmas holiday. Supreme units $15 night more. NO CREDIT CARDS.

1 BR 1 bath (2,max 4) $110/80, 2 BR 2 bath (4,max 6) $130/100

KOA RESORT

811 S. Kihei Rd., Kihei, Maui, HI 96753. (808-879-1161) 1-800-877-1314. 54 units (2,030 sq.ft.) on spacious 5 1/2-acre grounds in 2 five-story buildings across road from beach. 2 tennis courts, spa, jacuzzi, putting green. Units have washer/dryers. NO CREDIT CARDS. 10% monthly discount.

1 BR 1 bath (2,max 4) $100/800   Extra persons $10/day, children under 2 free
2 BR 1 bath (4,max 4) $115/ 95, 2 bath (4,max 6) $125/105   5-night minimum
3 BR 2 bath (6,max 8) $150/130, 3 bath (6,max 8) $175/155 $100 deposit

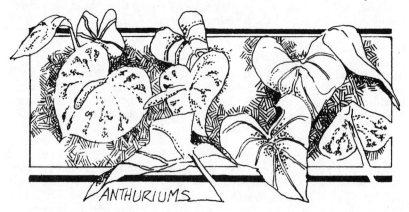

ANTHURIUMS

KAUHALE MAKAI (Village by the Sea)
930-938 S. Kihei Rd. Kihei, Maui, HI 96753. (808-879-8888)
Agents: Oihana 1-800-367-5234, Kihei Maui Vac. 1-800-542-6284, Kumulani 1-800-367-2954, RSVP 1-800-663-1118, Rainbow Rentals 1-800-451-5366, Maui Condos & Homes 1-808-879-5445, Island Discount Rentals 1-808-879-1466, VIP 1-808-879-5504. 169 air-conditioned units in 2 six-floor buildings with phones. Complex features putting green, gas BBQ's, children's pool, sauna, laundry center. The beach here is usually strewn with coral rubble and seaweed. $5 additional person. 5-night minimum.
Studio (2) $75/60, 1 BR (2) $105/90, 2 BR (4) $135/110

LUANA KAI ★
940 S. Kihei Rd., Kihei, Maui, HI 96753. (808-879-1268) Agents: Hawaiian Island Resorts 1-800-367-7042, Kihei Maui Vacations 1-800-542-6284, Rainbow Rentals 1-800-451-5366, More Hawaii 1-800-967-6687. 113 units with washer/dryers are located adjacent to a large oceanfront park with public tennis courts. The beach, however, is almost always covered with coral rubble and seaweed. The grounds are nicely landscaped and include a putting green, BBQ area, pool area sauna and jacuzzi. Towel service mid-week, linen service weekly. Children under 12 free. Extra person $10. 2-night minimum high season. Weekly discounts. 3 BR units may be available from some agents.
1 BR (2) g.v./o.v. $115-140/95-115, 2 BR (4) o.v. $160/135

MAUI SCHOONER RESORTS
980 S Kihei Rd, Kihei, Maui HI 96753. (808-879-5247) Completed in 1984, these 58 units have been tastefully decorated in mauves and blues and have washer/dryer, microwave, phones and maid service every other day. Full prepayment. Only one building has an elevator to the upper floors. Fronting these condos is a public park with 4 tennis courts and a beach that is seasonally strewn with coral rubble. On-site are a nice pool area, separate men's and women's saunas, wet bar area, and hot tub. Now a time share resort.
1 BR (4) g.v. $110/ 90, o.v. $125/105   7-nite/2-nite deposit
2 BR (6) g.v. $135/115, o.v. $150/130   7-day refund notice
3 BR (8) garden $160/140   persons under 18 free

LANAKILA
992 S. Kihei Rd., Kihei, Maui, HI 96753. No vacation rentals, long term only.

LEINAALA
998 S Kihei Rd, Kihei, Maui, HI 96753. (808-879-2235) 1-800-334-3305 U.S. & Canada. 24 one and two bedroom units in a 4-story building. Tennis courts at adjoining park. Pool, cable color TV. Oceanview. This property is fronted by a large grassy park which stretches out to the ocean. The beach is usually covered with coral rubble and much better beach activities would be enjoyed a short drive down to one of the Kamaole Beach Parks in Kihei. Monthly discounts. $200 deposit with 30-day refund notice. NO CREDIT CARDS. Extra persons $10 night. 4 night minimum. *Studio/no view (2) $55, 1 BR (2) $85/75, 2 BR (4) $110/100*

WAIPUILANI
1002 S. Kihei Rd., Kihei, Maui, HI 96753. (808-879-1465). 42 units in three 3-story buildings. No vacation rentals. Only long term.

MAUI SUNSET
1032 S. Kihei, Rd., Kihei, Maui, HI 96753. (808-879-0674) Reservation Assistance 1-800-843-5880. Agents: Kihei Maui Vac. 1-800-542-6284, Kumulani 1-800-367-2954, Maui Network 1-800-367-4221, Hawaiian Apt. Leasing 1-800-854-8843 (1-800-472-8449 CA), RSVP 1-800-663-1118. 225 air conditioned units in 2 multi-story buildings. Tennis courts, pitch and putt golf green, and sauna. Large pool, exercise facility, barbecues. Located on beach park with tennis courts, however, this beach is generally covered with seaweed and coral rubble. Extra persons $7/night. *1 BR $105/85, 2 BR $135/110, 3 BR available thru some agents*

LEILANI KAI
1226 Uluniu St.,(P.O. Box 296) Kihei, Maui, HI 96753. (808-879-2606). Eight garden apartments with lanais. $200 deposit. Extra person $7.50. Full payment prior to arrival. 3-day minimum stay. NO CREDIT CARDS. Monthly discounts. *Studio (2) $75/60, 1 BR (2) $100/75, 1 BR dlx (4) $115/85, 2 BR (4) $125/90*

KIHEI GARDEN ESTATES
1299 Uluniu St., Kihei, Maui, HI 96753. (808-879-6123), 1-800-827-2786.Agents: Kihei Maui Vacations 1-800-542-6284. 84 units in eight 2-story buildings. Jacuzzi, BBQ's. Across road and short walk to beaches. Monthly discounts. $100 deposit, full payment 30 days prior to arrival. NO CREDIT CARDS. Rates for 4-6 nights. Weekly discounts. *1 BR (2,max 4) $90-100/ 75-85, 2 BR (4,max 6) $110/85*

HALE KAI O KIHEI
P.O. Box 809, 1310 Uluniu Rd., Kihei, Maui, HI 96753. (808-879-2757). 59-oceanfront units with lanais in 3-story building. Sandy beachfront. Shuffleboard, putting green, BBQ's, laundry, recreation area. Maid service on request for extra charge. Extra person $9/night. 10% monthly discount. $150 deposit. 60-day/30-day cancellation notice (less $20 handling fee). NO CREDIT CARDS. Daily rates upon request. *1 BR (2) $575/395 weekly, 2 BR 2 bath (4) $725/545 weekly*

MAUI SUN   (Hotel)
175 East Lipoa, Kihei, Maui HI (808) 874-9000 or 1-800-762-5348 from Hawaii, Mainland or Canada. 229-rooms with tropical grounds including large pool and whirlpool spa, koi ponds, waterfalls. Two connecting six story buildings feature rooms with an interconnecting system allowing them to join together for a larger family. Each room is air conditioned with private lanai. There are also several suites available. This hotel is located several blocks away from the ocean. Hence, a good value! Rooms have garden views, some of the suites offer oceanviews. The Frangipani restaurant and lounge is located on the property, featuring breakfast, lunch, dinner and specialty buffets. Sunday night offers champagne brunch and a Hawaiian luau-style evening buffet. *Mountain view rooms with one king or 2 queen $79, garden view $89 partial ocean $99, suites available.*

WAIOHULI BEACH HALE
49 West Lipoa St., Kihei, Maui, HI 96753. (808-879-5396). Agents: Pali Kai 1-808-879-8550, Paradise Realty 1-808-874-8074. 52 units in four 2-story buildings. Large pool, BBQ area, shuffleboard, near shopping center. Located on beachfront that is poor for swimming or snorkeling, often covered with coral rubble and seaweed. Spacious park-like lawn area around pool. Extra person $8/night. Weekly discounts. *1 BR (2) $95/70 - 625/450 weekly; 2 BR (4) $115/100 - $800/700 wk*

KIHEI BEACHFRONT RESORT
Located at end of Lipoa St. Agent: Maui Condos & Homes 1-808-879-5445. Eight oceanview 2-bedroom units with washer/dryers, microwaves, dishwashers, and air conditioning in a single 2-story building. Large lawn area fronting units. Lanais on upper level. No elevator. Pool area jacuzzi. Five night minimum stay or cleaning fee required. $200 deposit. $10 additional person. Weekly, monthly discounts. *2 BR o.v./g.v. $130/95, 2 BR o.f. (4) $165/130*

KAPULANIKAI APTS
73 Kapu Place, PO Box 716, Kihei, Maui, HI 96753. Agent: Bello Realty 1-800-541-3060. 12 units are oceanview with private lanais or open terraces. Beachfront is poor for swimming or snorkeling. Grassy lawn area in front. BBQ's, laundry facilities, pay phone on property. *1 BR 1 bath $80/65*

ISLAND SURF
1993 S. Kihei Rd., Kihei, Maui, Hi 96753. Agent: Kumulani 1-800-367-2954. This property is turning many of its units into commercial offices and shops on the first three floors which really detracts from a resort-like setting, although the economy of the place may attract some. Across the road from the Kamaole I Beach Park. $100 deposit. Five day minimum. Extra persons $8. *Hotel rooms $50/$40, 1 BR $75/65, 2 BR $95/80*

KIHEI PARK SHORES   (No rental information available)

SHORES OF MAUI
2075 S. Kihei Rd., Kihei, Maui, HI 96753. (808-879-9140) 1-800-367-8002. 50-unit two-level complex in garden setting offers BBQ's, tennis courts, and spa. Located across the street from a rocky shoreline and 1½ blocks north of Kamaole I Beach Park. $100 deposit, 30-day cancellation notice, full payment 30 days prior to arrival. Extra persons $8/night, monthly discounts. 3-day minimum (Christmas holiday 1-week minimum). Monthly discounts. NO CREDIT CARDS. *1 BR $90/65, 2 BR $110/90*

PUNAHOA
2142 Iliili Rd., Kihei, Maui, HI 96753. (808-879-2720). 15-oceanview units with large lanais, telephones. No pool. Elevator, laundry facilities, beaches nearby. NO CREDIT CARDS. $400/200 deposit, 60-day refund notice. Extra persons $10/-night. Weekly/monthly discounts. 5-day minimum or pay $30 service charge. *Studio (2) $81/62, 1 BR (2,max 4) $111/84, 2 BR (2,max 6) $87-110 / $120-140*

KALAMA TERRACE   (No rental information available)

BEACH CLUB APARTMENTS
2173 Iliili Rd., Kihei Maui, HI 96753, (808) 874-6474. One block from beach, washer dryers, kitchens. Long term rentals only.

LIHI KAI COTTAGES
2121 Iliili Rd., Kihei, Maui, HI 96753. (808-879-2335) 1-800-544-4524. Nine beach cottages. All units are 1 BR 1 bath with kitchen and lanai. Self-service laundromat. Next to Kamaole I Beach. $100 deposit, 3-day minimum, 60/30 day refund notice. Maid service available at additional fee. *1 BR (2) $59/54*

117

MAUI VISTA

2191 S. Kihei Rd., Kihei, Maui, HI 96753. (808-879-7966) 1-800-367-8047 ext.330. Agents: Aston 1-800-922-7866, Oihana 1-800-367-5234, Kihei Maui Vac. 1-800-542-6284, RSVP 1-800-663-1118.

280 units in three 4-story buildings, across from the beach. Some units have air conditioning, some have washer/dryers. All have kitchens with dishwashers. The 2-bedroom units are fourth floor townhouses. Some oceanview units. 6 tennis courts, 3 pools, BBQ's. 5-night minimum low, 7-night high season. We had some problem with sound carrying from a neighboring unit, but overall, a good value. Extra person $10. One nights deposit. Rollaway $10 additional, $6 cribs.
1 BR (2,max 4) $95/80; 2 BR (2,max 6) $115/100

PACIFIC SHORES

2219 S. Kihei Rd. (808-874-3461) Residential and long term rentals only.

KAMOA VIEWS

2124 Awihi Place. (808-879-5335). Long term rentals only.

KAMAOLE ONE

2230 S. Kihei Rd., Kihei, Maui, HI 96753. (808-879-4811). 2-story building. Nine units. No elevators or pool, covered parking. Beachfront. Nice location. Telephones, washer/dryers, compactors, air conditioning, ceiling fans and cable TV. Some have microwaves. NO CREDIT CARDS. *2 BR ground floor $150-160/130-140*

MAUI COAST HOTEL   (Hotel)

2259 S. Kihei Rd., Kihei, Maui, HI 96753. (808) 874-MAUI. Operated by West Coast Hotels. Opening in late 1992. It will offer 264 guestrooms and each offers an oceanview from a balcony. The guest rooms will be suites providing separate sitting and bedroom areas, and refrigerators. There will be two "super suite" floor plans as well as a king room and a twin bed room. The hotel will offer two restaurants, two pool, outdoor spa, tennis court, fitness center, gift and sundry shop, shuttle service to local golf and shopping, complimentary laundry facilities and limousine service. No room rates available as we go to press.

KAMAOLE BEACH ROYALE

2385 S. Kihei Rd.,(P.O. Box 370) Kihei, Maui, HI 96753. (808-879-3131) 1-800-421-3661, FAX (808) 879-9163. 64 units with washer/dryers and single or double lanais in a single 7-story building across from Kamaole I Beach. Recreation area, elevator, roof garden. 10% monthly discount, 5-day minimum, $200 deposit, balance due 30 days prior to arrival. $25 service charge. NO CREDIT CARDS.

1 BR 1 bath (2) $ 90/65   Extra person $10 per night
2 BR 2 bath (2) $100-105 / $75-80
3 BR 3 bath (2) $110/85

KIHEI ALII KAI

2387 S. Kihei Rd., Kihei, Maui, HI 96753. (808-879-6770) Agents: Leisure Properties 1-800-888-6284, Kihei Maui Vacations 1-800-542-6284, RSVP 1-800-663-1118, Rainbow Rentals 1-800-451-5366.

127 units in four buildings. All units have washer/dryers. No maid service. Complex features pool, jacuzzi, sauna, two tennis courts, BBQ. Across road and up street from beach. Nearby restaurants and shops. Extra persons $7/night. $100 deposit, 3 night minimum. Full payment 30 days prior to arrival.

1 BR (2) $85/60, 2 BR (4) $95-115 / $70-80, 3 BR (6) $115/90

ROYAL MAUIAN

2430 S. Kihei Rd., Kihei, Maui, HI 96753. (808-879-1263) 1-800-367-8009. 107 units with lanai, washer/dryer, and phone in a 6-story building. Complex has shuffleboard, carpeted roof garden, and is next to the pleasant Kamaole II Beach Park. $12 extra person (no charge children under age 6), 5-night minimum, $200 deposit with $25 cancellation fee. 14-day discount summer, 30-day winter. Maid service every twice weekly.

1 BR 1 bath or 2 bath (2) $120-130/100-105
2 BR 2 bath (2) $150/128, 3 BR (4) $195/173
Side wing two bedroom, two bath units are $90 low season

KAMAOLE NALU

2450 S. Kihei Rd., Kihei, Maui, HI 96753 (808-879-1006) 1-800-767-1497. FAX (808) 879-8693. Thirty-six 2-bedroom, 2-bath units with large lanai, dishwasher, and washer/dryer in a 6-story building. Located between Kamaole I and II Beach Parks with all units offering oceanview. Weekly maid service during high season. $12 extra person. 3-day minimum. NO CREDIT CARDS. $200/100 deposit with $25 cancellation fee. Summer specials offered.

2 BR 2 bath (2) o.v. $130/95, o.f. $140/105

HALE PAU HANA

2480 S. Kihei Rd., Kihei, Maui, HI 96753. (808-879-2715) 1-800-367-6036, FAX (808) 875-0238. Agents: Condominium Rentals Hawaii 1-800-367-5242.

Seventy-eight oceanview units in four buildings. Laundry area, elevator. Located on Kamaole II Beach. Limited maid service. NO CREDIT CARDS. Weekly and monthly discounts. Extra person $15-25. $50 reservation cancellation fee. Special rates for November 1 - December 15th.

1 BR (2,max 4) $135-155 / $100-105
1 BR 2 bath (2,max 4) $155-160 / $105-110

KIHEI KAI NANI
2495 S. Kihei Rd., Kihei, Maui, HI 96753. (front desk: 808-879-1430) reservations 1-800-473-1493. Agents: Kihei Maui Vacations 1-800-542-6284, Hawaiian Apt. Leasing 1-800-854-8843.

180 one-bedroom units with lanai or balcony in a 2 and 3-story structure. This complex is one of the older ones along Kihei Rd. Laundry room and recreation center. Across from Kamaole II Beach. $7 extra person. 4-night minimum, $100 deposit, balance due 30 days prior to arrival. NO CREDIT CARDS thru front desk reservations. *1 BR (2) ($80-85/65-70)*

MAUI BANYAN
2575 S. Kihei Rd. Agents: Kihei Maui Vacations 1-800-542-6284, Hawaiiana Resorts 1-800-367-7040, Kumulani 1-800-879-9272. Overlooking Kamaole Beach Park II these suites feature kitchens, washer/dryer, lanai, air condition, cable TV and telephone. Facilities include tennis court, pool and jacuzzi, bbq. Hotel rooms have no kitchens or telephones. Daily maid service.
Hotel room (max. 2) g.v. $90/80, partial o.v. $100/90
1 BR (max. 4) g.v. $115/105, partial o.v. $130/120, o.v. $145/135
2 BR (max. 6) g.v. $155/145, partial o.v. $170/160, o.v. $185/175
3 BR (Max. 8) g.v. $195/185, partial o.v. $215/205

KIHEI AKAHI
2531 S. Kihei Rd., Kihei, Maui, HI 96753. (808-879-1881) Agents: Maui Condo & Home Realty (808-879-5445), Oihana 1-800-367-5234, Condo Rentals Hawaii (808-879-2778), Maui Condominiums 1-800-367-5242, CANADA 1-800-663-2101, Kihei Maui Vac. 1-800-542-6284, RSVP 1-800-663-1118.

240 units with washer/dryers. 2 pools, tennis court, BBQ's. Across from Kamaole II Beach. $5/nite discount after 6 nites. 10% monthly discount. Extra person $12. 4-day minimum, $125 deposit, full payment 30 days prior to arrival. NO CREDIT CARDS. *Studio (2) $75/65, 1 BR 1 bath (2) $95/80, 2 BR 2 bath (4) $120/$95*

HALEAKALA SHORES ★
2619 S. Kihei Rd., Kihei, Maui, HI 96753. (808-879-1218) 1-800-367-8047 ext. 119, 1-800-423-8733 ext. 119 Canada. Seventy-six, 2-BR units in two four story buildings. Located across the road from Kamaole III Beach. Maid service available for additional charge. Washer/dryers. Covered parking. They also have a very thoughtful policy where returning guests receive an extra discount. A very good value! Winter season seven night minimum, $200 deposit except Christmas season which requires a two week minimum with non-refundable full payment in advance. Summer season five night minimum, $100 deposit, 5% weekly discount. NO CREDIT CARDS. *2 BR (1-4) $115/85*

MAUI PARKSHORE
2653 S. Kihei Rd., Kihei, Maui, HI 96753. (808-879-1600. Agent: Oihana Properties 1-808-244-7685. Sixty-four, 2-bedroom, 2-bath oceanview condos with washer/dryers, and lanais in a 4-story building (elevator) across from Kamaole III Beach. Pool area sauna. 10% monthly discount. $100 deposit, payment in full upon arrival. NO CREDIT CARDS. Extra person $10/5 per night.
2 BR 2 bath (4) $100/80

KAMAOLE SANDS

2695 S. Kihei Rd., Kihei, Maui, HI 96753. (808-879-0666) Agents: Aston Resorts 1-800-922-7866, Kihei Maui Vacations 1-800-542-6284, Hawaiian Apt. Leasing 1-800-854-8843 (1-800-472-8449 CA), Kumulani 1-800-367-2954.

440 units in 10 four-story buildings. Includes daily maid service. 4 tennis courts, wading pool, 2 jacuzzi's and BBQ's. Located on 15 acres across the road from Kamaole III Beach. In 1992 they completed a $1.2 million renovation of their suites. Kamp Kamaole is the kids program offered seasonally for 8-12 year olds, hours 9 a.m. - noon and 1 - 3:30 p.m. and is free of charge for registered guests.
1 BR 2 bath (1-4) $135/110, 2 BR 2 bath (1-6) $160/135
3 BR 3 bath (1-8) $195/160

HALE KAMAOLE

2737 S. Kihei Rd., Kihei, Maui, HI 96753. (808-879-2698) 1-800-367-2970. Agents: Condo Rental Hawaii 1-800-367-5242, Kumulani 1-800-367-2954. 188 units in 5 buildings (2 & 3-story, no elevator) across road from Kamaole III Beach. Laundry building, BBQ's, 2 pools, tennis courts. Some units have washer /dryers. Courtesy phone at office. Limited maid service. $100 deposit per week, balance due 30-60 days before arrival. 3 night minimum stay. Monthly discounts. NO CREDIT CARDS. Extra person $8. *1 BR (2) $99/67, 2 BR 2 bath (4) $129/87*

MAUI KAMAOLE

2777 S. Kihei Rd., Kihei, Maui, HI 96743. (879-7668). Agents: Kihei Maui Vacations 1-800-542-6284, Maui Condo & Home Realty 1-800-367-5242, Pali Kai 1-808-879-8550, Condo Rental Hawaii 1-800-367-5242.

The newest development on South Kihei Rd. is on a bluff overlooking the ocean and across the street and a short walk down to Kamaole III Beach Park or Keawakapu Beach. 1 BR units are 1,000 - 1,300 sq.ft. and 2 BR units are 1,300 - 1,600 sq.ft. Some have oceanviews. This is a four phase development that will eventually have 316 residential units on 23 acres. They are low rise, four-plex buildings grouped into 13 clusters, each named after Hawaiian flora. Phase One is nearing completion, and Phase Two will include a pool, spa and pavilion. Phase four will add a second pool and two tennis courts.
1 BR $110-140/80-110, 2 BR $155-165/125-130

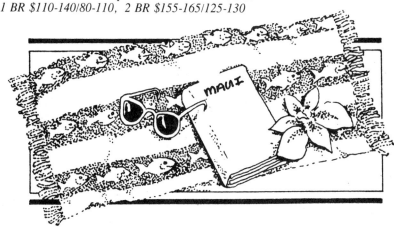

MAUI HILL ★

2881 S. Kihei Rd., Kihei, Maui, HI 96753. (808-879-6321) Agents: Aston Hotels 1-800-922-7866, Kumulani 1-800-367-2954, RSVP 1-800-663-1118. 140 attractively furnished units with washer/dryers, air conditioning, microwaves, dishwashers, and large lanais. Daily maid service. There are 12 buildings with a Spanish flair clustered on a hillside above the Keawakapu Beach area. There is a moderate walk down and across the road to the beach. Upper units have oceanviews. The 3-bedroom units are very spacious. Large pool and tennis courts. 1-night deposit.
1 BR (1-4) $165/135, 2 BR (1-6) $185/155, 3 BR 3 bath (1-8) $275/245

KIHEI SURFSIDE

2936 S. Kihei Rd., Kihei, Maui, HI 96753. (808-879-1488) 1-800-367-5240. Agents: Kihei Maui Vacations 1-800-542-6284. 83 units on rocky shore with tidepools, a short walk to Keawakapu Beach. Large grassy area and good view. Maid service every fourth day. Extra persons $6. 3-night minimum, 3-day deposit, 14-day cancellation notice. 10% monthly discount. This property has a three rate system. Summer, fall and winter are each priced at a slightly different rate. Rates shown are winter/summer. Extra persons $10.
1 BR 1 bath (2) $115/73, 1 BR 1½ bath (2) $125/80, 2 BR 2 bath (4) $160/130

MANA KAI ★

2960 S. Kihei Rd., Kihei, Maui, HI 96753. (808-879-1561) 1-800-525-2025 (FAX 808-874-5042). Agents: Kumulani 1-800-367-2954, Maui Condos 1-800-663-6962. 132 rooms in an 8-story building. The studio units have a room with an adjoining bath. The 1-bedroom units have a kitchen and the 2-bedroom units are actually the hotel unit and a 1-bedroom combined, each having separate entry doors. Complex has laundry facilities on each floor, an oceanfront pool, and a restaurant off the lobby. Daily maid service. The Mana Kai is nestled at the end of Keawakapu Beach, and offers a majestic view of the blue Pacific, the 10,000 foot high Haleakala and Upcountry Maui. It is the only major facility in Kihei on a prime beachfront location. Keawakapu Beach is not only very nice, but generally very under used. The Ocean Terrace restaurant as well as a small market is located on the property. 1-night deposit, balance due 30 days in advance of arrival summer season, 60 days winter season. 14-day cancellation notice. The rates include a late model car with unlimited mileage. Car user must be 21 years of age and have a valid drivers license.
S BR 1 bath (2) $ 95/ 90, includes breakfast & car (no kitchen)
1 BR 1 bath (2) $175/155, includes car
2 BR 1 bath (2) $195/175, includes car

WAILEA OCEANFRONT HOTEL   (Hotel)

2980 S. Kihei Rd., Kihei, Maui, HI 96753. (808-879-7744) Hawaiian Pacific Resorts 1-800-367-5004. Formerly the Surf and Sand the first thing to note is that it is now pink! Gone is the Oriental brown and orange look of the 1970's. They were not able to let us view any of the 88 units. In spite of the recent "renovation" it looked pretty funky. No pool, located on Keaweakapu Beach, but only the front unit has an oceanview. Several two story buildings, no lanais.
Standard $77/67 (3), Superior $85/75 (2), Deluxe $96/86 (2), 1 BR $144/134 (5)

HALE HUI KAI

2994 S. Kihei Rd. Kihei, Maui, HI 96753. On-site property rental agent "Ruth" (808-879-1219) - no credit cards. Other agents: Bello Realty/Maui Beach Homes 1-800-541-3060. Oceanfront on Keawakapu Beach. 5-night minimum, $200 deposit. Extra person $15-20. *2 BR 2 bath o.v. $135/115, side o.v. $115/90*

WAILEA

INTRODUCTION

Wailea is a well planned and well manicured resort on 1,500 acres just south of Kihei. Developed by Alexander and Baldwin, Wailea encompasses five resort hotels and four condominium complexes which offer high quality accommodations. Included are two 18-hole championship golf courses, a large tennis center and a shopping center. The spacious and uncluttered layout is impressive, as are its series of lovely beaches.

Besides visiting resorts and beaches, there isn't much to do. There is a small shopping center which will satisfy most basic needs. Tuesdays at 1:30 they feature a free Hawaiian show in the central courtyard of the Wailea Shopping Center that is quite good. Bring a towel or mat to sit on, you can pick up a cold drink, an ice cream cone or a sandwich to enjoy during the show.

The first two resort hotels were the 550-room Maui Inter-Continental Resort which opened in 1976, and the 350-room Stouffer Wailea Beach Resort which opened in 1978. During the past couple of years this area has been the hub of development on Maui.

The Palms at Wailea is the newest condominium property located at Wailea's entrance. The Four Seasons Hotel opened in the spring of 1990 and was followed by the September 1991 opening of the neighboring, 812 room Grand Hyatt Wailea. Kea Lani, an all suites resort, opened in November of 1992 with 450 rooms and 37 oceanfront villas on Polo Beach. The Diamond Resort, a private, primarily Japanese guest hotel, is located in the foothills above Wailea.

The Wailea condominium villages are divided into four locations, two are beachfront, while two are adjacent to the golf course. The newest of these villages is the Grand Champion Villas which opened in 1989.

The Polo Beach condominiums are located adjacent to Wailea resorts on Makena Road. Wailea Point, an exclusive condominium development, offers no vacation rentals.

WHAT TO SEE AND DO

The lovely Wailea beaches are actually well planned and nicely maintained public parks with excellent access, off-street parking and all but one have restrooms and rinse-off showers. Ulua Beach is our personal favorite. The Stouffer Wailea Beach Resort also offers lovely grounds you might want to enjoy.

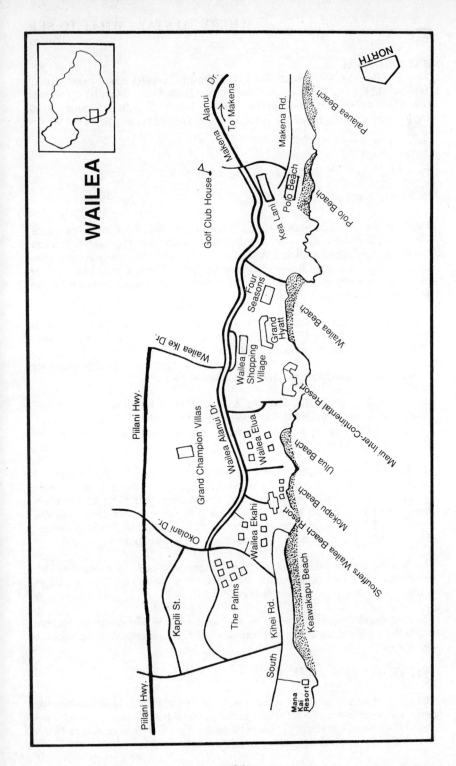

WAILEA

WHERE TO SHOP

Wailea Shopping Center is located at the southern end of Wailea. It offers a small pantry market, a mall of shops, and a restaurant. Each of the Wailea resorts also has an assortment of gift shops.

ACCOMMODATIONS - WAILEA

The Palms at Wailea   Maui Inter-Continental Resort
Wailea Villas   Diamond Resorts
  Ekolu Village   Wailea Point Village
  Ekahi Village   The Four Season Resort
  Elua Village   Grand Hyatt Wailea
  Grand Champion Villas   Kea Lani
Stouffer Wailea Beach Resort   Polo Beach Club

BEST BETS: It's hard to go wrong in wonderful Wailea. Affordable accommodations are not what the visitor will find here, but there are a variety of excellent condominiums and hotels among which to choose. Each is different, each is lovely and in fact there is not one property that we would not recommend. The choice is up to the personal preference of the guest. Here is a quick synopsis of each.

Wailea Villas - Our choice among the four areas would be the Elua Village. These are more expensive, of course, but beach aficionados will love having Ulua Beach at their front door.

Maui Inter-Continental Resort - A top notch resort hotel featuring a tropical flavor with lovely spacious grounds, excellent restaurants, and two great beaches. They recently completed a major renovation which involved a convention center and a magnificent new lobby and central stairway. An added plus here is their special children's program and room rates for kids.

Stouffer Wailea Beach Resort - This complex is smaller, and more intimate -- as resorts go -- it has lush, tropical grounds, and it is fronted by one of the island's finest beaches.

Four Seasons Resort - This resort is purely and simply elegant. From it's white porte cochere you enter a tranquil and serene environ. Simply sit by the pool or enjoy a day on the beach. No need to go further!

The *Grand Hyatt Wailea* - This is an enormous resort, but also enormous fun! The pools are incredible, but if you prefer the ocean, there is excellent Wailea Beach. There is something to do for everyone in the family. Just walking the grounds and touring the $40 million art collection could fill up a day!

The *Kea Lani* - This is an all suites resort, a blend of the best of resorts and the comforts of a condominium, all on Polo Beach. Want to really indulge? Then how about one of their private oceanfront villas with private swimming pool?

Polo Beach - Luxury condominium units with easy access to two small but good beaches.

THE PALMS AT WAILEA
3200 Wailea Alanui Drive, Wailea, Maui, HI 96753 (808) 879-5800. Agents: Hawaiiana Resorts 1-800-367-7040. Luxury units located with oceanviews in Wailea. One and two bedroom condominiums on a bluff overlooking the Wailea area with view of the islands of Kahoʻolawe and Lanaʻi. Each unit features air conditioning, washer/dryer. Guests have use of the recreation center which includes a pool and jacuzzi. As part of the Wailea destination, this property offers access to the two Wailea golf courses and tennis complex. Daily maid service.
1 BR g.v. (4) $150/140, o.v. $165/155; 2 BR (6) $185/175, o.v. $205/195

WAILEA VILLAS
3750 Wailea Alanui, Wailea Maui, HI 96753. (808-879-1595) 1-800-367-5246. Agents: Destination Resorts Wailea (808-879-1595) 1-800-367-5246, Kumulani (only Ekahi condos) 1-800-367-2954. Some agents may have a limited number of units for slightly better prices than those quoted below. The price range reflects location in the complex. Children under 16 free in parent's room.

EKOLU VILLAGE - located near the tennis center and the Wailea golf course.
1 BR (2) $160/135, 2BR (4) $200/160

EKAHI VILLAGE - on the hillside above the south end of Keawakapu Beach, some units are right above the beach.
S BR (2) $140/120, 1 BR (2) $170-190/140-160, 2 BR (4) $275/225

ELUA VILLAGE - located on Ulua Beach, one of the best in the area. We would recommend these units.
1 BR (2) g.v.-o.v. $195-230/165-200, o.f. $300/250
2 BR (4) g.v.-o.v. $275-315/225-270, o.f. $400/340
3 BR (6) g.v. only $375/300, o.f. $500/440

GRAND CHAMPION VILLAS - 155 Wailea Iki Place, Wailea, HI 96754. Agent: Destination Resorts 1-800-367-5246, Maui Network 1-800-367-5221, Kihei Maui Vacations 1-800-541-6284. The fourth and newest of the Wailea Villas, this is a sportsman's dream, located between Wailea's Blue Golf Course and the "Wimbledon West" Tennis Center. 188 luxury condominium units on 12 lush acres with garden view, golf view or oceanview units. Daily maid service, grocery delivery service, concierge service. Golf, tennis and/or car packages available.
1 BR (2) $140-160/120-135, 2 BR (4) $180-200/150-160

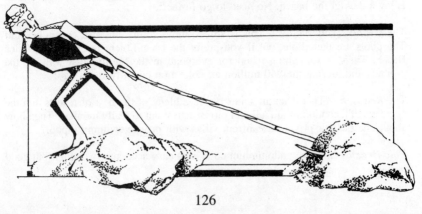

STOUFFER WAILEA BEACH RESORT ★ (Hotel)
3550 Wailea Alanui, Wailea, Maui, HI 96753. (808-879-4900) 1-800-992-4532.

347 units including 12 suites. This luxury resort covers 15.5 acres above beautiful Mokapu Beach. Each guest room is 500 sq.ft. and offers a refrigerator, individual air conditioner, a stocked mini-bar, and private lanai. The rooms have been recently redecorated in soothing rose, ash and blue tones. An assortment of daily guest activities are available as well as a year round children's program called Camp Wailea. The Mokapu Beach Club is a separate beachfront building with 26 units that feature open beamed ceilings and rich koa wood furnishings, plus a small swimming pool. The resort's restaurants are the Maui Onion, a pool-side gazebo; Palm Court, serving international buffets in an open air atmosphere; Raffles', an award-winning gourmet restaurant; Gion Hamasaka, serving authentic Japanese cuisine and a weekly Hawaiian luau. The Sunset Terrace, located in the lobby area, offers an excellent vantage point for a beautiful sunset and nightly entertainment 5:30 - 8:30. The beach offers excellent swimming. The best snorkeling is just a very short walk over to the adjoining Ulua Beach. The grounds are a beautiful tropical jungle with a very attractive pool area which was recently expanded to include additional lounging areas and more jacuzzi pools. They recently completed a major renovation of their resort that included redesign of their restaurants. The annual Marine Art Expo is held here every year.

They also offer several "breakation" options. These include a combination of room and car, room and golf or honeymoon options.
Mountainside & oceanside rooms $215 - $275, oceanview rooms $295
Mokapu Beach Club, beachfront $395, 1 & 2 BR suites $575-$1,500

MAUI INTER-CONTINENTAL RESORT ★ (Hotel)
3700 Wailea Alanui, Kihei, Maui, HI 96753. (808-879-1922) 1-800-367-2960, Honolulu 1-800-537-5589, Canada 1-800-268-3785.

In 1991 they completed a $40 renovation of their restaurants, public areas and new conference pavilion. The new coche porte greets your arrival with a grand entry and ocean view. Beautiful koa rockers temp guests to sit, ralax and enjoy the tranquil, gorgeous view. Just beyond, the new main stairway descends down and past a lily pond (a popular wedding site) to the new central pool area. The new oceanview, 34,000 sq. ft. conference pavilion is a topped with a rooftop observatory. Take the elevator or walk up for a panoramic view and an perfect vantage point for whale watching. The renovations blend in so well that it is hard to remember it ever being any other way. The design is unpretentious, old Hawaiian and classic. The artwork is subtle. Chests from Japan, huge stone mochi bowls, spirit houses from Thailand, roof finials from New Guinea, and calabashes from the Big Island.

Located on 22 acres they have 1/2 mile of oceanfront property and access to two great beaches, Ulua and Wailea. There are three pools, a seven-story tower and six low-rise buildings. The wonderful layout of this resort allows 80% of all guest rooms to have an ocean view and the grounds are spacious and sprawling. No "packing them in" feel here! The main pool area has two pools. One deeper and one a 4 1/2 foot depth all over. There is also a pint size slide into a small pool that is perfect for the pint size members in your family. Nothing exotic or fancy, just plain good water fun. A separate pool in the luau area is often uncrowded. The units located nearest the beach afford wonderful private ocean views.

The restaurants in this lovely resort include poolside Sun Spot, Hula Moons and the Lanai Terrace. There is also a Sunday brunch and seasonal Aloha Mele Luncheon offered in the Makani Room.

This resort takes a special look at family travel and offers a special family rate where a room is provided free for children if you book another room at standard rack rate. The Family Package is being revised for 1993 and we'll keep you advised of the changes in our MAUI UPDATE newsletter. Another plus for the family pocketbook is that kids eat free on the kids menu in the Hula Moons or the Lanai Terrace restaurants. An excellent children's day and evening program offered year round called Keiki's Club Gecko. Laundry facilities are coin-op and located in several areas on property. The resort offers many complimentary daily activities as well as one of Maui's best luaus. Pau Hana from 5:30 - 8 p.m. with live entertainment. A number of exciting annual events are sponsored by the resort. Golf, tennis and honeymoon package plans also available.

Room rates for 1992 were reduced by 25% from 1991 rates, making this an even better resort vacation option!
G.v. $159, m.v. $179, o.v. $199, o.f. $229, deluxe $279

DIAMOND RESORTS OF JAPAN (Hotel)
555 Kaukahi St., Wailea, HI 96753. (874-0500) This private resort, an extension of the Diamond Resort Corporation which manages a chain of 20 resorts throughout Japan, is located on 14.5 acres just above the Wailea Golf Course. The spa facility which includes a men's and women's daiyokujo (traditional Japanese bath), a waterfall to gently massage your neck and shoulders as well as a soothing Finlandia sauna is one of the resort's highlights. Recently, Diamond Resort has implemented the Diamond Spa Club program. Membership in the club provides the opportunity to experience the luxurious spa and spend a peaceful night in one of the exclusive hotel rooms. For rates and more information, contact a Spa Club representative.

INTER-CONTINENTAL, MAUI

It is a beautiful and interesting resort and the panoramic view from the lobby is dramatic! The artwork is primarily large tapestries which mimic the work of Van Gogh. They also have a private art gallery which is open upon guest request. The resort's chairman is particularly fond of Joan Miro and we viewed a new $7 million dollar acquisition that was on display. The restaurants are open to the public and the Sunset Bar offers freshly made $1 sushi, complimentary pupus, happy hour drinks and live entertainment plus a fabulous sunset view.

Their three dining facilities are Satoru, Le Gunji, both fine dining restaurants, and Island Terrace which serves "nutritionally balanced cuisine." See the restaurant chapter, Wailea section, for descriptions.

WAILEA POINT VILLAGE
4000 Wailea Alanui, Wailea, Maui, HI 96753. 136 luxurious oceanview and oceanfront condominiums arranged in four-plexes which are laid out in a residential plan on 26-oceanfront acres. Privacy is maintained by a gate guard at the entrance. Unfortunately, no rental properties available here!

THE FOUR SEASONS RESORT WAILEA ★
3900 Wailea Alanui, Wailea, Maui, HI 96753. (808-874-8000) (National reservations 1-800-332-3442). 380 over-sized guest rooms (600 sq. ft) on eight floors encompassing 15 beachfront acres on the beautiful white sand Wailea Beach. A full service resort featuring two pools, two tennis courts at the resort, croquet lawn, health spa, beauty salon, three restaurants and two lounges. The public areas are spacious, open and ocean oriented. A very different atmosphere from other Maui resorts with the blue tiled roof and creamy colored building creating a very classical atmosphere. Even the grounds, although a profusion of colors with many varied Hawaiian flora, are more structured in design with a vague resemblance to a Mediterranean villa. The focus of the resort is water. Throughout the resort's gardens and courtyards are an array of attractive formal and natural pools, ponds, waterfalls and fountains.

Their guest policy features real aloha spirit, with no charge for use of the tennis courts or health spa and complimentary snorkel gear, smash or volleyball equipment. Guests services, which distinguish the Four Seasons from other properties, include their early arrival/late departure program. These guests have their luggage checked and are escorted to the Health Club where a private locker is supplied for personal items. The resort makes available for these guests an array of casual clothing from work-out gear to jogging suits or swim wear. Another unusual amenity is provided periodically to pool and beachside sunbathers who are offered a refreshing iced towel, ice water or Evian mist. For the meeting planner, the Four Seasons features a 7,000 square foot ballroom, two banquet rooms and five conference areas situated adjacent to a 3,000 square foot hospitality suite. The suite offers a large living room, two bedrooms, another living space designed for private meetings, kitchen, and a 1,000 square foot lanai.

Amenities for guests on the club floor* include a private lounge, 24 hr. concierge, complimentary breakfast, afternoon tea, evening cocktails and after dinner liqueurs. Numerous special package offers include a room and car, golf, romance and family packages. (Note: The Golf package offers play at the exclusive new private Waikapu course.) Complimentary, year-round "Kids for All Seasons"

program designed for hotel guests aged 5 - 12 years. Restaurants include the Cabana Cafe, Pacific Grill and Seasons.
Partial o.v. $320, o.v. $400, Four Seasons executive suites o.v. $600
O.v. & o.f. suites $750-$1,400, additional suites $2,200 - $5,000
*Club floor plans available for additional $100 per night
Third adult in room $75 night, club floors $100 per night
Under age 18 complimentary when sharing same room with parents, except on club floor, add $50 per night per child ages 5 - 17. Adjoining children's room is available for $200 when parents pay standard room rate, except on club floors.

GRAND HYATT WAILEA ★

3850 Wailea Alanui Drive, Wailea, Maui, HI 96753 (808) 875-1234. The Grand Hyatt opened in September 1991 at a cost of $600 million with an additional $30 million in fine artwork. Quite frankly when we first heard the concepts planned for this new mega-resort we were concerned it would be another Kaua'i Lagoons, or take on aspects of Orlando or Anaheim. Wrong! The resort is a bit over-whelming, but it is tasteful, innovative and truly spectacular. Beautifully appointed with great attention to detail make it is a must-see, even if you aren't lucky enough to stay! In fact, make at least two trips... a second at night to enjoy dinner and tour the grounds when they are alight like a fairy land.

The sea remains the theme throughout the resort. Guests are greeted by a huge "drip wall" as they arrive. Look closely for the Hawaiian sea spirits which are hidden amid this interesting aquatic cascade. Each of the many Hawaiian sculptures has a legend or history -- King Kamehameha stands out near the entry and was created by Herb Kane, a noted specialist on Polynesian culture and history. He also created many of the mermaids, dancers and fisherman found by the resort's lagoons and streams. Inside the resort you'll find Hena, the mother of the demigod Maui. These are 18 bronzes around the grounds that were sculpted by world-famous artist Fernard Leger. Jan Fisher sculpted ten life-size pieces for the resort including the maidens bathing and the Fisher's trio of hula dancers at the entry of the atrium. Be sure to take note of the beautiful relief painted on the walls of the Grand Dining Room. The murals were painted by Doug Riseborough and depict his version of the legend of Maui. In the center of the dining room is a sculpture done by Shige Yamada, entitled "Maui Captures the Sun." Just outside the dining room is a small stage with a fabulous Hawaiian mosaic. The resort hopes to have an art tour.

The center courtyard is called the Botero Gallery. These sculptures seem to be getting the most discussion - both good and bad! Fernando Botero is a contemporary artist from Columbia and his work is "oversized." The huge Hawaiian woman reclined on her stomach (smoking a cigarette in the buff) weighs 600 pounds and is appraised at $2 million. If you're on the upper levels, be sure to look down to see her from another.... uh, interesting, perspective!

Over $20 million was spent on the waterfalls, streams, rapids, slides, reflecting pools, swimming pools, river pool, scuba pool, salt water lagoon and spa features. This is one of the most high-tech aquatic systems in the state. Strikingly beautiful, the formal pools rim the lobby and enter a 10,000 gallon reflecting pool in the atrium. Just beyond the atrium is a 200 foot long reflecting pool featuring a 5-story flowing fountain. Beyond this pool is a formal swimming pool with a terraced fountain, erupting over four stories. The "action pool" is a million gallon, 23,500 square foot pool with five large, free-form pools at various levels beginning at a height of 40 feet and dropping to sea level. The perimeter meanders over three-fifths of a mile and each pool has a different character and color with varying shades of green and blue mosaic tiles. Huge rocks and landscape features line the pools and a steam-spewing volcano top it all off. At one end of the pool is the Hyatt's largest waterslide, a 225 foot twisting ride that drops three stories. The "jungle pool" offers a rope swing. The pools are connected by a 220 foot river which carries swimmers at varying current speeds, ranging from white water rapids to a lazy cruise. Along the way are hidden grottoes, whirlpools and saunas, six slides, six waterfalls and a bumpy white water rapids that has been created by the use of special pumps and pipes. At the bottom of the river is a one-of-a-kind water elevator which lifts the swimmers back up to the top again. Below the rocky waterfall is the scuba pool which gets prospective divers in the mood with an underwater mural featuring a coral reef, and sea life made of tiles. Streams and pools also meander through elaborate gardens in Hawaiian and Japanese themes throughout the resort. It takes 68,000 gallons of water a minute to sustain their aquatic system.

The Spa Grande is Hawai'i's largest spa, and spans 50,000 square feet in the atrium wing of the resort. It is designed with Italian marble, original artwork, Venetian chandeliers and inlaid gold. It provides a blend of European, Japanese and America spa philosophies. The spa's central concept is based on a longevity program which allows guests to enjoy the fitness, beauty and health treatments as well as working out a regime that will continue once their vacation has ended. An in-house physician works with guests providing medical and fitness evaluations. Hawaiian therapies include a ti leaf wrap, limu (seawood) bath and a lomi lomi massage. The "Terme Wailea" is a 30-minute circuit on the spa's "wet" level which begins with a loofah scrub, followed by a trip to the Roman tub for a cool dip followed by a choice of specialty baths. The masso, thermo and hydrotherapy treatments are available in 42 individual rooms. Also available are a sonic relaxation room, cascading waterfall massage, authentic furo soaking tubs and white and black sand body treatments. An aerobics studio, weight room, cardio-vascular room, racquetball and squash court (the only ones on Maui), a full-service beauty salon, and game room are among the many spa options.

GRAND HYATT WAILEA

The Tsunami Nightclub (what great name!) offers 8,000 square feet of high tech lounge with black marble floors and would you believe it, hydraulic lifts under parts of the floor to give dancers a little extra rhythm! Couch potato and don't like to dance? Then they've a plan for you too... each table is be equipped with its own sound controls for one of fifty TV monitors spread about the room. The menus are intriguing plexi-glass boxes with an enclosed liquid that cause wave action! Five restaurants give guests plenty of choices. Kincha, features very authentic and expensive Japanese cuisine and is set amid a beautiful Japanese Garden. The Grand Dining Room Maui, situated 60 feet above sea level, offers a panoramic view of the Pacific, the gardens and Molokini Island from both inside or on a lovely outdoor eating veranda. Cafe Kula features spa foods. Humuhumu-nukunuku (Humuhumu) for short is named for the Hawaiian state fish. It sits surrounded by a saltwater lagoon filled with tropical fish. Pacific Rim/seafood cuisine is the fare here. Bistro Molokini serves California and Italian items and the Volcano Bar provides light dining and snacks. There is also a swim up bar. The food & beverage department has created an interesting assortment of original drinks. A Reeses peanut butter smoothie may be just the thing for sipping around the pool, or a liliokoi and orange juice splashed with champagne the ideal before dinner drink.

Now the rooms! There are 787 oceanfront rooms each 650 square feet and 53 suites. The Presidential suite (5,500 sq. ft.) is priced at a mere $7,000 per night and features what is lovingly referred to as a Imelda Marcos shoe closet, a private sauna, a room sized shower with ocean view in one bathroom and a black marble and teak soaking tub in the other. Lots of marble is used throughout all the rooms with subtle marble-ized wallpapers in huges of purple, mauve and peach. The resort was designed so that each room would provide an ocean view.

This may be the one resort that your kids will INSIST you come back to again and again. Or perhaps, after you visit Kamp Hyatt, you may wish to try and pass for a 10 or 11 year old. The 20,000 square foot camp operates year round and includes infants (from 6 months) as well as older kids. A huge area is designed with crafts in mind, even a pottery kiln has been installed. Adjacent is a kid's dining dream, resembling a 1950's style soda fountain. An outdoor area offers a toddler size whale shaped pool, cushy soft grass-like play-yard and playground equipment. Another room houses the infants, another the computer center, another the video arcade and yet another has a Hawaiian version of F.A.O Schwartz that will ensure that your kids may not be glad to see you upon pickup time. The price is $35 per day (9 a.m. - 3 p.m.) including lunch, with an evening schedule including dinner for $25.

The 38,000 sq. ft. ballroom is a convention planners dream, with concealed projection screens, specialized audio equipment, the works! The ballroom also has three huge, beautiful and unique artworks in gold and silver leaf which depict the story of Pele the fire goddess and her to sisters. Don't neglect a look up at the 29,000 pound Venetian glass chandelier imported from Italy.

We were frankly rather pleasantly surprised by the interesting blend of mega resort glitz and Hawaiian, themes tempered with outstanding craftsmanship. It seems to work. There is actually a great deal of fine craftsmanship (notice the twisted ohia wood rails that line the pathways) and we especially like the attention to the Hawaiiana aspects. The resort is visually very stimulating and each time you stroll the grounds you're sure to see something new. The chapel, set in the middle of the grounds, however, leaves us a bit puzzled. Looking as though it were snatched from Reno and transplanted to the beach in Wailea, we wonder why anyone would choose to be married inside, where the view of the ocean is obscured by stained glass, and when there are so many more beautiful sites around the hotel grounds, or on the beach. However, you should still inspect the Chapel. The woodwork and stained glass windows are absolutely beautiful, and take note the chandeliers, priced at $10,000 each!

All in all, if you're seeking a resort vacation, you'll find it all here. Not everyone wants the activity of a resort, but this one certainly has something for everyone. *Ocean $350, oceanfront $375, deluxe o.f. $425, Regency Club Floor $500*

KEA LANI ★
4100 Wailea Alanui Drive, Wailea, HI 96753. (808) 875-4100 1-800-882-4100. 413 suites plus 37 2 & 3 BR oceanfront villas. Designed after Las Hadas in Manzanillo, the name means "White Heavens." Its Mediterranean-style architecture is getting many mixed reviews. It seems to us that perhaps this might be the home of a Sultan with a dramatic style set on 22 acres, and seems very out of place in Wailea. However, it is a fabulous location and the roomy suites make for very comfortable vacation living. The landscaping softens the architecture as you enter the drive lined with Norfolk pines. Beyond the porte cochere is a large open lobby area with a fountain covered by 9 domes. Decorations are in Hawaiian florals, with mosaic tile ceilings and floors. There are 413 one-bedroom suites, each with a 100 square foot balcony. Views are garden, partial ocean, and oceanview. Each has a sunken marble tub, an enormous walk-in shower, king or two double beds, two closets, decorated in hues of cream and white. A cotton kimono is provided for guests. The living room features a state of the art cassette and laser disc system, 27 inch television and video recorder. Fresh ground coffee and coffee maker is provided daily in the suite and a mini-kitchen offers a microwave, a small sink, mini-bar and flatware. An iron and ironing board will also be available in each room. The spa is a 2,200 square foot exercise room with sauna, steam bath and equipment. The "Caffe Ciao" offers deli and bakery foods, pasta, pizza and an espresso bar. Polo Beach Grille & Bar has an outdoor setting

KEA LANI

under a canopy of coconut palm trees and serves kiawe grilled meats, seafood, salads, specialty ice creams and tropical drinks. The Kea Lani Restaurant offers casual meals all day with indoor and outdoor seating overlooking the formal pool. The 22,000 sq. ft. pool area is be a series of pools connected together. The upper level pool adjoins a swim up pool bar.

In addition to the suites, there are also 37 townhouse style villas, 24 are two bedroom and 13 are three bedroom, which overlook Polo Beach. An 1,800 sq. ft. two-bedroom villa runs $795 a night, and a 2,100 sq. ft three-bedroom unit runs $1195; both include either an Avis Cadillac or convertible. A little spendy, but it would be easy to feel at home here! Each has a private lanai, huge walk-in closets, full size kitchen and washer and dryer, and are decorated in very muted mauves. Each has a generous living room and eating area. If you don't want to make that walk to the beach, you can just meander out onto your lanai and take a dip in your private swimming pool. That's right. Each villa has its own pool!

The resort offers "Keiki Lani" (Heavenly Kids) for youths aged 4 to 11 years of age. Offered year round Monday thru Saturday from 9 a.m. until 3 p.m. includes lunch. Activities range from face painting to sailing, picnics to hula and off-property excursions. Children's menus available in the restaurant. Honeymoon, wedding, family, and sporting packages are available.
1 BR suite garden m.v. $225-245, partial o.v. $285, o.v. $325,
1 BR suite deluxe, o.v. or o.f. $355-395
2 BR villa (1-6 persons) $795, 3 BR villa (1-8) $1,195

POLO BEACH CLUB ★
20 Makena Rd., Wailea, Maui, HI 96753. (808-879-8847) Agents: Destination Resorts 1-800-367-5246 is the on-site rental agent, Hawaiian Apt. Leasing 1-800-854-8843 (1-800-472-8449 CA), Island Dreamscape 1-800-367-8047 ext. 216 U.S.

71 apartments in a single 8-story building located on Polo Beach. The units are luxurious and spacious. Underground parking, pool area jacuzzi. This once very secluded area is soon to be "discovered." Is located next to the Kea Lani Resort. Additional persons (over 4) $20 each. Three night minimum.
1 BR (2) o.f. $275-325 / $200-240, 2 BR 2 bath (max 6) o.f. $275-325 / $225-275

MAKENA

INTRODUCTION

The area just south of Wailea is Makena, and one of the newer resort developments on Maui. The project began with the completion of an 18-hole golf course in 1981. The Makena Surf condominium project opened in 1984. The Japanese conglomerate, Seibu, has a magnificent new resort, the Maui Prince Hotel, located at Maluaka Beach. Also in this area are several beaches with public access. They include Oneloa, Puuolai, Poolenalena, Palauea and Maluaka beaches. Since the area is not fully developed the end results remain to be seen.

WHAT TO DO AND SEE

Here are the last really gorgeous and undeveloped recreational beaches on Maui. Consequently, development in this area has met with a great deal of ongoing controversy. The new paved road (Makena Alanui) runs from Wailea past the Makena Surf and Maui Prince Hotel, exiting onto the Old Makena Rd. near the entrances to Oneuli (Black Sand) Beach and Oneloa (Big Makena)-Puuolai (Little Makena) Beaches. Past Ahihi Kinau Natural Reserve on Old Makena Rd. you will traverse the last major lava flow on Maui, which still looks pretty fresh after some 250 years and continues to La Perouse Bay. (See BEACHES). Hiking beyond La Perouse affords some great ocean vistas. You'll see trails made by local residents in their four wheel drive vehicles, and fishermen's trails leading to volcanic promontories overlooking the ocean. You may even spot the fishing pole holders which have been securely attached to the lava boulders. The Hoapili Trail begins just past La Perouse Bay and is referred to as the King's Highway. It is believed that at one time the early Hawaiians made use of a trail that circled the entire island and this may be the remnants of that ancient route. The state Forestry and Wildlife Division and volunteers worked together recently putting in place stone barricades to keep the four wheel drive vehicles and motorcycles from destroying any more of the trail.

GRATED RIPE COCONUT

135

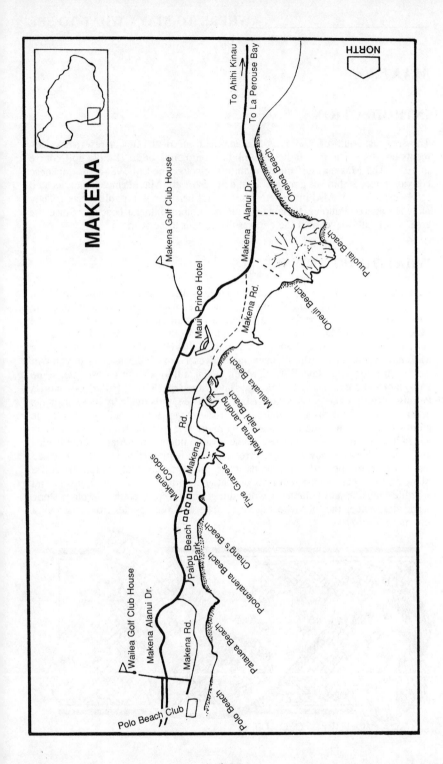

MAKENA

NORTH

To Ahihi Kinau
To La Perouse Bay

Makena Golf Club House

Makena Alanui Dr.

Ololoa Beach

Puolai Beach

Maui Prince Hotel

Makena Rd.

Oneuli Beach

Maluaka Beach

Makena Landing

Paipu Beach

Five Graves

Makena Rd.

Makena Condos

Paipu Beach

Park

Chang's Beach

Poolenalena Beach

Palauea Beach

Wailea Golf Club House

Makena Alanui Dr.

Makena Rd.

Polo Beach Club

Polo Beach

136

ACCOMMODATIONS - MAKENA

BEST BETS: The Maui Prince Hotel and **Makena Surf** - Both are first class, luxury accommodations (and the only ones available), on beautiful beaches.

MAKENA SURF ★
96 Makena Alanui Rd., Makena 96753, Destination Resorts 1-800-367-5146, Hawaiian Apt. Leasing 1-800-854-8843, Kihei Maui Vacations 1-800-541-6284. Located 2 miles past Wailea. All units are oceanfront and more or less surround Paipu (Chang's) Beach. These very spacious and attractive condos feature central air conditioning, fully equipped kitchens, washers and dryers, wet bar, whirlpool spa in the master bath, telephones and daily maid service. Two pools, and four tennis courts are set in landscaped grounds. Three historic sites found on location have been preserved.

1 BR (2) $250-325 / $200-275   *Prices listed are 2 or 3 nights*
2 BR (2) $300-375 / $240-315   *Discounts for 4 nights or longer*
3 BR (4) $450 / $395   *Extra person $15/night*

MAUI PRINCE ★
5400 Makena Alanui, Makena, Maui 96753. (808-874-1111) Reservations: 1-800-321-6284. In sharp contrast to the ostentatious atmosphere of some of the Kaanapali resorts, the Maui Prince radiates understated elegance. Its simplicity in color and design, with an Oriental theme, provides a tranquil setting and allows the beauty of Maui to be reflected. The central courtyard is the focal point of the resort with a lovely traditional water garden complete with a cool cascading waterfall and ponds filled with gleaming koi. The rooms are tastefully appointed in cool neutral hues and equipped with the comfort of the guests in mind. The units have two telephones and a small refrigerator which is stocked with complimentary fresh fruit and sparkling water. A yukata (summer kimono) is available for use during the guest's stay. A morning paper and 24-hour full room service add to the conveniences.

There is plenty of room for lounging around two circular swimming pools or in a few steps you can be on Maluaka (Nau Paka) Beach with its luxuriously deep, fine white sand and good snorkeling, swimming and wave playing. The resort is comprised of 1,800 acres including the Makena Golf Course, a 72-par 18 hole championship course designed by Robert Trent Jones, Jr. Restaurants include Prince Court serving Island Regional dishes (and one of the island's best Sunday brunches), al fresco dining in Cafe Kiowai and the Japanese restaurant and sushi bar at Hakone.

The Prince Kids Program is offered mornings 9 am. until noon during spring, summer and Christmas vacations. It is a complimentary program for kids ages 4 to 12, but a minimum of three children are required to run the program. Every child receives a logo tote bag, visor and beach ball upon registration. Activities are run by the pool staff and include arts and crafts, swimming, nature hikes.
Partial o.v. $210, o.v. $250, o.v. prime $290, o.f. $330, Suites $400-800
No charge for third person using existing beds

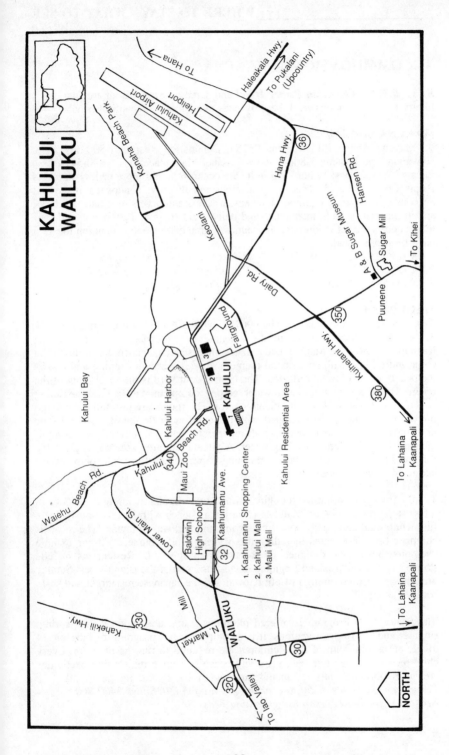

KAHULUI WAILUKU

1. Kaahumanu Shopping Center
2. Kahului Mall
3. Maui Mall

NORTH

WAILUKU AND KAHULUI

INTRODUCTION

The twin towns of Wailuku and Kahului are located on the northern, windward side of the island. Wailuku is the county seat of Maui and Kahului houses not only the largest residential population on the island, but also the main airport terminal and deep-water harbor. There are three motel-type accommodations around Kahului Harbor, and while the rates are economical, and the location is somewhat central to all parts of the island, we cannot recommend staying in this area for other than a quick stopover that requires easy airport access. This side of the island is generally more windy, overcast and cooler with few good beaches. Except for the avid windsurfer, we feel there is little reason to headquarter your stay in this area, however, there are good reasons to linger and explore.

WHAT TO DO AND SEE

Kahului has a very colorful history, beginning with the arrival of King Kamehameha I in the 1790's from the big island of Hawaii. The meaning of Kahului is "winning" and may have had its origins in the battle which ensued between Kamehameha and the Maui chieftain. The shoreline of Kahului Bay began its development in 1863 with the construction of a warehouse by Thomas Hogan. By 1879 a landing at the bay was necessary to keep up with the growing sugar cane industry. Two years later, in 1881 the Kahului Railroad Company had begun. The city of Kahului grew rapidly until 1900 when it was purposely burned down to destroy the spreading of a bubonic plague outbreak. The reconstruction of Kahului created a full-scale commercial harbor, which was bombed along with Pearl Harbor on December 7, 1941. After World War II, a housing boom began, with the development of reasonably priced homes to house the increasing number of people moving to the island. The expansion has continued ever since.

Wailuku is the county seat of Maui and has been the center of government since 1930. It is now, slowly, experiencing a rebirth. It is often overlooked by visitors who miss out on some wonderful local restaurants and limited, but interesting shopping.

Market Street in Old Wailuku Town is alive with the atmosphere of Old Hawaii. The area, rich in history, was built on the site of ancient Heiaus and witnessed decisive Hawaiian battles. Later the area hosted the likes of Mark Twain and Robert Redford. It is no wonder that such an area should re-emerge in the modern day with shops of a cultural nature. One-of-a-kind items can be found here, gathered from around the world and eras gone by. Such is the case with Old Wailuku Town and the cluster of interesting shops on the upper end of Market Street in an area known as Antique Row.

Set against the lush backdrop of the Iao Valley and the West Maui Mountains, Antique Row is a small area offering a quaint alternative to the hustle-bustle vacation centers of Lahaina and Kihei. Surrounding this area is a multitude of wonderful and inexpensive ethnic restaurants. So don't limit your excursion to the few shops on the corner of Market and Main streets.

Emura's at 49 Market Street has consistently proven to be the spot for the best buys of eel skin items. From wallets and purses, to shoes and attaches. Pay cash and get an extra discount!

The once Takata Market, a thriving butcher shop and grocery store in the 30's, is now home to *Memory Lane* (antique store) and *Traders of the Lost Art* (158 Market St). Operated by Tye Hartall, Traders of the Lost Art features a variety of native carvings and primitive ritual art, which he brings back regularly from the secluded Sepik River area of Papua in New Guinea. Next door was the B. Hotta General Store and residence, which now houses an art gallery. *Alii Antiques* is across the street.

Kaahumanu Church, Maui's oldest remaining church was built in 1837 at High and Main Streets in Wailuku.

Hale Hoikeike in Wailuku houses the *Maui Historical Society* and is known as the *Bailey House* (circa 1834). To reach it, follow the signs to Iao Valley and you will see the historical landmark sign on the left side of the road. It's open daily from 9 am - 3:30 pm, and a small admission is charged. Here you will find the Bailey Gallery, (once a dining room for the female seminary that was located at this site), with paintings of Edward Bailey done during the 19th century. His work depicts many aspects of Hawaiian life during earlier days. Also on display are early Hawaiian artifacts and memorabilia from the missionary days. The staff is extremely knowledgeable and friendly. They also have for sale an array of Hawaiian history, art, craft and photographic books, all available at prices LESS than other Maui bookstores. Originally, the Royal Historical Society was established in 1841, but it was not reactivated as the Maui Historical Society until 1956. The museum was dedicated on July 6, 1957, then closed for restoration on December 31, 1973 and reopened on July 13, 1975. Of special interest are the impressive 20 inch thick walls that are made of plaster using a special missionary recipe which included goat hair as one ingredient. The thick walls provided the inhabitants with a natural means of air conditioning.

KAAHUMANU CHURCH

The *Maui Jinsha Mission* is located at 472 Lipo Street, Wailuku. One of the few remaining old Shinto Shrines in the state of Hawaii, this mission was placed on the National Register of Historic Places in 1978.

The *Halekii and Pihana State Monuments* are among Maui's most interesting early Hawaiian historical sites. Both are of considerable size and situated on the top of a sand dune. These temples were very important structures for the island's early Alii. Their exact age is unknown, although one resource reported that they were used from 1765 to 1895. The Halekii monument is in better condition as a result of some reconstruction done on it in 1958. Follow Waiehu Beach Road across a bridge, then turn left onto Kuhio Place and again on Hea Place. Look for and follow the Hawaii Visitors Bureau markers. Some say the Pihana Heiau (temple) was built by the menehunes (Hawaii's little people), others believe by the Maui chiefton, Kahekili.

The Iao Valley is a short drive beyond Hale Hoikeike. Within the valley is an awesome volcanic ridge that rises 2,250 feet and is known as the Iao Needle. A little known fact is that this interesting natural phenomena is not a monolithic formation, but rather what you are viewing is the end of a large, thin ridge. A helicopter view will give you an entirely different perspective! Parking facilities are available and there are a number of hiking trails. A recent addition is the *Tropical Gardens of Maui*. This botanical garden features the largest selection of exotic orchids in the Hawaiian islands. For a small fee you can stroll the grounds where they grow, and visit their gift shop filled with tropical flowers and Maui made products. Plants can be shipped home. Snack bar and picnic tables available. Phone 244-3085.

The Heritage Garden - Kepaniwai Park is an exhibit of pavilions and gardens which pay tribute to the culture of the Hawaiians, Portuguese, Filipinos, Koreans, Japanese and Chinese. Picnic tables and BBQ's available for public use. Located on Iao Valley Rd. Free admission, open daily. Public swimming pool for children is open daily from 9 am - noon and again from 1 until 4:30. Also a popular site for weddings and other functions, it is available for rent from the Maui Parks Dept. A deposit is required and the Wailuku permit office (1580 Kaahumanu Ave., Wailuku, Maui (808) 243-7389) can provide the necessary forms.

Just outside Wailuku on Hwy. 30, between Wailuku and Maalaea, is Waikapu, home of the *Maui Tropical Plantation*. This visitor exhibit has become one of the top ten most heavily visited in the state of Hawai'i. The fifty acres, which opened in 1984, have been planted with sugar cane, bananas, guava and other island produce. A ten acre visitor center includes exhibits, a market place, nursery and restaurant. There is no admission for entry into the marketplace or the restaurant, however, there is an $8 charge for admission for the narrated tram ride around the fields. The tram ride, which departs every half hour, includes several stops for samples of fresh fruit. The plantation is open seven days a week from 9 a.m. until 5 p.m. (244-7643). Three nights a week the Maui Tropical Plantation features a Hawaiian Country Barbecue and dinner show featuring Buddy Fo and his Hawaiian Country Band. For reservations or more information call 242-8605.

Baldwin Beach - See the section on BEACHES for Baldwin Beach and others in the area.

The Maui Zoological and Botanical Gardens are open 9-4 daily with FREE admission. Go up Kaahumanu to Kanaloa Street and turn by the Wailuku War Memorial Center. The zoo is on the right hand side. This is a zoo Maui style, with a few pygmy donkeys, sheep, goats, monkeys, Galapogos turtles, birds and picnic tables.

The Kanaha Wildlife Sanctuary is off Route 32, near the Kahului Airport, and was once a royal fish pond. Now a lookout is located here for those interested in viewing the stilt and other birds which inhabit the area.

A popular Saturday morning stop for local residents and visitors alike is ***The Swap Meet*** ★ (877-3100) held at grounds around the Christ the King Church, next door to the Post Office off Pu'unene Hwy 35. You'll find us referring to this event for various reasons throughout this guide. For a fifty-cent admission (children free) you will find an assortment of vendors selling local fruits and vegetables, new and used clothing, household items and many of the same souvenir type items found at higher prices in resort gift shops. Here you can pick up some fantastic tropical flowers and for only a few dollars lavishly decorate your condo during your stay. Protea are seasonally available here too for a fraction of the cost elsewhere. This is also the only place to get true spoonmeat coconuts. These are fairly immature coconuts with deliciously mild and soft (to very soft) meat and filled with sweet coconut milk. We stock up on a weeks supply at a time. Another "must purchase" are some of the goodies from the Four Sisters Bakery! Free parking. Hours are 8 am - noon.

The ***Alexander and Baldwin Sugar Museum*** ★ is located at 3957 Hansen Rd., in Puuene. Puuene is on Highway 35 between Kahului and Kihei, the tall stacks of the working mill are easily spotted. The museum is housed in a 1902 plantation home that was once occupied by the sugar mills superintendent. Memorabilia include the strong-box of Samuel Thomas Alexander and an actual working scale model of a sugar mill. The displays are well done and are very informative. Monday thru Friday 9:30 - 4. Admission charge: $2 adult visitors, $1 adult Maui residents. Visiting students 6-17 years $1. Maui students 6-17, 50 cents. Children under 6 are free. Call 871-8058.

HAWAIIAN STILT

WHERE TO SHOP

There are three large shopping centers in Kahului, all on Kaahumanu Street. The *Maui Mall* is only a two-minute drive from the airport. It offers two large grocery stores, Star and Safeway, and a large Long's Drugs which is great for picking up sundry items. They also have a variety of small shops and restaurants. The older, local style *Kahului Shopping Center* is lined with Monkey pod trees and is filled with local residents playing cards. Check out the Toda Drug Store that has a very reasonable luncheonette, or Ah Fook's grocery for their bentos. The largest shopping center is *Kaahumanu* with 47 shops and restaurants. Two major department stores, Sears and Liberty House, anchor this mall with the island's largest selection of clothing and gift shops in between. If you don't have accommodations with a kitchen, you might want to pick up a styrofoam type ice chest at one of these centers and stock it with juices, lunch meats and what not to enjoy in your hotel room and for use on beach trips or drives to Hana and Haleakala. (Check with your hotel regarding small in-room refrigerators.) A new Kmart should be open by mid-1993 at the intersection of Dairy Road and the Hana Hwy.

Wailuku has no large shopping centers, but a cluster of shops down their Main Street makes for interesting strolling.

ACCOMMODATIONS - WAILUKU

BANANA BUNGALOW
310 North Market Street, Wailuku (808) 244-6880, 1-800-8-HOSTEL. Previously the old Happy Valley Inn and Valley Isle Lodge. They describe their accommodations as an international budget hotel and hostel, with clean and comfortable accommodations with a social atmosphere attracting budget travelers, wind-surfers and international backpackers. Rooms are equipped with closet, chair, mirror and night stand. Bathrooms are shared. The lounge offers a cable TV, refrigerator and pay phone. Laundry facilities on property. They do take Visa, Mastercard and American Express.
Shared room (sleeps 3-4) $15 per person
Single room with double bed #31.95
Double room with two twins or one queen bed #38.95

NORTHSHORE INN
2080 Vineyard St., Wailuku (808) 242-8999. Some major renovations at the Northshore Inn in Wailuku have increased the size to a sleeping capacity of 75 people. Owner Katie Moore has been operating the hotel for three years, but has been a resident on Maui for eight. The Inn features an informal, international atmosphere with windsurfers and budget backpackers from around the world staying as guests. Much of the accommodations available are shared dormitory rooms that sleep four or six to a room. Their motto is "Fun is Number 1 - come as guests, leave as friends." They also now offer laundry facilities and a storage room. The garden in the back of the building is gone, but there are still plenty of great ethnic restaurants up and down the street and a new European bakery and deli is located right beneath the hotel. A TV is provided in the lounge area. Rental cars can be arranged. Reservations accepted. Weekly discounts.
Shared rooms (sleep 4 - 6) $15 per night, single $33, double $43

ACCOMMODATIONS - KAHULUI

One advantage to choosing this area for headquarters is its proximity to the Kahului Airport and its somewhat central location to all other parts of the island. The motels are clustered together on the Kahului Harbor.

MAUI PALMS   (Hotel)
(808-877-0051) Agent: Hawaiian Pacific 1-800-367-5004. Also located on Kaahumanu Avenue. This property is a 103 unit low rise hotel with Polynesian decor. Restaurant on premises. They offer free airport pickup.
Room rates (3) $67-80/57-70

MAUI BEACH HOTEL   (Hotel)
(808-877-0051) 170 Kaahumanu Avenue, Kahului, Maui, HI 96732. Agent: Hawaiian Pacific 1-800-367-5004. Renovated in 1991, this two story, 152 room hotel is located oceanfront on Kahului Bay. All rooms have air conditioning, TV, some balconies. Complimentary airport shuttle service.
Room rates (3-4) $85-120/$75-110

MAUI SEASIDE   (Hotel)
1-800-367-7000 U.S., 1-800-654-7020 Canada, FAX (808) 922-0052. The older Maui Hukilau has been combined with the much newer Maui Seaside to form one property called the Maui Seaside. You might want to inquire when booking here about which of the buildings you will be in. The management, Sand and Seaside Hotels, tell us that all of their properties have been recently renovated and refurbished like new. Vi's Restaurant is right next door. Add $16 a day more for car.
Room rates $74-98/64-88

HIBISCUS & PALM

UPCOUNTRY and onward to HALEAKALA

INTRODUCTION

The Western slopes of Haleakala are generally known as Upcountry and consist of several communities including Makawao and Pukalani. The higher altitude, cooler temperatures and increased rainfall make it an ideal location for produce farming. A few fireplace chimneys can be spotted in this region where the nights can get rather chilly. Accommodations are limited to two small lodges in Kula and a few cabins which are available with the park service for overnight use while hiking in the Haleakala Crater.

WHAT TO DO AND SEE

Enroute to upcountry is Pukalani, meaning "opening to the sky," and it is the last stop for gas on the way to Haleakala. There are also several places to enjoy a hearty meal. (See RESTAURANTS).

Haleakala means "house of the sun" and is claimed to be the largest dormant volcano in the world. The crater is truly awesome and it is easy to see why the old Hawaiians considered it sacred and the center of the earth's spiritual power. There is a $3-per car charge for admission to the crater, U.S. residents age 62 and older enter free. The most direct route is to follow Hwy. 37 from Kahului then left onto Hwy. 377 above Pukalani and then left again onto Hwy. 378 for the last 10 miles. While only about 40 miles from Kahului, the last part of the trip is very slow. There are numerous switchbacks and bicycle tours doing the 38-mile downhill coast. Two hours should be allowed to reach the summit. Sunrise at the crater is a popular and memorable experience, but plan your arrival accordingly. Many visitors have missed this spectacular event by only minutes. The Maui News, the local daily, prints sunrise and sunset times. The park offers a recording of weather and viewing conditions which can be reached by calling 572-7749. The park headquarter number is 572-9306. A recording of hiking and camping information is available at 572-9177. Be sure you have packed a sweater as the summit temperature can be 30 degrees cooler than the coast and snow is a winter possibility. Mid-morning from May to October generally offers the clearest viewing. However, fog can cause very limited visibility and a call may save you a trip.

At the park headquarters, you can obtain hiking and camping information and permits. Day-hike permits are not required, however, they do request you complete a registration form at the trail head and deposit it in the box provided. The first stop is Kalahaku Overlook. Here you can see the rare silversword which takes up to 20 years to mature, then blooms once in July or August, only to wither and die in the fall. Keep your eye out for the many nene geese which inhabit the volcano.

Talks on Haleakala history and geology are presented several times daily in the summit building visitors center located at an elevation of 9,745 feet. It is open daily from 6 am - 3 pm (hours may vary). A short distance by road will bring you to the Sun Visitor Center located on the crater rim. This glassed-in vantage point (the Puu Ulaula outlook) is the best for sunrise and is the highest point on Maui. The rangers give morning talks here at 9:30, 10:30 and 11:30. The view, on a good day, is nothing short of awesome. The crater is seven miles long, two miles wide, and 3,000 feet deep. A closer look is available by foot or horseback (see RECREATION AND TOURS - Horseback riding.) A 2 1/2 hour hike down Sliding Sands Trail into the Haleakala Crater is offered by the park service every Saturday, Sunday and Tuesday. They depart at 10 am from the House of the Sun Visitor Center. A hike featuring native Hawaiian birds and plants is offered each Monday and Thursday mornings. Again, check with the ranger headquarters 572-9306 to verify trips, dates and times. A unique excursion begun by Cruiser Bob's and several other operations is a 38-mile downhill ride on a specially designed bike. (See RECREATION & TOURS - Biking).

The park service maintains 30 miles of well-marked trails, three cabins and two campgrounds. All are accessable only by trail. The three cabins are Holua, Kapalaoa and Paliku, all located within the Haleakala Crater. The closest cabin is about seven miles away from the observatory. Arrangements for these cabins need to be made 90 days in advance and selection is made 60 days prior to the dates requested by a lottery-type drawing. For more information, write: Superintendent, Haleakala National Park, P.O. Box 369, Makawao, Maui, HI 96768. Rates are $8 per night for each adult, and $5.50 for each child 12 and under. Minimum charge $20 per cabin. Maximum cabin occupancy is 12. $15 deposit to hold reservations.

Short walks might include the three-fourth mile Halemauu Trail to the crater rim, one-tenth mile to Leleiwi Overlook, or two-tenth mile on the White Hill Trail to the top of White Hill. Caution, the thin air and steep inclines may be especially tiring. (See RECREATION AND TOURS -Hiking.)

Science City can be seen beyond the visitor center, but it is not open to the public. It houses a solar and lunar observatory operated by the University of Hawaii, television relay stations, and a Department of Defense satellite station.

If time allows, there is more of Upcountry to be seen!

The Kula area offers rich volcanic soil and commercial farmers harvest a variety of fruits and vegetables. Grapes, apples, pineapples, lettuce, artichokes, tomatoes and, of course, Maui onions are only a few. It can be reached by retracking Hwy. 378 to the Upper Kula Road where you turn left. The protea, a recent floral immigrant from South Africa, has created a profitable business. *The Kula Botanical Gardens* (878-1715) charges an admission of $3 for adults, and children 50 cents, open 9 am - 4 pm. The *Maui Enchanting Gardens*, on Hwy. 37 in Kula, charges $3.50 for adults, $1.50 for children for a self guided botanical tour. The *Sunrise Protea Farm* (878-2119) in Kula has a small, but diverse, variety of protea growing adjacent to their market and flower stand for shipment home. Dried assortments begin at about $25. Picnic tables available and no charge for just looking!

Be sure and stop in Keoke at *Grandma's Coffee House*. This wonderfully cozy, two year old restaurant is the place for some freshly made, Maui grown coffee, hot out of the oven cinnamon rolls or a light lunch. See Upcountry restaurants for more information.

Poli Poli State Park is high on the slopes of Haleakala, above Kula at an elevation of 6,200 feet. Continue on Hwy. 377 past Kula and turn left on Waipoli Rd. If you end up on Hwy. 37, you've gone too far. The sign indicating Poli Poli is currently missing, so you could also look for a sign indicating someones home, it reads WALKER. It's another 10 miles to the park over a road which deteriorates to deep ruts and is often muddy. A 4-wheel drive is really a necessity for this road during wet weather. The park offers miles of trails, a picnic area, restrooms, running water, a small redwood forest and great views. A cabin, which sleeps up to 10, is available through the Division of Parks, P.O. Box 537, Makawao, Maui, HI 96768. For more information see the "Hiking" section in the RECREATION AND TOURS chapter

Approximately 9 miles past the Kula Botanical Gardens on Hwy. 37, is the Ulupalakua Ranch. *The Tedeschi Vineyards* (878-6058), part of the 30,000 acre ranch, made its debut in 1974. The tasting room is located at the Ranch in the old jail and provides samples of their pineapple, champagne and red table wines. Free daily guided tours are offered between 10 am and 5 pm. The tour begins at the Tasting Room then continues to view the presses used to separate the juice from the grapes, the large fermenting tanks, and the corking and the labelling rooms.

If you continue on past the ranch on Hwy. 37 it's another very long 35 miles to Hana with nothing but beautiful scenery. Don't let the distance fool you. It is a good 3-hour trip, at least, over some fairly rough sections of road, which are not approved for standard rental cars. During recent years this road has been closed often to through traffic due to severe washouts. Check with the county to see if it is currently passable. If you're not continuing on, we suggest you turn around and head back to Pukalani and Makawao. Unfortunately, the Ulupalakua Road down to Wailea has been closed due to a dispute between the Ranch and the county. It is hoped that this or some other access between Upcountry and the Kihei/Wailea area will soon be developed. On the way down you can go by way of Makawao, the colorful "cowboy" town, and then on to Paia or Halemaile. Both have several good restaurants. (See RESTAURANTS - Upcountry).

TEDESCHI WINERY

WHERE TO SHOP

The town of Makawao offers a western flavor with a scattering of shops down its main street, a few restaurants and numerous grocery stores. We recommend the *Komoda Store* for its popular bakery, but get there early! The Pukalani Shopping Center has a grocery store, and some small shops and restaurants. *Viewpoints Gallery*, 3620 Baldwin (572-5979) is a fine co-operative gallery featuring local artists and a clustering of interesting gift shops; a must see in Makawao.

WHAT TO SEE AND DO

The *Hui Noeau Visual Arts Center* may at first seem a little out of place, located at 2841 Baldwin Avenue, down the road from Makawao. However, there could not be a more beautiful and tranquil setting than at this estate, called Kaluanui, which was built in 1917 by famous Honolulu architect C.W. Dickey for Harry and Ethel Baldwin. The house was occupied until the mid-1950's and in 1976 Colin Cameron (grandson of Ethel Baldwin) granted Hui Noeau the use of Kaluanui as a Visual Arts Center. Near the entrance to the nine acre estate are the remains of one of Maui's earliest sugar mills. It utilized mule power and was the first Hawaiian sugar mill to use a centrifugal to separate sugar crystals. What were once stables and tack rooms are now ceramic studios. A gift shop is open year round and the first part of December they have a special Christmas boutique. Daily 9 am - 1 pm. 572-6560. Fourth of July weekend is wild and wonderful in Makawao. Festivities include a morning parade through town and several days of rodeo events. Check the local paper for details.

ACCOMMODATIONS - UPCOUNTRY

Accommodations are limited in Upcountry. Five and one-half miles past Pukalani is the Kula Lodge. See listings at beginning of Accommodations section for information on Upcountry bed & breakfast facilities.

KULA LODGE
RR 1, Box 475, Kula, Maui, HI 96790 (808-878-1535) 1-800-233-1535. FAX (808) 878-2518. Five rustic chalet-like cabins with restaurant on the property.
Chalet 1 & 2 $140 (queen bed, fireplace, lanai, stairs to loft with 2 twin beds)
Chalet 3 & 4 & 5 $120 (queen bed, ladder to loft with two futons)
Chalet 5 $120 (single story with double bed and studio couch)
An additional amount of $50 will be charged for more than two guests

KULA SANDALWOODS
There is supposed to be a reopening of the restaurant and the cabins at the old Silversword. Judging by the response we received on inquiry, and their uncooperative and uninterested attitude in supplying us with information, their outlook is bleak. Apparently they have the restaurant open for breakfast and lunch (878-3523) but opening of the rest may not be for several years. They requested not to be included rather than sending us any menus or information.

PUALANI RETREAT
PO Box 1135, Makawao, HI. See Bed and Breakfast section.

HANA

INTRODUCTION

If you do not plan an extended stay in Hana, you might consider at least an overnight stop at one of the facilities to break up the long drive to this isolated east coast of Maui. (Insiders secret! Hana can best be enjoyed before and after the throngs of visitors who daily make this drive, so plan a stay in Hana of several days or at least overnight!) Here is a different Maui from the sunny, dry resort areas on the leeward coast. The windward coast here is turbulent with magnificent coastal views, rain forests, and mountain waterfalls creating wonderful pools for swimming. However, DO NOT drink the water from these streams and falls. The water has a high bacteria count caused from the pigs which live in the jungle-like forests above. The beaches along the Hana Hwy. are unsafe for swimming.

The trip to Hana by car from Kahului will take at least three hours and plan on plenty of time to make some stops, enjoy these waterfalls up close and experience this unique coastline.

Accommodations vary from hotel/condo to campgrounds and homes at a variety of price ranges. The 7,000 acre Hotel Hana Ranch has achieved their goal of creating an "elegant ranch atmosphere." Several moderately priced condominiums and inexpensive cottages are also available. Waianapanapa State Park, just outside Hana, has camping facilities and cabins. (See the Camping section for more information.) Ohe'o also has a tent camping area, bring your own drinking water.

Hana offers a quiet retreat and an atmosphere of peace (seemingly undisturbed by the constant flow of tourist cars and vans) that has lured many a prominent personality to these quiet shores. Restaurant choices are extremely limited and shopping is restricted to the Hasegawa General Store, the Hana Ranch Store or a few shops at the Hana Hotel.

WHAT TO SEE AND DO

PAIA - ALONG THE ROAD TO HANA

If you'd like a self-guided, yet narrated tour, consider renting one of the "Best of Maui" cassette tours. The $25 charge includes a tape player, Hana Highway guidebook, blossoms of Hawaii guide book, tropical flower identification card, detailed route map and sometimes a special premium offer of a free T-shirt! The tape allows you to drive at your own pace while listening to information on the legends and history of the islands. You pick up the tape and player on Dairy Road just off Puunene Ave. For information or reservations phone 871-1555.

A little beyond Wailuku, and along the highway which leads to Hana, is the small town of Paia. The name Paia translated means "noisy," however, the origin of this name is unclear. This quaint town is reminiscent of the early sugar cane era when Henry Baldwin located his first sugar plantation in this area. The wooden buildings are now filled with antique, art and other gift shops to attract the passing tourist. (See RESTAURANTS for more information).

The advent of windsurfing has caused a rebirth in this small charming town and a number of new restaurants have recently appeared over the last few years with more to come.

The *Maui Crafts Guild*, a group of local artisans own and operate this store. Pottery, koa furniture, weaving, wall sculptures, wood serving pieces, prints and basketry are featured. Very lovely, but expensive, hand-crafted items. *Things from the Past* is housed in a former automotive garage and is easy to spot on the Hana Hwy. with its friendly Hawaiian Santa out front. A conglomeration of items that will be of interest to just about anyone.

Accommodations in Paia are a little scarce. There may be some bed & breakfast options and there has been talk of a lodging in the town of Paia, but still in the discussion stages.

KUAU COVE-MAUI - 794 Poho Place, Paia, Maui, HI 96779. (808) 579-9400. Book a 2-bedroom unit on ocean next to Mama's Fish House and receive a 20% discount when you eat at Mama's. Color TV, BBQ, Washer/dryer, VCR and stereo. Maid service weekly. Seventh night is free! One bedroom units also available. *1 BR $60, 2 BR $125*

HANA
Anyone who endures the three-hour (at least) drive to Hana deserves to sport the "I survived the Road to Hana" T-shirts which are sold locally. While it may be true that it is easy to fall in love with Hana, getting there is quite a different story. The drive to Hana is not for everyone, although many guide books claim other-wise. It is not for people who are prone to motion sickness, those who don't like a lot of scenery, those who are in a hurry to get somewhere or those who don't love long drives. However, it is a trip filled with waterfalls and lush tropical jungles (which flourish in the 340-inch average annual rainfall). Maps are deceiv-ing. It appears you could make the 53-mile journey much faster than three hours but there are 617 (usually hairpin) curves and 56 miniature bridges along this narrow road. And believe it or not, each of these bridges has its own Hawaiian name! Even with recent repaving, most cars travel in the middle of the road, making each turn a possibly exciting experience, especially at night.

The Hana Hwy. was originally built in 1927 with pick and shovel, which may account for its narrowness, to provide a link between Hana and Kahului. There can also be delays on the road up to two hours if the road is being worked on. In days gone by when heavy rains caused washouts, it is said that people would literally climb the mud barricades and swap cars, then resume their journey. Despite all this, 300-500 people traverse this road daily, and it is the supply route for all deliveries to Hana and the small settlements along the way.

Now, if we haven't dissuaded you and you still want to see spectacular undevel-oped scenery, plan to spend the whole day (or even better, stop overnight) in Hana. If you are driving, be sure to leave as early in the morning as possible. You don't want to be making a return trip on this road in the dark. Be sure to get gas, the last stations before Hana are in Kahului or Paia. With the exceptions of an occasional fruit stand, there is no place to eat and only limited stops for drinking water. Be sure you pack your own food and drink. Picnic's in Paia is a popular stop for a picnic lunch. For something a little more unusual try packing along some local style foods or a bento (box lunch). Takimaya's grocery story on Lower Market St. has an unbelievable assortment of cooked, pre-packaged food made fresh daily. Fried calamari, tako poki (raw octopus), kalbi ribs, baked yams, and much, much more. Packing some rain gear and a warm sweater or sweatshirt is a precaution against the sometimes cooler weather and rain showers. Don't forget your camera, but remember not to leave it in your car unattended.

We also might recommend that if you drive, select a car with an automatic transmission (or else be prepared for constant shifting). Another choice is to try one of the small van tours which go to Hana and leave the driving to them. Check to see whether the tours are operating their vans around the other side of the island. This will depend on the road conditions. It is also a road not recommended for rental cars. The scenery on this dry side is strikingly different from the northern coast rain forests. Good tour guides will also be able to point out the sights of interest along the way that are easy to miss! The only other alternative is to by-pass the Hana Highway by flying into Hana's small airport.

There are two good resources you might also consider taking along on your drive. Stop at the small booth on Dairy Road, across from the Shell service station. For about $25 you can rent a cassette player and narrated tape to follow along on your trip. *Maui's Hana Highway*, by Angela Kay Kepler, runs about $5.95 at local bookstores and it's eighty information filled pages include plenty of full color photos of the area. Especially good for identifying the flora and fauna in this area.

Ho'okipa, about two miles past Paia, is thought by some to offer the world's best windsurfing. There won't be much activity here in the morning, but if you are heading back past here in mid to late afternoon when the winds pick up, you are sure to see numerous windsurfers challenging wind and wave. These waves are enough to challenge the most experienced surfers and are not for the novice except as a spectator sport. You'll note that on the left are the windsurfers while the waves on the right are enjoyed by the surfers! A number of covered pavilions offer shaded viewing and the beach, while not recommended for swimming, does have some tidepools (of varying size depending on the tidal conditions) for children to enjoy a refreshing splash. This beach is also a popular fishing area for local residents and you may see some folks along the banks casting in their lines.

The next area you will pass through is ***Haiku***, which translated means abrupt break. It is not unusual to experience some overcast, rainy weather here. During 1989 this area had more rainy days than not! Enjoy the smooth wider highway here, the Hana Highway awaits you just ahead!

Two miles from the point where Hana Highway intersects Route 400 look for a small roadside trail marker by the Hoolawa Bridge. This area, known as ***Twin Falls***, offers a pleasant spot for swimming. The first pool has two waterfalls, but by hiking a little farther, two more pools of crystal clear water created by waterfalls can be easily reached. Remember, don't drink the stream water! Mosquitos can be prolific so pack bug spray.

There are no safe beaches along this route for swimming, so for a cool dip, take advantage of one of the fresh water swimming holes provided.

Waikamoi Ridge - This picnic area and nature trail is about 1/2 mile past roadside marker #9 and has no restrooms or drinking water. This area is noted for its stands of majestic bamboo, and you are sure to see wild ginger and huge ferns.

Puohkamoa Falls - Located near roadside Marker #11 is an area to pull off the road with parking only for a couple of cars. This small picnic area offers one covered (in the event of one of the frequent windward coast rain showers) table. A short tunnel trail through lush foliage leads to a swimming hole beneath the water fall.

Kaumahina State Park - Just past roadside marker #12 you'll find this lovely park. This area overlooks the spectacular Honomanu Gulch, the rugged Maui coastline and in the distance a view of the Ke'anae Peninsula. Believe it or not this is about the half-way point to Hana. A good opportunity to make use of the toilet facilities.

The YMCA's Camp Ke'anae - Offers overnight accommodations for men and women (housed separately). The rate is $8 a night. Arrival is requested between 4 pm and 6 pm. Bring your own food and sleeping bag. Phone (808-248-8355). Reservations and information number is (808) 242-9007.

Just past Camp Ke'anae is the ***Ke'anae Arboretum***. This free botanical garden is managed by the Department of Land and Natural Resources and is home to a myriad of tropical plants. A number of the plants have been labeled for your assistance in identification.

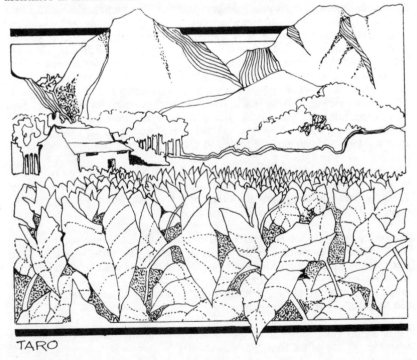

TARO

The ***Ke'anae peninsula*** was formed by a massive outpouring centuries ago from Haleakala. Today it is an agricultural area with taro the principal crop. The taro root is cooked and mashed and the result is a bland, pinkish brown paste called poi. Poi was a staple in the diets of early Hawaiians and is still a popular local food product which can be sampled at luaus or purchased at local groceries. Alone, the taste has been described as resembling wallpaper paste, (if you've ever tried wallpaper paste) although it is meant to be eaten with other foods, such as kalua pig. It is a taste that sometimes needs time to acquire. We have heard of island grandmothers sending fresh poi to the mainland for their young grandchildren. It is said to be extremely healthy, full of minerals and well tolerated by young stomachs. You'll see the fields filled with water and taro in varying stages of development. The Ke'anae Congregational Church, or ***The Miracle Church***, in Wailua is a historical landmark with a fascinating history. In the mid-1800's the community was lacking in building material for their church. Quite suddenly a huge storm hit and, by some miracle, deposited a load of coral onto the beach. The crushed coral church walls are still standing today.

If you'd like to explore Ke'anae more fully, check with Ekahi Tours (See Land Excursions). With a minimum number of people they will provide a van tour to Ke'anae which includes a tour of the poi factory.

The Shell Shop - Turn left at the Coral Miracle Church sign. The shop is located across the street from the church. Since 1974 local divers have been creating original shell jewelry from the limpet shell. The jewelry is sold exclusively at this location.

Wailua Lookout - Located just past Wailua on the roadside, look carefully for a turnoff. Park and follow the tunnel made by the hau plants, up the steps to the Lookout. The trek up is worth the excellent view.

The ***waterfalls*** are spectacular along the road, but consider what they are like from the air! We had no idea of the vastness of this tropical forest until we experienced it from a bird's eye view. Almost every waterfall and pool are preceded by another waterfall and pool above it, and above it there are yet others. The slice of this green wonderland seen from the winding Hana highway is just a small piece of the rugged wilderness above.

Puaa Kaa State Park - Fourteen miles before Hana, this park has two waterfalls and pools that are roadside. This picture perfect little park is a favorite stop for a picnic lunch. The waterfalls and large pool have combined with this lush tropical locale to make you feel sure a menehune must be lurking nearby. Restrooms and drinking water are available here too. Keep your eye out for mongoose. They have been "trained" by some of the van tour guides to make an appearance for a handout at some of these wayside stations. The best place to get a look at them is usually near the garbage cans. Toss a little snack and see if anyone is home.

With a little effort a sharp observer can spot the open ditches and dams along the roadside. These are the ***Spreckles Ditches*** built over 100 years ago to supply water for the young sugar cane industry. These ditches continue to provide the island with an important part of its supply of water.

Waianapanapa (pronounced WHY-A-NAHPA-NAHPA) *State Park* is four miles before Hana and covers an area of 120 acres. Translated it is said to mean glistening water. This area offers a number of historical sites, ancient heiaus (temples) and early cemeteries. You can spot one of the many stone walls used by the early Hawaiians for property boundaries, animal enclosures and also as home foundations. It is noted for its unusual black sand beach made of small smooth volcanic pebbles. The ocean here is not safe for swimming, but there is plenty of exploring! Don some mosquito repellent, tennis shoes are a good idea, and follow the well marked trails to the Waianapanapa Caves. The trail is lined with thick vines, a signal left by the early Hawaiians that this area was kapu (off limits). The huge lava tubes have created pools of cold, clear water. An ancient cave legend tells of a beautiful Hawaiian princess named Popoalaea who fled from Kakae, her cruel husband. She hid in the caves, but was discovered and killed. At certain times of the year the waters turn red. Some say it is a reminder of the beautiful slain princess, while others explain that it is the infestation of thousands of tiny red shrimp. Another three mile trail along the coast follows part of the ancient King's Hwy. which, in the days of the early Hawaiians, may have extended around the entire island. Several ancient heiaus can be found in this area. Another portion of the ancient highway can be found on the southern coastline past La Perouse Bay. Camping is allowed and there are rustic cabins available for rent (See ACCOMMODATIONS - "Hana," which follows).

The Helani Gardens (248-8274) is a self-guided botanical tour by foot or car through some very dense vegetation. Created by Howard Cooper it opened in 1970 after thirty years of development. The lower area consists of five acres with manicured grounds and a tropical pool filled with jewel colored koi. The upper sixty five acres are a maze of one-lane dirt roads through an abundant jungle of amazing and enormous flowering trees and shrubs. Wild plants from around the world are raised here and you'll see plenty of gigantic versions of your own house and garden plants from back home. Keep a sharp eye out for the large treehouse built by the Cooper grandchildren. This is really quite an enjoyable adventure, and one usually overlooked by those in a hurry to or from Hana and Ohe'o. Take your time and explore this unusual attraction. Admission $2 for adults, $1 children 6-16. Located about one mile before Hana. Picnic areas and restrooms available.

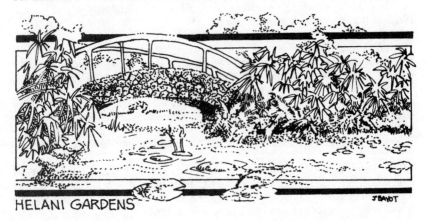

HELANI GARDENS

The last curve of the road will put you at **Hana's Gardenland**. There is no charge to browse through their flower displays and they thoughtfully provide picnic tables and a restroom. The plants sold here include the rare and beautiful and are available for shipping anywhere.

Now, back in the car for a drive into downtown Hana, but don't blink, or you might miss it. **Hana Cultural Center** (248-8622) opened in August of 1983. It contains a collection of relics of Hana's past in the old courthouse building and a small new museum. Open Monday through Sunday 10 am - 4 pm. Located near Hana Bay, watch for signs.

Hana Bay has been the site of many historical events. It was a retreat for Hawaiian royalty as well as an important military point from which Maui warriors attacked the island of Hawaii, and then were in turn attacked. This is also the birthplace of Ka'ahumanu (1768), Kamehameha's favorite wife. (See Beaches for more information.)

The climate on this end of Maui is cooler and wetter, creating an ideal environment for agricultural development. The Ka'eleku Sugar Company established itself in Hana in 1860. Cattle, also a prominent industry during the 20th century, continues today. You can still view the paniolos (Hawaiian cowboys) work at nearby Hana Ranch. There are 3,200 head of cattle which graze on 3,300 acres of land. Every three days the cattle are moved to fresh pastures. (Our family was thrilled when a paniolo flagged us to stop on the road outside Hana, while a herd of cattle surrounded our car enroute to fresher pastures.)

Hana has little to offer in the way of shopping, however, the **Hasegawa General Store** offers a little bit of everything. It has been operated since 1910, meeting the needs of visitors and local residents alike. Several years ago the original structure was burned down, but they reopened in the old Hana Theatre location. Hours are Monday thru Saturday 8 am - 5:30 pm an Sunday 9 am - 5:30. This store has even been immortalized in song.You may even run into one of the celebrities who come to the area for vacation. The Hana Ranch Store is open daily and the Hana Resort has a gift shop and boutique.

SOME LOCAL HANA INFORMATION:

St. Mary's Church (248-8030) Sat. Mass 6 pm, Sun. 9 am
Wananalua Protestant Church (248-8040) Built in 1838. Services 10 am Sundays
Hana Ranch Store (248-8261) 7:00 am-7 pm daily
Hasegawa General Store (248-8231) 8 am-5:30 pm, Mon.-Sat., Sun. 9 am-3:30
Hana Medical Center (248-8294) Emergencies 24 hours. Mon.-Fri. 8 am-noon
    and 2 pm-5 pm. Sat. 8 am-noon. Closed Sunday.
Bank of Hawaii (248-8015) Mon.-Thur. 3-4:30 pm and Fri. 3-6 pm
Library (248-7714) Tues.-Fri. 8-5 pm, Mon. 8-8 pm
Post Office (248-8258) 8 am-4:30 pm, Mon.-Fri.

The oldest building in town, built in 1830, currently houses the laundry facility for the Hana Hotel.

On Lyon's Hill stands a large stone cross in memory of Paul Fagan. It was built by two Japanese brothers from Kahului in 1960. Although the access road is chained, the front desk of the Hotel Hana will provide a key. The short trip to the top will reward the visitor with a spectacular panoramic view of Hana Bay and the open pasture land of the Hana Ranch.

Kaihalulu Beach (Red Sand Beach) is located in a small cove on the other side of Kauiki Hill from Hana Bay and is accessible by a narrow, crumbly trail more suited to mountain goats than people. The trail descends into a lovely cove bordered by high cliffs and is almost enclosed by a natural lava barrier seaward. For more details see BEACHES.

Hamoa Beach - This gorgeous beach has been very attractively landscaped and developed by the Hotel Hana Maui in a way that adds to the surrounding lushness. The long sandy beach is in a very tropical setting and surrounded by a low sea cliff. As you leave Hana toward Ohe'o Gulch look for the sign 1½ miles past the Hasegawa store that says "Koki Park - Hamoa Beach - Hamoa Village." Follow the road, you can't miss it.

You quickly pass fields of grazing world-famous Maui beef and reenter the tropical jungle once more. Numerous waterfalls cascade along the roadside and after ten curvy, bumpy miles on a very narrow two-lane road, and a 45-60 minute drive, you arrive at one of the reasons for this trip, the Kipahulu Valley and *Ohe'o Gulch*. Popularly known in the past as the Seven Sacred Pools as a tool for attracting tourists, the original and proper name is trying to be reclaimed by the Park Service.

The 100 ft. *Wailua Falls* cascades beneath the narrow bridge (a great place for a photo) flowing over the blue-grey lava to create these lovely lower pools. The pools you see below the bridge are just a few of the more than 20 that have been formed as the water of this stream rushes to the ocean. The pools are safe for swimming so pack your suit, but no diving is allowed. Swimming off the black sand beach is very dangerous and many drownings and near drownings have occurred here.

COMMON 'AMAKIHI

The best time to enjoy these falls may be in late afternoon, when the day visitors have returned to their cars for the drive home. (Another good reason to make Hana an overnight trip.) The bluff above the beach offers a magnificent view of the ocean and cliffs, so have your camera ready. This area is of historical significance and signs warn visitors not to remove any rocks. A pleasant hike will take you to the upper falls. *Makahiku Falls* is 185 feet high and is a fairly easy half mile hike that passes through some cattle pastures. *Waimoku Falls* is another mile and a half. Three to four hours should be allowed for this hike which traverses across the stream and through a bamboo forest. Heavy rains far above in the mountains can result in flash floods. Avoid swimming in these upper streams or crossing the stream in high water. Check with the park rangers who keep advised as to possible flooding conditions. Also check with the park service (248-8251) to see if the free Saturday 9 am, ranger-guided hikes are available. One interesting fact about Ohe'o is that many of the marine animals have evolved from saltwater origins. Others continue to make the transition between the ocean's salty environment and the fresh water of the Ohe'o stream. One of the most unusual is the rare oopu which breeds in the upper stream, migrates to the ocean for its youth and then returns to the stream to mature. After a glimpse of the many waterfalls, this appears to be a most remarkable feat. The ingenious oopu actually climbs the falls by using its lower front fins as a suction cup to hold onto the steep rock walls which form the falls. Using its tail to propel itself, the oopu travels slowly upstream.

The upper *Kipahulu Valley* is a sight visitors will never see. Under the jurisdiction of the park service, it is one of the last fragments of the native rain forests. The native plants in the islands have been destroyed by the more aggressive plants brought by the early Hawaiians and visitors in the centuries which followed. Some rare species, such as the green silversword, grow only in this restricted area.

Two miles further on is the *Charles Lindbergh grave*, located in the small cemetery of the 1850 *Kipahulu Hawaiian Church*. He chose this site only a year prior to his death in 1974, after living in the area for a number of years. However, he never envisioned the huge numbers of visitors that would come to Hana to enjoy the scenery and visit his gravesite. Please respect the sanctity of this area.

It is sometimes possible to travel the back road from Hana thru Upcountry and back to Kahului. This is Maui's desert region and it is a vivid contrast to the lush windward environs. While very parched, this route presents a hazard which can take visitors unaware. Flash floods in the mountains above, which are most likely November to March, can send walls of water down the mountain, quickly washing out a bridge or overflowing the road. The road is sometimes closed for months due to serious washouts. Check with the county to see the current status of this route. Car rental agencies post warnings that travel is not advised on this route for standard cars and that renters are responsible for all damage. If this route is passable (which at the time of printing was not) consider stopping at *The Kaupo General Store*. It has been operating for years and is open based upon the whim of the management. Take note of the many rock walls. This area supported a large native Hawaiian population and these walls served as boundaries as well as retaining walls for livestock, primarily pigs. The walls are centuries old and unfortunately have suffered from visitor vandalism and destruction by the range cattle. Cattle are now the principle area residents.

As you enter Upcountry and civilization once more, look for the **Tedeschi Winery**. Located at the Ulupalakua Ranch it offers tasting daily from 9 - 4. They began in 1974 and produced only a pineapple wine until 1983 when they harvested their first grapes. They also offer a champagne and a red table wine. On the way back down you might stop at **The Maui Botanical Gardens** which feature a close up look at the unusual protea flowers. Admission is charged. (See Upcountry for more information.)

ACCOMMODATIONS - HANA

Aloha Cottages   Waianapanapa State Park
Hana Bay Vacation Rentals   YMCA Camp Ke'anae
Hana Plantation Houses   Hana Kai Maui Resort Apts.
Hotel Hana Maui   Heavenly Hana Inn

ALOHA COTTAGES
PO Box 205 Hana, Maui, HI 96713 (808-248-8420). Six simple, clean two bedroom cottages with electric kitchens, (some with oceanview) $68 for party of two for one night, $5 additional for use of second bedroom, $10 each additional person. Two or more nights discounted to $65 per night. Downstairs studio for two is $55. Large house is available (no children allowed) $75 for two persons, $20 each additional person.

HANA BAY VACATION RENTALS ★
Stan Collins, PO Box 318 Hana, Maui, HI 96713 (808-248-7727) 1-800-651-7970. As an alternative to condominium and hotel living you might be interested in one of eight private homes available in and around Hana. They offer fully equipped one, two or three bedrooms homes with ocean or bay views. Prices range from $65 for the Kauiki Cabin to $150/night for a newly constructed Philippine Koa and Mahogany hand crafted duplex located 50 yards from Hana Bay. Payment in full in advance for 7 days or less, please include a SASE w/ 9.43% tax added. Stay 7 nights pay for 6! There is a 10% cancellation fee. Rates are $20 higher November 15th - March 30 and June 1 - August 30. We stayed in one of their oceanview homes and found it roomy, comfortable and clean. The surrounding yard was well maintained and a great opportunity for the kids to romp around while we enjoyed sitting on the porch with a peaceful view of Hana Bay.

HANA PLANTATION HOUSES ★
Operated by Blair Shurtleff and Tom Nunn who also now operate the Hana Gardenland. At this time they offer six varied options. The Plantation House, a one bedroom cedar plantation style home with vaulted ceiling, jacuzzi tub/shower, two covered lanais, runs $140. The Hale Kipa, House of Hospitality, is located in the town of Hana, a short walk to Hana Bay. Newly remodeled, this two story plantation style house is located on grounds that include a private spa. Hale Kipa has two separate accommodations, each with it's own entrance. The upstairs is a split level that sleeps four with one bedroom, one bath, kitchen, private sundeck, while the downstairs sleeps two. Upstairs rents for $135, downstairs for $100. Their Waikoaloa Beach House is a mile from the town of Hana and this solar-powered home accommodates up to four guests. There is also a separate sleeping structure with outdoor private bath/shower facility that is adjacent to the main house that will accommodate two guests. The "annex" rents for $35, the Beach

House for $160. Rates are for single or double occupancy, each additional person is $10 per night. Full payment is required in advance. They have a new condo on Moloka'i too! For information on their additional accommodations contact them at PO Box 489 Hana, Maui, HI 96713. (808) 248-7248.

HOTEL HANA-MAUI ★

P.O. Box 8, Hana, Maui, Hi 96713 (808-248-8211) 1-800-321-HANA. FAX (808) 248-7202. Discounts on extended stays. Special honeymoon package is available. *Garden accommodations $305, Garden Jr. suites $365, Garden 1 BR suites $525 Sea Ranch Cottage $425, Sea Ranch Cottage 1 BR Suites $795*

This is the most secluded Maui resort, and a Hana landmark that has been called an island on an island. Five plantations were consolidated when Paul Fagan saw that the end of the sugar industry in Hana was close at hand. There had been 5,000 residents in Hana in 1941, and only 500 remained when he began the hotel and cattle ranch which rejuvenated Hana. Approximately 1/3 of Hana's population of over 1,000 are employed in some fashion by the hotel, ranch or flower nursery. Hotel Hana Ranch opened for public use in 1947 and was later renamed Hotel Hana Maui. The 97-room hotel resembles a small neighborhood with the single story units scattered about the grounds. The rooms are simple, but elegant with hardwood floors, and tiled bathrooms with deep tubs. The resort prides itself on the fact that it has no televisions or room air conditioning. Newer additions are the 47 sea ranch cottages located oceanview at Kaihalulu Bay. These resemble the early plantation style houses. These cottages include oceanview and the majority offer spas on the lanais.

The Wellness & Fitness Retreat is five days and four nights at $1570 per couple, $2200 including meals. It offers a complimentary upgrade to Garden Jr. Suite or sea ranch cottage, hiking excursions and nature walks, exercise classes, one 1-hour massage or one 1 1/2 hour facial, and specially planned healthy cuisine menu. Resort guests can also join the complimentary aquasize, breakfast walks or the exercise classes and hiking excursions for a small fee.

The Historic Plantation House has been restored to its original elegance. Built in 1928, the 4,000 square foot building was the home of August Unna, Hana's first plantation owner. The surrounding four acres are filled with beautiful plants and trees that are more than 100 years old. The Plantation House is available as a guest home and offers two bedrooms and baths, a large living room with fireplace, dining room, library, bar and complete kitchen. To provide the latest technology for private business gatherings and meetings, it has been equipped with electronic data transmission equipment and audio-visual equipment that includes a large screen closed circuit television system. An adjacent pavilion and covered deck area add outdoor meeting areas. The site is also the location of the Hotel Hana Maui's weekly Manager's cocktail party.

Activities include a weekly luau, many trails for hiking or horseback riding, or cookouts at Hamoa beach. A shuttle provides convenient transportation for the three mile trip to beautiful Hamoa Beach with private facilities for hotel guests. Tours are also available to Ohe'o Stream. Two swimming pools are located on the hotel grounds. They also offer a dining room as well as an informal family dining restaurant. (Restaurant dining and the weekly luau are available to non-hotel guests on a space available basis. Call for reservations.) Children's activities and overnight sitters are available. A bar with a large fireplace and an open deck with a quiet lounge adjoining invite guests to enjoy a peaceful atmosphere for conversation or reading. The restaurant has a 35-foot ceiling with skylight, hardwood floors and a deck opening to a magnificent oceanview and excellent food. The library contains rare volumes of early Hawaiiana as well as popular novels. There is also a small boutique with resort fashions and jewelry in addition to a beauty salon. The "golf adventure" is three holes in the midst of the resort. The Club Room has a television, and evening lectures are sometimes given here. A more peaceful and beautiful setting is difficult to imagine.

WAIANAPANAPA STATE PARK
54 S. High Street, First Floor, Wailuku, Maui, HI 96793. (808-243-5354) The State Park Department offers cabins that sleep up to six people. The units have electric lights and hot water, showers and toilet facilities. There is a living room and one bedroom with two bunks in the bedroom and two singles in the living-room. Completely furnished with bedding, bath towels, dish cloth, cooking and eating utensils. Hot water. Showers and toilet facilities. Electric range (no oven) and refrigerator. No pets are allowed and bring your own soap! A five-day maximum stay is the rule and guests are required to clean their units before departure, leaving soiled linens. A 50% deposit is required for reservations and they are booked way ahead (6 months to one year). Children are considered those ages 11 and under, adults are counted as being 12 years and above. A pro-rated list of rates will be sent to you by the Parks Department on request. Included here are a few sample prices. The beach is unsafe for swimming, however, there are some interesting trails, pools, and lava tubes. The beach is not sand, but actually very small, smooth black pebbles. Mosquito repellent is recommended, even for a short walk through the pool area. Six persons maximum.
1 adult-$10/day, 2 adults-$14, 4 adults-$24, 6 adults-$30
1 adult 1 child-$10.50, 2 adults 2 children-$18, 2 adults 4 children-$20

YMCA CAMP KE'ANAE
In Ke'anae. (808-248-8355) Bring your own sleeping bag and food. Separate facilities for men and women. Accommodations are dormitory style. *$8 a night.* Reservation number (808) 242-9007.

HANA KAI MAUI RESORT APARTMENTS
P.O. Box 38, Hana, Maui, HI 96713 (808-248-8426) or (808-248-7346) 1-800-346-2772 U.S. & Canada. 13 oceanfront units on Hana Bay, fully furnished including kitchens. Maid service is daily and there are laundry facilities available. Attractive and well kept grounds with ornamental lava rock pool, no swimming pool. Extra persons $10 per night. No charge for children under age 12.
Studio (2) $110, 1 BR (2) $125

HEAVENLY HANA INN
P.O. Box 146, Hana, Maui, HI 96713. (808-248-8442) 4 modern units in a single Japanese-style inn. Each unit is 2-bedroom, with bath, dinette and lanai that sleeps 2 - 6 people. Payment in full is requested in advance to hold reservations. NO CREDIT CARDS. Rates are *$85 for two, up to $115 for four.* They also offer two "rustic" cottages that sleep four or five persons. *Rates are $75 - $110 per night.*

BOOKING AGENTS

ASTON HOTELS & RESORTS
2255 Kuhio Avenue
Honolulu, Hi 96815
1-808-931-1400 1-800-321-2558
From Canada 1-800-445-6633

Kaanapali Villas	Maui Vista
The Mahana	Kaanapali Shores
Maui Hill	Maui Lu Resort
Kamaole Sands	Maui Park

CLASSIC RESORTS
50 Nohea Kai Drive
Lahaina, Maui, HI 96761
1-800-642-6284 (808-667-1400)
From Canada call collect

Kaanapali Alii
Lahaina Shores
Puunoa

CLASSIC RESORTS
175 Lipoa St.
Kihei, HI 96753
1-800-762-5348
Canada - call collect
(808-875-9000)

Maui Sun

COLONY RESORTS
32 Merchant St.
Honolulu, HI 96813
1-808-523-0411 1-800-777-1700

Napili Shores

CONDOMINIUM RENTAL HAWAII
2439 S. Kihei Rd., Suite 205A
Kihei, Maui, Hi 96753
1-808-879-2778 1-800-367-5242

Hale Kamaole	Maui Kamaole
Hale Pau Hana	Sugar Beach
Kihei Akahi	

DESTINATION RESORTS ★
3750 Wailea Alanui
Wailea, Maui, HI 96753
1-800-367-5246 1-808-879-1595

Grand Champions
Makena Surf
Polo Beach Club
Wailea Condominiums

GENTLE ISLAND HOLIDAYS ★
PO Box 1441, Kihei, Maui, HI 96753
1-808-877-3945   1-800-544-6050,
FAX (808) 874-3966

Bookings for the majority of condos
with a broad selection of units. We
found them very congenial and
helpful, with some units below
standard front desk prices. During
low season, seventh night free at
some properties.

HAWAIIAN APT. LEASING
479 Ocean Avenue, Suite B
Laguna Beach, CA 92651
1-800-472-8449 CA
1-800-854-8843 U.S. except CA
1-800-824-8968 Canada

Kaanapali Alii	Milowai
Kaanapali Royal	Mahana
Kaanapali Shores	Makena Surf
Kahana Villas	Maui Eldorado
Kamaole Sands	Maui Sunset
Kapalua Villas	Napili Bay
Kihei Bay Surf	Napili Shores
Kihei Bay Vista	Papakea
Kihei Holiday	Polo Beach Club
Kihei Kai Nani	Sands of Kahana
Kihei Resort	Sugar Beach
Laule'a	The Whaler
Maui Kaanapali Villas	
Maalaea Yacht Marina	

HANA BAY
VACATION RENTALS ★
PO Box 318
Hana, Maui, HI 96713
1-808-248-7727
Stan Collins has a great alternative
to condo vacationing. Choose one of
his Hana cottages or homes.

HAWAIIAN PACIFIC RESORTS
1150 South King St.
Honolulu, HI 96882
1-800-367-5004
FAX 1-800-477-2329

Maui Beach   Wailea Oceanfront
Maui Palms

HAWAIIANA RESORTS INC.
1270 Ala Moana Blvd.
Honolulu, HI 96814
1-800-367-7040 U.S. Mainland
1-800-877-7311
1-800-232-2520 inter-island

Kaanapali Royal
Kihei Bay Vista
Maui Banyan
Maui Kaanapali Villas
Palms at Wailea

KAANAPALI VACATION
RENTALS PO Box 384900
Waikoloa, Hawaii 96738
1-800-822-4252
1-808-667-9559 US & Mainland

Hale Mahina   Maui Eldorado
Kaanapali Royal   Sands of Kahana
Kuleana   The Whaler
Maui Kaanapali Villas
4-Bedroom home at Napili

KIHEI MAUI VACATIONS ★
P.O. Box 1055
Kihei, Maui, HI 96753
1-808-879-7581 1-800-542-6284 U.S.
1-800-423-8733 Ext. 4000 Canada

Maalaea Yacht Marina
Kauhale Makai   Maalaea Kai

Maui Kamaole   Kamaole Sands
Grand Champions   Kihei Holiday
Maui Banyans   Kihei Kai Nani
Maui Sunset   Luana Kai
Pualani   Makena Surf
Kihei Resort   Menehune Shores
Kihei Akahi   Milowai
Kihei Alii Kai   Maui Vista
Kihei Bay Surf   Homes-Cottages
Kihei Garden Estates (good range of
South Maui properties-extra charge
for cleaning if stay less than 4 nights)

KLAHANI
PO Box 11108
Lahaina, Maui, HI 96761
1-800-669-MAUI (U.S. & Canada)
FAX 1-808-661-5875

Hale Mahina   Hoyochi Nikko
Hale Ono Loa   Mahina Surf
Honokowai Palms   Puamana

KUMULANI
PO Box 1190, Kihei, Maui, HI 96753
1-800-367-2954 U.S. & Canada
1-808-879-9272

Hale Kamaole   Maui Banyan
Island Surf   Maui Sunset
Kamaole Sands   Royal Kahana
Kauhale Makai   Wailea Condos
Mana Kai Maui

MAALAEA BAY RENTALS ★
RR 1 Box 389
Wailuku, Maui, HI 96793
1-808-244-5627   1-800-367-6084

Hono Kai   Maalaea Kai
Kanai A Nalu   Makani A Kai
Maalaea Banyans Milowai
Maalaea Yacht Marina Lauloa

MARC RESORTS GROUPS
2155 Kalakaua Ave., 7th floor
Honolulu, HI 96815
1-800-535-0085 (808) 922-9700
FAX (808) 922-2421
Kahana Villa   Maui Eldorado
Kahili at Kapalua Paki Maui

MAUI CONDOMINIUMS
PO Box 1089
ALDERGROVE, BC,
CANADA V0X 1A0
1-800-663-6962 Canada

Aston Maui Park	Mahana
Hale Kamaole	Maui Islander
Hono Koa	Kamaole Sands
Island Sands	Napili Bay
Kihei Akahi	Paki Maui
Kihei Bay Surf	Papakea
Kihei Garden Estates	
Kihei Holiday	Royal Kahana
Kihei Kai Nani	Sugar Beach
Maui Palms Hotel	
Maui Kaanapali Villas	
Valley Isle Resort	
Village By the Sea	
Whaler	

MAUI NETWORK LTD.
PO Box 1077
Makawao, Maui, HI 96768
1-800-367-5221 U.S. Mainland
1-808-572-9555 Canada

Grand Champions	Kuleana
Hale Mahina	Maui Sunset
Kihei Beach Resort	
Kihei Baysurf	Papakea

MELE ADVENTURES
Ron and Judy Brown
880 Front St. Suite 575
Lahaina, Maui, HI 96761
1-800-657-7714 HI & U.S. Mainland
Vacation rentals in addition to
arranging activities and tours.

MORE HAWAII FOR LESS
5324 Kester Ave. Suite 4
Van Nuys, CA 91411
1-800-967-6687 U.S. & Canada
1-808-986-7420

Hale Ono Loa	Papakea
Luana Kai	Sugar Beach
Maalaea Banyans	

OIHANA PROPERTY MANAGEMENT
840 Alua
Wailuku, Maui, HI 96793
1-808-244-7684 or 1-808-244-7491
1-800-367-5234 U.S. & Canada

Island Sands	Leinaala
Kamoa Views	Maalaea Banyans
Kana'I A Nalu	Maui Parkshore
Kauhale Makai	Maui Vista
Kealia Puuamana	
Kihei Akahai	

OUTRIGGER HOTELS HAWAII
2335 Kalakaua Ave.
Honolulu, HI 96715-2941
1-800-367-5170
FAX 1-800-4564329

Kaanapali Beach Hotel

OVER THE RAINBOW, INC.
186 Mehani Circle
Kihei, Maui, HI 96753
(808) 879-5521

Specializes in assisting the disabled
traveler with any physical limitations.
Booking accommodations, tours,
personal care.

PLEASANT HAWAIIAN HOLIDAYS
2404 Townsgate Rd.
Westlake Village, CA 91361
1-800-242-9244 U.S. Mainland & HI

Inter-Continental
Kahana Beach
Kamaole Sands
Maui Marriott
Royal Lahaina

The above plus other hotels &
condos. Bookings are for package
plans of 7 to 14 nights on one or
more islands and includes airfare
and rental car.

RSVP
1575 W. Georgia St., 3rd Floor
Vancouver, BC Canada V6G 2V3
1-800-663-1118 U.S. and Canada

Following is a partial list of
properties. Ask about specials
they may have for free rental
cars, senior rates etc.

Kaanapali Royal	Maui Hill
Kaanapali Shores	Maui Park
Kahana Sunset	Maui Sunset
Kahana Villa	Maui Vista
Kahana Village	Menehune Shores
Kauhale Makai	Napili Shores
Kihei Akahi	Paki Maui
Kihei Alii Kai	Papakea
Kihei Holiday	Sands of Kahana
Kihei Resort	Sugar Beach
Mahana	The Whaler
Maui Kaanapali Villas	

RAINBOW RENTALS
CONDOMINIUM MANAGEMENT
PO Box 1893, Kihei, Maui, HI 96753
1-800-451-5366 U.S. Mainland
1-808-874-0233

Kauhale Makai	Luana Kai
Kealia	Maalaea Surf
Kihei Alii Kai	Sugar Beach
Kihei Resort	

RAINBOW RESERVATIONS INC.
PO Box 11453
Lahaina, Maui, HI 96761-6453
1-800-367-6092 U.S. & Canada
1-808-669-5550

Hale Mahina	Maui Sands
Hololani Resort	Napili Shores
Kahana Outrigger	
Lahaina Shores	Papakea
Lokelani	Pohailani
Valley Isle Resort	

RIDGE REALTY RENTALS ★
10 Hoohui Rd. Suite 301
Kahana, HI 96761
1-800-326-6284 U.S. & Canada
1-808-669-9696

The Ridge (Kapalua)

WHALER'S REALTY ★
Whaler's Village, Suite A-3
2435 Kaanapali Parkway
Lahaina, Maui, HI 96761
1-800-367-5632 U.S.
1-808-661-8777

Kaanapali Alii
Kaanapali Royal
Kaanapali Plantation
Kaanapali Shores
Kaanapali Villas
Kanaha Sunset
Kapalua Golf Villas
Mahana
Papakea
Sands of Kahana
The Whaler

(They offer high quality
condos at fair prices)

WINDSURFING WEST
1-800-782-6105
(808) 572-5601
FAX (808) 871-4624

Vacation packages include car,
windsurfing equipment and condo.
Properties include

Kihei Bay Surf	Sugar Beach
Maui Sunset	Maalaea Surf

Ttownhouses at Sugar Cove
Basic or deluxe houses
and studios or cottages
on the North Shore
Windsurfing lessons available

RESTAURANTS

INTRODUCTION

Whether it's a teriburger at a local cafe or a romantic evening spent dining next to a swan lagoon, Maui offers something for everyone. We're confident that you will enjoy exploring Maui's diverse dining options as much as we have!

The majority of restaurants in the Maalaea to Makena, and Lahaina to Kapalua areas have been included, and for the adventurer or budget conscious traveler, take special note of the wonderful local dining opportunities in Kahului and Wailuku.

Needless to say, we haven't been able to eat every meal served at every restaurant on Maui, but we do discuss with a great many people their experiences in order to get varied opinions. We also welcome your comments. (See READER RESPONSE.)

Following this introduction, the restaurants are first indexed alphabetically and then also by food type. The restaurants are then divided by geographical area, separated by price range, and listed alphabetically in those price ranges. These are: "INEXPENSIVE" under $10, "MODERATE" $10 to $20, and "EXPENSIVE" $20 and above. As a means of comparison, we have taken an average meal (usually dinner), excluding tax, alcoholic beverages and desserts, for one person at that restaurant. The prices listed were accurate at time of publication, but we cannot be responsible for any price increases. For quick reference, the type of food served at the restaurant described is indicated in Italic type next to the restaurant name. Sample menu offerings are also included as a helpful guide. An important postscript here is the rapidity with which some island restaurants open and close, change names, and raise prices. Our quarterly newsletter, THE MAUI UPDATE, will keep you abreast of these changes.

The Kaanapali Beach Hotel is expected to close for a year for renovations. No word yet as to the dates, so we are including the restaurants.

Some of the popular fast food/chain restaurants, such as Subway Sandwiches, Jack-in-the Box and Pizza Hut are not included.

Dinner cruises are covered in the Recreation and Tour section of this book.

Our favorite restaurants are generally either a real bargain for the price, or serve a very quality meal, and are indicated by a ★.

BEST BETS

TOP RESTAURANTS

Our criteria for a top restaurant is excellence of food preparation and presentation, a pleasing atmosphere, and service that anticipates or responds promptly to one's needs. While the following exemplify these criteria they are also all "deep pocket" restaurants, so expect to spend $70 - $100 or more for your meal, wine and gratuity for two. Generally, anything you have will be excellent. Remember, even the best restaurants may have an "off" night, but these are seldom. Also, chefs and management do change, rendering what you may have found to be excellent on one occasion quite different the next. However, the following have proven to be consistent through the years. Enjoy your meal, enjoy being a little bit spoiled, and remember those muumuus are great for covering up all those calories!!

Bay Club, Kapalua Resort Hotel
David Paul's Lahaina Grill
Grand Dining, Grand Hyatt Wailea
Hakone, Maui Prince Hotel
Koele Lodge - Island of Lana'i
Prince Court, Maui Prince Hotel
Raffles', Stouffer Wailea Beach Resort
Sound of the Falls, Westin Maui Resort
Spats, Hyatt Regency at Kaanapali
Swan Court, Hyatt Regency at Kaanapali

TOP RESTAURANTS IN A MORE CASUAL ATMOSPHERE

While these restaurants are less expensive, it is still easy to spend $60 or more for dinner for two. They serve a superior meal in a less formal atmosphere.

Avalon, Lahaina
El Crab Catcher, Whaler's Village at Kaanapali
Haliimaile General Store, Haliimaile
Humuhumunukunukuapua'a, Grand Hyatt Wailea
Kapalua's Garden Restaurant, Kapalua Resort Hotel
Kapalua Grill and Bar, Kapalua
Longhi's, Lahaina
Mama's Fish House, Paia
Plantation House, Kapalua
Roy's, Kahana
The Villa, Westin Maui
Waterfront, Maalaea

RESTAURANTS WITH THE BEST VIEW

Plantation House Restaurant at Kapalua
Grand Dining Room at Grand Hyatt Wailea

LA CUISINE FRANCAIS

Maui's French restaurants fall in the "champagne" price range. Both Gerard's in Lahaina and Chez Paul in Olowalu offer outstanding fair, although the atmosphere at Gerard's is one of the Maui's best.

BEST SEAFOOD
All of the top restaurants plus:
Mama's Fish House, Paia
The Villa, Westin Maui
Gerard's, Lahaina

BEST SEAFOOD BUFFET
All of the top restaurants have wonderful seafood, but an All-You-Can-Eat is a seafood lovers dream come true! Try the Kapalua Bay Hotel each Friday evening for an outstanding selection.

The Villa Terrace, next to the Villa Restaurant at the Westin Maui, also has a nightly seafood buffet, and Palm Court at Stouffer Wailea Beach Resort has seafood featured on their buffet each Friday.

BEST BREAKFAST / BRUNCH BUFFETS
Buffets are a good way to enjoy a great meal with a wide selection of food at a moderate price. And you may not have to eat for the next two days! The best Sunday brunches are Prince Court at the Maui Prince Resort in Makena and Raffles at Stouffer Wailea Resort, both in South Maui. In West Maui, Kapalua's Garden Restaurant has a wonderful brunch, as does the Weston Maui's Sound of the Falls.

Swan Court features West Maui's best daily breakfast buffet. In South Maui, The Grand Hyatt has an outstanding daily breakfast buffet for $15.50. The Inter-Continental's breakfast buffet at the Lana'i Terrace is good at $12.95. The best priced Sunday brunchs are at the Kaanapali Beach Hotel $16.95, and the Royal Ocean Terrace at the Royal Lahaina Resort $16.75, followed closely by the Sunday champagne brunch at the Maui Sun's Frangipani Restaurant at $17.95.

The following buffets are listed in alphabetical order.

Benihana Restaurant in Lahaina has a Sunday brunch with four Oriental entrees.

The Frangipani Restaurant (Maui Sun in Kihei) offers warm bread pudding, pies, brownies, local style salads, and a pianist! $17.95 adults, Children 6 - 10 years $10.95, kids five and under are free.

The Garden Restaurant ★ (Kapalua Bay Resort) features an artistic presentation and unusual variety of gourmet specialties in an open-air setting for their Sunday brunch.

The Grand Dining Room ★ (Grand Hyatt Wailea) has a delicious daily breakfast buffet at $15.50 but, for a gourmet treat, try their Sunday brunch at $32 and sample Hawaiian regional cuisine. Selections include ham with mango chutney, Hawaiian bread sweet rolls, starfruit (fresh off the trees on the property), local gourmet Hawaiian dishes made with natural ingredients, such as jicama salad, guava pastries and kim chee too! How about a lilikoi guava mousse, Oriental cole slaw, or lomi lomi salmon. But save room for dessert!

Haliimaile General Store in Upcountry has a great Sunday brunch.

Makani Room (Maui Inter-Continental Resort) has a fine Sunday brunch that is in a little more casual setting. 9 am-1 pm $26.

Old Lahaina Cafe, 505 Front St. in Lahaina has a Saturday and Sunday brunch.

Palm Court (Stouffer Wailea Beach Resort) has a daily champagne breakfast buffet for $14.50.

Prince Court ★ (Maui Prince Hotel, Makena) features a spectacular display of over 160 food choices at the Sunday brunch, each arranged as a work of art. Each taste as good as they look! 9:30 am-1:30 pm $25.

Raffles' ★ (Stouffer Wailea Beach Resort, Wailea) has a true taste extravaganza for their champagne Sunday brunch with Tony Van Steen at the piano. You'll be sure to see some dishes here that you've never sampled before. 9 am-2 pm $23.50.

Royal Ocean Terrace (Royal Lahaina Resort) provides one of the best values for a Sunday brunch. Not an exotic or highly gourmet selection, but good fare at $16.75 for adults.

Sounds of the Falls ★ (Westin Maui, Kaanapali) serves an elegant Sunday champagne brunch in a beautiful atmosphere. Some people come just for the sushi bar! 9 am-2 pm, $19.75.

Swan Court ★ (Hyatt Regency, Kaanapali) features a lovely breakfast buffet daily in an elegant atmosphere. 6:30-11:30 am, until 1:30 pm on Sunday $13.50.

BEST DINNER BUFFETS
Frangipani Restaurant (Maui Sun Hotel, Kihei) offers Friday Seafood Buffet and Saturday prime rib buffet $16.95 adults, $12.95 kids.

Lana'i Terrace (Maui Inter-Continental Resort) offers nightly theme buffets $14.95 - $17.95

Moana Terrace (Marriott Hotel) has evening buffets for $18.95,m or arrive between 5 and 6 pm and enjoy a $3 discount. Kids 6 - 12 years are $8.50, no discount for early dining, children five and under eat free.

Palm Court (Stouffer Wailea Beach Resort) serves a dinner buffet three nights weekly, Prime rib, Italian and Seafood $24-$28.

Royal Ocean Terrace is a great dining value. International themes change nightly. Priced at $10.50 adults, $5.25 children 5 - 12 years and under age 5 are free.

BEST SALADS
The hands down winner are the Chinese chicken and Gado Gado salads, both available at Avalon restaurant in Lahaina.

TOP "LOCAL" RESTAURANTS (Kahului/Wailuku)

We have delighted in exploring the many small, family-owned "local" restaurants in Kahului, and especially in Wailuku. The food in these establishments is not only plentiful and well prepared, but also very inexpensive. The service is often better and friendlier than at many of the resort establishments.

Aki's Hawaiian Food and Bar (Hawaiian)
Fujiya's (Japanese)
Mama Ding's (Puerto Rican)
Saeng's Thai Cuisine (Thai)
Sam Sato's (Japanese/noodles)
Siam Thai (Thai)
Tasty Crust (Home style)
Tokyo Tei (Japanese)
Tsuru (Asian)
Vietnam Cuisine (Vietnamese)

BEST PIZZA

With the closure of Pizza Circus, we were left with the dilemma of who had the best pizza. We invited over 40 distinguished guests to serve as judges for a Maui Pizza War competition. The pizzas were rushed to a central location and judges enjoyed the difficult task of sampling over twenty five, piping hot pizza varieties.

Of most interest was the fact that there was no run-away winner. Tastes were diverse and what one judge considered a "10" for best crust, another would rate as a "4" for too doughy. Definite trends were evidenced by an assortment of unusual and creative pizza toppings. The pizza of today is innovative! So here is the run down of the many and varied winners!

The overall best pizza was judged to be a tie between Wiki Wiki Pizza of Maui in Kihei (not affiliated with Wiki Wiki in Lahaina) for their Maui Garden and sausage and onion pizzas, and Charleys of Paia for their vegetarian and spicy Tex-Mex selections. In second place was Dollies of Honokowai, and Lahaina Coolers rounded out this category in third position.

Dollies Pizza scored highest for "best cheese" and tied with Shaka Pizza of Kihei creating a stir with their gourmet white cheese pizza with garlic and broccoli and New York style cheese entries. Lahaina Coolers came in third and Charleys placed fourth.

Dollies also took first for best crust with Wiki Wiki Pizza of Maui in Kihei in second. Charleys came in a very close third and Luigis was fourth.

The most unusual pizza category found Ferraris taking a strong lead with their duck, roasted red pepper and eggplant combination impressing the judges. Casanovas finished second with their Greco, Genoa, Romana and Neapolitan pizzas, and Lahaina Coolers finished third with their local style and Evil Jungle entrees. Village Pizzeria was fourth for their clam and garlic with pesto pizza.

Wiki Wiki Pizza of Maui took top honors for the gooiest pizza and was followed by Ferraris in second and a third place tie between Sandcastle and Charleys.

RESTAURANTS
Best Bets

In the most (visually) appealing category, Casanova claimed the lead with Dollies and Wiki Wiki Pizza of Maui in a second place tie and Lahaina Coolers in third. The best cold pizza was a late evening category, and Lahaina Coolers was deemed best, Dollies and Wiki Wiki Pizza of Maui rounded out the honors in 2nd and 3rd position.

The peoples' choice honored those entrants whose pizzas were selected and sampled by the most judges. Lahaina Coolers, Shaka Pizza and Casanova took the top honors. The most talked about pizzas were Charleys for their spicy Tex-Mex creation, Shaka Pizza for their simple and delicious, cheese, broccoli and garlic pizza, and Ferraris for their exotic duck combination.

Although it didn't win top honors from our judging panel, our personal favorite was the entry from Shaka Pizza and Sandwich in Kihei, a New York subway style pizza that was wonderful and very cheesey.

BEST SANDWICHES
Paradise Fruits in Kihei with its "health conscious" menu. Also, the island's best shakes and fruit smoothies.

BEST HAMBURGER
Best hamburger with a view goes to Cheeseburger in Paradise.

GOOD AND CHEAP
Some restaurants continue to offer a discounted meal for early diners. Hours vary with the restaurant, but usually begin between 5 and 5:30 and end between 6 and 6:30. Generally, the meals are almost the same ones that you would pay more for an hour later, but you are limited in your selections. The following are ones that we recommend. We suggest you call to verify!

China Boat, Kahana
El Crab Catcher (poolside), Whaler's Village, Kaanapali
J.J's, 505 Front Street, Lahaina
Kihei Prime Rib and Seafood House, Kihei
Lahaina Fish Company (Also two for one coupons in drive guides)
Mickey's, Kahului
Moana Terrace, Marriott Hotel, Kaanapali (buffet)
Nanatomi's, Kaanapali (offers two for one early bird dinners most of the year,
        except high season)
Orient Express, Napili
Rusty Harpoon, Whaler's Village, Kaanapali

No early bird specials, but the Koffee Shop at the Kaanapali Beach Hotel has a $9.95 all you can eat prime rib dinner buffet, a breakfast or lunch for $5.95 and an afternoon deli buffet with make your own sandwiches along with salads, soups and desserts for $4.95.

BEST HAWAIIAN
Aki's, located on Market Street in Wailuku, is small, quaint, and very inexpensive. In West Maui check out the Lahaina Cafe at 505 Front St.

BEST FAST FOODS
Azeka's Market and Paradise Fruits in Kihei offer good food.

BEST SHAVE ICE
Shave Ice has almost disappeared on Front Street, but a few places have revived it. Shave ice, however, should not, in our opinion, be confused with a "snow cone." Both are cold and sweet, but a shave ice should be fine bits of ice crystals. Lappert's, with two locations in Lahaina, serves what they call a Shave Ice. We thought it should have been called a snow cone! Azeka's Market has a snack bar out front that also serves them. But they just aren't what they used to be! If you find a REAL shave ice on Maui, let us know!

BEST RIBS
Chris's Smokehouse features great ribs at their Lahaina restaurant. In Kihei, stop at Azeka's Market for their specially marinated ribs that you can cook.

FAVORITE BREAKFASTS
Pioneer Inn has it hands down as our favorite local breakfast stop in West Maui. The French toast, made of Portuguese Sweet Bread, is fabulous. The pancakes are pretty good, but skip the eggs and hashbrowns. The rustic atmosphere is reminiscent of by-gone days, and the prices reasonable. All of the waitresses are terrific, but if you're lucky enough to have Ma serve you, you'll get an especially warm aloha along with your meal. In an atmosphere of tropical delight a breakfast buffet is served daily at Swan Court. The macadamia nut pancakes are light and fluffy, and cooked to order. On the other side of the island in Wailuku is Tasty Crust, an inexpensive local restaurant, where unusual crusty pancakes are their specialty. Kapalua's Plantation House Restaurant offers a la carte menu items and a view that is spectacular!

MOST OUTRAGEOUS DESSERT
The Lahaina Provision Company's Chocoholic Bar at the Hyatt Regency Kaanapali is a chocolate lover's dream come true. This dessert buffet features soft, self-serve vanilla and chocolate ice cream and an array of toppings. Hot milk chocolate sauce, hot fudge or hot caramel. Strawberries, bananas, shredded coconut, m & m's, fresh fruits, granola, nuts, lady fingers, and they've added some cookie bars, cookies, mousse and even chocolate truffles. You can make the trip through as many times as you or your waistline can tolerate.

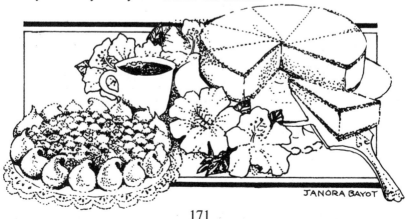

JANORA BAYOT

BEST BAKERY

Our favorite Lahaina bakery is cleverly named, The Bakery, and an early stop will ensure you the best selection of their wonderful French pastries. Cheese and luncheon meats are also available.

In central Maui don't miss a stop at the Homemade Bakery at 1005 E. Lower Main Street, their bread pudding is fantastic.

And be sure to stop at the Four Sisters Bakery at Vineyard St. at Hinano in Wailuku. Melen, Mila, Beth and Bobbie arrived from the Philippines eleven years ago. Their father had operated a Spanish Bakery in Manila for 15 years before moving the family to Maui. Not a large selection, but the items are delicious and different. One sweet bread is filled with cinnamon pudding, a sponge cake with a thin layer of butter in the middle of two moist pieces. The butter rolls are very good and the Spanish sweet and cinnamon rolls delicious. They sell their items only at this location and at the Swap Meet each Saturday morning. Hours are Monday thru Thursday and Saturday and Sunday 5 am until 8:30 pm, Friday until 10 pm.

A new one has joined the competition. Located on Vineyard Street, The Maui Bake Shop is a European-style bakery with fancy pastries and cakes run by Jose and Claire Fjuii Krall. Jose was previously the executive pastry chef at the Maui Prince Resort in Makena.

BEST VEGETARIAN

The only strictly vegetarian fare is available at The Vegan restaurant in Paia. The Garden Cafe and Bakery in Haiku also has a good selection of vegetarian foods.

BEST LUAU (See luau section which follows)

BEST DISCOUNTS

In the summer of 1992, Paradise Television network inaugurated a new Destination Maui program. The concept is similar to the Entertainment book. Members receive a card and a restaurant and activity review guide and are eligible for discounts at a variety of restaurants and for a number of activities. The current issue we examined included 43 restaurants and a dozen air, land and sea activities. The $30 membership fee is good for 30 days. Discounts range from 10-20% in the edition we examined.

In their review guide they include a list of the top twenty island restaurants, as rated by local residents. The top ten were Gerard's, Raffles, Avalon, Mama's, David Paul's, Chez Paul's, Seasons, Prince Court, Sound of the Falls and Roys. Eight of the top ten are included in the discount membership program, Seasons and Prince Court are not. With the exception of only one or two of the restaurants listed in the membership book, all are very good choices and an added 10% or more off your dinner may soon pay for the membership fee. The book notes that it is updated quarterly, so whether the same caliber of restaurants will continue to participate is yet to be seen. For more information call (808) 661-1111.

ALPHABETICAL INDEX

FOOD TYPE INDEX

CATERING

CLAMBAKE HAWAIIAN STYLE, INC.
A full catering service providing breakfast, brunch, lunch dinner and cocktail parties. Lite lunches $7 - $11 per person, barbecues, combination dinners $17 - $22 include seafood, steak and chicken selections. Theme parties are also available and include a sushi bar, pasta bar, oyster bar, thai chicken bar, or baron of beef. Pupu (appetizer parties) that serve 25 people run $176 - $310. The meals are cooked on location in their self contained steam cookers and grill. All seafood is cooked in its own shell with Hawaiian salt and butter. They require minimal space for cooking and cleaning, which can be done indoors or outdoors. Their prices include paper products, utensils, buffet service, set up and clean up. Available seven days a week. No delivery charge for a minimum of 20 people. Additional charge for groups of less than 20. Minimum is 6 people. Children's prices available. Bartender service available by the hour. RR 1 Box 52, Wailuku, Maui, HI 96793. (242-5095)

CHEZ-VOUS
Looking for something unique... elegant... and personal? Then enjoy in-home catering provided by Cyrille & Shirley Lecomte. Or perhaps the "Honeymoon Menu" prepared in your room highlighted by fresh Hawaiian Lobster and Crepes Suzette flambe. For more information contact Chez-Vous catering at 191 Wahikuli Rd., Lahaina, Maui, HI 96761 or phone 667-0636.

DANI'S CATERING
If you've never been to the Takamiya Market, you're missing a culinary experience. Dani's is the kitchen for Takamiya's market and they specialize in American, Japanese, Hawaiian and even some Filipino foods. Catered parties have a 20-person minimum. They also provide Central Maui delivery at no charge. Set menus range from $10.75 to $11.25 per person and include warmers, plates, napkins, chopsticks. Takamiya is at 359 N. Market, Wailuku. (242-6652)

TABLESIDE CHEFS OF MAUI
They offer three, four or five course meals for two or more people. Breakfast in bed and brunch for $150 per couple. 875-0823.

KOI

J BAYOT

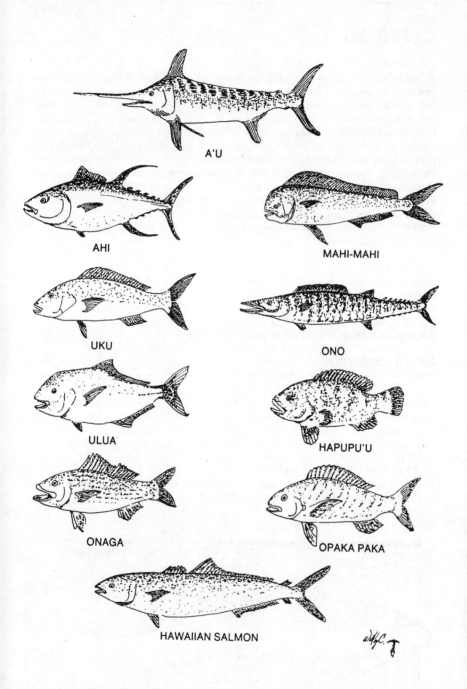

A'U

AHI

MAHI-MAHI

UKU

ONO

ULUA

HAPUPU'U

ONAGA

OPAKA PAKA

HAWAIIAN SALMON

A FEW WORDS ABOUT FISH

Whether cooking fish at your condominium or eating out, the names of the island fish can be confusing. While local shore fishermen catch shallow water fish such as Goatfish or Papio for their dinner table, commercial fishermen angle for two types. The steakfish are caught by trolling in deep waters and include Ahi, Ono, and Mahi. They sometimes provide a healthy struggle before being landed. The more delicate bottom fish include Opakapaka and Onaga which are caught with lines dropped as deep as 1,500 feet to ledges or shelves off Maui's west shoreline. Here is a little background on the fish you might find on your dinner plate.

A'U - The broadbill swordfish averages 250 lbs. in Hawaiian waters. Hard to locate, difficult to hook, and a challenge to land. Considered a steakfish.

AHI - The yellow fin tuna (Allison tuna) is caught in deep waters off the Kaua'i coast. The pinkish red meat is firm yet flaky. This fish is popular for sashimi. They weigh between 60 and 280 pounds.

ALBACORE - This smaller version of the Ahi averages 40 - 50 pounds and is lighter in both texture and color.

AKU - This is the blue fin tuna.

EHU - Orange snapper

HAPU - Hawaiian sea bass

KAMAKAMAKA - Island catfish, very tasty, but a little difficult to find.

LEHI - The Silver Mouth is a member of the snapper family with a stronger flavor than Onaga or Opakapaka and a texture resembling Mahi.

MAHI - Although called the dolphin fish, this is no relation to Flipper or his friends. Caught while trolling and weighing 10-65 lbs. this is a seasonal fish which causes it to command a high price when fresh. *Beware*, while excellent fresh, it is often served in restaurants having arrived from the Philippines frozen and is far less pleasing. A clue as to whether fresh or frozen may be the price tag. If it runs less than $10 it is probably the frozen variety. Fresh Mahi will run $16 - $20 a dinner. This fish has excellent white meat that is moist and light. It is very good sauteed.

MU'U - We tried this mild white fish at the Makawao Steak House and were told there is no common name for this fish. We've never seen it served elsewhere in restaurants.

ONAGA (ULA) - Caught in holes that are 1,000 feet or deeper, this red snapper has an attractive hot pink exterior with tender, juicy, white meat inside.

ONO - Also known as Wahoo. ONO means "very good." A member of the Barracuda family, its white meat is flaky and moist. It is caught at depths of 25-100 fathoms while trolling and weighs 15 to 65 pounds.

'OPAE - Shrimp

OPAKAPAKA - Otherwise known as pink snapper and one of our favorites. The meat is very light and flaky with a delicate flavor.

PAPIO - A baby Ulua which is caught in shallow waters and weighs 5 -25lbs.

UKU - The meat of this grey snapper is light, firm and white with a texture that varies with size. It is very popular with local residents. This fish is caught off Kaua'i, usually in the deep Paka Holes.

ULUA - Also known as Pompano, this fish is firm and flaky with steaklike, textured white meat. It is caught by trolling, bottom fishing, or speared by divers and weighs between 15 and 110 pounds.

LUAUS AND DINNER SHOWS

For a local luau, check the Maui News. You may be fortunate to find one of the area churches or schools sponsoring a fund raising luau. The public is welcome and the prices are usually half that of the commercial ventures. You'll see spontaneous, local entertainment.

Most of the luaus are large, with an average of 400 - 600 guests, with one of the smallest being the Old Lahaina Luau with only 280. Most serve traditional Hawaiian foods. The entertainment ranges from splashy broadway-style productions to a country barbecue, or a more authentic Hawaiian dance and song. In general there are a few standard things to be expected at most luaus. These are shell leis, photos, an imu ceremony, playing the Hawaiian wedding song, kalua pig, poi, and coconut pudding. Upon arrival there may or may not be some waiting in line before it's your turn to be greeted with a shell lei and a snapshot of your group (available for purchase after the show). However, the Grand Hyatt includes the photo free!

It is very difficult to judge these luaus due to their diversity. While one reader raves about a particular show, another reader will announce their disappointment with the same event. Read carefully the information provided keeping in mind that the performers do come and go. We will note changes in our newsletter THE MAUI UPDATE.

Luau prices run $42.50 - $55 for adults.

OVERALL BEST BETS
Best Dinner Show - Hyatt Regency
Best Atmosphere and Luau - South Maui - Maui Inter-Continental Resort
Best Atmosphere and Luau - West Maui - Old Lahaina Luau
Best Luau Food - Maui Inter-Continental Resort

GRAND HYATT WAILEA RESORT & SPA
In Wailea. Includes a fresh flower lei, 5 x 7 photo, unlimited Mai Tais (with or without alcohol), other bar beverages available for fee. Currently offered one night a week, they serve Maui short ribs, kalua pig, steamed clams and mussels, baked onaga, beef teriyaki, chicken long rice, poki, poi, haupia (coconut pudding) and pineapple cake. The show includes approximately 20 performers and musicians and they perform both the ancient hula (Kahiko) and contemporary hulas (Auana), as well as Tahitian numbers and fire dancers. Show is 5:30 - 8 p.m. $55 adults, children 6 - 12 years $25 and under six are free. We were unable to personally review this luau, so drop us a note and let us know how you like it!

HOTEL HANA MAUI AT HANA RANCH
Hamoa Beach Luau is held at Lehoula Beach on Tuesdays at 6 pm. Open to non-hotel guests based on availability for $50. Guests of the hotel are transported via hay wagon or van to the beachfront luau location. A very local and family oriented production. Many of those involved in the entertainment are folks you might see working in another capacity around the hotel. Phone 248-8211.

HYATT REGENCY

In Kaanapali. The "Drums of the Pacific" is more a dinner show than a luau format. It is held on the grounds of the Hyatt, however, there is no ocean view. A 5:30 p.m. arrival was suggested, which meant standing in line until 6 pm. Pictures were taken while waiting prior to being admitted to the grounds, where you were greeted with a lei and taken to a table by your server. The dinner buffet features Polynesian foods such as saimin noodles, kalua pork, shoyu chicken, sweet coconut beef and ono fish. A very brief imu ceremony was presented on the edge of the grounds with people viewing from their seats as best they could. The pig was then paraded through the center aisle. While dinner was being enjoyed we were entertained with Hawaiian melodies. Cocktail only seating began at 7 pm and then began a very fast paced one hour show. The costumes were excellent, and the dances performed were from various Polynesian isles. They offered not one, but an impressive three fire dancers. This show was very professionally done, with excellent performers and a host that resembled a young Wayne Newton. All in all, it was a show worth seeing. Currently four nights a week. Prices $44 for adults, juniors $36. Cocktail seating $26 adults, $23 for children.

MAUI INTER-CONTINENTAL RESORT ★

The Intercontinental refers to their luau as "Wailea's Finest Luau" and we'd have to agree! The fabulous outdoor setting in their luau garden is both beautiful and spacious with a sublime ocean view. The stage is set up to offer the ocean and beautiful sunset as backdrop. An open bar is available with drinks other than fruit punch at extra charge. Dinner moves swiftly through several buffet lines serving mahi mahi, chicken chow mein, and kalua pig and is overall the best food at any of the island's luaus. The best dessert table was also found here with a selection of macadamia cream pie, coconut cream pie, banana cream pie, coconut macaroons, and pineapple cake squares. The show begins just as the sun is setting with Ka Poe o Hawaii and Paradyse. Not an elaborate show, but one featuring a good range and quality of entertainment. And, of course, a firedancer. For overall food, entertainment and setting, this is the best of the luaus in South Maui. Tues.-Thur.-Sat., 5:15-8 p.m.. Adults $47, children 6-10 $23.50, under 6 free. Phone 879-1922.

OLD LAHAINA LUAU ★

The Old Lahaina Luau at 505 Front Street in Lahaina is situated right on the beach and offers the most beautiful luau setting in West Maui. A celebration of aloha in the traditional Hawaiian style is emphasized with guests greeted by shell leis and offered a choice between table setting or mats on the ground. You will note the many young Hawaiians that form their helpful and friendly staff dressed in colorful Hawaiian garb. One beautiful young lady demonstrates and sells leis by the water's edge.

This luau is one of Maui's smallest, with a maximum of 280 people. Following the imu ceremony it's time to visit the buffet where selections include a pleasing array of half a dozen salads and entrees such as chicken, fish and, of course, kalua pig! There are four buffet lines which speed the guests through smoothly and an open bar. Get your cameras ready as the show begins with a bit of a surprise. The show changes from time to time, but it is strictly Hawaiian, no fire dancers here. Auntie Eileen and Piilani Jones perform the duties of show hostesses. For food, atmosphere and good Hawaiian entertainment this gets the overall rating for the best luau in West Maui. Make sure you make your reservations in advance, this has become a popular attraction. Held Tues.-Sat. at 5:30. Phone 667-1998. Adults $46, Children $26.

RITZ CARLTON

At Kapalua. There are luau grounds with seating for 550, but the show is not up and operating as we go to press, and it is not known if they will have regularly scheduled public luau performances.

ROYAL LAHAINA RESORT

In Kaanapali. We arrived at 5:15 for a 45 minute wait until gate opening. It's worth the wait for a good seat. Ready-made mai tai's, fruit punch, open bar and shell leis were the first order of business. The luau grounds are much like those at the Hyatt. Near the ocean, but without an oceanview and seating at padded picnic table benches. While people were settling in, Makalapua, the hostess, invites folks up for a hula lesson. They also had a little humorous presentation about the luau foods to be served. Just the right amount of audience interaction. The imu ceremony was the shortest. (Some people hadn't even reached the pit before it was over.) Dinner began at 6:45 with four tables and eight lines allowing people to flow quickly through. Real "glass" glasses for drinks were a pleasant surprise, although the coffee cups were plastic. Large wooden trays offered plenty of room to pile on the teri beef, kalua pig, pineapple chicken, lomi lomi salmon, poi and salad bar. Desserts were not memorable as evidenced by the many tables littered with uneaten cake.

The show begins with the legend of the naupaka. A beautiful story of a lost love performed not on the main stage, but on a side stage with the sunset sky for an impressive backdrop. Dances from Samoa, Tahiti and Hawai'i are performed and the costumes were excellent. This was a very good luau show, but expect mediocre fare for your meal. Seven days a week. If the weather is uncooperative, they move the luau into their indoor Alii Room. Phone 661-9119. Adults $42.50, children 5 - 12 $19.95, under 5 free.

SHERATON MAUI HOTEL

At Kaanapali. After nearly a dozen luaus they all start looking a lot alike. What is unusual here at the Sheraton is an opportunity to learn a little more personally about some Hawaiian culture and activities. Following the lei greeting there is a chance to mingle with the staff to test your ability at twirling the poi balls or throwing the spear between two sticks imbedded into the ground and learn how to tie a ti leaf skirt. An open bar runs until 7 pm after which rum punch is available. The dinner buffet includes pineapple chicken, island snapper, teri beef steak and of course, kalua pig. The hostess is the very talented Alaka'i and the show includes the hula of the past (Kahiko) and the present (Auana), along with dances of the South Pacific. The outdoor setting here is a plus, set on the Sheraton's lush grounds. A rapid weather change during our visit here offered an opportunity for us to discover what happens when it rains at a luau! The show goes on! Brightly colored rain ponchos are passed to the guests while the dancers get wet! $42 plus tax, children 6 - 12 $19 plus tax. 661-3500.

STOUFFER WAILEA BEACH RESORT

3550 Wailea Alanui, Wailea. Offered Monday and Thursday in their outdoor luau gardens. Seating for up to 350 guess at roomy round tables. Not surprising is the prescribed ritual of shell leis and photo taking. Arrive early for the best seats. The buffet line moved quickly with two tables set up with two lines each. A selection of salads were followed by entrees that included mahi, teri beef, kalua pig, and chicken hekka. Desserts included banana cream pie, haupia, and pineapple upside down cake. An open bar was available and waitresses served fruit, mai tai or pina colada punch from large pitchers. The setting was lovely with the full ocean view. Our recommendation is that they move the stage so that the ocean and sunset form a backdrop for the stage. As it is now, you have the view to your back while the show is performed. The performers were good, although not the best. Audience entertainment included a couple of women and men volunteering to try their hand (or rather hips) at the hula. $45 adults, $26 for children. Phone 879-4900.

TROPICAL PLANTATION COUNTRY PARTY

Waikapu. Each Mon., Tues. and Wed. the charcoals are fired up for an all-you-can-eat BBQ feast. Grilled steaks, BBQ chicken, chili, corn on the cob, corn bread, fresh fruits, and a dessert table which includes a variety of pies. Tropical drinks, fruit punch, or iced tea. Entertainment includes plantation cowboys and cowgirls who sing and danced to some Hawaiian and country favorites, as well as a tour of the plantation. Adults $46.95, children 5 - 17 years $19.95, under five no charge. For a fee they can supply transportation from your accommodations to the Tropical Plantation. Inquire when making reservations, 244-7643.

DID YOU KNOW?

Luaus are definitely not low-calorie dining options. So eat and enjoy, but just in case you are interested, here is the breakdown! Kalua Pig 1/2 cup 150 calories, Lomi Lomi salmon 1/2 cup 87 calories, Poi 1 cup 161 calories (but who could eat that much!), fried rice 1 cup 200 calories, fish (depending on type served) 150-250 calories, chicken long rice 283 calories, haupia 128 calories, coconut cake 200-350 calories, Mai Tai 302 calories, Pina Colada 252 calories, fruit punch 140 calories, Blue Hawaii 260 calories, Chi Chi 190 calories.

LAHAINA

INEXPENSIVE

AMILIO'S DELICATESSEN   *American*
840 Wainee St., Lahaina Square (above Lahaina Shopping Center - north end of town) (661-8551) HOURS: Breakfast/lunch and dinner. COMMENTS: Take out or eat in. Deli sandwiches ($4.10 -$5.45), plate lunches ($3.95-$4.85).

ARAKAWA ★   *Chinese*
Lahaina Center. (661-8811) Hours: Daily 11 am-8 pm. COMMENTS: There are very few really good dining values in West Maui. Arakawa's Chinese food, tucked in the middle of Lahaina Center, is a great new "find!" Primarily for takeout, there are a few tables out in the courtyard. They have daily specials and a surprisingly large assortment of dishes and the fare is very good. We had enough for dinner for two adults and two kids for $13.

THE BAKERY ★   *French/American*
911 Limahana (turn off Honoapiilani Hwy. by Pizza Hut) (667-9062) HOURS: Mon.-Sat. 7 am-5 pm, Sun. 7 am-noon. SAMPLING: Whole wheat cream cheese croissants also ham, or turkey stuffed croissants, or small sandwiches such as turkey dijon. Huge fresh fruit tortes, fudge, and fresh breads are made here daily. COMMENTS: There is no seating area. Arrive early in the day to insure getting the best selections. It's well worth the stop if you are a lover of pastries. The selection is delicious!

BLACKIE'S BAR   *Mexican*
On Hwy. 30 between Lahaina and Kaanapali (667-7979) Look for the tree house structure with the orange roof. HOURS: Daily, 10 am-10 pm SAMPLING: Burritos, enchiladas, tacos, nachos, smoked hot dogs, burgers and Louisiana hot links. COMMENTS: Incredible photos of boat wrecks and memorabilia line the walls. Jazz on Fri. and Sun., 5-8 pm. Not a family restaurant.

BLUE LAGOON   *American*
Located on the lower level of the Wharf Shopping Center (661-8141) HOURS: 11 am-9:30 pm. SAMPLING: Sandwiches include prime rib, BLT, Turkey or club $5.25 - $6.95, soup $1.95 - $2.95, entrees offer Mahi Mahi Cajun Style $11.95, Fish and Chips $10.25, Baby Back Ribs $11.95, shrimp platter $10.95. COMMENTS: This is a "self-serve" style restaurant. Place your order at the counter and pick it up on a tray and find a table in the courtyard.

BURGER KING   *American*
632 Front St., (667-6162) South end of Lahaina by the Banyan Tree. HOURS: 6:30 am-1 am serving breakfast, lunch, and dinner. SAMPLING: Breakfast sandwiches, salad bar, and the usual burgers at prices slightly higher than the mainland. (Another Burger King located at the Cannery Mall, 661-4395)

CHEESEBURGER IN PARADISE ★   *American*
811 Front St., Lahaina (661-4855) HOURS: Lunch/dinner served 10 am-11 pm SAMPLING: Select from their Classic BLT $5.95, Polynesian shrimp and fries

$8.95, aloha fish and fries $7.95, cheeseburger $6.95 or with recipes from Picnics Restaurant in Paia, they now offer a tofu burger or spinach nut burger. Chili Fries $5.95, upcountry salad $5.95. COMMENTS: A casual dining atmosphere located in the upstairs loft-like setting with open-air dining and wonderful views of the Lahaina Harbor and Front Street. Very good hamburgers, plus a view at no charge! Live music nightly 4 - 7 and 8 - 11. They also have created some new tropical drinks. The Lahaina Sunburn, the Lahainaluna Swirl or how about Trouble in Paradise?

CHILI'S *Southwestern Grill*
Lahaina Center. (661-3665) HOURS: 11 am-11 pm, daily. SAMPLING: The grilled Caribbean chicken salad at $7.95 was quite good, except for the canned pineapple. The Southwest Grill offers fajitas, BBQ baby back ribs, grilled chicken $8.95 - $13.95. The frozen Oreo pie at $3.75 might better be called a "Kilauea Pie" as the frozen yogurt in Oreo cookie crust was swimming in a hot lava flow of chocolate fudge. COMMENTS: Begun in 1978 they now have 262 restaurants in 38 states. A good restaurant value. A kid's menu is available. Another Chili's is planned for Waikiki and four more are planned for other islands.

CHRIS' SMOKEHOUSE ★ *American*
New location on Honoapiilani Hwy. near Pizza hut. (667-2111) HOURS: Lunch 11 am-4 pm; dinner 5-10 pm. SAMPLING: BBQ ribs, steak, fish, and chicken. Lunch menu $4.95 - $7.95. Ribs, chicken, steak, fish, dinners available a la carte $8.95 - $17.95.

CHUN'S KOREAN BBQ *Korean*
658 Front St., Lahaina Cinema Center. (661-9207) HOURS: Lunch and dinner 10 am-10 pm. SAMPLING: The first price is a lunch size portion, the second is a larger dinner entree. Beef bul ko gi $7.50/$12.50 (thinly sliced BBQ marinated meat), Meat Jun $5.75 (tender BBQ beef in egg batter), Kook soo $4.75/$8.50 (noodles, vegetables and egg in a clear broth) or Yuk ke jang $5.75/$9.25 (spicy beef soup with vegetables and rice noodle). COMMENTS: Opened the summer of 1992 in the Pizza Patio location, in the rear on the lower level of the center. The owner and chef was formerly with the Tiger restaurant in Lahaina.

DENNY'S *American*
Lahaina Square Shopping Center (667-9878) HOURS: 24 hours a day. SAMPLING: Breakfast served anytime. Burgers and local style dishes. Dinners include steak, seafood and chicken $6.79 - $10.79.

DOMINO'S *Italian*
888 Wainee at Papalua Street. (661-9000) HOURS: 11 am until midnight, Friday and Saturday until 1 am. Three Domino's locations, one in Lahaina, another in Kihei and a third in Kahului. This is a chain of restaurants that offer local delivery.

GOLDEN PALACE *Chinese*
Lahaina Shopping Center (661-3126) HOURS: Lunch 11-2, dinner 5-9. Also take out. SAMPLING: A large variety of selections with Chinese and some Szechuan dishes. Affordably priced from $4 - $11. COMMENTS: Beer, cocktails, and Chinese wine are also available.

GREAT JANE'S EATERY   *American*
888 Wainee St., Lahaina (661-5733) HOURS: Mon.-Fri. 7-4, Sat. 7-2, closed on Sun. Breakfast offers only wheat toast $.72. Deli style sandwiches and salads are luncheon fare $2.65 - $5.50. COMMENTS: 4 tables outside, 2 inside. Food to go.

HARD ROCK CAFE ★   *American*
Lahaina Center. (667-7400) HOURS: Daily from 11 am, bar opens 12:30. SAMPLING: Grilled burgers or chicken breast sandwiches $5.60-$6.95, lime BBQ chicken $10.95, HRC famous baby rock watermelon ribs $12.50, grilled marinated vegetables on a skewer $3.50. COMMENTS: A lively atmosphere, if the music isn't too loud for you. Fun and interesting memorabilia line the walls and you'll no doubt want to pick up one of their T-shirts for someone back home. A very popular eatery, possibly due to the great prices and good food, so expect it might be crowded or even a waiting line to get in during peak dining hours.

HARPOONER'S LANAI ★   *American/Local*
On Front St., wharfside at the Pioneer Inn, (661-3636) HOURS: Daily, breakfast 7-11 am, lunch 11:30 am-2 pm. SAMPLING: Eggs with ham, links, Portuguese sausage, or bacon for $4.25. Coconut, banana, macadamia nut, or blueberry pancakes at $4.95. French toast runs $3.25. Lunches might include Portuguese bean soup at $3, or a hamburger at $5.75. COMMENTS: Our usual order is their French toast which is four half-slices of Portuguese Sweet Bread that are thick and custardy. The pancakes are okay too, but skip the hashbrowns (they are the fast-food variety). The atmosphere is rustic, casual, and makes one feel almost as if the clock had been turned back.

HONEY SWEET YOGURT & ICE CREAM SHOP   *Sandwiches*
180 Dickenson St., (661-8256) SAMPLING: Sandwiches include light mayonaise, sprouts and tomatoes on whole wheat bread or French roll. $3.49 - $4.29 include french dip, avocado, egg salad, roast beef, ham or turkey. Soups and salads.

JUICY'S SANDWICH AND JUICE BAR   *Vegetarian*
505 Front St. #142, Lahaina (667-5727) HOURS: 8:30 am-8:30 pm Monday thru Saturday, 11 am-6 pm on Sunday. Fresh squeezed juices $2.75 - $4.50, wheat grass juice pressed twice daily. Entree prices $2.95 - $5.95, tofu burgers $4.95 and cholesterol, fat free, non-dairy whipped frozen dessert called Fruitage. Made of blended fruit juices it's delicious and only 20 calories per fluid ounce.

KENTUCKY FRIED CHICKEN   *American*
Lahaina Shopping Center (661-3422)

LAHAINA BROILER   *Seafood/American*
887 Front Street (661-3111) HOURS: Lunch 11-2, late lunch 2-5 pm, dinner 5-11 pm. SAMPLING: Lunch sandwiches, salads or entrees $4.95 - $9.25. Dinner entrees served with seafood chowder, bean soup or tossed salad. Entrees include chicken, teriyaki steak, top sirloin, seafood fettucini, chioppino $11.95 - $23.50. Currently they have a "Mai Tai Sunset Dinner" served from 5-8 pm. which is a mahi and chicken combination for $12.95. COMMENTS: A wonderful, open ocean view setting done in hues of grey, green and mauve. While the atmosphere is great the food has not proven to be so. A great location for an evening beverage. Karaoke entertainment evenings.

LAHAINA TREEHOUSE RESTAURANT   *Seafood-American*
Lahaina Marketplace on Front St. (661-3235) HOURS: Lunch 11 am-5 pm, dinner 5-9 pm. SAMPLING: Lunch selections are served with fries or salad, mahi sandwich, pirate shrimp, N.Y. steak philly sandwich, grilled chicken breast sandwich, luncheon salads $6.95-$7.95 Pupus available at lunch and dinner $2.50 - $5.50. Dinner soups and salads $2.50 - $7.95, fresh fish of the day served sauteed, grilled, tempura or "pirate" style as well as coconut shrimp $11.95, steak sticks $12.95 (N.Y. steak grilled and marinated in a ginger and basil sauce) or noodle stir fry $9.95.

LANI'S PANCAKE COTTAGE ★   *American*
658 Front St., Wharf Cinema Center, across from the Banyan Tree (661-0955) HOURS: Breakfast and lunch 6:30 am-2:30 pm. SAMPLING: In addition to the popular breakfast fare they offer entrees such as fish and chips or chili burgers $4.50 - $6.50. COMMENTS: Very busy during breakfast hours, offering seating indoors or on the patio. A landmark in Lahaina and still owned by Lani Moore.

MARIE CALLENDER   *American*
Located at the Lahaina Cannery Mall, Kaanapali side of Lahaina (667-7437) HOURS: 7 am-10 pm Mon.-Thurs. and Sun. Until 11 pm on Fri. and Sat. SAMPLING: Breakfast omelettes served all day from $6.95 - $7.50 or choose a fresh fruit waffles. Lunches include pasta, hamburgers, salads, and sandwiches. Dinner entrees begin daily at 4 pm, Marie's quiche $7.95, pasta primavera $8.25, full meals $10.95 - $14.95 include oven roasted chicken, BBQ style ribs or homestyle pot roast. COMMENTS: Great pies, but the food nothing special.

MCDONALD'S   *American*
Located at Lahaina Shopping Center. HOURS: Open for breakfast, lunch, and dinner. SAMPLING: The usual for McDonald's with a few added items such as Saimin. COMMENTS: Indoor eating and also a drive-through.

MOONDOGGIES   *Italian-American*
666 Front St., Lahaina (661-3966) HOURS: Daily 10 am-10 pm. SAMPLING: Breakfasts $4.95 - $5.95, sandwiches $5.55 - $6.95, pizzas $7.70 - $15.75, pasta and steak $8.95 - $15.95. COMMENTS: The new owner is Koji Takashima and manager is Mary Jo Berkely, formerly with Lahaina Coolers. It's very "surf bistro" in decor, similar to Lahaina Coolers with white tables, turquoise and green director chairs and big plants, making a very light and spacious atmosphere and a good use for this open-air location. The menu is served all day from 10 am until midnight. They plan to start serving breakfast later in the year. The prices are reasonable, not gourmet or innovative, but simple and familiar which should be appealing to many. The Italian food is better than average, with good spaghetti and meatballs even! The "Big Curls" is a sort of combination between calzone and cornish pastie, baked dough stuffed with several options. The spinach was excellent using fresh leaves that had been lightly marinated. The curls could well become their signature dish! The sliders are mini-burgers. Or how about the apple pizza pie a la mode! You can get a whole "pizza" or just a slice. Basically it is a slice of pizza with apple pie topping and a big scoop of ice cream, served warm! The prices are reasonable and the music was pleasant without being overwhelming. The view adds to the appeal as well and this could become a great family dining location.

MOOSE McGILLYCUDDY'S *American*

844 Front St., upper level of Mariner's Alley, a small shopping alley at the north end of town (667-7758) HOURS: Breakfast from 7:30 am-11 am., also lunch and dinner. SAMPLING: The really big eater may want to tackle a moose omelette consisting of 12 eggs with two types of cheese, bacon, sausage, mushrooms, sprouts, spinach, and onion for $17.95. Regular omelettes $5.95. Half dozen types of burgers $4.75 - $7.95. Pizza's, salads, sandwiches, Mexican selections and a kid's menu. Ice cream and non-alcoholic drinks. COMMENTS: A very affordable, not overly exotic atmosphere. Moose operates an alcohol awareness service and offers a designated driver program. The selected individual wears a special badge and gets served free non-alcoholic drinks. Very popular place for their breakfasts, $3.59 for their early bird special of eggs, bacon, potatoes, rice or toast and orange juice served 7:30-9 am. Their early bird dinners are just as popular with a choice of prime rib, chicken or mahi for $7.95. Evening music on the wild side. Large screen sports TV.

PAPA'S MEXICAN FOOD *Mexican*

At Lahaina Business Plaza behind the Chevron Station. (667-7615) HOURS: 11 am-2 pm, 5 pm-8 pm. Take out orders or seating available. SAMPLING: Hawaiian burrito is made with kalua pork, refried beans, cheese and salsa $3.75, tacos, tamales, enchiladas $2.50 - $3.75, plate lunches $6.

PIZZA HUT *Italian*

127 Hinau, Lahaina, (661-3696) They now have five locations on Maui. In Kihei at the Dolphin Plaza, in Kahului there are two locations, a new location in Honokowai and another in upcountry at Pukalani. We've heard some good reports on their salad bar.

PLANET HOLLYWOOD *Burgers etc.*

Scheduled to open in late 1992 somewhere in Lahaina. Could offer some competition to the Hard Rock Cafe!

S.W. BAR-B-QUE *American-Local*

At Lahaina Square (661-4156) HOURS: Breakfast 6-11 am, lunch 11 am-2 pm, dinner 5-9 pm daily. SAMPLING: BBQ chicken, short ribs, pork or steak. Also Chinese cuisine.

SAENG'S THAI ★ *Thai*

1312 Front St. (667-0822) HOURS: lunch 11 - 2:30 Mon. - Fri. and dinner 5 - 9:30 daily. COMMENTS: Saeng's Thai cuisine, one of our favorites in Wailuku, opened a new West side in 1992. Located on the outskirts of Lahaina across from the Cannery. Same menu as the Wailuku location, only here you can enjoy the ocean view and the sunset.

SIR WILFRED'S ESPRESSO CAFE

Lahaina Cannery Mall, Kaanapali side of Lahaina (667-1941) HOURS: 9 am-9 pm. SAMPLING: Small seating area, limited menu includes quiche $2.95 - $3.95, pastries, cookies, cheesecake. COMMENTS: A very small, pleasant eatery. Great coffee and espresso. Gourmet coffees available for purchase.

SONG'S *Chinese-Hawaiian*
658 Front Street at the Wharf Shopping Center (667-1990) HOURS: Daily for lunch and dinner. SAMPLING: This is okazayu style buffet with chicken adobo, kim chee, stir fry vegetables and more. After viewing the selections in the display case, your plate is dished up for you. Only a single table near the door offers seating, or get yours to go. Saimin, lomi lomi, stuffed cabbage, prices $1.50 - $5.

SOUTH SEAS/SNUG HARBOR *American-Seafood*
At Pioneer Inn, harborside (661-3636) HOURS: Open only for dinner. SAMPLING: Dinners include salad bar, cup of soup, vegetables and rice or potatoes. Teriyaki steak $14.95, Shrimp tempura $16.95, prime rib "bones" $12.50. Nightly specials. COMMENTS: Seating at South Seas is poolside at the very rustic Pioneer Inn Hotel. The Snug Harbor has indoor seating at the same location, same menu. Very casual atmosphere and they do offer a children's dinner menu $4.95.

SUBWAY *Sandwiches*
658 Front St., Wharf Cinema Center (667-9999) Deli sandwiches.

SUNRISE CAFE *French*
693A Front St., (661-3326) HOURS: 5:30 am-9:30 pm. SAMPLING: All menu items under $5. Homemade soups, salads, quiche, cheesecake. COMMENTS: This is a very small, quaint eatery with food available to go.

TACO JOE'S CANTINA *Mexican*
658 Front Street at the Wharf Cinema Center on the courtyard level in the rear (667-2917) HOURS: Daily 11 am-midnight, food served until 10 p.m. SAMPLING: Fajitas $12.95, chille rellenos $11.95, two tacos $7.95, chimichanga $9.95, tostada $8.95. COMMENTS: Formerly Pancho and Lefty's. They feature an "all virgin bar" - just sodas, coffee, tea and lemonade.

TAKE HOME MAUI *American*
121 Dickenson (661-8067) SAMPLING: Fresh fruit smoothies $3.25, toffuti, sandwiches $4.55 ice cream and sodas in the freezer. Fruits and Hawaiian coffee are among the items to be shipped or taken home. COMMENTS: Limited seating. Fruit smoothies are delicious!

THAI CHEF *Thai*
Lahaina Shopping Center (667-2814) HOURS: Lunch 11-2:30 Mon.-Fri., dinner 5-10 nightly. SAMPLING: Entrees such as Thai crisp noodles, green papaya salad and garlic squid are $5 - $10. COMMENTS: We were disappointed with the quality and size of the portions. None of the dishes we ordered were memorable and it was an expensive meal for the amount of food served. However, others seem to like it and the Thai toast comes highly recommended.

VILLAGE PIZZERIA *Italian*
At 505 Front St. (661-8112) HOURS: Lunch and dinner daily SAMPLING: Pizza is available in Neapolitan style (thin crust) or Sicilian (thick crust). A 14" plain pizza starts at $10, a combo of 4 items $14.25. COMMENTS: The clam and garlic pizza is a specialty here!

MODERATE

ALEX'S HOLE IN THE WALL *Italian*
834 Front St. (661-3197) HOURS: Dinner 5:30 pm, Mon.- Sat. SAMPLING: Chicken parmigiana, shrimp Alfredo, lasagna, ravioli, linguine & sausage or chicken marsala $17 - $24. COMMENTS: Our dinner was well prepared, although after a day on the beach the portions were a little small for hearty appetites. A popular place for local residents, but we tend to prefer our Maui dining to include some of those magnificent ocean vistas or warm sunsets instead of dark inside atmosphere. Located up a flight of stairs, difficult for anyone handicapped.

BENIHANA *Japanese*
658 Front Street at the Wharf Cinema Center on the upper level (667-2244) HOURS: Lunch 11:30 - 2 pm, dinner 5-10 pm. SAMPLING: Lunch selections include chicken, filet mignon, daily specials or a bento lunch. Complete dinners with chicken, steak or seafood. COMMENTS: This well known mainland chain has joined the ever increasing number of teppanyaki style restaurants on Maui. This method of cooking involves a great deal of flourish and preparation by a chef who cooks your meal at the table in front of you. Part of the price of the dinner is for the show! They also serve Sunday Champagne brunch on their lana'i. Four entrees run $9.25 - $10.50 and include chicken katsu, mahi mahi, omrice or seafood salad.

BETTINO'S *American-Local*
At 505 Front St. (661-8810) Currently new owners are taking over the place. No word on any name change or menu.

BLUE TROPIX NIGHTCLUB *Italian*
900 Front St., Lahaina (667-5309) Opening in late 1992, but inside information reports this nightclub and restaurant will feature dinner and dancing from 5 pm-2am with a California/Italian menu served until 1 am. From 9 pm-2 am enjoy music from the 30s, 40s, 50s and 60s. In addition to a live DJ and their will be live entertainment some nights. Located on the waterfront in Lahaina, there will be a cover charge of $5 between 8 pm and 2 am. Dinner entrees will be priced under $20.

CAFE MAESTRO *Italian*
608 Front St., Lahaina (661-8001) HOURS: Lunch 11:30 - 5 pm, dinner 5 - 10:30 pm. SAMPLING: Lunch selections include pasta pesto $8.50, pasta Napolitaine $7 or linquini Mediterranean $12.50. Dinner selections feature fettucini primavera $8.50, duck lasagna $11.50, salmon stuffed black pasta rolls in pepper sauce $13.50, beet pasta with veal $11.50, entrees including soup or salad are Veal Scallops Gypsi $14. Appetizers and salads from $2.95. COMMENTS: The bread is multi-grain bread served with extra virgin olive oil and seasonings which would be better with a French or sourdough bread. The spinach salad with smoked chicken, artichoke and macadamia nuts ($7.50) had very good flavor and was a hearty enough salad to share. The beet pasta was very good with a pink hue and the gorgozola cheese sauce complimented nicely. The black pasta was fun - little oval-shaped slices with black pasta borders, attractively presented on a plate in sauce. The veal scallops was another interesting entree. The scallops were part of the veal stuffing, kind of an Italian version of Veal Cordon Bleu and an interest-

ing combination of flavors. Since they recently opened, the menu is new and there may be changes. They have pizza too. The dinners, which include soup or salad, are a good value. With the extended evening hours it is a nice option for late diners! You'll also find some decorating changes with some vivid new art work, red chairs and green ceilings.

CHART HOUSE ★ *American*
1450 Front St. (661-0937) HOURS: Dinner daily 4:30-9:30 pm. SAMPLING: Baked scallops or sweet & sour chicken priced $16.95, teriyaki top sirloin $18.75, pepper steak $22.95 and their popular 20 oz. prime rib at $25.75. Daily specials and fresh fish selections. Entrees are served with a hot squaw bread and sour dough breads and a choice of Chart House salad or New England clam chowder. Their salads are either a fresh Caesar, a spinach topped with poppy seed dressing or a garden salad. The children's menu includes small sirloin, ground sirloin, broiled chicken or beef kabob plus salad, potato or rice and soft drink $3.25 - $6.95. COMMENTS: The combination appetizer is $12.75 and offers a good size sampling of shrimp, oysters, teriyaki and chicken sticks. They have added a non-smoking section and have enlarged the parking lot. They no longer offer their salad bowl, but do have a nice selection of salads. The desserts are limited, but very good. The Key Lime pie is really Key Lime pie ($3.95) and of course for the chocolate lover there is mud pie or chocolate mousse pie!

There is a comfortable atmosphere with lots of wood and lava rock. The limited number of oceanview tables are a hot commodity and require that you arrive when they open. Potatoes and rice are available at an extra charge. They provide one of the best keiki menus we've seen. The menu serves as a coloring book and a small pack of crayons are thoughtfully provided. The children's selections include four very reasonably priced dinners, $2.95 for ground sirloin, chicken teriyaki or beef kabobs at $4.95, and a small sirloin steak at $6.45. The entree portions were large. Included with the meal was salad, rice or potato and a soft drink. The adult entree prices may be slightly higher than other restaurants, but the cut of prime rib was enormous and the fresh fish portion very ample. They now do take reservations! They also have a Chart House restaurant in Kahului and in Wailea.

HARBOR FRONT *Ethnic Asian - Japanese-Thai-Chinese*
658 Front Street, Wharf Cinema Center, top level (667-5122) HOURS: Lunch 11 am-3 pm, dinner 5pm-10pm. SAMPLING: Pad Luk Chin (Thai pork balls with vegetables), Donbori steak (Japanese steak and rice dish), Chinese fried ribs, Eruasian potatoes with corned beef, Kara age (Japanese style fried chicken) $6.95 - $9.95. COMMENTS: New owners took over this restaurant at the Wharf Cinema Center. The fresh fish display in front is gone and there are some new Asian flags draped from the ceiling. It is Chinese/family style dining where the various dishes are ordered and shared. The Eruasian specialties are an interesting concept, European preparation of Asian dishes. Opened too late to do a personal review.

J.J.'S BEACH GRILL *American-Seafood*
505 Front Street (667-4341) HOURS: Daily 10 am until midnight, cocktails until 1 am. SAMPLING: Lunch menu includes Eggs Benedict, pasta, french dip, salads from $6.95. All dinner entrees include J.J.'s special bread, tossed Caesar salad, baked potato, pasta or french fries. Kiawe broiled rack of lamb $20.95, cajun shrimp pasta $19.95, roast duckling with green peppercorn sauce $17.95. COM-

MENTS: J.J. McGibboney (of The Kapalua Grill and Bar) Lucien Charbonnier (of Chez Paul and Orient Express) and Steve Smith (chef of Chez Paul) have collaborated on this oceanfront dining location. Upstairs is Studio 505 with nightly entertainment. Early bird specials.

KIMO'S ★ *American/seafood*
845 Front St. (661-4811) HOURS: Lunch 11:30 am-2:30 pm. Dinner daily 5-10:30 pm. SAMPLING: Fresh fish prepared three different ways $16.95 - $19.95, Pacific seafood fettucini $14.95, baked scallops $15.95, vegetarian lasagna $9.95, ginger chicken $12.95. COMMENTS: They have a waterfront location and, if you're really lucky, you'll get a table with a view. Opinions vary greatly about Kimo's. Some really like it and others really don't. Our experience has been very good service and well prepared fresh fish. They must be doing something right - - one of a handful of restaurants to continue in Lahaina. They also have a bar on the lower level and an ocean view which provides a pleasant sunset view.

KOBE JAPANESE STEAK HOUSE ★ *Japanese Dining-Sushi Bar*
136 Dickenson (667-5555) HOURS: Dinner from 5:30. SAMPLING: Teriyaki chicken $13.90, Hibachi steak $19.50, Sukiyaki steak $15.90, lobster & steak combo $32.90. Dinners include soup, shrimp appetizer, vegetables and rice.COMMENTS: A sister of the Palm Springs and Honolulu restaurants, they offer teppan cooking (food is prepared on the grill in front of you) and the show is as good as the meal. They have a small parking lot adjacent to the building. Keiki menu. Reservations are recommended.

LAHAINA COOLERS *American*
180 Dickenson St., Dickenson Square, (661-7082) HOURS: Breakfast, lunch, dinner 7 am until midnight. SAMPLING: Pasta dishes available in appetizer or entree portions $5.50 - $12.90 includes chicken Azteca (bacon, tomato cilantro and wine), or Zebra ravioli in gorgonzola sauce. Shrimp scampi ala cerutti $15.75, Moroccan chicken spinach enchilada $8.50, bistro burger $8.75. Full bar service and tables inside or out. COMMENTS: They have a great slogan, "Because Life is Too Short to Eat Boring Food." We found the food items exotic and unique. Their chocolate taco filled with tropical fruit and berry "salsa" is a wonderful combination of flavors! The pizzas $8.50 - $10.50, are pretty much a single serving. The portions are ample for lunch, a little too small for a hearty dinner eater. They plan on opening another branch on the Big Island.

LAHAINA FISH COMPANY *Seafood*
831 Front St. (661-3472) HOURS: Lunch 11 am - 4 pm. Dinner 5 pm-11 pm. No reservations. SAMPLING: Available in their Hammerheads Fish Bar are a selection of menu items ranging from burgers and sandwiches to deep fried chicken, fried shrimp or fish and chips. $5.95-$9.95. Their dinner menu provides seafood selections such as fresh Pacific oysters, shrimp scampi or catch of the day, as well as chicken and beef entrees. Prices $7.95 - $21.95. COMMENTS: Nice oceanview setting. Check for 50% off the second dinner or buy one get one free coupons in This Week, The Maui Drive Guide and the Lahaina Historical Guide. Early bird dinner specials 5 - 6 p.m.

MUSASHI   *Japanese*
Lahaina Shopping Center (667-6207) HOURS: Lunch 11:30 am-2 pm, dinner 5:30-9:30 pm. SAMPLING: Beef or chicken teriyaki, sukiyaki, or nabe. Lunches run $5.25 - $9.75. Dinners include soup, side dish, pickles and rice with chicken or salmon teriyaki, the catch of the day fresh fish, or Unaju (barbecued eel over rice) $9.95-$17.

OLD LAHAINA CAFE ★   *Hawaiian*
505 Front Street. (661-3303) HOURS: Lunch 11-3. Dinner 5:30-10 pm COMMENTS: Nothing "old" about this place. Located on the beachfront with a breezy atmosphere. Operated by the same folks that run the beachfront luau. They recently remodeled and expanded. It has an even better open-air look and feel, just the kind of place visitors might imagine a Hawaiian restaurant would be. The new chef is Michael Ducheneau, formerly with Mango Jones. The food is good, even better than before. Their dinner rolls are fabulous, "poi rolls" made with taro that come out purple. A nice touch is the complimentary plate of tiny minted pineapple cubes served before the meal. The calamari salad is excellent and the chicken black bean and fettucini primavera are very good and a great value for $12.95. The chef offers a different potato each night, it might be roasted with wine and basil or speared and baked in a custard. The Chicken Pua Mana was a pleasing presentation of medallions of chicken in a very good sauce with lobster-in-the-middle. The shrimp done in the ti leaf was a very light preparation. Desserts range from light and fresh to decadent. The melon Anglaise is cantaloupe and honeydew cubes with a custard cream sauce with little strawberry drizzles on top and the chocolate Suicide Cake is a layered cake, very dense and very chocolatey served in a pool of white chocolate sauce. As before a wonderful ambience is added by the beach atmosphere, and lighted tiki torches with the pleasant sounds of Hawaiian music drifting in from the luau outdoors. They've really done a wonderful job renovating and improving the food without losing the Hawaiian ambience and flavor.

They recently added a Sunday brunch, served 8 am - 3:30 pm, which offers build your own omelete, Belgium waffles, Moloka'i French toast or Hawaiian Pancakes, as well as salads, sandwiches and local style plate lunches. This is not a buffet, simply off the menu a'la carte selections.

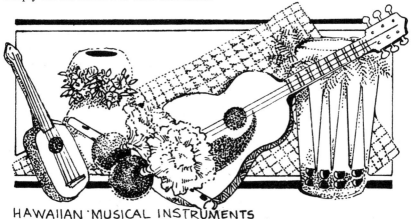

HAWAIIAN MUSICAL INSTRUMENTS

EXPENSIVE

AVALON ★ *Hawaiian Regional Cuisine*
844 Front St., (667-5559) HOURS: Daily 12-12. SAMPLING: A number of the dishes may be prepared to your liking, mild, medium or spicy. In addition to daily chef's specials, sample Avalon summer rolls for an appetizer $7.95, palani steak and Asian Prawns $23.95, Asian pasta made with shrimp, clams, scallops and fresh island fish $17.95, Chinese Duck, or fresh island fish prepared with shitake mushrooms in ginger sauce, in garlic black bean sauce, wok charred in asian spices, basil coulis, in sun dried tomato with basil cream sauce, Thai style with lemon grass, lime leaf with island salsa or in an herb sauce. One of many good reasons to come to Avalon is for salad. Not just any ordinary salad, mind you, but something special. The Gado Gado salad $10.95 comes from the island of Bali and is a tasteful blend of romaine lettuce, cucumbers, tofu, steamed vegetables on a bed of brown rice and topped with peanut sauce. Equally delicious is the Chinese tofu salad at $8.95. Both are huge portions. And, if you dare, some extraordinary Caramel Miranda for dessert. COMMENTS: The name Avalon, according to Celtic or Gaelic legend, is the West Pacific island paradise where King Arthur and other heroes went following death. The look here is 40s Hawaiian with antique aloha shirts adorning the walls, ceiling fans whirring and wonderful multi-colored oversized dishes. This one is a favorite of ours and we don't visit Maui without stopping by at least once! They recently added a new Juice and Elixer bar featuring fresh juices and exotic elixers! Avalon has won a number of awards and deservedly so. Be sure to not miss having at least one meal here!

CHEZ PAUL ★ *French*
Five miles south of Lahaina at Olowalu (661-3843) HOURS: Dinner 5:30-10:30 pm. SAMPLING: Dinners run $21 for vegetarian fare, $25 - $31 for other meals. The menu includes veal, fish, duck, and beef in wonderful French sauces. Dinners include French bread, soup or salad and two vegetables. Pate, escargot, and shrimp are available as appetizers. Save room for some very special desserts. COMMENTS: This small restaurant has maintained a high popularity with excellent food and service. It's not surprising they have won numerous dining awards. The wine list is excellent, although expensive. Wines are also available by the glass. Two seatings for dinner are offered, 6:30 or 8:30. Reservations are a must.

DAVID PAUL'S LAHAINA GRILL ★ *New American*
127 Lahainaluna at the Lahaina Hotel. (667-5117) SAMPLING: The menu is described as New American Grill Cuisine with a Southwestern flair. The menu changes, but you might enjoy for your dinner an entree of pan fried soft shell crab, ravioli's for Michelle (fresh saffron pasta filled with lobster and scallop hash and seasoned with shallots and chives), Kona coffee roasted lamb, or Tequila shrimp with firecracker rice $17.95 - $23.95. COMMENTS: David Paul was formerly with the Black Orchid on O'ahu and chef at Chez Michelle and the Hyatt Regency on O'ahu. The seating area is attractively furnished in French impressionism. Black and white floors are contrasted with a beautifully detailed fresco blue/green ceiling, peach table cloths and French impressionist art. While beautiful, it somehow lacked the cozy ambiance of one of our favorite restaurants

just across the street, Gerard's. Perhaps it was because we were one of only a few tables dining, but voices really carried and we could hear the conversation at the next table clearly. The food here is excellent and David Paul's has a continually changing menu, which keeps things interesting! We sampled their Caesar salad, which was excellent and an ample portion for two people. The soft shelled crab was very unusual and the pasta was delicately seasoned. The crab is cooked shell and all! Shipped in from the east coast, these crabs are "harvested" when they are in the molting process so that their shell is very soft. The fresh fish, opakapaka, was again a hearty portion served grilled with an accompanying tomato/onion zucchini sauce served finely chopped over eggplant. The Tequila Shrimp is available in mild, medium or hot. Medium proved to be plenty warm!

GERARD'S ★ *French*
In the lobby of the Plantation Inn at 174 Lahainaluna Rd. (661-8939) HOURS: Dinner only. SAMPLING: Dinner selections in the $22-$36 range. Selections might include Millefeuille of Salmon and Avocado with Vanilla Mousseline Sauce, seafood paella with lobster, old-fashioned coq au vin. COMMENTS: We were recently thinking back to the first time we dined at Gerard's, in its old, small, hole-in-the-wall location. It was wonderful then and it still is today! No one on vacation should deny themselves at least one night of special fine dining enjoyment. And if we have to pick among only one, Gerard's might well win out over several of our other favorites. Although partial to Maui's sunset ocean views while dining, sitting beneath a mango tree on the veranda of the Plantation Inn while dining at Gerard's is hard to beat. Just a short walk up Lahainaluna Road off Front Street in Lahaina, you are swiftly moved worlds away to a picturesque atmosphere reminiscent of a Gone with the Wind era. Crisply attired in green and peach the restaurant offers indoor or outdoor seating. A wine list features a range of moderate to expensive selections from California, France and the Pacific Northwest.

On a recent evening we began with a wonderful rich crab bisque followed by Ulua, the fresh fish and the evening special, a calamari with pasta dish. Our guidelines for a restaurant review center around the fresh fish. In other words a restaurant is as good as its fish! And Gerard's did not disappoint. The entrees

arrived, complimented with miniature vegetables. The calamari was a healthy portion in a wonderfully seasoned sauce. The fish was prepared with a spinach and bernaise sauce and not only was it excellent, but it was the best fish meal in recent memory and a good size filet too! The desserts, wonderful of course, vary nightly. Try the chocolate decadence complimented by a cafe au lait or a cappucino. The perfect evening was rounded out with background guitar music.

LONGHI'S ★ *Continental*
888 Front St. (667-2288) HOURS: 7:30 am - 10 pm; dessert served until 11 pm. SAMPLING: The menu is given orally by the waiter. A possible selection of a'la carte entrees might include Fettucini Alfredo, lobster and chicken canneloni, shrimp longhi, prawns amaretto and Venice. Seafood $20-$24, meat and poultry $17.50 - $26, pastas $13 - $21, salads, vegetables desserts from $4. COMMENTS: This is another of those Maui restaurants that people either love or they hate. In any case, they have become a near legend in Lahaina. The setting is casual, with lots of windows open to the bustling Lahaina streets. Personally, we have enjoyed our meals here, although the oral menu can sometimes mean you spend a little more than planned! An early breakfast before the visitors arrive in Lahaina is a great way to start the day. They offer espresso and a good wine selection. Valet parking nightly. Entertainment and dancing Friday and Saturday evenings.

SCAROLES *New York style Italian*
930 Wainee St., Lahaina (661-4466) HOURS: Lunch 11:30 - 2 pm, Dinner 5:30 - 9 pm daily. SAMPLING: Lunch items are light fare pasta, sandwiches and pizza $4.95 - $13.95. Dinner $17.95 - $23.95. COMMENTS: Scaroles advertises itself as "The New York side of Lahaina" and since they opened have been getting the thumbs up from locals and visitors alike and we'd tend to agree. Located on the Kaanapali side of Lahaina the restaurant is an open air, smallish, but cozy, dining room for 30 inside and a table or two outdoors. A basic Italian black and white color scheme is the decor here.

Being rather investigative dining reporters we noted that the appetizers at our neighbor's table looked great! An order of the calamari appetizer and a salad would have sufficed for a meal! For dinner you can sample homemade lasagna, seafood platter (a little too seasoned in our opinion), chicken served parmigiana, franchaise, marsala a la crema or saltimbocca. Daily specials are featured. All entrees are served with homemade minestrone soup or a salad that is presented with a bit of tomato and cucumber and fabulous warm-from-the-oven onion rolls. We're told by those who know that it is authentic New York Italian-style food. The pizza is available to eat in or take out. Reservations advised given the limited dining area.

KAANAPALI

INEXPENSIVE

BEACH BAR *American*
Westin Maui. (667-2525) Located atop the center island of the pool/deck area.
HOURS: 10 am-4:30 pm. SAMPLING: Services three pools with hot dog, shave
ice cart, and light menu to go. COMMENTS: The Beach Bar is by the pool and
the Garden Bar is by the beach. Why you may ask? Apparently the plate glass
names were switched and installed wrong, so rather than change the glass they
switched the names of the dining areas.

BURRITO BROTHERS *Mexican*
Located on the Kaanapali Parkway. (661-4500) SAMPLING: Complete taco
dinner $4.99, enchilada $5.99, Fiesta Chicken salad or taco salad $7.49, BBQ
burger 5.99, BBQ pork ribs $14.99, BBQ half chicken $9.99. COMMENTS: A
fairly new addition to the Kaanapali area and they deliver!

FOOD COURT *International*
Whaler's Village Shopping Center at Kaanapali. A 5,400 square foot lower level
food court is a recent addition to the center. The area features a contemporary
nautical architectural theme and will include a Chinese restaurant, Italian pizza
parlor, delicatessen and bar. Indoor/outdoor dining will accommodate about 150
people. Not open as we go to press.

GARDEN BAR *American*
Westin Maui, located near the beach (667-2525) HOURS: 9-9 pm. SAMPLING:
Kowabunga Tuna Sandwich $6.95, Pesto grilled chicken breast sandwich $8.25,
Ahi Sandwich with Wasabi mayo $8.25, Hang Ten Hot "Dawg" $4.50.

KAANAPALI BEACH HOTEL KOFFEE SHOP *American-Hawaiian*
Kaanapali Beach Hotel (661-0011) COMMENTS: The best value at Kaanapali.
The hotel is preparing in the near future to close for a year of renovations, but
until then sample their prime rib dinner buffet 4-9 pm for $9.95, breakfast buffet
6-10:45 am for $5.95, lunch buffet 11 am-2 pm for $5.95, or their afternoon deli
buffet 2 pm-4 pm with cheese and cold cuts to create your own sandwich plus
soup, salad and desserts for $4.95.

KAU KAU GRILL BAR *American*
Poolside at the Maui Marriott. (661-1200) HOURS: Continental breakfast 5:30-7
am, breakfast 7-11 am, lunch and snacks 11-4 pm. SAMPLING: Lunch menu
includes cheeseburgers, pizzas by the slice, salads, and sandwiches. The most
popular item is their Chicken Caesar salad. The connected bar serves cheese
sticks, calamari, onion rings.

THE MAKAI BAR *American*
Maui Marriott. (667-1200) HOURS: 4:30 pm-12:30 am. Located lobby level,
Lanai wing. COMMENTS: Open air cocktail lounge with sweeping ocean view
of the island of Lana'i. Great gathering place and nice sunset vistas. Voted by the
Maui News "Best of Maui" contest as having the best pupus! Stop by and judge
for yourself! Evening entertainment too.

MAUI YOGURT   *American*
Whaler's Village (661-8843) SAMPLING: Sandwiches such as cheese and egg salad, turkey or avocado and garden or fruit salads in the $4-$5 range. COMMENTS: No seating in the restaurant, but a few tables outside. Call ahead and order a picnic lunch.

OHANA BAR AND GRILL   *American-Italian*
Embassy Suites Resort (661-2000) HOURS: 10 am-10 pm daily. SAMPLING: If you are a guest of the hotel, this is where you'll find your morning breakfast cooked to order. They also offer poolside lunch and dinner selections. Sandwiches include Ohana burger, beef skewers Oriental style, grilled chicken breast, pizza.

MODERATE

CHICO'S   *Mexican*
Whaler's Village Shopping Center (667-2777) HOURS: Daily for lunch 11:30 am-2:30 pm, taco bar 11:30 am-11 pm and dinner 5-10 pm. SAMPLING: Dinner combination from $9.50, fajitas $9.95 and American fare such as London broil $9.95, cajun shrimp $10.95, BBQ ribs or mango fettucine with smoked chicken $9.95. Children's menu items include burgers, grilled cheese or hot dog $3.95-$4.50. COMMENTS: A good variety of Mexican fare with their freshly made flour tortilla shells enticing you as you enter.

CHOPSTICKS   *Pacific Rim*
Royal Lahaina Resort (661-3611) HOURS: Dinner nightly 6-9:30 pm. SAMPLING: Features Chinese, Japanese, Polynesian and Thai foods. All items are a la carte. From mainland China try thirteen dragon soup $4.75 or Hunan firecracker prawns $8.75. From Japan there is katsu $6.75 or tempura $9.25. The Polynesian offerings include Bahala na ribs $7.75 or coconut shrimp $9. From Hong Kong there is nutty chicken $7.50 or sample Thai fare such as spring rolls $4.75 or Thai basil chicken $8.75.

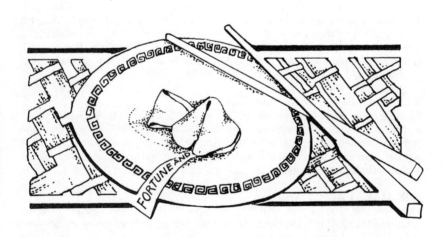

COOK'S AT THE BEACH ★ *American*
Westin Maui, north side of the swimming pool (667-2525) HOURS: Breakfast
6:30-11:30, lunch 11-2 and dinner 6-11 pm. SAMPLING: Daily breakfast buffet
is served Monday thru Saturday $13.95 adults, children $1.25 per year. Other
breakfast menu items available include Belgian waffle $7, makai omelette $9.25.
Lunch offers ono-licious sandwiches such as pesto grilled breast of chicken $8.25,
hamburgers or upcountry salads such as cashew chicken $8.50. Pizza from $8.50.
In the evenings they feature a prime rib buffet plus shrimp scampi pasta, Caesar
salad, fresh catch, seafood stir fry and more for $20.75 adults, children $1.25 per
year. The dinner menu ranges from pizza $8.50 and up, hamburgers and sand-
wiches from $7.50, and entrees such as seared sesame shrimp $13.95 or Szechuan
chicken $12.50. And not forgetting the younger traveler, a kid's menu served all
day $3.50-$4.75. COMMENTS: A good family restaurant with a varied assortment certain to please everyone and fairly reasonable prices for a resort!

EL CRAB CATCHER ★ *American-Seafood*
Whaler's Village Shopping Center (661-4423) It's a little hidden on the ocean
side. HOURS: Lunch 11:30-3 pm, poolside pupus 3-10 pm and dinner 5:30-10:30
pm. SAMPLING: Lunch offers French dip, burgers, salads and sandwiches.
Dinner entrees are served with soup or salad, vegetable and bread basket. Marine-
r's platter $14.95, crab alfredo $18.95, fresh crab stuffed fish $21.95, fish of the
day $19.95, Hawaiian chicken $13.95 or N.Y. steak $17.95 are among the options.
The poolside cafe menu features sunset specials served 5:30-6:30 pm, choice of
fresh fish, N.Y. steak, cajun mahi or steamed clams for $9.95 and other light fare
later in the evening such as grilled chicken or mahi mahi sandwiches $7.95 or
burgers $6.95-$7.95. COMMENTS: This was once an athletic club and the pool
remains beachside around which you can dine or enjoy a sunset and cool drink.
Some have been known to even take a dip! They do a wonderful job with their
fish preparation. Save room for one of their scrumptious desserts. This is a very
popular place and reservations are a good idea unless you want to wait an hour
or more for restaurant dining. They also have evening Hawaiian musical entertainment which is a great compliment to the oceanfront location.

LEILANI'S ★ *American-Seafood*
Whaler's Village Shopping Center, on the beach (661-4495) HOURS: Lunch
11:30-4, dinner 5-10:30, pupu bar 4 pm-midnight. SAMPLING: Ginger chicken
$12.95, quarter pound cheeseburger $7.95, spinach, mushroom and cheese raviolis
$9.95 and Malaysian shrimp $16.95, fresh fish $16.95-$19.95. COMMENTS: This
restaurant is a branch of the Kimo's and the Kapalua Bar and Grill operations.
They also offer a limited children's menu, and some luscious desserts. A reliable
stop for a good meal. Their Seafood Bar is located on the lower level with lighter
fare and is open to the beach.

LUIGI'S PASTA PIZZARIA *Italian*
Kaanapali Resort, by the golf course (661-4500) HOURS: Daily 11:30 am-
midnight, bar until 2 am. SAMPLING: Lunch selections include pasta or pizza as
well as sandwiches such as submarines, French dip or club. Dinner selections
$12.99-$18.99. How about a roasted garlic bulb served in butter sauce and served
with fresh pasta.... your friends are gonna love you!

MAUI ROSE   *American-Seafood*
Embassy Suites Resort (661-2000) HOURS: Dinner 5-10 pm. SAMPLING: Entrees Flambe'd Tiger Prawns $21.75, Fresh fish $22-$31.25, broiled black angus steak $16.95-$21.95. COMMENTS: A gracious floral setting adjacent to Kaanapali Beach provides a relaxing eating environ. The Maui Menus brochure has a two for one discount coupon.

MOANA TERRACE ★   *American-Buffet*
Maui Marriott Hotel (667-1200) HOURS: 6:30 am-11 pm. SAMPLING: Daily breakfast buffet 6:30-11 am, adults $13.95, children 6-12 years $6, under 6 are free. Includes cheese blintz, omelettes, Belgian waffles, breakfast meats, muffins and hot cakes. Lunch menu offers Cobb salad $8.95, Grilled swordfish $12.95, N.Y. strip steak $12.95, or Maine lobster BLT $10.95. Rainbow's End Dessert Bar is an all you can eat buffet available 5-9 pm. Nightly buffets are $18.95, but early diners received $3 off an adult meal. Children 6-12 years $8.50 no early dining discount. Sunday, Tuesday and Thursday is their Prime Rib buffet, Monday is Pacific Rim cuisine, Wednesday and Saturday are seafood buffets and a BBQ buffet is held on Fridays. Espresso bar.

MOBY DICK'S   *American-Seafood*
At the entrance to the Royal Lahaina Resort (661-3611). Currently closed for renovations. No word on when they will open or if they will have a name change.

NANATOMI   *American-Japanese*
Kaanapali Golf Course Club House (667-7902) Lunch served 11-3, dinner 5-10 pm. SAMPLING: Sandwiches, salads and local style plate lunches $.95-$6.95. Dinners $13.95 for tempura vegetables, teriyaki chicken or beef, N.Y. steak, fresh fish, sukiyaki, shabu shabu $13.95-$25.95. COMMENTS: Two for one dinner specials may be offered seasonally to early evening diners.

PAVILLION   *American-Cuisine Naturelle*
Hyatt Regency Maui, lower level (661-1234) Daily for breakfast and lunch. SAMPLING: Both their breakfast and lunch menu feature "cuisine naturelle" which offers some very healthy alternatives. Selections include an egg white and chive omelette topped with fruit and strawberry coulis ($8.50), chicken florentine is sauteed chicken on a bed of fresh spinach served with whole wheat toast ($8.50). Their all you can eat breakfast buffet served 6:30-11:30 am is $12.50 for adults, $6.50 children and features juices, fresh fruits, pastries, cereals, breakfast meats, egg dishes and tropical crepes. Luncheon selections offer healthy alternatives such as a chicken burger served on a whole wheat bun, or classic vegetable club sandwich which includes fresh vegetables, lean turkey and low fat swiss cheese on whole wheat bread. But not to fear, for those of you cholesterol loving travelers they also have roast beef, reuben sandwiches, hamburgers and pizza!

ROYAL OCEAN TERRACE ★   *American*
Royal Lahaina Hotel (661-3611) HOURS: Daily for breakfast, lunch and dinner 6 am-10 pm. Sunday brunch served 9-2 pm. SAMPLING: Sunday brunch $16.75 adults, $8.50 children 5-12 years, under 5 years, free. Features an omelette station, a baron of beef and glazed ham carving station, a waffle station, a pasta isle, a sushi bar, a fruit station, a salad bar, a seafood and cheese display, a hot line with eggs, rice, hash browns, kalua pig, stuffed pancakes and more plus a dessert and

breakfast pastry area and, if that isn't enough visit, the build your own sundae station. The International Buffet is offered 6-10 pm and offers Oriental, Italian, Mexican, Polynesian, Seafood and Paniolo fare for $10.50 adults, $5.25 children 5-12. In addition to their buffet they offer a dinner menu which includes pastas and pizzas $7.50-$12.25, and entrees $14.50-$18.25 of Australian lamb, mahi chicken, sauteed sea scallops, opakapaka with lilikoi lime butter or filet mignon. COMMENTS: The Royal Ocean Terrace is really aiming to meet the needs of the conservative, budget minded traveler, give them the most for their vacation dining dollars. The salad bar is not quite as extensive as it was previously, but still a good selection. This is a very attractive, airy restaurant.

THE RUSTY HARPOON   *American*
Whaler's Village (661-3123) HOURS: Daily breakfast 8-11 am, lunch 11-5, happy hour special and burger/beer special 3-5 pm, early bird dinner specials 5-6, dinner menu 5-10 pm and dinner 5-10 pm. SAMPLING: Breakfast specialty is their "Grill Your Own" waffle with trimmings to top it. Lunches run $7.50-$10.50 for hot entrees, salads and sandwiches, and burgers. Dinners offer prime rib, stir fry beef, fresh catch and crab, kalbi ribs $16.95-$22.95. Kid's menu offers four selections $5.75. Good selection of appetizers, try the bucket of clams!

SOMEPLACE DIFFERENT   *American*
Poolside at the Sheraton Hotel (661-0031) HOURS: Lunch served 11:30 am-2:30 pm, dinner 6-10 pm. COMMENTS: Something old, something new, Someplace Different! Someplace Different, the new restaurant at the Sheraton, is located in the old site of the Black Rock Terrace Restaurant. The Sheraton still features the popular evening sunset ceremony. Beginning about 6--ish, the cliff diver lights the torches by the pool, runs up the hill and lights another three then goes to the edge of the cliff, blows a conch shell and holds out a lei to the sky then dives. It is as fun to watch as ever. Follow the ceremony by dining at Someplace Different! The newly renovated restaurant has a brighter, whiter look with a whimsical sporty feel with brightly colored napkins, big paper palm tree in the middle and beer and Pepsi designer neons on the back wall.

The menu is unusual and most of it works. The Al Capone's Chicken Pocket appetizer ($6.75) and the Mama Mia's Ravioli ($5.25) were both good, however, the sauce was the same, while the menu described the chicken appetizer served with a basil cream sauce and the ravioli with a roasted red bell pepper sauce. The Cappelini Kaanapali which is lobster, julienne mushrooms in lobster sauce ($17.25) entre was very good, a very large portion that came loaded with fresh vegetables in the sauce with mushrooms and lots of lobster pieces, topped with a big piece in the shell. It was even better than the menu description. The Whiskey ribs ($17.25) were excellent, with a fabulous sauce that smelled so good that the people at the neighboring table commented on it! It was served with yummy baked beans and potatoes. Other dinner selections include Island fresh catch $23.50, dinner size sandwiches $9.95-$11.95, brochette of beef with salmon $19.50. The best of the three desserts sampled was the rainbow ice cream torte, a triangle slice of three layered neapolitan-like ice cream cake with a delicious banana flavor substituted for vanilla. Then layered with chiffon and topped with baked meringue. Refreshing and very good. Something different about the dessert menu was the lack of anything chocolate! They also offer nightly dinner specials for $24.95.

TIKI TERRACE   *American-Hawaiian*
Kaanapali Beach Hotel (661-0011) HOURS: Breakfast 7-11 am, Sunday breakfast menu is served 7 am-8:45 am followed by their Sunday champagne brunch 9 am-2 pm. SAMPLING: Scampi, T-bone steak, pasta ohana, Hawaiian calabash (bamboo basket filled with fresh vegetables and tofu then steamed and served with a ginger-soy sauce. COMMENTS: Complimentary hula show nightly with Hawaiian entertainment throughout the evening while you dine. Note that the Kaanapali Beach Hotel is slated for closure for a year of renovation. We were not able to determine closure date prior to going to press, so call to be sure they are still open!

VILLA RESTAURANT ★   *American-Seafood*
Westin Maui (667-2525) HOURS: Dinner only 6-10 pm. SAMPLING: Seafood is the specialty! Pacific Spicy prawns and soba noodles $18.75, Pacific salmon $20, grilled eggplant and zucchini $13.95 or crispy ginger chicken $14.95. Fresh fish $16.95-$21. COMMENTS: One of our best bets for fresh island fish and a beautiful setting. All tables look out onto the lagoon where swans and exotic ducks float along peacefully. Check for nightly dinner specials. The Villa Terrace, next to the Villa Restaurant at the Westin Maui, also has a nightly (except Monday) seafood buffet $21.75 adults, children $1.25 per year. Guitarist entertains.

EXPENSIVE

DISCOVERY ROOM   *Continental-American*
Sheraton Hotel, atop picturesque Black Rock (661-0031) HOURS: Breakfast 6:30-10:30. Dinner daily. SAMPLING: Breakfast buffet and a la carte breakfast service available until 10:30 am daily. Dinner choices range from spiral of lamb $22.95 to grilled scallops $26.95 or Fettucini Ala Neptune $23.95 to Island shrimp curry $21.50. Dinners are a la carte. Complete dinners available at $32.50. Nightly dinner buffets $18.95.

LAHAINA PROVISION COMPANY ★   *American*
Hyatt Regency Maui (661-1234) HOURS: Lunch 11:30-2 pm and dinner 6-11 pm. Chocoholic bar 6-11 pm, lounge from 11 am-11 pm. SAMPLING: Luncheon items run $6.50-$9.50 for sandwiches, salads. Dinner selections include Maui clambake $26 which is a combination of spiny lobster, clams, shrimp and fish, Hawaiian paella also $26, pork chops with apple chutney, cajun prime rib $18. COMMENTS: This restaurant is cleverly perched above the pool and on the edge of one of the Hyatt's waterfalls. Dinners here are very pleasant. Warm caraway bread begins the meal and the fettucini that accompanied the meal was outstanding. Ask whether they have a children's Camp Hyatt menu or children can order most entrees on the menu at 1/2 price for 1/2 size. This place may be a favorite if you're a chocolate lover. They have a CHOCOHOLIC BAR that features rich ice cream with an incredible choice of terrific temptations to top it. If you have dinner, it's an additional $3.95, but you can come later for dessert only and indulge for $6.95. We recommended this dessert as a definite Maui Best Bet! Reservations are recommended for dinner or dessert. Major credit cards are accepted.

LOKELANI ★ *American-Seafood*
Maui Marriott Hotel (667-1200) Dinner served 5:30-10 pm. All of the fish is market priced daily and your selection may be prepared a variety of ways. Appetizers, soups, salads such as seafood chowder, seafood Caesar salad or mussels. Entrees start at $18 and include fresh fish, seafood and selections of duck, lamb venison and steak.

NIKKO JAPANESE STEAK HOUSE *Japanese*
Maui Marriott Hotel (667-1200) Dinner only. Samari Sunset Menu is served only from 6-6:30 pm daily and prices are considerably less, for example chicken ($12.95), scallops ($17), sukiyaki steak ($14.95) are served with steamed rice, teppan-yaki vegetables, Japanese green tea and green tea ice cream. Children's menu for 10 and under $8.95. After that the menu selections increase in price with a sesame chicken dinner ($19.95), filet mignon ($25.95), shrimp ($24) or scallops ($24). Part of the price is the "show." The chef works at your table and is adept at knife throwing and other dazzling cooking techniques. Note: The menu states that a 15% service charge will be added to your check. Voted the best ethnic Japanese restaurant in 1992 by the Maui News in their "Best of Maui" contest.

SOUND OF THE FALLS ★ *French-Oriental Influences*
Westin Maui (667-2525) Champagne brunch served Sunday brunch 10-2 pm. Dinner 6:30-9:30 pm. Begin your dinner with an appetizer of ahi carpaccio with wasabi sabayon $11 or warm calamari on crispy noodles with rice vinaigrette $8.75, and follow it up with a kona crab bisque $5.75 or a wilted upcountry spinach salad with smoked wild boar $9.50. Beluga caviar for two runs $75. Five entrees each designed to serve two include veal shank forestier $62 or whole baked onaga $54, or single entrees of kiawe grilled scallops $28, island seafood potpourri in chervil flavored broth $27 or enjoy the chef's daily selection of meats, poultry from "The Roast Cart" $36. The Sunday brunch is outstanding with seafoods including spiced shrimp, kiawe smoked mahi or peppered mussels. Breakfast items such as omelettes, Belgian waffles and eggs Benedict or cheese blintz as well as smoked baby ribs, cajun style mahi and prime rib. Some folks simply fill their plate with items from the sushi bar. The Sound of the Falls merits our Best Bet for one of the best brunches in West Maui. For the sushi lover it is worth the price alone for all you can eat! Desserts are fit for royalty and beautifully presented. Add to all this a very lengthy wine selection. A beautiful setting plus excellent service makes this a highly recommended dining experience.

SPATS ★ *Northern Italian*

Hyatt Regency Maui (661-1234) HOURS: Dinner Tuesday-Saturday, 6:30-9:30 pm. SAMPLING: Appetizers, soups (minestrone or cioppino), and salads (warm lobster salad, buffalo mozzarella) $6.25-$12.50. Pastas are available in two sizes, appetizer or entree. Fettucini $9.75/$18.50, Potato Gnocchi $7.50/$14 and entrees such as Filetto di Blue $25 (basil and garlic marinated beef tenderloin in zucchini pancake) or Costoletta di vitell $28.50 (veal chop with pizzaiolo sauce and grilled polenta.) Entrees $18.75-$28.50.

The interior resembles more an elegant British pub than a restaurante Italiano. The food and service are both excellent. The a la carte pasta appetizers proved sufficient for a child's portion or would be adequate for a light eater. Excellent fare. Reservations recommended. "Top 40" music is played in their lounge from 10 pm-midnight Tuesday-Thursday and until 2 am on Friday and Saturday. Dress code requires slacks, shirts with collars and covered shoes.

SWAN COURT ★ *Continental*

Hyatt Regency Maui (661-1234) HOURS: Open for breakfast buffet 7 am-11:30 a.m Monday-Saturday and until 12:30 pm on Sunday. Dinner 6-10 pm daily. SAMPLING: Their breakfast buffet is $14.50 and includes fresh-squeezed orange juice, macadamia pancakes with a variety of toppings, French toast, cereals, yogurt, fresh fruits, and a good choice of hot breakfast foods. Breakfast items off the menu also available. Dinner menu includes salads and soups $6-$8. Entrees are a la carte $23-$35 and include veal chop saute armagnac, champagne chicken, or fresh island fish Eichenholz (baked on a plate of oakwood, with capers and mushroom garnish - and it is delicious!). Save room for dessert. Chocolate aficionados must try the Swan Court mousse! It is a chocolate swan filled with chocolate mousse accompanied by little clouds of whipped cream topped with macadamia nuts that are rich enough for 2! $7.

The atmosphere and the view of the Swan Court are worth it for a special treat! Our "best bet" for a daily breakfast buffet. The dinners are excellent and many unusual preparations are offered. Our only criticism is the proximity of other tables and noise seems to carry. Reservations are advised. Major credit cards accepted.

KAHANA - NAPILI - KAPALUA

BAR ONLY

KAPALUA BAY RESORT - BAY LOUNGE ★
Kapalua Bay Resort. (669-5656) HOURS: 4:30-8 pm. COMMENTS: Enjoy a fabulous sunset in this elegant setting. Pupus served are complimentary. The tropical drinks, including non-alcoholic, run $4.50-$6.50 with some the size of small fishbowls. Currently they are offering complimentary pupus 4:30-6 pm with flavors from around the world. Sunday will please those with a yen for oriental food with sushi, spring rolls, teriyaki beef sates featured. Other evenings sample French, Italian, or Mexican items. Live soft background music is provided.

THE LIBRARY LOUNGE
Ritz Carlton at Kapalua. Offers oceanviews. Not open as we go to press.

THE SUNSET LOUNGE
Ritz Carlton at Kapalua. Continental breakfast, cocktails throughout the day, afternoon tea and classical entertainment combined with a spectacular ocean view.

INEXPENSIVE

CHINESE GO GO   *Chinese*
3481 L. Honoapiilani, located near the Kaanapali Shores. (669-5725) HOURS: Lunch 11 am-4 pm. Dinner 4-9 pm. SAMPLING: Your choice of any two lunch entrees plus steamed rice, fried rice or noodles $4.95, three entrees $5.95, four entrees $6.95. Entrees include sauteed calamari with black bean sauce, pepper steak or kung pao chicken. Dinner with two entrees $6.95, three entrees $7.95, four entrees $8.95. Dinner entrees include sweet and sour pork, sauteed shrimp with snow peas or curry scallops and shrimp. A la carte items are served in pint size containers and do not include noodles or rice $5.95-$7.95. COMMENTS: This was previously the site of our favorite, Fat Boy's, restaurant. We weren't able to review this new restaurant before press time.

DOLLIE'S   *American-Italian*
4310 Honoapiilani Hwy. at the Kahana Manor (669-0266) HOURS: 10 am-midnight. SAMPLING: Pizzas, sandwiches, and pasta $5-$10 COMMENTS: Dollie's scored high marks in several categories of our pizza contest, scoring second place for best overall pizza, top honors for best cheese and for best crust and even scored well in the best cold pizza category! You'll also find one of the best selections on Maui with more than 40 domestic and imported beers. Espresso too! Food to go. Very popular spot with local residents.

GAZEBO   *American*
Poolside at the Napili Shores. HOURS: 7:30 am-2 pm breakfast and lunch. SAMPLING: Breakfast offers omelettes and an assortment of tropical pancakes or "eggs 'n things" from $3.50. Lunch selections include burgers, sandwiches and salads $4.75-$5.95. COMMENTS: Popular with Maui residents for the friendly atmosphere with a wonderful ocean view.

HONOLUA GENERAL STORE   *American*
Above Kapalua as you drive through the golf course. HOURS: 6:30 am-8 pm. COMMENTS: The Kapalua Hotel refurbished this once funky and local spot. The front portion displays an assortment of Kapalua clothing and some locally made food products. Breakfasts include pancakes, eggs and such. Lunches include four local plate lunches daily which might include stew or teri chicken $4.75-$5.50 or a smaller portion called a hobo which is just a main dish and rice for $2.95. Sandwiches and burgers from their deli too.

MARKET CAFE   *American-Italian*
Kapalua Bay Hotel Shops (669-4888) HOURS: Daily for breakfast, lunch and dinner. Open 8 am-10 pm. SAMPLING: Breakfast served daily until 11 am, Sundays until 1 pm. Omelettes, tropical pancakes, hot oatmeal with blueberries $4.95-$8.95. Breakfast special $2.99. Lunch items include house specials such as three cheese lasagna or a beef tenderloin sandwich, grilled mahi or chicken sandwiches, soups and salads $6.95-$9.95. The lunch menu continues thru dinner with hamburgers, sandwiches etc. Dinner is served from 5 pm with selections leaning to an Italian flare with pasta, fish, chicken and veal dishes $11.95-$17.95. Offerings include veal piccata, eggplant parmigiana, shrimp parmigiana and linguini marinara. Full bar. COMMENTS: This small restaurant has good, affordable fare and is part of a market that carries some unusual imported foods.

McDONALD'S OF KAHANA   *Fast food*
Located in the Kahana Gateway shopping center, a large indoor dining area. Breakfast, lunch and dinner served.

SUBWAY   *Deli sandwiches* - 5095 Napilihau. (669-0099)

VILLAGE CAFE   *American*
Village Golf Course at the first hole. (669-1947) HOURS: 6:30 am-6:30 pm. SAMPLING: Breakfasts $2.95- $4.95. They serve Lappert's Kona Coffee roasted daily on Kaua'i $.96. Sandwiches such as The Village Cheeseburger $5.95, as well as grilled cheese steak, deli delights, grilled chicken, and salads. COMMENTS: They make a great burger here! Let us know what you think!

MODERATE

BEACH CLUB   *American*
Kaanapali Shores Resort (667-2211) HOURS: Breakfast 7-11 am, lunch 11:30-3:00, the cafe menu includes sandwiches, soups and light fare served 3 - 9:30 pm. and dinner from 5:30-9 pm. SAMPLING: Dinners range from seafood and chicken to steak, special each evening runs $10.95.

THE CAFE AND TERRACE - Ritz Carlton. Not open as we go to press.

CHINA BOAT   *Cantonese-Szechuan-Mandarin*
4474 L. Honoapiilani (669-5089) HOURS: Lunch daily 11-3, dining nightly 5-10 pm. Karaoke and cocktails 10 pm until 1:30 am. SAMPLING: Shrimp with vegetables, beef with broccoli, and some hot and spicy dishes as well. Entrees from $8.95 for lemon chicken to Peking duck at $28.95.

ERIK'S SEAFOOD GROTTO   *American-Seafood*
4242 Lower Honoapiilani Hwy. on the second floor of the Kahana Villa Condo (669-4806) HOURS: Dinner daily 5-10 pm. SAMPLING: Dinners include chowder or salad, potatoes or rice, and bread. BBQ shrimp, steaks, seafood brochette $14.95-$19.95. COMMENTS: Check for early bird dinner specials. This is one of those restaurants that we don't hear much good about, but then we don't hear anything bad either! Kind of a middle of the road dining experience. Currently, early bird specials from 5-6 pm for $10.95 - $12.95 includes N.Y. steak, island mahi, lobster stuffed boneless chicken breast or crab stuffed prawns.

THE GARDEN RESTAURANT ★   *Continental*
Kapalua Bay Resort Hotel (669-5656) HOURS: Breakfast 6:30-11 am, Sunday brunch 11:30 am-2 pm and dinner nightly 6-10:30, except Seafood Buffet which is Fridays 5:30-9:30 pm. SAMPLING: In keeping with the trend to more casual and affordable fine dining, The Garden restaurant has a completely revised new menu. Kiawe grilled lemon chicken $16.95, fresh Hawaiian tuna $15.75, "hot and spicey crab pot with udon noodles" $13.50 or pasta selections in two sizes, such as seared ahi angel hair "Mediterranean" $10.95/$14.95 or smoked tea ducking pasta $8.95/$13.25. Take note that their Executive Chef, Henry Clay, makes an offer that if you're craving something that is not on the menu, if he has the ingredients, he'll prepare it! The Mayfair buffet served Sunday served 11:30-2 pm.

Enjoy continental dining in this semi-open tropical setting. Excellent food and service make this a pleasant dining experience. With the closing of the Plantation Veranda this is the only full service dining room at the Kapalua Hotel. Our recent dinner was fantastic. The fish was perfectly prepared, the service was excellent. Reservations recommended, a must for Sunday brunch. They recently began a wonderful Friday evening seafood buffet which is a deal and proving very popular at $22.95 adults, $16.95 under 12.

KAHANA KEYES   *Seafood-American*
Valley Isle Resort in Honokowai. (669-8071) HOURS: Dinner only. SAMPLING: Early bird specials 5-7 pm. Regular menu $9.95-$14.95. COMMENTS: Live entertainment and dancing nightly.

KAHANA TERRACE   *American*
4299 L. Honoapiilani Hwy., Sands of Kahana Resort (669-5399 ext. 22) HOURS: Breakfast 7:30-11, lunch 11 am until closing and dinner 5:30-9. SAMPLING: Pupu menu at bar. Lunch menu offers sandwiches, salads, hamburgers $5-$8. Complete dinners with entrees of N.Y. steak, Maui ribs, vegetable stir fry, fresh catch of the day, fish and chips, steamed clams $7.95-$14.95. COMMENTS: Very quiet dining, this restaurant seems to be primarily used by the resort guests. A good selection of menu items and lunch items available at dinner too. Check on nightly dinner specials $11.95-$14.95.

KAPALUA GRILL AND BAR ★   *American-Continental*
200 Kapalua Drive, just across the road from the Kapalua Hotel and a short drive up Kapalua Drive (669-5653) HOURS: Lunch 11:30-3 pm and dinner 5-10 pm. SAMPLING: With a constantly changing menu you will never know what to expect, but it will all be great! Soft shell crab $18.95, muscovy duck $16.95, seafood marina $15.95-$19.95. Lunches run $7.95-$9.95.

A new menu is printed daily and they include a list of birthday celebrities on the top. If you call in the morning, they'll add the name of your birthday person. Won't they be surprised at dinner! An admirable wine list begins at about $16-$18 with more extravagant selections such as a '45 Chateau Lafit Rothschile at $990. Tank tops are okay daytime attire, but not appropriate for evening. This is a sister facility to Leilani's and Kimo's, but its menu is a little more gourmet. A golf course and ocean view add to the pluses of this restaurant. It's a popular restaurant, so you might want to call ahead for reservations.

KOHO GRILL AND BAR ★ *American*
5095 Napilihau St., Napili Shopping Center. (669-5299) HOURS: Daily 11 am until midnight. SAMPLING: Soup, sandwiches, salads, $4.75-$5.95 include club sandwich, veggie sandwich, chicken, fajita or taco salad. Entrees range from shrimp scampi $9.25, blackened catch of the day $8.65, koho chicken $8.95, fettucini primavera $7.65. COMMENTS: A great new addition to West Maui. Koho's is a popular stop offering a diverse menu and affordable prices which boils down to great family dining. The same operators run this restaurant and also the beautiful new Plantation House in Kapalua and another Koho Grill and Bar in Kahului. They also have a great keiki (kids) menu and, knowing how fussy some kids can be, they'll even cut the crusts off the sandwiches!

ORIENT EXPRESS *Thai-Chinese*
Napili Shores Resort, one mile before Kapalua (669-8077) HOURS: Dinner 5:30-10 pm. SAMPLING: Ginger beef, garlic shrimp, seafood in clay pot, and spinach pork are priced $7.95-$14.95. COMMENTS: This restaurant is run by the same folks who operate Chez Paul. They have an early bird special for $11.95.

PINEAPPLE HILL *Continental*
Up past Napili on the "freeway to nowhere," turn left for Kapalua and you will see the entrance. (669-6129) HOURS: Dinner 5-10 pm with cocktails beginning at 4:30. SAMPLING: Dinners include a house salad, vegetables and rolls. Entrees begin at $9.95 for linguine with herb sauce to $24.95 for shrimp Tahitian. Other selections offer New York pepper steak, rack of lamb and fresh island fish.

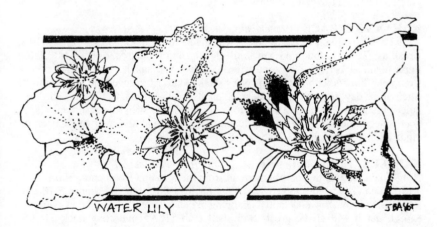

WATER LILY

This was once the home of plantation manager David Fleming. He was one of Maui's early agricultural pioneers who helped establish mango, liche, pineapple and other exotic plants and trees. Just past Kapalua is the beach park bearing his name. He completed the plantation house in 1915 and planted those beautiful Norfolk Pines which line the drive. It opened for dining in the early 1960s. Pineapple Hill has one of the loftiest settings for sunset viewing. We recommend enjoying cocktails out on the front lawn while watching the sun descend. Recent renovations have freshened up the interior. Several recent reports indicate that both service and food have improved, although in the past we have had mixed reviews.

PIZZA FRESH *Italian*
Napili Plaza, 5095 Napilihau St., (669-6180) HOURS: Open for lunch and dinner 11:30 am-9 pm. SAMPLING: Pizzas are served in four sizes and available with white or wheat crust in thick or thin varieties. Grilled chicken, capers, fresh basil or garlic, sun dried tomatoes or zucchini are among the many varied toppings offered. In addition to pizza, owners Elizabeth and Craig Blum have added an Italian deli. Items include lasagna, eggplant parmesan, prawn and tomato concasse, and more. Salads include garden Greek or Caesar. Catering available through their "Unlimited Pastabilities" and orders to go. They also have TCBY yogurt and dessert items.

THE POOL BAR AND RESTAURANT
At the new Ritz Carlton in Kapalua. Indoor and outdoor dining. Not open as we go to press.

POOL TERRACE RESTAURANT AND BAR *International*
Kapalua Bay Hotel, poolside (669-5656) HOURS: Lunch 11 am-5:30 pm. SAMPLING: Open only for lunch, with occasional special dinner functions. Overstuffed sandwiches include Mexican club, reuben on rye or albacore tuna salad $7.95-$9.95. Pizzas $11.75-$12.50 and entrees such as stir fry shrimp $16.95, cashew chicken $13.50 or shabu shabu $8.95. COMMENTS: The beautiful location of this casual poolside setting features an ocean view from every seat.

ROY'S KAHANA BAR AND GRILL ★ *Pacific Rim Cuisine*
4405 Honoapiilani Hwy., Kahana Gateway (669-6999) HOURS: Currently dinner only, but plans are to add a Sunday brunch. SAMPLING: Chef's nightly specials include an ever-changing assortment of pasta, pizzas and variations of local lamb and beef, Northwest salmon and fresh Hawaiian fish, priced $18-$23. Crispy lemon grass chicken $11.95, grilled shrimp & clam linguine $8.50/$16.95, mongolian style loin of lamb $16.75, individual size pizzas include grilled shrimp and eggplant or Szechuan Shrimp pizzas $6.95.

We've heard from visitors and locals alike that this is a terrific new addition to the Kahana area and Maui as well. The food is better than good, it's great. The only negative is that because of the popularity and crowds, the noise level has proven a little too loud for some. The high ceilings with no insulation also contribute to the noise, even when it isn't crowded. Roy's was rated as the top overall restaurant for 1992 in the "Best of Maui" in a survey conducted by Maui News.

SEA HOUSE   *American-Local style*

5900 Lower Honoapiilani Rd., beachfront at Napili Kai Beach Club (669-1500) HOURS: Breakfast 8-11, lunch 12-3, and dinner 6-9. Taco bar Fridays only 3-7 pm, weather permitting. SAMPLING: Luncheon fare includes sandwiches and salads $5.25-$7.25. Their dinner menu offers items in either full or light portions. Light suppers include bucket of little neck clams with garlic bread $11.95 or tempura shrimp and vegetables $14.95. Other entrees are served with kula green salad, rice or potato, vegetable and rolls and include scampi Olowalu $19.50, veal forestiere $17.95 or roast rack of lamb $21.95. Nightly specials are complete dinners with entrees of prime rib and scampi on Saturday $12.95, mahi with lemon caper sauce on Monday $11.95 or baked lobster tail on Thursday $12.95. Friday evenings is their Foundation Dinner Show, adults $25, children $20. COMMENTS: One reader reports that they sampled the Thursday evening lobster special and found it to be very good! A nice oceanfront location is a plus too! Local entertainment most nights 8-10 pm.

EXPENSIVE

THE PLANTATION HOUSE ★   *Seafood-Continental*

2000 Plantation Club Drive, Kapalua (669-6299) HOURS: Lunch 11 am-4 pm, dinner from 5:30 pm, Saturday and Sunday brunch 8 am-3 pm. SAMPLING: Serves a la carte Sunday brunch featuring french toast, potato pancakes, Eggs Benedict or Eggs Blackstone or a smoked salmon benedict. $4.75-$7.95. Lunch offers wok fried vegetables with meat, pizza, salads and sandwiches $5.95-$8.25. Dinner specialties include fresh fish prepared a choice of six ways, pork chops, "pepa" steak, mixed grill, "duck under the influence," home on the range chicken and pasta $14.95-$21.95. COMMENTS: Someone had fun writing this menu! This is one of the best new additions to the Maui dining scene in recent memory. The food is great and complimented by what is, no doubt, the best oceanview dining location in West Maui. Located in the clubhouse of the Plantation Golf Course, the management is well experienced with the dining scene on Maui. This restaurant is affiliated with the popular Koho Grill & Bar in Kahului and in Napili. If you have a sweet tooth, don't miss the "Brownie to Da Max." It is sure to become the Hula Pie of the '90s. It is served in a huge dish and it is plenty big for two to enjoy. Plan to come a half hour or so before sunset to experience the view!

PLANTATION HOUSE RESTAURANT

THE BAY CLUB ★ *French-Seafood*
At Kapalua near the entrance to the resort (669-8008 after 5 pm, 669-5656 before 5 pm) HOURS: Lunch 11:30-2 and dinner 6-9:30 pm. SAMPLING: Lunches include Mediterranean prawns served on angle hair pasta with artichoke hearts and capers $14.50 or Bay Club House sandwich $8.50. For dinner select from the soups salads or appetizer categories and sample an avocado and papaya salad, fresh oysters on the half shell or seafood chowder $5.50 - $12.50. Entrees of fresh fish, bouillabaisse, shellfish, lamb, capon, chicken, veal or duck $22-$28.95.

The restaurant is situated on a promontory overlooking the ocean, a perfect spot from which to enjoy the scenic panorama along with pupus and cocktails. You might want to indulge in one of their ice cream libations, such as a Bay Lounger (dark rum, fresh pineapple and ice cream) or the Bay Club Delight (Kahlua, Grand Marnier, Amaretto and ice cream) $6 ish. Extensive wine list. The dress code requires swimsuit coverups for lunch and, in the evening, long sleeve dress shirts or jackets for men and no denim. A pianist serenades you through dinner adding a romantic touch. With the changes in ownership over the last few years, service has suffered. We hope that the current management can restore the impeccable service and food; because, for us, this has always been a very special restaurant.

THE SUNSET GRILL
At the Ritz Carlton at Kapalua. Seating for 130 in main dining room plus a 15-seat private dining facility. Not open as we go to press.

KIHEI

INEXPENSIVE

ALEXANDERS FISH, CHICKEN AND RIBS
1913 S. Kihei Rd. (874-0788) HOURS: 11 am-11 pm daily. SAMPLING: Meals $4.95-$9.95. Mahi, scallops, oysters, calamari, clams, chicken, ono, BBQ chicken sticks, and shrimp yakitori. Fish available by the piece. A la carte items include zucchini sticks, cornbread, french fries, rice, coleslaw, onion rings or a broiled ono or broiled chicken sandwich. Dine in with limited seating or take out. Received the 1992 award for Best Fish and Chips in the Maui News dining contest.

AZEKA'S SNACK SHOP *Local Style*
Azeka's Place Shopping Center on South Kihei Rd. HOURS: 9:30-4 pm Mon.-Sat. SAMPLING: Plate lunches $3.10-$4.15, tuna sandwiches $1.05, teriburger $1.80, hamburger $1.10. COMMENTS: The teriburger contains marinated beef and is quite tasty. Among the plate lunch selections are teriyaki beef or meat loaf, served with rice and macaroni salad and packed in a styrofoam carton for convenience "to go." Several picnic tables offer limited outdoor seating.

CHUMS ★ *Local Style*
2439 S. Kihei Rd., Suite 20-A, Kihei (874-9000) HOURS: Daily 6:30 am-11 pm. Entertainment nightly. SAMPLING: The menu at this new location is exactly the same as the Wailuku location, although the prices are just a little higher on some

items. A huge bowl of saimin $3.75, French dip $5.45, hot turkey, roast pork or roast beef sandwich $5.25, island style meals such as pork katsu, roast pork, teri beef from $5.10-$6.75. COMMENTS: Breakfast served 6:30-11 am, menu is the same for lunch and dinner. A great family dining spot and a nice alternative to Denny's! Evening entertainment is Hawaiian contemporary music or karaoke.

DENNY'S   *American*
Kamaole Shopping Center HOURS: 24 hours daily. SAMPLING: Burgers, local style dishes and dinners which include steak, seafood and chicken $6.79-$10.79. Breakfast served anytime. COMMENTS: From 5 am until 2 pm, Monday thru Friday they have "stopwatch specials" served in 10 minutes or less, guaranteed. Also available are senior specials.

DOMINO'S PIZZA   *Italian*
2349 S. Kihei Rd. in ABC Shopping Center (874-6000) HOURS: 11 am until midnight, Friday and Saturday until 1 am. Three Domino's locations, one in Lahaina, another in Kihei and a third in Kahului. This is a chain of restaurants that offer delivery.

HENRY'S BAR AND GRILL   *American*
Lipoa Shopping Center (879-2849) HOURS: 10 am-2 am SAMPLING: Grill your own steak or chicken, served with salad bar and roll $8.75. COMMENTS: Four televisions, one a big screen, for sporting events or stop by to see your favorite soap opera!

INTERNATIONAL HOUSE OF PANCAKES   *American*
Azeka's Place Shopping Center on South Kihei Rd. HOURS: Sun.-Thurs. 6 am-midnight, Fri. and Sat. 6 am-2 am. SAMPLING: Breakfast, lunch, and dinner choices served anytime. The usual breakfast fare and sandwiches. Dinners run $5.95-$10.95 and include soup or salad, roll and butter. COMMENTS: A children's menu is available. Very crowded on weekends.

McDONALD'S   *American*
1900 area of South Kihei Rd. at the Kihei Shopping Center HOURS: Breakfast, lunch, and dinner. Breakfast served only from 6 am-10 am. SAMPLING: There are a few unusual island items added to the menu. For breakfast, you can have Portuguese sausage with rice, and chase it down with chilled guava juice. COMMENTS: Indoor seating available. Prices slightly higher than mainland.

MARGARITA'S BEACH CANTINA   *Mexican*
101 N. Kihei Rd., Kealia Village (879-5275) HOURS: Lunch 11:30-2:30 and dinner 5-10 pm, bar from 5 pm. SAMPLING: Enchiladas, tamales, tacos, burgers and sandwiches $7.95-$10.95, full dinners $11.95-$13.95. COMMENTS: Outdoor dining.

NEW YORK DELI   *American*
2395 S. Kihei Rd., (879-1115) HOURS: 10 am-9 pm. SAMPLING: In addition to luncheon meats there is a wide selection of salads and entrees such as lasagna. Bagels, in every variety, are flown in fresh from New York! Sandwiches run $5-6.

PANDA EXPRESS *Northern Style Chinese*
At Azeka Place II Shopping Center. COMMENTS: Report that they offer a complete meal for under five dollars. They will feature a deli-style roasting department offering dishes such as roast duck, Chinese spare ribs and shoyu chicken. A separate noodle department and full service catering available as well. A chain restaurant which is based in California. Not open as we go to press.

PARADISE FRUIT ★ *Healthy American*
Located at the Rainbow Mall (879-1723) HOURS: 6 am-10 pm. Food served until 9 pm. SAMPLING: "Healthy oriented" sandwiches, salads, and smoothies. Veggie or turkey sandwich $4.25, salads $2.50-$5.50, smoothies and shakes $3.25-$3.50. COMMENTS: This is a fruit and vegetable market, including organic produce, that also sells some sundry items. Tucked in the back is their snack bar. Their yogurt shakes and smoothies are delicious! The also have breakfast items, lasagna, tortelli, chow fun and burritos.

PERRY'S SMORGY *American*
1819 S. Kihei Rd., (874-7616) HOURS: Lunch 11 am-2:30 pm, dinner 5 pm-9 pm seven days a week. Breakfast 7:30-11 am on Saturday and Sunday, serving breakfast seven days a week during high season. SAMPLING: Adult breakfast $4.95, lunch $5.95 and dinner $8.95. Kids are charged by the pound, 5 cents a pound for breakfast, 10 cents for lunch or dinner. COMMENTS: Quantity is the key word here. A great place for the teenage appetite that knows no limits. The fare ranges from chicken to fish, roast beef to casseroles, desserts too.

PIZZA FRESH *Italian*
2395 S. Kihei Rd. in Dolphin Plaza (879-1525) HOURS: Daily 3-9 pm. SAMPLING: White or whole wheat crust pizza that they make and you bake. Available in four sizes, small to X-large and thirty-five toppings from which to choose. One topping small $7.75, in X-large it's $20.55. They also deliver!

UPCOUNTRY PRODUCE

ROYAL THAI CUISINE   *Thai*
1280 S. Kihei Rd. at Azeka's Shopping Center (874-0813) HOURS: Mon.-Fri. 11-3 for lunch, daily 5-9 for dinner. SAMPLING: Appetizers, soups, salads and entrees such as chicken cashew basil, evil prince chicken or garlic cabbage $4.75-$6.95. COMMENTS: The prices are pretty decent, but the portions are a little small. Food was good, but nothing outstanding.

THE SANDWITCH   *American*
145 North Kihei Rd., by Sugar Beach Condos (879-3262) HOURS: Mon.-Sat. 11-11, Sunday noon to 11. SAMPLING: Sandwiches, burgers, salads.

SHAKA SANDWICH AND PIZZA ★   *American-Italian*
Located behind Jack 'n the Box in Paradise Plaza on South Kihei Rd. near Azeka's market (874-0331) HOURS: 10 am-9pm Monday thru Saturday, closed Sunday. COMMENTS: If you like New York subway-style pizza you're in for a real treat. If you have no idea what New York subway-style pizza is, you're also in for a real treat. When Paradise Publications sponsored a pizza contest, Shaka Sandwich and Pizza was fairly new and a bit of an unknown to most of the island residents who served as judges. Their gourmet white cheese pizza with garlic and broccoli was outstanding. Don't miss stopping by for a piece of the pie!

THE SPORTS PAGE GRILL AND BAR   *American*
2411 S. Kihei Rd. (879-0602) HOURS: 11:30 am-11:30 pm. SAMPLING: New York Yankees Hot Dogs, Foul Ball Burger, Edmonton Oilers Tuna Melt, Dick Butkus Corned Beef and Cheese, Flo Jo Roast Beef. Also hot dogs and salads.

You probably already have the idea! This is definitely the spot for the sports aficionado. With confident good humor their menu resembles a newspaper tabloid and reads, "You will be served in 5 minutes...or maybe 10 minutes...or maybe even 15 minutes...relax and enjoy yourself." It may take at least 15 minutes to read over the menu. The front page covers exotic beverages and a hearty selection of imported beers, followed on the inside by dugout dogs, champion burgers, sport fishing sandwiches, bowl games (those are salads), and "game favorite" sandwiches. Not much on the menu over $5.95. A big screen TV with remote monitors and satellite reception should ensure plenty of good conversation for the athletic enthusiast! They have added live entertainment with comedy performers on Saturday night.

SUBWAY SANDWICHES   *American*
Kukui Shopping Center (879-9955) HOURS: 9 am-midnight. Sandwiches $2.69-$7.39, salads include roast beef, seafood, chef or tuna $3.29-$5.99.

SUDA SNACK SHOP   *Local Style*
61 S. Kihei Rd. by the gas station along S. Kihei Rd. (879-2668) Pizza after 3 pm phone (879-7133) HOURS: 5 am-1 pm, pizza after 3 pm. SAMPLING: Plate lunch $4.75, burgers $1.65-$2.40, chow fun $2.40. The pizza portion of the restaurant is open 3 pm-9 pm. Both closed Sunday. COMMENTS: We were disappointed that this little "dive" wasn't one of the island's best kept secrets. The burgers were so-so, the french fries were pricey for the portion and the chow fun wasn't a meal, it was snack size. See you in Wailuku for burgers and chow fun!

MODERATE

AKINA'S ON THE BEACH
760 S. Kihei Rd., in the Menehune Shores condominium (879-0076) Former location of The Breakers Restaurant. Not open as we go to press. We'll update you in our Maui newsletter!

BUZZ'S WHARF *American-Seafood*
Maalaea Wharf area (244-5426) HOURS: Everyday 11 am-3 pm for lunch, 5-9 for dinner. SAMPLING: Lunch includes sandwiches, salads and hot entrees $3.95-$12.95. Dinners include shrimp, trout, oysters, spaghetti, BBQ ribs and scallops $9.95-$26.95. COMMENTS: Offers a lovely Maalaea harbor view. The service remains mediocre to poor, but the food, particularly their specialty Tahitian shrimp, is very good. Bar/lounge area.

C & R CANTINA *Mexican*
2463 South Kihei Rd., Kamaole Shopping Center (879-4488) HOURS: Lunch 11 am-2:30 pm, Dinner from 5 pm. SAMPLING: Dinner selections include Mexican omelet, machamacha (scrambled eggs with shredded beef, onions, peppers), calamari steak or mucho relleno, prices range from $8.95-$11.95. Children's menu available.

CANTON CHEF *Cantonese-Szechuan*
Kamaole Shopping Center (879-1988) HOURS: Lunch 11-2 pm and dinner 5-9:30 pm. SAMPLING: Vegetable, chicken, beef, duck, seafood and pork dishes priced $5.50-$11. COMMENTS: Owned in conjunction with the Hong Kong Restaurant. Orders to go.

CHUCK'S ★ *American*
Kihei Town Center (879-4488 or 879-4489) HOURS: Lunch Monday to Friday 11 am-2:30 pm, interim menu Mon.-Fri. 2:30-5:30, dinner 5:30-10:00 pm daily. SAMPLING: Dinner selections include rice or baked potato or fries and salad bar and bread. Beef kabobs $11.95, chicken teriyaki $13.95, kalbi ribs $14.95, baby back ribs $14.95. Fresh and imported fish $18.95. COMMENTS: No reservations taken. Children's menu $6-$11. Especially popular for its salad bar.

ERIK'S SEAFOOD BROILER *American-Seafood*
2463 S. Kihei Rd., Kamaole Shopping Center (879-8400) HOURS: Dinner 5-10 pm. SAMPLING: Fresh Hawaiian fish dinners include soup or salad, potato or rice, vegetable and bread $20.95. Other entrees include stuffed prawns $19.95, coquilles St. Jacque $17.95, BBQ shrimp $18.95, rack of lamb $24.95 and filet and scampi $25.95.

FRANGIPANI *American*
175 E. Lipoa St., at the Maui Sun Hotel (875-9000) HOURS: Breakfast 6:30-11 am, Sunday brunch 8:30 am-2:30 pm, lunch 11 am-2:30 pm., pupus 2:30-9 pm, dinner 5:30-9 pm, lounge open until 11 pm, and on Friday and Saturday until 1 am. SAMPLING: Sunday champagne brunch offers a 12 item entree with an omelette station, salad bar and sundae bar $17.95 adults, $10.95 kids. Daily breakfast buffet is $7.95 adults, $5.95 children. Items off the menu are available as well. Lunch features soup, salads and sandwiches, burgers $4.95-$7.95.

Dinners are moderately priced with lighter fare including Oriental stir fry $12.95, honey stung chicken $5.95, steak sandwich $9.95 and entrees such as Sun Prawns $17.95, Seafood Medley $19.95, and their special inflation fighter prime rib $12.95. Friday seafood buffet $16.95 adults/$12.95 kids, Saturday is a prime rib buffet for the same price. COMMENTS: Dining room entertainment ranges from talent night, to country western music, to ballroom dancing.

FRESH ISLAND FISH   *American-Seafood*
Maalaea Harbor (242-5364) HOURS: 10 am-5 pm Mon.-Sat. SAMPLING: Menu changes daily. COMMENTS: This restaurant/seafood market is not inexpensive, but you can pick up some fresh fish to cook at your condo. Varied fish entrees served daily.

GREEK BISTRO ★   *Greek*
Kai Nani Shopping Center, 2511 South Kihei Rd. (879-9330) HOURS: Dinner served 5-9:30 pm. SAMPLING: Prawns Island style $12.95, mousaka $10.95, lamb shishkabob $12.95 or Mediterranean chicken $10.95. COMMENTS: This little restaurant is a delightful surprise. We tried the Greek Gods Platter which was a combo of Greek specialties for $11.95 and found it excellent. Table seating is limited to a small outdoor area. Check this one out!

ISANA SHOGUN   *Japanese Teppanyaki*
515 S. Kihei Rd., (874-5034) HOURS: Teppan dinner 5-9 pm sushi bar 5:30-10 pm, bar 5 pm, karaoke from 8:30 pm. SAMPLING: Sushi bar available as well as seven teppanyaki tables which serve entrees ranging from $15.95 for chicken teppanyaki, $29.95 for steak and lobster. All entrees include shrimp appetizer, salad, soup, teppan vegetables, rice and Japanese tea along with two dipping sauces. COMMENTS: Isana means "big fish" or "whale" in Japanese and a giant whale sculpture by James Hagedorn graces the central stairway. Upstairs in the Mermaid Lounge is a karaoke bar.

ISLAND FISH HOUSE   *American-Polynesian-Seafood*
1945 South Kihei Rd. (879-7771) HOURS: Dinner from 5:30 pm. SAMPLING: Complete dinners include chowder or salad, au gratin potatoes or island rice, fresh vegetables and homemade bread. Chicken teriyaki $12.95, scallops $16.95, shrimp polynesian $17.95, or their daily fresh fish which is offered cooked six different ways. COMMENTS: Well it is sad, but true. One of our favorite island restaurants seems to have slipped a bit and we've found it necessary to take away the "star" rating. Our favorite carrots were even a disappointment, and the interior is sadly overdue for some refurbishing. During our recent visit the fish was adequately cooked, but not memorable. The owners also operate Ferrari's restaurant right behind Island Fish House. We found it excellent, so perhaps the newer restaurant has involved the energies of the owners/operators and Island Fish House has suffered. We'll update you in our quarterly newsletter about any changes!

KIHEI PRIME RIB AND SEAFOOD HOUSE ★   *American*
2511 South Kihei Rd., in the Nani Kai Village (879-1954) HOURS: Dinner from 5-10 pm. SAMPLING: Ribs $17.95, polynesian chicken $17.95, prime rib in varied cuts from $19.95. Salad bar a la carte is $8.95. Early bird dinner special of chicken, prime rib or fish $10.95-$12.95. COMMENTS: Dinners include a salad bar, Caesar salad, or red snapper chowder, and is served either with fettucini

noodles or rice. Homemade bread also accompanies your meal. The salad bar was very good, and the choices included sweet Kula onions. The high-beamed ceilings with the hanging plants compliment the gorgeous wood carvings done by Bruce Turnbull and paintings by a German artist, Sigrid. They offer piano entertainment nightly. A long time Kihei favorite.

LA BAHIA   *Mexican*
2511 S. Kihei Rd., at Kai Nani Village, formerly the location of La Familias (875-1007) HOURS: dinner 4-10 pm daily, the lounge is open 11:30 am-midnight, pupus served 2 pm until midnight, 99 cent margaritas 2-6 pm daily. SAMPLING: Fajitas, chimichangas, tostadas, enchiladas, burritos $7.95-$12.95. Specialties include fresh island fish $16.95, nopales (cactus) chicken $11.95, carne picado $12.95 or camarones (shrimp) tigre $14.95.

LUIGI'S PASTA PIZZARIA   *Italian*
Azeka's Shopping Center on S. Kihei Rd. (879-4100) HOURS: Daily 11:30 am until midnight, bar until 2 am. SAMPLING: Lunch selections include pasta or pizza as well as sandwiches such as submarines, French dip or club. Dinner selections $12.99-$18.99

MAUI LU LONGHOUSE   *Polynesian*
Maui Lu Resort, 575 South Kihei Rd. (879-5881) HOURS: 7 am-9 pm. for breakfast, lunch and dinner. Jesse Nakooka has returned to the Maui Lu and entertains several evenings a week.

OCEAN TERRACE   *Polynesian-American*
2960 South Kihei Rd., Mana Kai Hotel (879-2607) HOURS: Breakfast, lunch and dinner served between 7 am and 10 pm. SAMPLING: Breakfasts include specialty pancakes, i.e. coconut or macadamia. Lunches offer salads, sandwiches and hot entrees $3.95-$10.95. Dinner selections include teriyaki chicken, veal marsala, prawns Tahitian. COMMENTS: Operated by the owners of Island Fish House, this restaurant has a contemporary look enhanced by its oceanfront location. A wonderful spot to enjoy cocktails and the sunset. Pupu items range from local dishes to Polynesian foods. Children 12 and under half portions for price. Early bird specials 5-6 pm.

SILVERSWORD GOLF CLUB RESTAURANT   *American-French*
Located at the Silversword Golf Course (879-0515) HOURS: 10:30 am-3 pm for lunch daily SAMPLING: Sandwiches, hamburgers, soups, salads and lunch entrees are affordably priced $3.25-$5.75. Located on a lofty setting with a pleasant view of Kihei and beyond Kaho'olawe and Molokini.

SURFER JOE'S GRILL & BAR   *American*
61 South Kihei Rd. is located next to Suda's Store in Kihei. (Formerly the location of the Hong Kong Restaurant.) (879-8855) SAMPLING: A limited, but interesting! A South Swell Burger is a mahi filet at $5.50. Hookipa Sandwich is a vegetarian blend of lettuce, tomato, onions, cheese, cream cheese and sprouts $4.50. "Totally Awesome Honey Chicken" $6. Also available are Groomed Shrooms, tempura deep-fried or sauteed mushrooms, "Totally Tubed Calamari," "Duke's Fried Zukes" and fresh fruit ice cream smoothies. A funky bar with booths and a patio. Food available TO GO! No personal checks or credit cards.

EXPENSIVE

CARELLI'S ON THE BEACH   *Italian*
2980 S. Kihei Rd. at the Wailea Oceanfront Hotel (875-0001) HOURS: Dinner only 6-10 pm nightly. No reservations, valet parking. SAMPLING: Pastas selections include spaghetti con vongole (fresh clams, garlic, parsley, olive oil and white wine) $17, rigatoni alla napoletana (tomato sauce with beef short ribs and lamb sausage) $16. Specialties of the house offer Carelli's zuppa di mare cioppino $28, fresh island fish $22, or scaloppini di vitello (veal served either marsala or piccata) $26. Rocco's after hours mangia menu (10 pm until closing) offers seafood cannelone $12, fettucine alfredo $8 or pizzas $6-9. COMMENTS: One of a handful of restaurants on Maui that are really on the beach. There is a minimum food charge of $15 per person at dining tables, no minimum at Rocco's Angia Bar.

FERRARI'S ★   *Californian-Mediterranean*
1945 S. Kihei Rd. behind Island Fish House. (879-1535) HOURS: Dinner only 5-9 pm. SAMPLING: Fresh seafood and freshly made pastas. Try fettucine carbonara $13.95, seafood marina $21.95, or fettucine primavera $14.95, pizza $9.95-$12.95.

The menu is Italian with a 'California flair. The dining room is highly stylized, with lots of tile and glass and sets a rather elegant mood. Ferrari's participated in our Pizza contest and shocked the judges with an innovative smoked duck creation. It isn't on their menu, but ask and they'll make it for you! The items we sampled included scampi, fettucini and fish, and were all excellent and the service was friendly and efficient. Check on early bird specials, and look for their brochures in the restaurant/activity display racks. It has a coupon for a 20% discount on two regularly priced entrees.

WATERFRONT ★   *Seafood*
At the Milowai Condo, Maalaea (244-9028) HOURS: Dinner only from 5 pm. SAMPLING: Tournedos of beef au poivre $23.95, chicken piccata $16.95, veal scaloppine ala marsala $23.95 and fresh fish, cooked 6 - 8 different ways.

A family operation, the Smith's have done a great job with this oceanfront location. The meals, especially the fresh fish are fabulous and it is quickly garnering a popular following of repeat customers. The dinner entrees are all served with garden salad with a choice of four homemade dressings, vegetables and rice or potatoes. The Scallops au gratinee ($22.95) included lots of very big and flavorful scallops and loaded with cheese. The Chef Ron's Wild Game du Jour is an interesting option that might range from pheasant to rabbit or venison. The En Bastille was "ono" as well at $26 was a huge portion of angel hair pasta sauteed with fresh scallions, mushrooms and tomatoes. Our original impression of the dessert was that they looked better than they tasted, and we're glad to report the quality has improved. Selections range from white chocolate cheesecake with sour cream topping to an apple pear pie with macadamia nut ice cream. They have been receiving numerous accolades and they are well deserved.

WAILEA-MAKENA

Many new resorts and restaurants opened in Wailea during 1990 and 1991 and we will keep you updated with restaurant reviews in the *MAUI UPDATE*. Be sure and share with us your comments as well!

LOUNGES

KEA LANI SUNSET TERRACE ★
The Kea Lani resort presents evening contemporary music, appetizers and special prices on beverages. Each week a different selection of appetizers is offered including tastes from Mexico Sicily, China and the Pacific Rim. The appetizers are complimentary, and at a chef's saute station additional items availalbe at nominal prices. There is also the Kea Lani Lounge which overlooks the Pacific Ocean and tropical gardens and features a very different atmosphere with couches and overstuffed chairs.

MOLOKINI LOUNGE ★
Maui Prince Hotel, Makena (874-111) A wonderful opportunity for a sunset view. Entertainment and complimentary pupus served 4:00-6:30 pm daily. Call to check on entertainment available. Currently the entertainment schedule is as follows. Contemporary Hawaiian sounds of Mele Ohana nightly from 4:30-6:30 pm in the Molokini lounge; Out in the atrium, a classic duo, The Sterling Strings, plays Sat.-Thurs. evenings 6:30-8:30 pm; Ron Kualaau entertains 9-11 pm Tuesday thru Sunday.

SUNSET TERRACE ★
Stouffer Wailea Beach Resort, on the lobby level. (879-4900) HOURS: open nightly 5-10 pm. Pleasant evening entertainment seven nights a week 5:30-9:30. You can order pupus.

SUNSET BAR ★
Diamond Resort, Wailea (874-0500) HOURS 4-11 pm. Located in the foothills, overlooking Wailea, West Maui, Molokini and the beautiful blue Pacific is this hidden gem. One of the best views on the island is featured at this exclusive resort. The good news is that the restaurants and bar are open for non-resort guests. They currently feature a special Aloha Friday event offering drink specials, complimentary pupus, live entertainment and freshly made $1 sushi is available on Fridays from 5:30-7:30 pm. A real find and a best bet for a great sunset view, but arrive early!

VOLCANO BAR
Located at the Grand Hyatt Wailea (875-1234) HOURS: 7 am until dusk, continental breakfast 7 am-11 am. Sandwiches and salads served 11 am-6 pm.

INEXPENSIVE

CAFFE CIAO ★ *Italian*
Kea Lani (875-4100) HOURS: 6:30 am-8 pm. SAMPLING: Full bakery, capuccinos, deli items, Italian gelatos, homemade sausages, antipasto items. Sandwiches $5-9, pastries $.60-$2.40, specialty dishes $5-$9, giant pizza bread $8.95. COMMENTS: Black and gold decor with high stools and tables. Enjoy indoor and outdoor patio seating along the row of shops. While dining you can relax by reading one of a variety of complimentary newspapers, from the San Francisco Chronicle to the Australian News. The sausages are made in-house and they have several varieties, Italian, Portuguese, French and garlic, or try one of several salami varieties including wild boar! They smoke their own salmon and produce their own private label of products, macadamia nut honey, peppercorn ketchup, Maui poha berry butter or pineapple jam. Other items sold are imported from Italy. Jumbo oatmeal or chocolate chip cookies, freshly made cheese Danish croissants, macadamia nut pies, Italian tiramisu, banana nut bread, are just a few of the items tempting the visitor. But don't forget, they also have deli style sandwiches! Also "gelati" and Italian sodas.

ED & DON'S *American*
Wailea Shopping Village. (879-1227) HOURS: 9 am-7 pm Mon. thru Sat. 10 am-6 pm on Sunday. SAMPLING: Sandwiches, ice cream and candies available here.

MAKENA GOLF COURSE RESTAURANT *American*
5415 Makena Alanui. At the Golf Course, just beyond Wailea (879-1483) HOURS: Lunch 10:30 am-3:30 pm, pupus 3-6:30 pm. SAMPLING: Salads, soup and sandwiches $4.25-$8.50. COMMENTS: Furnished in a tan and green theme, this open-air restaurant features an outstanding golf and ocean view.

MAUI ONION *American*
Stouffer Wailea Beach Resort, poolside (879-4900) HOURS: Lunch 11 am-3:30 pm, bar open until 6:30 pm. Take out sandwiches for golfers $4. SAMPLING: Salads, burgers and sandwiches $5.25-$9.50. Lunches include cajun grilled chicken breast sandwich $9, maui onion rings $4.75, sashimi $9.50, cheeseburgers $8. COMMENTS: Great onion rings and burgers!

POLO BEACH GRILLE AND BAR *American*
Kea Lani, poolside. (875-4100) HOURS: 11 am-6 pm. Luncheon menu priced $6-$13 offers local tuna salad, thai chicken wings, Caesar salad or grilled shrimp. Or sample some refreshing ginger sorbet. Also features a swim up bar.

SET POINT CAFE *American*
131 Wailea Ike Place atop the pro shop at the Wailea Tennis Center. (879-3244) Daily 8-11 am for breakfast, lunch 11-2 pm. SAMPLING: Breakfast runs $3-$6, lunch selections include pasta dishes, sandwiches, soup or salad $5-$8.25.

WIKI WIKI PIZZA OF KIHEI ★ *Italian*
2411 S. Kihei Rd. (874-9454) HOURS: 11 am-10 pm. SAMPLING: Limited table seating outside. Pizzas are baked and available to go. Pizzas from $8.95 for a 12 inch cheese. A vegetarian delight, large is $18.95. Co-winner of our pizza contest in the over all best pizza category.

MODERATE

BISTRO MOLOKINI ★ *"Light" California-Italian*
Grand Hyatt Wailea (875-1234) HOURS: 11:30 am-2:30 pm, dinner 6-10:30 pm.
SAMPLING: Lunch selections include grilled mahi $13.50, proscuitto and roasted pepper served on a rosemary baguette $9, California cobb salad $9, pizzas from $8. Save room for some of their delicious gelatos. Smaller children's portions available at half price. Dinner menu changes daily, runs $12.50-$25 includes pizzas, ravioli fruitti di mar $17, fettucini carbona $12.50, grilled veal chop with rosemary $25 or branzino al livornese (sea bass roasted with bell peppers, potatoes and black olives) $19. For dessert sample their tiramisu molokini, Yum! COMMENTS: The menu is definitely Italian, but very light and innovative. The ravioli is not the traditional stuffed pasta squares, but more like squares of pasta with whole pieces and bites of seafood and sauce on top, then more pasta squares laid on top of that. More like seafood with pasta accompaniment than pasta with a little seafood. The sea bass was very good, a thin layer of potato slices baked on top of the fish kept it very moist. The antipasto misto had shrimp, white beans, artichokes, olives, peppers and homemade boccini mozzarella balls, all lightly marinated. The sour dough bread is served with a bottle of extra virgin olive oil mixed with bits of whole garlic, cerrano chili, oregano and rosemary, rather than the ordinary butter option. If you request butter, however, they brought it in little fish shaped "pats"! Capuccino is served with a rock candy swizzle stick to stir it with. And as for desserts - the pizza with raspberry sauce, sweet ricotta and fresh fruit was very good, but far too heavy after a big meal. Perhaps on its own with coffee for a late night meal would be great. The Tiraisu was very good and rich, chocolate and coffee with cream and liqueur, but still light and fluffy tasting. And once again, we appreciate their offering a children's menu! Pizza, burger or chicken nuggets at $3.

CABANA CAFE *American*
Four Seasons, Wailea (874-8000) COMMENTS: A casual atmosphere serving lunch and an afternoon bar with pupus out of doors.

CAFE KIOWAI *Polynesian-American*
Maui Prince Hotel, Makena (874-1111) HOURS: Breakfast, lunch and dinner are served daily with snacks available between regular meal service 6:30 am-10:30 pm. SAMPLING: Breakfasts include old fashioned malted waffles with strawberries and pecans $7, or three egg omelettes including one with smoked salmon, caviar, mushrooms and brie $10.25. Lunches include grilled chicken sandwich $6.75, prime rib and sliced turkey sandwich $12.50 or grilled skirt steak on french bread $12.50. Dinner is served 5-9:30 pm and offers boboli pizzas and pastas $9-$16, wok seared dishes $13.50-$17.50, in addition to jumbo tiger prawns, chicken with soy and ginger glaze or grilled catch of the day $16-$27. The iced tea comes in mango, papaya or peach flavors! COMMENTS: Keiki menu available. Kiowai pronounced "Key-oh-wy" means "fresh flowing water."

CHART HOUSE *American*
100 Wailea Ike Drive, Wailea (879-2875) HOURS: Dinner nightly 5-10 pm. SAMPLING: Seafood selections include swordfish $16.95, coconut shrimp $21.45, prime rib from $18.95, fresh fish and steaks $16.95-$22.95. Former location of the Wailea Steak House. Kids menu available!

FAIRWAY ★ *American-Continental*
100 Kaukahi St., at Wailea Golf Course Clubhouse (879-4060 or 879-3861) HOURS: Breakfast from 7:30, lunch 11-3:30 pm. No longer serving dinner. SAMPLING: Breakfast selections include pancakes $4 and eggs benedict $7.75. Lunch offers burgers $6.25 or turkey clubhouse $6.75. COMMENTS: This restaurant is open-air with outdoor seating available. It offers a beautiful ocean view. Cocktails are available from the adjoining bar, the Waterhole. Their ice cream drinks are richly refreshing any time of day. Here is a sampling to tempt your palate: Fairway Grasshopper - creme de menthe, creme de cocoa, and ice cream all blended together, and topped with chocolate mint liqueur and chocolate sprinkles. Wailea Almond Joy - Amaretto, Kahlua, ice cream, blended and topped with whipped cream and almond slices. Brandy Alexander - Brandy, ice cream, and creme de cocoa blended and sprinkled with nutmeg. These wonderful concoctions run $6-ish.

HARRY'S SUSHI AND PUPU BAR *Japanese*
See Lobster Cove which follows. (879-7677)

ISLAND TERRACE *"Nutritional Cuisine"*
Diamond Resort. 555 Kaukahi St., Wailea (874-0500). HOURS: Breakfast 6-10:30 am, lunch 11 am-2:30 pm. SAMPLING: This restaurant is on the upper level of the Diamond Resort. An exclusive resort which makes their restaurants available to the general public. The menu features eating right selections for the health conscious and describes the theme of this restaurant as nutritionally balanced cuisine in harmony with fitness and longevity.

LANAI TERRACE ★ *International*
Maui Inter-Continental Wailea (879-1922) HOURS: 6-11 am for breakfast. 5-11 pm for dinner. SAMPLING: Breakfast fare ranges from a Continental breakfast or pancakes to the New York breakfast with salmon lox, bagels and cream cheese or the Japanese breakfast of miso soup, butter fish Nitsuki, Tsukemono, rice and tea. $6.95-$12. The breakfast buffet is offered daily at $14.50. Dinners for the light appetite include salads, sandwiches, egg or pasta dishes or indulge in an all-you-can-eat theme buffet nightly. COMMENTS: An attractive, bright and cheery atmosphere. Check out their "theme" nights - Monday and Wednesday are pasta nights, Tuesday its a Mexican Fajita Festival, Oriental Stir Fry is enjoyed on Thursdays, Fridays is a Bavarian Buffet and Saturday rounds out the week with Prime Rib. Buffets run $14.95-$17.95, served 5-9 pm. Early bird specials currently offers adults dining between 5 and 6 pm an additional $3 discount off an adult entree. Indoor or outdoor dining on the Lanai.

SANDCASTLE ★ *American*
3750 Wailea Alanui, Wailea Shopping Center (879-0606) HOURS: Lunch menu 11:30 am-9 pm and dinner daily from 5 pm. SAMPLING: Lunch selections includes soup, salads, and sandwiches $5.95-12.95. Dinner choices of fresh fish, shellfish, pasta, meat and fowl $9.95-14.95. COMMENTS: Their menu has changed a great deal from the last edition of our guide. There are a good variety of selections and since they serve from their lunch menu all day, a good affordable dining option for families.

EXPENSIVE

CAFE KULA *Spa Cuisine*
Located at the Grand Hyatt Wailea (875-1234) HOURS: Breakfast, lunch and dinner. SAMPLING: Breakfasts entice with blueberry stuffed crepe $8, pecan waffles with raspberries $8.50. Lunch and dinner selections vary daily, depending on what the chef finds to be the best and freshest of ingredients. Menu itmes might include rilled breast of chicken with mango-chili sauce and Hawaiian mahi mahi with Kula corn on the cob, Maui snap peas with roasted red peppers served with Kona orange and Maui basil vinaigrette. COMMENTS: Chef Kathleen Daelemans was recently on several television spots showing a bit of what spa cuisine really is. She reported on the Home Show that since beginning as a chef for this trendy new cuisine cookery, she lost 34 pounds. And had a photo to prove it! She describes spa cuisine as food for life, for better living. This means organic produce, local fish and the freshest poultry and meats available all prepared with low sodium, low cholesterol and, of course, low fat. She works with Kula farmers to get the freshest hand-picked produce delivered daily. For the hearty eater, we found the "Nouveau Health" cuisine was a little expensive with tiny portions of food. The multi-grain bread was great though!

GION HAMASAKU ★ *Japanese*
Stouffer Wailea Resort (879-4900) HOURS: Open daily, except Thursday, 6-10 pm, reservations are required for teppanyaki seating and recommended for restaurant dining. SAMPLING: The restaurant offers a selection of complete dinners including Kaiseki (traditional Japanese Table D'hote), Teppanyaki, Tempura, Nabemono and cook your own meals which include Sukiyaki, Shabu Shabu, Yosenabe and Chicken Mizutaki. The meals range $20-$80. A Sushi bar is also available. COMMENTS: The decor of the new Gion Hamasaku is as authentic as its cuisine. Woodwork, screens, stone flooring, bamboo trim, and decorative artifacts were all produced in Japan to exacting standards. In fact, parts of the dining area were actually constructed in Japan before dismantling them for shipment to Stouffer Wailea. The name Gion originates from the Gion district of Kyoto and the Hamasaku family, Kyoto restaurateurs, lend their name and

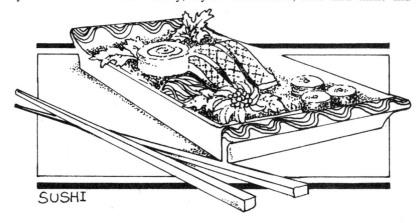

SUSHI

225

culinary expertise to this newest dining establishment. Offering such traditional Japanese fare emphasizes freshness, subtle flavors and delicate preparations. Reserved teppanyaki seating is offered three times nightly. The main dining room seats 22, while private dining rooms seat four to six guests each. The sushi bar accommodates only ten. The restaurant is designed to promote the feeling of privacy and intimacy.

GRAND DINING ROOM ★
Grand Hyatt Wailea (875-1234) HOURS: Sunday champagne brunch 9 am-1 pm. Daily (Mon.-Sat.) breakfast buffet 6:30-11 am. Dinner served nightly 6-10 pm. SAMPLING: Their daily breakfast buffet is $15.50 adults, $7.25 children, but for a gourmet treat try their Sunday champagne brunch at $32 adults, $16 children and indulge in some excellent Hawaiian regional cuisine. Selections include ham with mango chutney, Hawaiian bread sweet rolls, starfruit (fresh off the trees on the property), local gourmet Hawaiian dishes made with natural ingredients, such as jicama salad, guava pastries, chocolate bread pudding, rice pudding and kim chee too! How about a lilikoi guava mousse, Oriental cole slaw, or lomi lomi salmon. But save room for dessert and try marzipan clowns or chocolate whales. Begin your dinner with baked crab cake in sea urchin $12.50 or a warm jade salad with seared sea scallops $10.50. Entrees are priced $27-$35 and include tournedos of veal, five spice pork tenderloin, Shanghai bouillabaisse. COMMENTS: A fabulous dining setting and outstanding food. A great way to pamper yourself.

HAKONE ★ *Japanese*
Maui Prince Resort, Makena (874-1111) HOURS: Dinner only, 6-9:30 SAMPLING: A la carte dinners include nikujaga (boiled thinly sliced pork, potatoes and onion), breaded pork tonkatsu or assorted tempura and begin at $12. Complete dinners $21, kaiseki courses at $43. COMMENTS: Authenticity is the key to this wonderful Japanese restaurant, from its construction (the wood, furnishings and even small nails were imported from Japan) to its food (the rice is flown in as well). The food and atmosphere are both wonderful here, and of course even the presentation of the food is artistic! Their Maui roll is a specialty here, made with smoked salmon, Maui onions and cucumbers. The bento plate is a smaller version of the kaiseki dinner, and more affordable. It includes ahi sashimi, nimono, tempura and mushimono. Nimono is a pickled vegetable while mushimono is a steamed egg custard filled with shrimp, chicken, shitake mushrooms and ginko nuts. The sukiyaki is very good, but it requires a minimum of two orders along with advance reservations. Appetizers range from marinated octopus to chicken yakitori. There is also a sushi bar.

HULA MOONS *Seafood-American*
Maui Inter-Continental Resort (879-1922) HOURS: 11 am-5 pm daily for lunch and dinner. SAMPLING: Lunch includes sandwiches and burgers $7-11. Hula Moons has a wonderful salad bar, $11.50. Entrees include lemon & herb flavored chicken breast $17, lamb chops $24 or an incredible steamed seafood basket filled with scallops, fish, prawns, lobster, Chinese dim sum, Alaska king crab legs and dipping sauces $38. COMMENTS: Hula Moons is dedicated to the spirit of Don Blanding, Hawai'i's well known poet, artist and musician. "Hula Moons" was the title of one of his most popular books. The restaurant is located on the pool level and flickering torches and live Hawaiian music add to the ambiance of this ocean view restaurant. Hula moons provides either indoor or outdoor dining. Early bird

specials are 5-6 pm nightly and are $3 off an adult entree. Live entertainment evenings from 5:30-8 pm.

HUMUHUMUNUKUNUKUA'PUA'A ★ *Seafood*
Grand Hyatt Wailea (875-1234) HOURS: Dinner only 5:30-10:30 pm. SAMPLING: Baked opakapaka in ti leaves with lilikoi butter $22.50, Big Island salmon $23, roast five spice duck on stir fry cabbage $22, lamb shish kebob $23. COMMENTS: This restaurant is named for the trigger fish, the state fish of the islands. Rather a mouthful, so the eatery is more affectionately referred to as humu-humu for short. It is a wonderful dining location. Tucked in the front grounds of the resort it is situated on top of a saltwater pond filled with aquatic life. They also offer smaller size portions for children 12 and under. Entrees are a la carte.

KEA LANI, THE RESTAURANT *Euro-Pacific Cuisine*
4100 Wailea Alanui, Kea Lani Resort (875-4100) HOURS: Breakfast 6:30-11 am and dinner 5:30-11 pm. SAMPLING: Dungeness crab cakes in dill butter sauce $9 or Thai chicken and coconut soup $3.50 can begin your meal, followed by pan seared black angus tenderloin with sweetbreads $24, Ewa chicken breast with sundried tomatoes $17 or grilled New Zealand boneless lamb chops $22. Menu changes daily. Breakfast offers Japanese and American fare $6-$8.50. Coffee $3. COMMENTS: The Kea Lani features their own specialty line of gourmet products which they use in the restaurant and also sell at Caffe Ciao. They include garlic peppercorn catsup, guava catsup, banana nut bread and macadamia nut honey. They utilize fresh island ingredients and have their own Kea Lani herb garden. The hotels fine dining restaurant features 40-foot vaulted ceilings designed in a southern Mediterranean style and offers great ocean views. The menu is termed "Euro-Pacific" cuisine which is a combination of classic cooking styles of Europe with the flavors and foods of the Pacific.

LE GUNJI ★ *Japanese*
555 Kaukahi St., located at the Diamond Resort (874-0500) HOURS: Dinner only. SAMPLING: A teppan-yaki restaurant which requires reservations for the Chef's special be made no later than 4 pm on the day you dine. The Special Course includes a choice of entree, fresh catch, fresh Maine lobster or filet mignon $80 per person. Other meals are the Diamond Course $65, Seafood Course or Beef Steak Course at $50. Two dinner seatings at 6 or 7:30 pm. Newly added is a mini-diamond course for $45. SAMPLING: Not quite a mega-expensive restaurant, but with $50 the cheapest entree, it is getting up there. The dining room is small and intimate with a beautiful garden courtyard located behind where the chef cooks. This style of Teppan-yaki is a bit different in that it is cooked with a French flair. Perfectly logical since their Chef Gunji Ito, from Osaka, previously cooked French cuisine.

LOBSTER COVE-HARRY'S SUSHI BAR *Seafood-Japanese*
Located next to the Chart House in Wailea (879-7677) HOURS: Nightly from 5:30-10:30, Harry's Sushi, operated by Harry Okumara is located adjacent to Lobster Cover and is open until 1 am. Lucien Charbonnier of Chez Paul, Orient Express, J.J.'s and Studio Five recently opened this new restaurant in the former Sakura location. The Sushi Bar remains and is now called Harry's Sushi and Pupu Bar. At Lobster Cove the menu focuses on lobster almost exclusively. Lobster

entrees are $24 and up and they have three kinds of lobster to choose from at $20 - $24 a pound. A 1 1/2 lb. selection was a tail and a couple of claws and the body filled with rice pilaf and accompanied by black beans for $36. The lobster was served with a whiskey sauce which was not exceptional. The Mussels Poulette was described as "in a special cream sauce" which proved to be more like a milky bouillon, lacking in flavor. The Lobster salad was good with more lobster here than in the entree, and the ginger dressing went well with the lobster. However, the salad greens were a lot of unusual varieties that are currently "in" and may or may not be to the taste of all diners. The raviolis were served in an interesting and flavorful sauce with a hint of curry. Served on a square of pasta with scallop and shrimp halves it was then covered with another pasta square and more sauce on top. The lobster in a fish shaped puff pastry looked very nice, but also suffered from a boring sauce. In few of the small quantities and flavorless sauces, a drawn or spicy butter might have better enhanced the lobster which did have good texture and flavor. You also have the opportunity of being introduced to your lobster before it is cooked. The desserts were good and included an excellent flan tart and a chocolate truffle cake served with a very good creme anglaise sauce. Our dining reviewer didn't stop in to try Harry's Sushi and Pupu Bar, but reported that the place was busy! The menu includes maki sushi, nigiri sushi and sashimi.

MAKANI ROOM ★ *American*
Maui Inter-Continental Wailea (879-1922) HOURS: Sunday brunch only, 9 am-1:00 pm. COMMENTS: The buffet is $26 adults, $13 children. Seating is on the large lanai with a scenic view of the neighboring islands or at indoor tables. The feeling at this brunch is enjoyably casual, however, there is nothing casual about their lavishly laden tables. Omelets are cooked to order, as well as other choices which vary but may include fresh seafood, beef or lamb entrees as well as eggs benedict or crepes. Don't forget to save room for at least two trips to the dessert table. The pastry chef here has a wonderful way with the more unusual fruits - we tried a gooseberry pie. Reservations are a really good idea.

PACIFIC GRILL *East-West*
Four Seasons Resort in Wailea (874-8000) HOURS: 6 am-11 pm for breakfast, lunch, dinner and Sunday brunch. SAMPLING: Breakfast is a la carte or from a buffet. Lunch features an informal setting with sandwiches, hamburgers, hot entrees such as fresh fish or pasta and a salad buffet. Dinner features Pacific Rim Cuisine, Asian-Oriental, complimented by continental fare such as lamb and steak. COMMENTS: In addition to Western style selections, guests can choose Oriental Pacific Rim cuisine. Three Chinese chefs are in view at the restaurant's entrance preparing Thai, Vietnamese, Chinese and Japanese dishes. Indoor or lana'i dining.

PALM COURT ★ *International-Buffet*
Stouffer Wailea Beach Resort (879-4900) HOURS: Breakfast 6-11 am, Dinner 6-10 pm. SAMPLING: Daily, except Sunday, champagne breakfast buffet is $14.50. On Sundays an a la carte breakfast menu is offered $2.75-$8 from 6 until 9 am. From 9 am until 2 pm the restaurant shares Sunday Brunch with the adjoining Raffles restaurant. Three evening buffets a week will feature Prime rib on Tuesday $24, Italian buffet on Wednesday $18 and Seafood Buffet on Friday $28. All other nights feature an a la carte menu with prices $5-$22. This open-air dining hall is festively decorated in reds and greens and offers evening breezes and an ocean view. Reservations are accepted only for a group of 5 or more.

PRINCE COURT ★ *Hawaiian Regional Cuisine*
Maui Prince Hotel, Makena (874-1111) HOURS: Dinner 6-9:30 pm, Sunday brunch 10 am-1:30 pm. SAMPLING: Appetizers, soups, and salads $5.25-$12.50 are the prelude to an outstanding selection of delicious entrees. Sample veal chop with Hana apple bananas, grainy mustard and rum cream $28, Kiawe grilled jumbo prawns with basil and ogo cream with black pasta $29 or Medley of fresh vegetables with roasted onion pasta $18. Sunday brunch, $24 adults/$15 children, is an outstanding selection of over 160 items. Items that might be found on the buffet include croissants stuffed with Portuguese sausages or ham, smoked oysters, octopus or island fish, avocados stuffed with crab, or an unusual and delicious midora bisque soup. Brunch entrees during our visit ranged from roast lamb or prime rib to veal piccata. The dessert table is beyond belief! Reservations recommended. COMMENTS: Hawaiian Regional Cuisine is the new "buzz" word in dining experiences in the islands. It is simply the opportunity to experience the many varied selections of fresh foods grown, raised or caught in the islands. The culinary cuisine of the Prince Court is an incredible blend of flavors which highlight the best and freshest Hawaiian produce, meats and fish. Chef Roger Dikon is perhaps one of the best and most innovative chefs in all of Hawai'i and a main force behind the emergence of H.R.C. (Hawaiian Regional Cuisine.) Beautifully situated the dining room offers a splendid view of the ocean and hotel grounds. The Sunday brunch is tops on our list for a tasteful extravaganza.

RAFFLES' ★ *Pacific Rim Cuisine*
Stouffer Wailea Beach Resort (879-4900) HOURS: Sunday brunch 9-2 pm, dinner Mon.-Sat. 6:30-10 pm. Closed Sunday evenings. SAMPLING: Brunch includes champagne, and entrees of chicken, veal, beef and fish which vary weekly. A salad bar, variety of egg dishes and omelets made to your request. Pastries and desserts to delight any sweet tooth. The buffet runs $26 for adults, $14 for children ages 5 - 12. Reservations are accepted and highly recommended for larger groups. The Raffles' dinner menu showcases fresh fish, lamb, veal and lobster dishes with preparations adding an imaginative twist to classically popular dishes. Sort of American flavors with island flair! Sample wok seared mahi mahi with green papaya relish and lilikoi shallot butter or roasted rack of lamb with Moloka'i herbs and garlic potato flan. Entrees run $22-$31. Salads, soups or appetizers $5-$12.50. Desserts, with selections varying daily, $6. They serve dinner nightly at Raffles' from 5-10 pm, and the Sunday Brunch is offered 9 am-2 pm. The wine list includes Italian, French, California, Washington State, Australian, and German selections.

Raffles' recently underwent some renovations. The most distinctive difference is their new intimate dance floor and live music nightly. The decor has changed making the restaurant lighter, more open and spacious, but still very elegant and romantic. They've gone from a very British, with a touch of Singapore, atmosphere to one more like Singapore with a touch of British. The remodeling has made Raffles' a bit smaller, so they now extend out into the Palm Court for their popular Sunday brunch seating. Week nights piano music is featured and on Friday and Saturday a jazz duo perform. The restaurant seats 126 for dinner and a small lounge featuring fine wines by the glass adjoins. Raffles' is named for Sir Thomas Stamford Raffles (1781 - 1826), the British founder of the city of Singapore where the Raffles' Hotel has become a legend. The buffet is a terrific splurge. The dessert bar was constantly being replenished and each new offering looked better than the last. The chocolate mousse merited a second serving and the chocolate rum cake was rich and moist. Aloha wear is acceptable - an extra large muu muu might not be a bad idea!

SATORU RESTAURANT *Japanese*
Diamond Resort, 555 Kaukahi St., Wailea (808) 874-0500. HOURS: Dinner only 6-9 pm. SAMPLING: Wafuu Kaiseki is a set menu for $60. Included in the many varied items is tempura of shrimp, chicken stuffed with strips of burdock, sashimi, marinated dish of seaweed and jellyfish in vinegar. Sushi Kaiseki is $80 per person. Chef's Special courses run $40-$50 per person. Yosenabe $35, Sukiyaki $30, Sashimi $35, Tempura $30. Single dishes or side dishes $5-$20. COMMENTS: This restaurant is located on the lower level of the resort. An exclusive property that makes their fine restaurants available to the general public. The dining hall is large with cathedral-like ceilings and lots of attractive rockwork. Very simple, elegant decor.

SEASONS *Continental-Californian*
Four Season's Resort in Wailea (874-8000) HOURS: Dinner only 6-10 pm. SAMPLING: Pan fried opakapaka with steamed fennel and apple raisin curry sauce, blue Hawaiian prawns and green lip mussels with olive oil and shaved asiago. COMMENTS: Terrace seating with an ocean view combined with background music performed by a jazz trio. The Four Season's Sunset Lounge offers nightly entertainment and dancing 6 pm-1 am.

MEGA-EXPENSIVE

KAISEKI RYORI *Japanese*
Grand Hyatt Wailea (875-1234) Hours: Dinner only. COMMENTS: The "mega-expensive" is a new category this year, since just "expensive" really isn't descriptive enough for this new, very authentic Japanese restaurant. It appears the race is on for which Japanese Restaurant in Wailea can charge the most for a meal. The Japanese restaurant at the Grand Wailea Resort, Kaiseki Ryori, appears to be taking the lead with a per dinner per diner price of $500. Yes, that is not a typo,

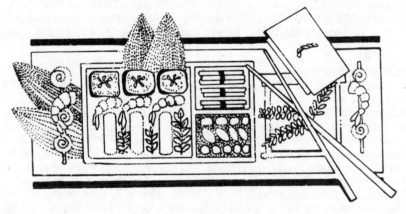

and it is dollars, not yen. This premium dining experience affords the guest to enjoy a Miyabi meal, translated it means elegance. Their menu reads, "Finest complete dinner of super deluxe authentic Japanese culinary art served with Home Made Fruit Wine Sakizuke, Appetizer, Clear Broth Soup, Sashimi, Refreshing Hassun, Broiled Fish, Boiled Vegetables, steak, deep fried Onmono, Vinegared Vegetable, Rice (sushi or noodle), Season's Fruit, Finest Green Tea." Two other set meals, the Aya (coloration) and the Nishiki (golden embroidery), are available at $200 and $100 per person. The Chef's Suggested Kaiseki is for those on a budget, ranging from $70-80 per person. There are two dinner seatings 6-7:30 pm and 8-10:30 pm. Sushi and tempura counters are also available. The sushi counter has a capacity for only 17 people and the tempura bar 15. While we may find these prices outrageous, the Japanese visitor on Maui, accustomed to paying the high "yen" for a meal in their homeland, may not be in for a shock. We're told that a fine meal in Japan runs several hundred dollars or more.

KAHULUI-WAILUKU

Along Lower Main Street in Wailuku are a number of local restaurants which are not often frequented by tourists and may well be one of the island's best kept secrets! Don't expect to find polished silver or extravagant decor, but do expect to find reasonable prices for large portions of food in a comfortable atmosphere. Note that many of these local restaurants may not accept credit cards. Dairy Queen, Pizza Hut, McDonald's, Burger King, and Jack in the Box are a few of the restaurants in and around Kahului and the Maui Mall. These don't require elaboration. Orange Julius at Kaahumanu Mall offers top your own waffles and seafood and turkey pita sandwiches.

INEXPENSIVE

While not restaurants, two of our favorite haunts bear mention here. The *Home Made Bakery* at 1005 Lower Main, open 6 am-9 pm daily, is an island institution. More than just donuts, you'll find unusual specialties such as empanadas, manju, and bread pudding. You can also pick up their items in selected grocery stores. Phone 244-7015.

Nearby is the *Four Sisters Bakery* on Vineyard and Hinano in Wailuku. It is run by Melen, Mila, Beth and Bobbie who arrived from the Philippines after helping their father run a Spanish Bakery in Manila for fifteen years. Not a large selection, but delicious and different items. One is a sweet bread filled with a cinnamon pudding, a sponge cake "sandwich," as well as cinnamon rolls and butter rolls. The only place you can purchase these delicacies is at their bakery or at the Saturday Swap meet in Kahului. 244-9333. Hours 5 am-5 pm Saturday and Sunday, 5 am-8 pm Monday thru Friday.

AKI'S HAWAIIAN FOOD AND BAR   *Hawaiian*
309 N. Market, Wailuku (244-8122) HOURS: Mon.-Sat. 11 am-10 pm, Sunday 5-9 pm. Chicken hekka, Hawaiian favorites such as kalua pig with cabbage and a wonderful octopus soup. The prices remain in the very affordable $4-$6 range for lunch or dinner. A good stop if you want to try some local Hawaiian food.

ARCHIE'S *Japanese*
1440 Lower Main St., Wailuku (244-9401) HOURS: Mon. through Sat. 10:30-2 pm, and 5-8 pm. Closed Sundays. SAMPLING: Their specialty is (Hama'ko) Teishoku $8.50. Don't know what that is? You'll have to stop in and find out. Sandwiches priced $1.30-$3, saimin $1.90, plate lunches run $3-$8. Dinners come with soup, rice and tea $4.80-$8. Sashimi available too! COMMENTS: The food is good and the prices are reasonable.

BACK STREET CAFE *American*
335 Hoohana Blvd., #7A, Kahului (877-4088) HOURS: Mon.-Fri. 10:30 am-2 pm SAMPLING: Daily homemade specials, salads and sandwiches. Take-out lunches available as are catering services. Very popular with the local residents. Daily lunch special is $4.50.

CAFE KUP A KUPPA ESPRESSO BAR-CAFE *International*
79 Church St. (244-0500) HOURS: Mon.-Fri. 7 am- 4:30 pm., Sat. until 1 pm. Possibly opening for dinner. SAMPLING: Breakfast burrito $3.50, frittata $5, belgian waffle $4.50 or "lunch things" which include four kinds of pizza fresca ($6) healthy sandwiches or quesadilla $4-$5. Salads range from Caesar to Oriental chicken $5, and desserts are homemade at $2.75. Bruce Mann, formerly at the Wailuku Grill and Dennis Mitchell, formerly with Stardancer combine for a great new dining addition to Wailuku!

CHINA CHEF *Chinese*
275 Kaahumanu Ave., Kaahumanu Center, Kahului (871-8111) HOURS: Lunch 11-2, dinner 5-9. Dim Sum served daily 11 am- 2 pm. COMMENTS: Stop in for Dim Sum! Most dishes are priced at $2 or $2.50 and include such tasty treats as Chinese malsada or black bean with spare rib. COMMENTS: Chef Sum Lau, who has two Chinese restaurants in Kihei, has opened a third restaurant in the Kaahumanu Mall called the China Chef. They serve a variety of oriental dishes okasuya style, or sit down in their dining room.

CHINA EXPRESS *Chinese*
At Safeway, 170 E. Kamehameha Ave., Kahului (877-3377) SAMPLING: Items available in 1/2 pint, pint, quart or two quart size and items prepared in their Chinese roasting oven are available by the pound. Plate lunches $4.29-$5.99.

CHUM'S *Local Style*
1900 Main Street, Wailuku (244-1000) HOURS: 6:30 am-10:30 pm Monday thru Saturday, Sunday 7 am-10 pm. SAMPLING: Homemade soups, stew, local style meals include beef tomato, mahi mahi, roast pork, fried chicken $5.15-$6.60 and chili, priced $2.50-$5.95. Breakfast served until 11 am, same menu for lunch and dinner. COMMENTS: Food good and filling and a good option for a late evening snack after a movie in Kahului!

THE CLASS ACT ★ *Continental*
Maui Community College Campus, Kahului (242-1210) HOURS: Lunch only Wednesday and Friday 11 am-12:30 pm. COMMENTS: This is one of Maui's best kept secrets. Insiders know they are in for a treat when they stop by for a five-course gourmet lunch for $7.50. The Food Service students of the Maui Community College prepare and wait on the tables as well, with a varied selection

of entrees weekly. Two selections are prepared, one is a healthy heart selection which is low in sodium and fat. The program is only offered during the school year, so be sure and call to check on availability and schedule a reservation.

THE COFFEE STORE
Kaahumanu Center (871-6860) HOURS: Mon., Tues. Wed. 7 am-6 pm, Thurs., Fri 7 am-9 pm. Saturday 8:30 am-6 pm, Sunday 9 am-4 pm. SAMPLING: Muffins $1.85, lasange, $4.50, strudel, cheesecake, assorted pastries $2-$3.50, quiche of the day $3.50. COMMENTS: They are planning to open another store at Azeka's II in Kihei in the fall of 1992 and another is tentatively scheduled for 1993 in Napili. In addition to freshly roasted coffee, they serve locally made fresh pasta dishes, croissants, salads and sandwiches. Voted as having the best capuccino on Maui in the "Best of Maui" contest conducted by the Maui News. They roast their own beans and mail order coffees are also available.

DOMINO'S PIZZA *Italian*
180 E. Wakea Ave., Bay H, Kahului (871-5000) HOURS: 11 am until midnight, Friday and Saturday until 1 am. Three Domino's locations, one in Lahaina, another in Kihei and a third in Kahului. This is a chain of restaurants that offer delivery.

FUJIYA'S ★ *Japanese*
133 Market Cafe, Wailuku (244-0206) HOURS: Lunch 11-2 Mon.-Fri., Dinner 5-9 Mon.-Sat. SAMPLING: Tempura $9.50, teriyaki $6.50, chicken $5.75. Five dinner choices include a combination such as tempura with yakitori, fried ahi, tsukemono, miso soup and rice. Combination plate $9. Beer & sake available. COMMENTS: One of our best bets for Japanese food. Sushi lovers will appreciate their sushi bar where a large variety of selections are available at half the usual resort area price.

HAMBURGER MARY'S *Mexican*
Corner of Main and Market St., Wailuku (244-7776) HOURS: Daily 10 am-10 pm. COMMENTS: Currently in the process of turning over to new owners. Our understanding is that the name will remain the same, but there will be a new menu and policy changes when the new ownership takes over sometime in the fall of 1992. We'll update you in the Maui newsletter.

ICHIBAN THE RESTAURANT *Japanese*
Kahului Shopping Center (871-6977) HOURS: Breakfast and lunch 7 am-2 pm, dinner 5-9 pm. SAMPLING: Tempura Don, Katsu chicken, teri steak, sukiyaki. Breakfast $3.65-$4.25, lunch $5.50-$5.75, dinner $5.60-$11.95, combination dinner plate $9.25. COMMENTS: Located in the older Kahului Center, this restaurant doesn't stand out as memorable for its food or ambiance.

IMPERIAL TEPPANYAKI *Japanese*
Maui Palms Hotel, Kahului (877-0071) HOURS: Nightly from 5:30-8:30 pm. SAMPLING: A buffet with different items prepared by teppanyaki chefs at the buffet. Entrees might include fried fish, ika tempura, chicken yakitori. From the salad bar sample miso soup, tofu with ginger sauce, sashimi and other local favorites.

INTERNATIONAL HOUSE OF PANCAKES   *American*
Maui Mall, Kahului (871-4000) HOURS: Sun.-Thurs 6 am-midnight, Fri. and Sat. until 2 am. COMMENTS: A very large facility with a menu that is popular with all family members. Something for everyone and at reasonable prices. Basic dinners begin in the $5 range.

KALEO'S KAU KAU   *Local Style-Filipino-Hawaiian*
Lower Main Street, Wailuku (244-2040) HOURS: Lunch 11-2:30, Dinner from 5:30-9 pm. SAMPLING: Plate lunches include tripe stew or chop steak $4.75, and a number of Hawaiian dishes include luau stew, squid with coconut or opihi (only place we've ever seen this on the menu) and Filipino dishes such as pork sari sari. An opportunity to sample some unusual and authentic local dishes.

KEN SAN   *Japanese*
2051 Main Street, Wailuku (242-2971) HOURS: Mon.-Sat. 10:30 am-2 pm. SAMPLING: A self serve counter with a variety of hot and cold selections, all priced under $1.65. Choose chicken katsu, mahi, noodles or fried shrimp. Scoop out a portion of apple or macaroni salad, fried or white rice too. A sushi tray for $2.60 includes two pieces of shrimp sushi and six pieces of California roll. COMMENTS: Formerly a head chef at a Lahaina restaurant this owner/chef runs a new and highly popular spot for the Wailuku work force. A few seats along the counter up front and four tables in back, or fill up your carton to go. Saturday is the best time to visit when it is not only quieter, but the selection is better. The sushi especially gets pretty well picked over if you don't get there REAL early during the week. But it is no wonder - where else can you get four California rolls for $1!

KOHO GRILL AND BAR ★   *American*
Kaahumanu Shopping Center, Kahului (877-5588) HOURS: Daily for breakfast 8-11 am, lunch and dinner until 9:30 pm on Mon.-Thurs., 11 pm on Fri. and Sat., and 9 pm on Sun. Happy Hour daily 3-6. SAMPLING: Quiche $4.65, fajitas $6.95 blackened chicken breast sandwich $4.75, soups, salads, burgers and sandwiches $1.95-$4.95. Dinners are served from 5 pm and include pasta, stir fry and cajun as well as trout almondine, T-bone steak, shrimp scampi $6.45-$11.95. COMMENTS: A great family dining spot. Dinners are affordable and the menu is broad enough to offer something for everyone with sandwiches available for dinner as well as lunch. One of only a few restaurants in the area open on Sundays! Convenient for a bite enroute to the airport, with fast and friendly service.

LOPAKA'S BAR AND GRILL   *American*
161 Alambra, Kahului Industrial Area (871-1135) HOURS: 11 am-9 pm. SAMPLING: Same menu for lunch and dinner. Burgers and sandwiches $3.95-$7, plate lunches such as Korean ribs and BBQ beef $6.95-$7.95. COMMENTS: More a bar atmosphere than restaurant.

LUIGI'S   *Italian*
Maui Mall, Kahului (877-3761) HOURS: 11:30 am-4 pm for lunch, 4-10 pm for dinner. SAMPLING: Lunch offers potato skins, saimin, calamari strips, pasta, pizza and burgers $3.99-$8.99. Dinner offers veal marsala, steamed mussels, more pasta and pizza $10.99-$18.99. COMMENTS: Daily specials.

MAMA DING'S PASTELES RESTAURANT ★ *Puerto Rican-Local*
255 E Alamaha St., Kahului (877-5796) HOURS: Breakfast/lunch 6:30 am-2 pm.
Mon.-Sat. You can have lunch at 7 am and breakfast at 2 pm! SAMPLING: Eggs
Bermuda (2 eggs whipped with cream cheese and onion) served with potatoes or
rice and toast $3.95, fresh fruit pancakes $3.95. Sample bacalao salad, a tossed
green creation with codfish bits, green banana and dressing for $2.25 small, $4.50
large. For the less adventurous try a grilled chicken breast sandwich! COM-
MENTS: Ready for a different breakfast? Skip IHOP and try this cozy restaurant
tucked away in the Kahului Industrial Area. Or try a pastele which has an exterior
of grated green banana and a filling of pork, vegetables and spices that is then
steamed. Delicious! We've tried several breakfasts, all were good! Looking
forward to going back for lunch! Stop by after the Saturday Swap Meet or order
a picnic to go to Hana or Haleakala. No credit cards.

MAUI BAKE SHOP & DELI LDT. ★ *European Pastries-Deli*
2092 Vineyard St., Wailuku (242-0064) HOURS: Mon.-Sat. 5 am-5 pm, Sunday
until 1 pm. They seem to be getting a thumbs up from visitors and tourists alike.
An early morning arrival assures a greater selection from the many varied goodies.
This European style bakery is a combination of efforts between Jose and Claire
Fjuii Krall, a French husband-chef and his Japanese wife. They have pizzas,
quiches and sandwiches on French bread or croissant sandwiches. The big stone
oven is still there, left over from the Yokouchi family that was in this location in
the 1930s. Pastries include cakes, napoleans and other very fancy pastries. One
was a hollowed sweet roll filled with custard, then topped with marzipan leaves
and a bit of round orange marzipan and they called it a "peach" -- cute and it
looked just like a peach, but we were surprised that the custard flavor was vanilla.
At Christmas holiday time check out their stollen gingerbread and yule logs, at
Easter indulge in a marzipan egg. There are a few ice cream tables and chairs.
Jose Krall began cooking in 1976 in France and since then has trained in Belgium
and France before becoming Executive Pastry Chef at the Maui Prince in Wailea,
where he left to open this bake shop in Wailuku in the fall of 1991. Yum!!

MAUI BOY *Hawaiian-Local Style*
2102 Vineyard St., Wailuku (244-7243) HOURS: Monday thru Thursday 7 am-9
pm, Friday and Saturday until 10 pm, Sunday until 8 pm. SAMPLING: Hawaiian
favorites such as Kalua pig and poi or lau lau. Local style plate lunches available
for lunch and dinner include chicken or pork teriyaki, roast beef or pork priced
$5.95-$7.95. Breakfast served to 11 am, lunch begins then until 5 pm when dinner
entrees are served.

MAUI COFFEE ROASTERS (BEAN'S WORLD)
444 Hana Hwy., Kahului (877-CUPS) HOURS: 7:30 am-6 pm. SAMPLING:
Caesar salad $4.81, basmato sandwich $4.33, bagel and cream cheese $1.44.
Turkey sandwich $5.77 or ultimate veggie burger $6. COMMENTS: Cute little
shop, where you can purchase a broad array of freshly roasted coffees and enjoy
great prices on food and beverages. Sample fresh Maui lemonade made with
honey and served on the rocks $2.16 or ginger blast, a blend of fresh ginger juice
and bee pollen $2.16 or Thai iced coffee $3.12. Brewed regular or decaf Kona
coffee $.48, espresso $.96, a depth charge (a shot of espresso in their kona coffee)
$1.44 or a capuccino $1.92.

MING YUEN   *Chinese*
162 Alamaha, Kahului (871-7787) Lunch daily 11:30 am-5 pm, dinner 5-9 pm. Cantonese and Szechuan style foods, dishes $6 and up. A little off the beaten track, you'll find it tucked behind Safeway off Kamehameha Ave. in the industrial area. Not as inexpensive as some of the other local eateries, but they do a great job. They celebrate the Chinese New Year, in Jan. or Feb. - it varies, with a very popular ten course meal. In fact the event has become so popular, they have expanded to run it several nights.

MOON HOE CHINESE SEAFOOD RESTAURANT   *Oriental*
752 Lower Main St., Wailuku (242-7778) HOURS: Mon.-Sat. lunch 11 am-2 pm. Dinner daily 5-9 pm. SAMPLING: Huge menu selection including a variety of preparations for duck, pork, beef, chicken, vegetables and fish. Prices generally run $4.95-$7.95. They specialize in seafood dishes.

NAGASAKO FISH MARKET   *Seafood-Local*
1276 Lower Main St., Wailuku. (242-4073) Store hours Mon.-Sat. 6 am-8 pm, Sun. 7 am-5 pm. Lunches served Mon.-Fri. 9 am until they are all gone, which is usually about 1 pm. Operated by Jordan Nagasako of the Lahaina Nagasako grocery family. As a fisherman, he can buy and sell fish wholesale, thus offering an amazing variety of fish and shellfish for you to cook in your Maui home. Exotic reef fish include opelu, akule, weke or oio. Live clams and crabs too!! Looking for something more unusual? Then try some of their poke (marinated raw fish) A very interesting assortment that might include conch-shell poke with flying-fish eggs. Plate lunches run $4-$6 and include stews, chicken or fresh fish and are served with rice and macaroni salad. As of now, this is a "to go" eatery.

NAOKEES   *Hawaiian-Local*
1792 Main St., Wailuku. (244-9444) A fire destroyed this restaurant mid-1992. No news on whether or not they will reopen.

NAZO'S   *Hawaiian-Local Style*
1063 Lower Main St., Wailuku, at Puuone Plaza (244-0529) HOURS: Mon.-Sat. 6 am-9 pm. SAMPLING: Sandwiches include egg salad at $1.75, or grilled ham and cheese $2.25. Entrees include soup or salad, rice or mashed potatoes, coffee, tea or fruit punch. Selections include liver with bacon, shrimp tempura for $5-6. A tossed salad adds 80 cents. Luau stew is featured on Wed., pig feet on Thurs. and Sat. COMMENTS: A small, family-owned restaurant which is very affordable and prides themselves on their home-style cooking. No credit cards.

PINATA'S   *Mexican*
395 Dairy Rd., Kahului. (877-8707) Mon. to Sat. 10:30 am-7 pm. Tostados, quesadillas, Mexican salads, nachos $2.45-$4.95. Combination plates $5.65-$6.95. COMMENTS: Owner Steve Waller reports that everything is made from scratch, from the beans to the salsa (two kinds, blended and smooth or chunky) and they use only 100% cholesterol free oils. A family operation, they wanted to keep the prices affordable, yet maintain a high standard. Transplanted from Southern California, they wanted to bring to Maui the Mexican flavors of food found in the Los Angeles and San Diego area. They offer quite a few vegetarian selections as well. Mexican food is kind of a personal thing, so perhaps that is why the reviews on this place are a bit mixed. A very convenient stop enroute to the airport.

RED DRAGON CHINESE RESTAURANT *Chinese*
Maui Beach Hotel, Kahului (877-0051) HOURS: Nightly 5:30-8:30 pm, closed Mon. SAMPLING: Cantonese buffet dinner with over fifteen selections which change nightly. Entrees may include haposai, clams in hot sauce, sweet and sour pork or roast chicken. Reservations required. On Tuesday and Thursday every fourth adult eats free with minimum 10 persons. Buffet runs $12.95 plus tax.

SAENG'S THAI CUISINE ★ *Thai*
2119 Vineyard St., Wailuku, (244-1567) HOURS: Lunch Mon.-Fri. 11 am-2:30 pm, dinner daily 5-9:30 pm. SAMPLING: Basil chicken, shrimps asparagus, sate or tofu with peanut sauce $4.50-$9 with seafood selections slightly more expensive $10.95 and up. COMMENTS: This wins hands down for the most attractive local restaurant in Wailuku. Owners Toh, Tom and Zach Douangphoumy have created a little Eden with lots of plants providing privacy between tables. They also know how to cook Thai. Traveling in India, Laos, Vietnam and Thailand in their youth they had an opportunity to sample a diversity of foods. 1989 seemed to be the year of the Thai on Maui and we tried them all. This newcomer is far and away the best of the bunch. Not only was the service attentive, but the portions generous and every dish better than the last. We were especially partial to the peanut sauce. In fact it was so good that enroute to the airport and bound for the mainland we picked up some peanut sauce "to go!" Don't miss this one! They recently opened a second location in Lahaina!

SAM SATO'S *Local Style-Hawaiian*
318 North Market St., Wailuku (244-7124) HOURS: Breakfast and lunch 8 am-2 pm, pastries served until 4 pm. Closed Thurs. & Sun. SAMPLING: Noodles are their specialty. Breakfast includes eggs or pancakes. Lunch options include combination plates $3.50-$4 such as teriyaki beef, stew, chop steak or spare ribs. Sandwiches and burgers. Saimin and chow fun are served in small portions for $1.70-$1.85, or large portions for $2.10-$3.70. COMMENTS: The homemade pastries are wonderful. The peach, apple and coconut turnovers were fragrant and fresh. In addition to noodles they specialize in manju, a Japanese tea cake. It may come as a big surprise when you discover that these tasty morsels are actually filled with a mashed version of lima beans!

SAM SATO'S

RESTAURANTS

SIAM THAI   *Thai*
123 N. Market St., Wailuku. (244-3817) Lunch Mon.-Fri. 11-2:30, dinner daily
5-9:30. Exotic green papaya salad $4.95, eggplant tofu $5.95, Thai ginger beef
$5.95. COMMENTS: The white table cloths give this restaurant an elegant air.
According to our waiter we dined at the same table Robert Redford used when he
visited. Very good Thai food although the competition is now stiff with the new
Saeng Thai just around the corner. New owners took over in the spring of 1992.

SIR WILFRED'S ESPRESSO CAFE   *American*
Maui Mall, Kahului. (877-3711) Mon.-Thurs. 9-5:30 pm, Fri. 9-9 pm, Sat. 9-5:30
pm, Sun. 11 am-5 pm. SAMPLING: Continental breakfasts with fresh pastries.
Bagels or deli-style sandwiches are available for lunch as well as a variety of
salads or quiche. Also a selection of gourmet teas, coffees or beer and wine.

SIZZLER   *American*
355 E. Kamehameha Hwy, Kahului (871-1120) HOURS: 6 am-10 pm, until
midnight on Fri. and Sat. SAMPLING: Sirloin steak, sizzler steak, chicken dishes
all in the $8-$15 range. All you can eat salad bar includes soup, salad and tostada
bar for only $7.99. A keiki (children's) menu offers a choice of steak, shrimp,
burger, fish platter, or salad bar, all for $5 or less. Steak and lobster $17.99.
COMMENTS: As Sizzlers go, this is one of the better ones. A good selection of
entrees at family prices and a very good salad bar as well!

SUBWAY SANDWICH
1955 Lower Main, Wailuku, in the Wailuku Industrial Center, 244-9999. Also at
737 Lower Main, Wailuku, 242-1900 and at 340 Hana Hwy, Kahului, 877-7272.

TASTY CRUST ★   *Local Style*
1770 Mill St., Wailuku. (244-0845) HOURS: Daily 5:30 am-1:30 pm for breakfast
and lunch daily, 5-10 pm for dinner except Mon. SAMPLING: Unusual and
delicious crusty hotcakes are their specialty, two are a meal for $1.80, or French
toast $1.70. Add an egg for 50 cents. Lunches and dinners a la carte. Spare ribs
$4.25, fried shrimp $3.95, roast beef $4.75 and served with rice and a salad.
Sandwiches and hamburgers $1.35 and up. COMMENTS: Local atmosphere and
no frills, just good food at great prices.

TIN YING   *Chinese*
1088 Lower Main St., Wailuku (242-4371) HOURS: Daily 10 am-9 pm. SAM-
PLING: Selections include Hong Kong or Szechuan style with prices ranging from
$5.75-$8.75. Eat in or take out. COMMENTS: Okasuya style lunches at $2.75
include an entree and fried rice or noodles and are a real good value.

TOKYO TEI ★   *Japanese*
1063 E. Lower Main St., Wailuku. (242-9630) Lunch 11-1:30 Mon.-Sat., dinner
daily 5-8:30. Sunday dinner served until 8 pm. Lunch runs $3.75-$11.75.
Teishoku trays include shrimp tempura, sashimi, fried fish, teriyaki pork or steak.
Dinner selections such as hakata chicken, seafood platter, and a number of others
that are difficult to pronounce run $5-$11.75 and include rice, miso soup, namasu
and ko-ko. COMMENTS: Small and cozy atmosphere. Great food! Take out
meals also available. Cocktails. Very popular with local residents and tourists and
deservedly so. Winner of one of our top three awards for best local restaurants.

TSURU ★ *Japanese*
2080 Vineyard St., (244-1900) HOURS: Breakfast 7-11 am, lunch followed until 3 pm, dinner 5-9 pm. closed Sunday. (Former location of Hazel's). SAMPLING: Grilled shrimp and tortilla salad with mixed greens corn tortillas, black beans, tomato, cucumber, onions, cheese, pico degrallo and vinaigrette $7.95, BBQ chicken salad $6.50, teppanyaki selections $5.95-$7.05, pasta dishes $3.50-$6.95, burgers and hot dogs or sandwiches $3.50-$4.95. Not just the usual sandwiches mind you, how about grilled asparagus and cream cheese or hot black forest ham and mozzarella cheese? Soups are served with fresh cornbread and honey butter. Breakfast items $3.50-$4.95 including huevos rancheros or loco moko. Steak and eggs $6.95. COMMENTS: Owner Rob Meyers has had plenty of experience cooking on Maui, both at Kobe Japanese Steak House and at David Paul's Lahaina Grill. Here at his new restaurant they serve Japanese food too, but other dishes include vegetarian eggplant torte, barbecue chicken salad and grilled rock shrimp tortilla salad.

VIETNAM CUISINE ★ *Vietnamese*
1246 Lower Main St., Wailuku (244-7845) HOURS: Daily 10 am-10 pm. COMMENTS: This restaurant wins for the most confusing. They opened, moved across the street, reopened, closed, and are now open again. Olivia, daughter of the original owner Yen Nguyen Walker, has taken over the restaurant and we're glad they're back! If you love Asian food and aren't familiar with Vietnamese fare, you'll be pleasantly surprised. Very delicate flavors and interesting combinations of spices and blending of foods. Sample bun cha gio, steamed rice noodle with fried spring roll $5.50, rau muong xao voi tom, water spinach stir fried shrimp with shrimp sauce $9 or hu tieu xao rau, Cambodian style noodle stir fry with vegetables $7.50.

MODERATE

AURELIO'S *Continental*
55 Kaahumanu Ave., Kahului, across from the Maui Mall (871-7656) HOURS: Breakfast 7 am-11 am, dinner to 10 pm Monday thru Saturday, until 5 pm on Sunday. SAMPLING: Lunch and dinner selections $5.50-$12.95.

CHART HOUSE ★ *American-Seafood*
500 N. Puunene Ave., Kahului (877-2476) HOURS: Dinner 5:30-10 pm. SAMPLING: Prime rib is their specialty, also fresh seafood and chicken priced $15-$23. COMMENTS: Large portions, excellent children's menu $3.25-$6.45. You can be sure it will be less crowded on this side of the island. A pleasant ocean view.

MICKEYS ★ *American-Seafood*
Kahului Bldg., 33 Lono Ave. (871-7555) HOURS: Lunch Monday to Friday 11 am-2 pm and dinner nightly 5:30-9 pm. SAMPLING: Lunches run $6.50-$12.95. Dinners range from $12.95 for chicken to $22.95 for seafoods. Their "king" platter for two is $69.95. Fresh fish priced daily, children's portions 1/2 price. COMMENTS: Excellent fresh fish! Early bird dinners $12.95.

UPCOUNTRY

INEXPENSIVE

BULLOCK'S OF HAWAII   *Local Style-American*
Just past Pukalani Shopping Center on the right side going up the mountain. HOURS: Breakfast 7:30-11:30 am, lunch 11:30 am-3 pm. SAMPLING: Usual breakfast items, omelettes from $3.25, French toast $2.50. A moonburger runs $4.50 (it was lunchtime here when the first astronaut walked on the moon), a guava shake at $2.95, sandwiches from $9.95, and plate lunches $4.25-$7.50. COMMENTS: A landmark in Upcountry, celebrating their 25th year in business October 1992! Still operated by Palu and Hazel Elkins. And in case you're interested, Hazel's maiden name was Bullock.

COURTYARD DELI
3620 Baldwin Ave. #102A, Makawao (572-3456) SAMPLING: Tempeh salad $4.75, tarragan chicken salad $4.95, or personal sandwiches created from a choice of a variety of "elements." Breakfast offers Belgiam waffles, mauka morning burrito, papaya with bananas and walnuts, eggs $3.50-$4.25. Courtyard coolers include honey lemonade, real orange juice and fruit smoothies. Courtyard creams are a selection of flavors combined with milk or soy milk or half and half and served over ice. Espresso drinks too.

DAIRY QUEEN - MCDONALD'S - Pukalani

FU WAH   *Chinese-Szechuan*
Pukalani Shopping Center (572-1341) HOURS: 10:30 am-3 pm Tuesday to Sunday 5-9 pm. SAMPLING: Dinner entrees from $5.75 or choose family dinner combinations $12-$25. Sizzling platters and braised pot courses from $6.50.

GRANDMA'S COFFEE HOUSE ★   *Local Style*
Located in Keokea (878-2140) HOURS: Tuesday thru Saturday 7 am-5 pm., Sunday 7 am-3 pm. Closed Monday. COMMENTS: This is a family operation run by Alfred Franco, his wife and their two young children (son Derek is known as "the boss" and a younger sister Alyson). Alfred is encouraging the return of the

coffee industry in Upcountry Maui. Born and raised in Upcountry, his grandmother taught him how to roast the coffee beans to perfection. He does this several times a day in his 104 year old coffee roasting machine that was brought from Philadelphia by his great grandmother. The coffee is sold by the pound in a blend known as "Maui coffees." Some of the beans used are grown on Moloka'i which is part of Maui County. Prices are high, and there is no decaf available. (Grandmother never taught Alfred how to do that.) A few tables are an invitation to visitors to sit down, enjoy a cup of coffee, espresso, capuccino, or fresh fruit juice along with cinnamon rolls, muffins, and more, all fresh from the oven. A bit more of an appetite might require one of their fresh avocado sandwiches, a bowl of chili and rice or homemade Portuguese bean soup. With the popularity of this place among locals and visitors alike, it is tough for them to keep up with the demand for these goodies. So if you're hungry in Upcountry, be sure to stop in at Grandma's, just five miles before the Tedeschi Winery. Alfred's goal is to put Keoke on the maps and minds of everyone. And he just may do it!

KITADAS RESTAURANT   *Local Style*
3617 Baldwin Avenue, Makawao. PHONE: 572-7241 HOURS: 6 am-1:30 pm daily except Sun. COMMENTS: Popular local eatery.

PIZZA FRESH   *Italian*
1043 Makawao Ave., Unit 103. (572-2000)

UPCOUNTRY CAFE   *Local style*
7-2 Aewa Place, Pukalani (572-2395) HOURS: Sunday breakfast only 6:30 am until noon. Monday and Wednesday thru Saturday open 6:30 am-3 pm. Closed Tuesday. SAMPLING: Loco Moo-co includes two eggs, Upcountry hamburger patty smothered with brown sauce and steamed rice $5.75, vegetable fritatta $4.25, or raisin cinnamon French toast $4.25. Lunch selections include teriyaki beef burger $4.95, crab supreme, crab and melted mozzarella on boboli bread $7.25, entrees such as sauteed mahi $5.75, beef curry stew $4.95 or kalbi ribs $5.95. COMMENTS: The theme here is "cow" and the cow pie dessert is a rich blend of macadamia nuts and chocolate cream cheese filling a chocolate cookie tart, this was created by chef Aaron Heath's wife Tammy, who is the head baker at one of the resort hotels in Kaanapali. They also make all their own salad dressings, jams and jellies! Recently one in the best "mom and pop" restaurants of the Maui News dining contest. Co-owners Shirley Buetler and Aaron Heath have been in operation at this location for about two years but have years of restaurant experience on Maui and elsewhere. This is a great addition to Upcountry dining.

MODERATE

CASANOVA ITALIAN RESTAURANT AND DELI   *Italian*
1188 Makawao Ave., Makawao (572-0220) HOURS: Deli from 8:30 am-7:30 pm. Lunch and dinner at the restaurant. SAMPLING: The deli offers hot sandwiches, pastries, capuccino and fresh juices. Pizza too! For lunch there is roast beef, chicken or fresh catch sandwiches $7.95-$9.95, pasta $7.50-$8.75, antipasti & insalate $5.95-$6.95. Dinner selections include gamberoni giganti $19.50, jumbo prawns broiled with fresh rosemary or sauted in brandy sauce, fusilli vesuvio $8.95 corkscrew pasta in tomato sauce, baked eggplant, goat cheese, basil and garlic, or gnocchi $9.75 potato-spinach dumplings with three sauces from which

to choose. Pizzas made in their wood burning oven $8.95-$14.50. Menu spans from $7.95-$18.95. COMMENTS: Evening entertainment. This is another of those restaurants that seems to span the gamut of tastes. We have heard raves from some and others didn't think it was anything memorable. Our meal wasn't outstanding.

HALIIMAILE GENERAL STORE ★ *Continental*
Haliimaile Rd., Haliimaile (572-2666) HOURS: Lunch 11-3, dinner 6-10 and Sunday brunch 10-3. SAMPLING: Lunches include a creative selection of sandwiches and salads $5-$8 served with unusual salad accompaniments. Dinners run $13-$24. Sunday brunch offers breakfast brunch and lunch brunch items. Lox and bagel $9, Bev's boboli (pizza topped with crab dip) $6, eggs Blackstone $8, Vegetable frittata $7 or Chicken club sandwich $8, fresh catch sandwich $9. While the items change, standard items include an entree of Rack of lamb Hunan style $24 or paniolo ribs $16 and the popular blackened sashimi appetizer $10. Other menu items might include paniolo stuffed artichoke $8, Thai coconut fettucini $13, shrimp scorpio $19. Lunches offer Chinese chicken salad $9, Caesar salad $7, vegetable torte $9, sandwiches and weekly specials.

This restaurant has put Haliimaile on the map since it opened several years ago. The original structure dates back to the 1920s when it served as the General Store and hub of this community. The 5,000 square foot restaurant has two main dining rooms. Jeremy Realton assisted with the interior design (among his many accomplishments is the set for the Pee-Wee Herman show.) The high ceiling is the original and the floors are refurbished hardwood. The tables are set with cloths in green and peach and there is a huge beautifully designed bar in the front dining room. The menu rotates stressing quality in their food preparation and includes the fresh herbs they cultivate in their own garden. The dinner menu features an interesting selection of dishes with unusual and creative preparations. An admirable wine list that includes some nice ports, sherrys and cognacs too. Our only previous complaint was the lack of choices for the traveling toddler in the group. Well, thanks to Bev and Joe Gannon, for adding a Haliimaile style peanut butter and jelly sandwich served on raisin bread of course!

KULA LODGE *American*
Five miles past Pukalani on Haleakala Hwy. (878-1535) HOURS: Breakfast 7-11:30 am, lunch 11:30-5 pm; dinner 5-9:30 pm. Dinner is served only on Sat. and Sun. reservations are recommended. SAMPLING: Lunches include sandwiches, salads, and burgers from $5.25-$6.95, also hot entrees. Dinners include rice or potato, vegetable and range from carpetbagger steak $20, rack of lamp $22, raviolis of the day $14, prawns Molokini $18. COMMENTS: An added benefit here is the fireplace, a warming delight after a cold trip to the mountain top, a panoramic view, and cocktails. Children's portions available. They've recently added several vegetarian specials which include stuffed eggplant with spaghetti squash and feta cheese and vegetarian crepes with non-dairy bernaise.

KULA SANDALWOODS
Haleakala Hwy. (878-3523) Menu items for lunch and breakfast under $10. Formerly Silversword Inn. New owners and new name.

MAKAWAO STEAK HOUSE   *American*
3612 Baldwin, Makawao. (572-8711) HOURS: Dinner nightly 5-9:30, weekends until 10 pm. SAMPLING: Chicken Zoie $17.50 (breast stuffed with creamed spinach), Scampi $21, N.Y. steak $19.95, fresh fish varies daily. Dinners includes choice of eight salads and freshly baked bread.

POLLI'S   *Mexican*
1202 Makawao Ave., Makawao (572-7808) HOURS: 11:30-2:30, Sunday brunch 10:30-2:30, Happy hour 2:30-5 pm, dinner 5-10 pm. SAMPLING: Dinner combinations run $8-$12. Vegetarian dishes available. COMMENTS: New owner Tim Ellison has been making some changes to this popular Upcountry restaurant, including adding BBQ chicken and baby-back ribs to the menu.

PUKALANI TERRACE COUNTRY CLUB   *American-Hawaiian*
360 Pukalani Rd. (572-1325) Turn right just before the shopping center at Pukalani and continue until the road ends. HOURS: Open 10-2 for lunch, 5-9 for dinner. SAMPLING: Lunch offers a Kalua pig Hawaiian plate for $7.50 or tripe stew for $6.65. Dinner menu offers similar selections at slightly higher prices. Salad bar $6.85, salad bar with dinner $2.85. COMMENTS: Check for early bird dinners and nightly dinner specials. A great view of Maui from here. You might consider a stop on the way down from Upcountry for a drink and tropical sunset.

PAIA

INEXPENSIVE to MODERATE

CHARLEY'S   *American-Italian*
142 Hana Hwy. in Paia (579-9453) HOURS: Breakfast, lunch and dinner. SAMPLING: Cheese omelette, steak and eggs, huevos rancheros $4.25 -$7.95, lunch items sandwiches, hamburger, burittos $4.25-$5.95, dinners include two home-made garlic rolls and a dinner salad. Selections include pizza, ribs, fresh fish, calzone, fettucini, $7-13. COMMENTS: Renovations are expected to double the size of their sports bar which has a 70 inch TV and enlarge the eating area.

GARDEN EARTH CAFE & BAKERY   *Vegetarian*
100-A Haiku Rd., across from the Haiku Post Office (575-2000) HOURS: Open Monday to Saturday 6 am-6 pm. SAMPLING: Breakfast $2.25-$4.25 includes whole wheat pancakes, smoothies, granola, fruits, fresh juices. Lunch and dinner $3-$4 offers vegetarian daily specials, salads, sandwiches, soups. Pizza special is $2 per slice and made with whole wheat dough. Whole pizza $12-$18.

KIHATA RESTAURANT   *Japanese*
115 Hana Hwy., Paia (579-9035) HOURS: Closed all day Monday, hours 11 am-1:30 for lunch Tuesday thru Saturday, open for dinner only on Sunday. SAMPLING: Lunches include chicken katsu, noodle dishes, beef teriyaki $5-$8. Dinner Teishoku meals include miso soup, rice, shrimp tempura, chicken teriyaki and fish for $12-$15. Bento lunches and sushi also available. COMMENTS: Good food, but prices are slightly higher than similar restaurants in Wailuku.

PAIA FISH MARKET RESTAURANT   *American-Seafood*
101 Hana Highway, on the corner of Baldwin Ave. and Hana Highway (579-8030) HOURS: Lunch noon to 5 pm and dinner 5-9:30 pm. SAMPLING: Lunch and dinner selections similar to lunch plates around $10.95, two or three dollars less expensive than the dinner counterpart. A blackboard slate recounts the selections such as fish tacos, fish chowder, shrimp fajitas, ahi burgers. Fresh fish is selected from the case and runs $10-$16.95 for a dinner portion served with rice or home fries and coleslaw. Beer, wine and champagne. COMMENTS: This is the sixth restaurant for owner Warren Roberts from Malibu California. Our trial here was disappointing. Order at the counter and then pick up your meal and seat yourself at a half dozen over-sized picnic tables. A dark interior at night with interesting and humorous artifacts lining the walls. The fish in the display looks fresh, but filets of such fish as mahi or onaga are dried out when charbroiled. Our fish was accompanied by a pile of fried potatoes that filled up the plate. No good selections for children.

PEACHES AND CRUMBLE   *American-Healthy*
On Baldwin Ave. just off Hana Hwy. (579-8612) HOURS: 6:30 am-7 pm, seven days a week. SAMPLING: No meals, just sandwiches and bakery items. Unusual baked items include carrot cake with guava filling, lilikoi cheesecake, "jungle bars" (dried organic bananas, coconut, macadamia nuts and passion fruit). Sandwiches such as salmon with cream cheese or Mexican avocado are made on their own freshly baked bread. Specials include pizza. A few counter seats.

PICNIC'S   *American-Healthy*
30 Baldwin Ave, a few blocks off the Hana Hwy. (579-8021) HOURS: 7:30 am - 7 pm, 7 days a week. Closed Thanksgiving and New Years. SAMPLING: The Plantation breakfast includes eggs scrambled with cheddar, coffee and toast $3.75. Their lunch specialty is the spinach nutburger $4.79, Mahi mahi supreme $5.26, turkey $4.69, avocado and swiss $4.79. Countryside box lunch at $8.58 includes a choice of sandwich, drink, cookie, chips and fruit. COMMENTS: A very popular place to pick up some lunch goodies for the road to Hana or Haleakala. Anything on their menu is available to go and everything is ready from 7:30 am. No need to call ahead, just stop by enroute.

THE VEGAN RESTAURANT *American-Vegetarian*
115 Baldwin Ave., a few blocks off the Hana Hwy. (579-9144) HOURS: 11:30 am-8:30 pm. SAMPLING: Serves only vegetarian foods. Tofu omelette $2.50, lasagna tofucci $3.95, sweet and sour tofu $4.50, carrot salad $2.95, sandwich platters $4, complete dinners vary daily $8.95. COMMENTS: It is hard to believe with the wealth of restaurants that this is currently Maui's only vegetarian. It opened in late 1989 with an aim to create foods with tastes and textures to resemble meat products, but without the use of animal products or cholesterol in any of their food. Vegan is a non-profit organization that has been doing vegetarian nutrition seminars for more than six years before opening this restaurant. Seating for a dozen people. Catering also available.

WUNDERBAR *German*
89 Hana Hwy. in Paia (579-8808) Breakfast 7:30-11 am daily except Monday, and lunch 11:00-2 pm. Dinner served 5-10 pm. SAMPLING: Most entrees run $13-$17 and include Wiener Schnitzel, Piccata Milanese, Hungarian goulash, peppersteak, Bavarian hunter steak served with spaetzle and fresh seafood entrees which are priced daily. Desserts run $4-$6 and range from fresh baked apple strudel to a Grand Marnier souffle or chocolate mousse. Cocktails, wine and beer available.

It took several years after Benard Weber and Birgit Schaefer first came to Maui and discovered the town of Paia before their dream of opening a European style restaurant was realized. The restaurant is in affiliation with several restaurants in Germany. Located in the former Dillon's site, they have completely renovated the restaurant into a cozy, warm and friendly European style atmosphere and decorated it with memorabilia such as a black forest clock, an old piano from Vienna, big railway signs and beer ads. Their chef/manager Benard Weber is from Switzerland. Birgit Schaefer, co-manager is from Germany. The chef trained in many restaurants in Switzerland as well as working in various European countries and experienced their diverse cuisines. They hope to add more European menu items in the future. In sampling the menu items the pasta proved hearty, basic and homemade. The basil bread was unusual and aromatic but a bit overdone. The sauerkraut with potatoes was a nice blend of flavors. The sauce on the grilled Mediterranean style fish was a bit pungent. Overall, the food was a little different, and would certainly satisfy the meat and potatoes palate. Some dishes were a bit too salty, but generally good, healthy food in a homemade fashion. The use of Kula vegetables is a nice feature. The desserts are a European style and not overwhelmingly sweet. The Schoggimousse is a chocolate mousse from Switzerland that was not too airy or too pudding-like, but just right. They also serve the only German beer on Maui, but due to popularity, it might not be in stock. It's like an Inn with a very family feel.

EXPENSIVE

MAMA'S FISH HOUSE ★ *Continental-Seafood*
On Hwy. 36 just 1 1/2 miles past Paia, look for the ship's flagpole and the angel fish sign (579-8488) HOURS: Lunch served 11-2, happy hour and pupus 2:30-4:30, dinner from 5:30 pm. SAMPLING: Lunch appetizers include poisson cru, a traditional fish of Tahiti marinated in coconut milk and lime $10.95. Entrees include grilled shrimp kuau $16.95, Chicken teriyaki $13.95, Tahitian salad $13.95, mama's crabcakes $16.95, fish salad sandwich $10.95, fresh fishburger

$12.95. Dinner selections include fresh fish served nine different ways (at least) cioppino $26.95, fresh scallops with Maui onions $23.95, or Pineapple chicken teriyaki $15.95. COMMENTS: Mama opened her home, located on a peaceful beachfront in 1973, as Hawai'i's first fresh fish house. Her mission was "to serve creative seafood dishes with that elusive taste of Maui island cooking." Mama engages her own fishermen to catch their daily fare. Samples include Ono sauteed in mango butter and Baked Opakapaka Hana. Non-seafood entrees such as Kalbi ribs or chicken in papaya are available. Some great desserts too, mango or banana crisp, kula lime pie, fresh homemade ice cream or macadamia nut cheesecake with butterscotch and macadamia liqueur. It is a little out of the way, but you can be assured of a quality seafood meal. One of the more expensive seafood restaurants, but worth it. Reservations suggested.

HANA

INEXPENSIVE

HANA RANCH STORE - Open daily, ready-made sandwiches and hot dogs.
HASEGAWA GENERAL STORE - Open daily, a little bit of everything!!
TUTU'S - Hana Bay, 8:30-4 pm. Sandwiches, plate lunches.

MODERATE

HANA RANCH RESTAURANT *American*
Downtown Hana. (248-8255) 6:30-10 am daily for breakfast (take out only), lunch takeout available from 10 am - 4 pm daily, lunch in dining room is 11 am-3 pm daily. Pizza night every Thursday from 5:30-8 pm. A la carte dinner menu on Friday and Saturday evenings only from 6-8 pm. Reservations required. Take out menu varies in price from $4-$7 for sandwiches, burgers, plate lunches. All you can eat luncheon buffet is $12.95 adults, $7.95 adults for salad bar only. Children under 12 are $6.95. Buffet includes BBQ ribs, chicken, baked potatoes, baked beans, assorted breads and full salad bar. Dinner menu is served only Friday and Saturday nights, with pizza on Thursdays. Menu items include guava smoked baby back ribs for $18.95, N.Y. steak $22.50, prime rib $18.95, and $37 for lobster. Attire is casual. Full bar service. Dinner reservations recommended.

TUTU'S

EXPENSIVE

HOTEL HANA MAUI DINING ROOM ★   *Continental*
(248-8211) HOURS: Breakfast 7:30-10 am, a la carte or buffet lunch 11:30-2 pm, dinner 6:30-8:30. SAMPLING: Lunch offers wok seared ahi yellow fin tuna on dill bread $14.95, smoked turkey bacon, avocado club sandwich $12.95, or entrees such as daily special pasta $12.95, Hana ranch burger $12.95, or cobb salad $16.95. Dinners are a la carte and include "Hana's own" fresh catches $31, veal piccata "Milanaise" $31, double cut lamb chop with roasted garlic sauce $32.25 or chicken breast, flame broiled served with shredded daikon and teriyaki sauce $25. COMMENTS: Wonderful food served with unusually, light, delicious sauces. Prices are a little high, but when you're the only place in town, I guess you're entitled!

SUNSETS AND NIGHTLIFE

Here are a few suggestions as to what to do when and after the sun goes down on Maui. These locations usually offer entertainment, however, call to see what they are offering and which night, as it varies. Check This Week or the "Scene" section of the Thursday edition of the Maui News, which lists current late night happenings. Another good source for what is happening is "The Maui Bulletin," another free publication found around town.

SUNSET WATCHING SUGGESTIONS

The new Plantation House Restaurant, Kapalua
On the front lawn of the Pineapple Hill Restaurant, Kapalua
From the lobby bar of the Kapalua Bay Resort with their wonderful pupus
The Kapalua Grill and Bar
On the promontory at the Bay Club, Kapalua
Atop Black Rock in the Sheraton's Discovery Room
At the Hyatt Regency's Lahaina Provision Company
Enroute down from Haleakala, the Pukalani Country Club
The Fairway at the Wailea Golf Course (try an ice cream drink)
Enjoy the lobby bar at Stouffer Wailea Beach Resort
The Sunset bar at the Diamond resort has a fabulous panoramic view and good pupus!

NIGHT SPOTS & ENTERTAINMENT

Consult "The Scene" section of the *Maui News*, Thursday edition, to see who is playing when and where. The following spots generally offer entertainment, but as everything else, things change quickly!

LAHAINA - KAANAPALI - KAPALUA AREA

Lahaina: Moose McGillycuddy's is always hopping for the young crowd. You'll find jazz at Blackie's Bar four nights a week. Lahaina Broiler offers entertainment several nights a week, dance floor. Moondoggies has musical entertainment. Now popular is the Karaoke Entertainment at a number of restaurant/lounges. Karaoke is where a member of the audience selects a song that has music only, no words. They are given a sheet with the words and they sing along. There is usually a fee to entertain. The Maui Marriott hosts karaoke parties every Thursday, Friday and Saturday in their lobby bar. Admission is free, phone 667-1200 for information. Lahaina Broiler has karaoke as well. Studio 505 has varied entertainment. Kobe Japanese Steakhouse and Lahaina Coolers have entertainment, and the Blue Tropix Nightclub is scheduled to open, but no word yet.

Kaanapali: Spats at the Hyatt Regency is open nightly until 2 am, 4 am on Saturday, with a dress code of closed toe shoes, collared shirts and slacks for men, and closed toe shoes for women. Cover charge for non hotel-guests. At the Marriott, the Makai Bar features entertainment and a very small dance floor with karaoke entertainment in their lobby bar. El Crab Catcher has live Hawaiian style musical entertainment and Nanatomi features karaoke. The Royal Lahaina resort has a group that performs authentic and traditional Hawaiian music. At the Westin Villa Lounge is a varied selection of musicians from country to rock or blues and jazz. The show runs between 9 pm and midnight with no cover charge.

KIHEI - WAILEA - MAKENA AREA NIGHTSPOTS

Chum's restaurant in Kihei, the Inu Inu Lounge at the Maui Inter-Continental Wailea, and the Sunset Lounge at The Four Seasons Resort are the prime spots for late night entertainment in South Maui. In Makena, The Maui Prince has something special planned each evening, for more information see the Makena area listing under Molokini Lounge. The new Maui Sun hotel has entertainment which varies from pianists to talent night or dance bands. The Maui Lu frequently has shows that benefit a variety of worthwhile causes. Check "The Scene" in the Maui News.

ELSEWHERE
Check Wunderbar Restaurant in Pai'a for varied entertainment. Casanova's in Makawao features blues, jazz, western, disco and a bit of anything else.

BEACHES

INTRODUCTION

If you are looking for a variety of beautiful, uncrowded tropical beaches, nearly perfect weather year round and sparkling clear waters at enjoyable temperatures, Maui will not disappoint you.

With beaches that range from small to long, white sand to black sand or rock, and from well developed to (at least for a little longer) remote and unspoiled, there is something for everyone. The lay-on-the-beach-under-a-palm-tree type, or the explorer-adventurer will not want for the appropriate beach.

Maui's beaches are publicly owned and most have right-of-way access, however, the access is sometimes tricky to find and parking may be a problem! Parking areas are provided at most developed beaches, but are generally limited to 30 cars or less, making an early arrival at the more popular beaches a good idea. In the undeveloped areas you will have to wedge along the roadside. It is vital that you leave nothing of importance in your car as theft, especially at some of the remoter locations, is high.

At the larger developed beaches, a variety of facilities are provided. Many have convenient rinse-off showers, drinking water, restrooms, and picnic areas. A few have children's play or swim areas. The beaches near the major resorts often have rental equipment available for snorkeling, sailing, boogie boarding, and even underwater cameras. These beaches are generally clean and well maintained. Above Kapalua and below Wailea, where the beaches are undeveloped, expect to find no signs to mark the location, no facilities, and sometimes less cleanliness.

Since virtually all of Maui's good beaches are located on the leeward side of East and West Maui, you can expect sunny weather most of the time. This is because the mountains trap the moisture in the almost constant trade winds. Truly cloudy or bad weather in these areas is rare but when the weather is poor in one area, a short drive may put you back into the sun again.

Swells from all directions reach Maui's shores. The three basic swell sources are the east and north-east trade winds, the North Pacific lows, and the South Pacific lows. The trades cause easterly swells of relatively low heights of 2 - 6 feet throughout most of the year. A stormy, persistent trade wind episode may cause swells of 8-12 feet and occasionally 10-15 feet on exposed eastern shores. Since the main resort areas are on leeward West and East Maui, they are protected.

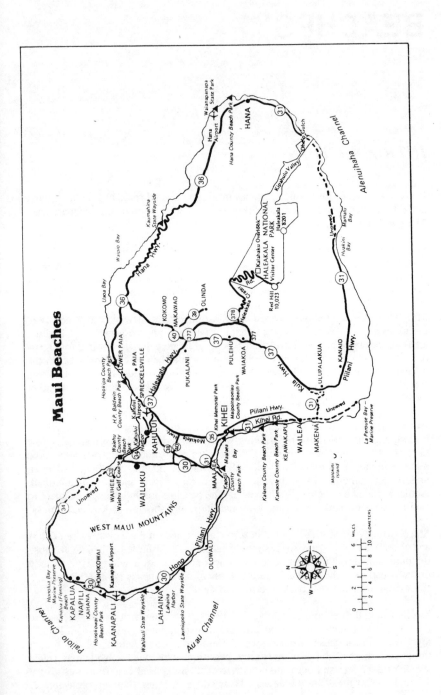

Maui Beaches

North Maui and Hana are exposed to these conditions however, along with strong ocean currents, therefore very few beaches in these areas are considered safe for casual swimming.

Kona winds generated by southern hemisphere storms cause southerly swells that affect leeward Maui. This usually happens in the summer and will last for several days. Surf heights over eight feet are not common, but many of the resort areas have beaches with fairly steep drop offs causing rather sharp shore breaks. Although it may appear fun to play in these waves, many minor to moderate injuries are recorded at these times. Resorts will post red warning flags along the beach during times of unsafe surf conditions. Most beaches are affected during this time causing water turbidity and poor snorkeling conditions. At a few places, such as Lahaina, Olowalu and Maalaea, these conditions create good surfing.

Northerly swells caused by winter storms northeast of the island are not common, but can cause large surf, particularly on the northern beaches, such as Baldwin, Kanaha and Hookipa Beach Parks.

Winter North Pacific storms generate high surf along the northwestern and northern shores of Maui. This is the source of the winter surf in Mokuleia Bay (Slaughterhouse), renowned for body surfing, and in Honolua Bay which is internationally known for surfing.

Land and sea breezes are local winds blowing from opposite directions at different times depending on the temperature difference between land and sea. The interaction of daytime sea breezes and trade winds, in the Wailea-Makena area particularly, produce almost daily light cloudiness in the afternoon and may bring showers. This is also somewhat true of the Honokowai to Kapalua region.

Oceanic tidal and trade wind currents are not a problem for the swimmer or snorkeler in the main resort areas from Makena to Kapalua except under unusual conditions such as Kona storms. Beaches outside of the resort areas should be treated with due caution since there are very few considered safe for casual swimming and snorkeling except by knowledgeable, experienced persons.

Maui's ocean playgrounds are probably the most benign in the world. There is no fire coral, jelly fish are rare, and sharks are well fed by the abundant marine life and rarely come into shore. However, you should always exercise good judgement and reasonable caution when at the beach.

1. "Never turn your back to the sea" is an old Hawaiian saying. Don't be caught off guard, waves come in sets with spells of calm in between.
2. Use the buddy system, never swim or snorkel alone.
3. If you are unsure of your abilities, use flotation devices attached to your body, such as a life vest or inflatable vest. Never rely on an air mattress or similar device from which you may become separated.
4. Study the ocean before you enter; look for rocks, breakers or currents.
5. Duck or dive beneath breaking waves before they reach you.
6. Never swim against a strong current, swim across it.
7. Know your limits.

8. Small children should be allowed to play near or in the surf ONLY with close supervision and should wear flotation devices.
9. When exploring tidal pools or reefs, always wear protective footwear and keep an eye on the ocean. Also, protect your hands.
10. When swimming around coral, be careful where you put your hands and feet. Urchin stings can be painful and coral cuts can be dangerous.
11. Respect the yellow and red flag warnings when placed on the developed beaches. They are there to advise you of unsafe conditions.

Paradise Publications has endevored to provide current and accurate information on Maui's beautiful beaches, however remember, nature is unpredictable and weather, beach and current conditions can change. Enjoy your day at the beach, but utilize good judgement. Paradise Publications cannot be held responsible for accidents or injuries incurred.

Surface water temperature varies little with a mean temperature of 73.0 in January and 80.2 in August. Minimum and maximum range from 68 to 84 degrees. This is an almost ideal temperature (refreshing, but not cold) for swimming and you will find most resort pools cooler than the ocean.

BEST BETS
On South Maui our favorite beaches are Makena for its unspoiled beauty, Maluaka for its deep fine sand and beautiful coral, Wailea and Ulua-Mokapu for their great beaches, good snorkeling and beautiful resorts, and Keawakapu and Kamaole II which offer gentler offshore slopes where swimming is excellent. A good place for small children is the park at the end of Hauoli Street in Maalaea, just past the Makani A Kai condos. There are two small, sandy-bottomed pools protected by reefs on either side of the small rock jetty.

On West Maui, Kapalua offers a well protected bay with very good swimming and snorkeling. Hanakaoo Beach has a gentle offshore slope and the park has lots of parking, good facilities, numerous activities, and is next to the Hyatt. Olowalu has easy access and excellent snorkeling. An excellent place for small children to play in the sand and water is at Pu'unoa Beach, which is well protected by a large offshore reef.

BEACH INDEX

MAALAEA TO LAHAINA

The beaches are described in order from Maalaea to Lahaina and are easy to spot from Honoapiilani Highway. They are all narrow and usually lined by Kiawe trees, however, they have gentle slopes to deeper water and the ocean is generally calmer and warmer than in other areas. The offshore coral reefs offer excellent snorkeling in calm weather, which is most of the time. These beaches are popular because of their convenient access and facilities as well as good swimming and snorkeling conditions.

PAPALAUA STATE WAYSIDE PARK

As you descend from the sea cliffs on your way from Maalaea you will see an undeveloped tropical shoreline stretch before you. At the foot of the cliffs at mile marker 11, Papalaua Park is marked by an easily seen sign. There are picnic tables, BBQ grills, and portable restrooms. The beach is long, (about 1/2 mile) and narrow and lined with Kiawe trees that almost reach the water's edge in places. The trees provide plenty of shady areas for this beautiful beach. Good swimming and fair snorkeling, popular picnicking area.

UKUMEHAME BEACH PARK

The entrance to the park is near mile marker 12, but there is no identifying sign. There is off-street paved parking for about 12 cars. Five concrete picnic tables. This is also a narrow 1/2 mile long sand beach with lots of Kiawe trees providing shade. Good swimming, fair snorkeling.

OLOWALU BEACH ★

About 2/10 mile before and after mile marker 14 you will see a large, but narrow stand of Kiawe trees between the road and the beach, followed by a few palm trees, then a few more scattered Kiawe trees. Parking is alongside the road. No facilities. This narrow sand beach slopes gently out to water four or five feet deep making it good for swimming and beach playing. There are extensive coral formations starting right offshore and continuing out a quarter mile or more, and a fair amount of fish expecting handouts. The ocean is generally warmer and calmer than elsewhere, making it a popular snorkeling spot.

AWALUA BEACH

The beach at mile marker 16 may be cobble stone or sand depending on the time of year and the prevailing conditions. No facilities. At times when Kona storms create a good southern swell, this becomes a very popular surfing spot for a few days until the swells subside.

LAUNIUPOKO STATE WAYSIDE PARK

This well-marked beach park near mile marker 18 offers a large paved parking area, restrooms, many picnic tables, BBQ grills, rinse-off showers, drinking water, pay phone, and a large grassy area with trees, all of which makes for a good picnic spot. There is a large man-made wading pool constructed of large boulders centered in the park. (Sand has accumulated to the extent that even at high tide there is no water in the pool). To the right is a rocky beach and to the left is a 200-yard dark sand beach with fairly gentle slope. It looks nice, but signs posted warn "Sharks have been seen in the shallow water off this beach. Entry into the water is discouraged." This area is rumored to be a shark breeding ground with shark fishing done here in the past. There is also a no alcohol sign posted. For some reason the beach does not seem to be used for much besides picnicking! However, a couple hundred yards offshore is good snorkeling and you may see snorkel excursions visit this shoreline when the weather prohibits a trip to Lana'i.

PUAMANA BEACH PARK
Well marked beach park near mile marker 19, just south of the Puamana Resort complex. Parking for 20 cars in paved parking area, with additional parking along the highway. Nice grassy park with seven picnic tables and plenty of shade trees. At the park itself there is no sandy beach, only a large pebble beach. The only beach is a narrow 200 yard long white sand beach just north of the park and fronting Puamana Resort. Fairly gentle slope to shallow water.

LAHAINA AND KAANAPALI

LAHAINA BEACH
There is a large public parking lot across from the 505 Front Street shopping center with easy access to the beach through the mall. There is also on-street parking near the Lahaina Shores with public right of way to the beach at the south end of the complex. Restrooms and showers are only available at the resort. The Lahaina Sailing Center is located on the beach. This narrow sand beach fronts the Lahaina Shores and 505 Front St. and is protected by a reef 30 - 50 yards out. The beach is generally sandy offshore with a gentle slope. The water stays fairly shallow out to the reef and contains some interesting coral formations. The area offers fair snorkeling in clear water on calm days. A good place for beginning snorkelers and children, but not good for swimming due to shallow water and abundant coral.

PUUNOA BEACH ★
The beach is at the north end of Lahaina between Kai Pali Rd. and the old Mala Wharf and can be seen as you leave Lahaina on Front St. Southern access: Take Kai Pali Rd. off Front St. Parking for about 20 cars along the road which is the entrance for the Puunoa Beach Estates. Public Beach access sign with concrete sidewalk to the beach. Mid beach access: Take Puunoa Place off Front St. at the Public Beach access sign. Parking for about four cars at the end of the road which ends at the beach. A rinse off hose here is the only facility for the beach. North Access: Take Mala Wharf off Front St. Parking for approximately 20 cars along the road just before the entrance to the Mala boat launching parking area.

This narrow, dense, darker sand beach is about 300 yards long and well protected by a reef approximately 100 - 150 yards offshore. The beach slopes gently to water only 3 - 4 feet deep. Unfortunately, rock and coral near the surface make swimming unadvised. There are areas of the beach clear of coral 10 - 15 feet out where children can play safely in the calm, shallow water. At high tide there are more fish to see while snorkeling. This continues to be a favorite with our children because of the calm, warm water.

WAHIKULI STATE WAYSIDE PARK

There are three paved off-street parking areas between Lahaina and Kaanapali. Many covered picnic tables, restrooms, showers, and BBQ grills are provided. The first and third parking areas are marked but have no beach. The second unmarked area has an excellent, darker sand beach with a gentle slope to deeper water. There is some shelf rock in places but it's rounded and smooth and not a problem. With the handy facilities, trees for shade, and the nice beach, this is a good, and popular, spot for sunning, swimming, and picnicking.

HANAKAOO BEACH PARK ★

Off Honoapiilani Highway, immediately south of the Hyatt Regency, there is a large, well-marked, off-street parking area. The park has rinse-off showers, restroom, and picnic tables. Wide, darker sand beach with gentle slope to deeper water. This is a popular area because of the easy parking, facilities, good beach, shallow water and good swimming, and you are right next to the Hyatt.

HANAKAOO BEACH ★ (Kaanapali Beach)

The beach fronts the Hyatt Regency, Marriott, Kaanapali Alii, Westin Maui, Whaler's Shopping Center and condos, Kaanapali Beach Hotel, and the Sheraton, and is known as Kaanapali Beach. Access is through the Kaanapali Resort area. Turn off Honoapiilani Highway at either of the first two entrances. This area was not designed with non-guest use in mind, and parking is definitely a problem.

A) The Hyatt end of the beach is only a short walk from the large parking area of Hanakaoo Beach Park.

B) Public right-of-way with parking for 10 cars at the left of the Hyatt's lower parking lot.

C) Public right-of-way between the Hyatt and Marriott, no parking.

D) Public right-of-way between Marriott and Kaanapali Alii with parking for 11 cars only.

E) Public right-of-way between Kaanapali Alii and Westin Maui, no parking.

F) Public right-of-way between Kaanapali Beach Resort and the Sheraton with parking for 11 cars only.

G) The Whalers Shopping Center has a three-story pay parking lot, but with beach access only through the complex.

H) There is no on-street parking anywhere in the Kaanapali Resort complex.

The Hyatt, Marriott, Westin Maui, and Sheraton all have restrooms, showers, bars, and rental equipment. There is a beautiful, long, wide, white sand beach with an abrupt drop-off to deep water. There are small areas of offshore coral from the Hyatt to the Westin Maui at times, but no true offshore reef. Great swimming and good wave playing with the exception of two or three points along the beach where the waves consistently break fairly hard. In the winter, snorkeling can be fair off the Westin Maui when the coral is exposed underwater. The best snorkeling is at Black Rock, fronting the Sheraton Hotel. The water is almost always clear and fairly calm, with many types of nearly tame fish due to the popularity of hand feeding by snorkelers. (Bread, frozen peas and packaged dry noodles seem popular). Not much colorful coral. The best entrance to the water is from the beach alongside Black Rock.

KAANAPALI BEACH (South End)

This beach begins at the north side of Black Rock and runs for over a mile to the north fronting the Royal Lahaina Resort and the Maui Kaanapali Villas. Turn off Honoapiilani Road at the last Kaanapali exit at the stop light by the Maui Kaanapali Villas. There are a few places to park on the side of the road near the Public Access beach sign. With the airport now closed there is more parking available. This area is being prepared for future hotel and condo developement and should eventually have much improved public access, facilities and parking. The only facilities now are those of the nearby hotels. This wide, (usually) white sand beach has a steep drop-off to deep water and is usually calm - a good place to swim. Snorkeling around Black Rock is almost always good.

KAHANA - NAPILI - KAPALUA AND BEYOND

KAANAPALI BEACH (North End)

This section of beach fronts the Mahana Resort, Maui Kai, Embassy Suites, Kaanapali Shores, Papakea, Maui Sands and Paki Maui from south to north, and ends at the Honokowai Beach Park. Access is generally only through the resorts. Most of the resorts have rinse-off showers convenient to the beach, however, no other facilities are available. This is a long, narrow, white sand beach which is fronted by a close-in reef. All the resorts except the Kaanapali Shores and Embassy Suites have retaining walls along the beach. The Kaanapali Shores has, over the last couple of years, suffered considerable erosion of its once wide beach and has recently completed an expensive new under-the-sand retaining wall in an effort to stabilize and restore it. There is also a cleared area through the coral in front of the resort. This is the only good swimming area on the north section of the beach and is the only good access through the reef for snorkeling.

The reef comes into shore at the south end of Papakea and again at the Hono-kowai Beach Park. At low tide the reef fronting Papakea can be walked on like a wide sidewalk. (See GENERAL INFORMATION - Children, for night walking on the reef) The reef is generally only 10 - 20 yards offshore and the area between is very shallow with much coral and rock making it undesirable for swimming and snorkeling. The middle section of beach, fronting the old Kaana-pali Airport, is slated for future development.

HONOKOWAI BEACH PARK

Turn off the Honoapiilani Hwy. on the first side street past the airport (at the Honokowai sign) and get onto Lower Honoapiilani Hwy., which parallels the ocean. The park is across the street from the Honokowai Grocery Store. There is paved off-street parking for 30 cars. There are 11 picnic tables, 5 BBQ pits, restrooms, showers, and a grassy park with shade trees. Grocery store across the street with pay phone outside. The white sand beach is lined by a wide shelf of beach rock. Between the shelf rock and reef there is a narrow, shallow pool with a sandy bottom which is a good swimming area for small children. There is a break in the reef at the north end of the beach where you can get snorkeling access to the outside reef. Water sport equipment for rent at the Honokowai Store.

KAHANA BEACH
In front of the Kahana Beach Condominiums, Sands of Kahana, Royal Kahana, Valley Isle Resort and Hololani from south to north on Lower Honoapiilani Hwy. There is limited off-road parking at the south end of the beach. Other access would be through the condos. The only facilities available are at the condos, usually rinse-off showers. There are several grocery stores, one at the Valley Isle Resort, the other at the Hololani condos. This white sand beach varies from narrow to wide and its offshore area is shallow with rock and sand, semi-protected by reef. Good swimming, fair snorkeling. Beach may be cool and windy in afternoons.

During the past years, from about 1989, this area has been particularly plagued by the unexplained green algae bloom which tends to concentrate here due to the wind, current and shoreline continues. The beach is fequently unappealing for swimming and beach use due to the amount of slimy green algae on the beach and in the water. One possible cause of this unsightly mess may be the nitrates and other chemicals which are used for agriculture and golf course maintainence, flowing into the ocean. The county is continuing to investigate and may find it necessary to institute some controls.

KEONENUI BEACH ★
The beach is in front of and surrounded by the Kahana Sunset with no convenient public access. A lovely wide crescent of white sand with a fairly gentle slope to water's edge, then fairly steep slope to deeper water. The beach is set in a small shallow cove, about 150 yards wide, which affords some protection. At times, especially in winter, rough seas come into the beach. When calm (most of the time), this is an excellent swimming and play area with fair snorkeling.

ALAELOA BEACH ("The Cove")
This miniature, jewel-like cove is surrounded by low sea cliffs. The small, approximately 25 - 30 yard long, white sand beach has a gentle slope with scattered rocks leading into sparkling clear waters. Pavilion and lounge chair area for use by Alaeloa guests. Good swimming and snorkeling with very clear and calm waters except when storm-generated waves come in. Fortunately, or unfortunately, depending on your point of view, this small cove is surrounded by the Alaeloa residential area which has no on or off-street public parking, therefore, public access to this beach is very difficult.

NAPILI BAY ★
There are two public accesses to this beautiful beach. There is a small, easily missed, public right-of-way and Napili Beach sign just past the Napili Shores at Napili Place Street. On-street parking at sign for Napili Surf Beach Resort. The public beach right-of-way sign shows the entrance to the beach. Public telephone in parking lot of Napili Surf. The second entrance is at the public beach right-of-way and Napili Sunset, Hale Napili, and Napili Bay signs on Hui Street. On-street parking and pay phone at entrance to beach walk.

This is a long, wide crescent of white sand between two rocky points. The offshore slope is moderately steep. Usually very safe for swimming and snorkeling except during winter storms when large waves occasionally come into the bay.

At the south end of the beach are a series of shallow, sandy tide pools which make an excellent place for children, but only under close supervision. Coral formations 30 - 40 yards offshore can provide fair snorkeling on calm days especially at the northern end of the beach and decent boogie boarding with mild swells. No facilities other than at the hotels along the beach. There is a grocery store just past the second entrance at the Napili Village Hotel. Look for the Napili Grocery Store sign.

KAPALUA BEACH ★ (Fleming Beach)
Just past the Napili Kai Beach Club you will see a public beach right-of-way sign. Off-street parking area for about 30 - 40 cars. Showers and restrooms. A beautiful crescent of white sand between two rocky points. The beach has a gentle slope to deeper water, maximum about 15 feet. From the left point, a reef arcs toward the long right point creating a very sheltered bay, probably the nicest and safest swimming beach on Maui. Shade is provided by numerous palm trees lining the back shore area. Above the beach are the lovely grounds of the Kapalua Bay Resort. Swimming is almost always excellent with plenty of play area for children. Snorkeling is usually good with many different kinds of fish and interesting coral. *REMEMBER*, this popular beach has limited parking.

NAMALU BAY ★
Park at Kapalua Beach and take the concrete path along the beach, up through the hotel's grounds, and out to the point of land separating Kapalua Bay from Namalu Bay. This small bay has a shoreline of large lava boulders, no beaches. On calm days snorkeling is very good and entry and exit over the rocks is easy. This little known spot is definitely worth the short walk down the trail.

ONELOA BEACH
Enter at the public right-of-way sign just past the Kapalua Bay Resort. Paved off-street parking for 12 - 15 cars only, no other facilities. Long, straight white sand beach with a shallow sand bar that extends to the surfline. The beach is posted with a warning sign "No swimming at time of high surf due to dangerous currents." This area tends to get windy and cloudy in the afternoons, especially in the winter months. We have usually found this beach deserted.

D. T. FLEMING BEACH PARK
Off-street parking on both sides of the road. Restrooms, showers, picnic tables, and BBQ's on the grassy dunes above the beach. The long white sand beach is steep with an offshore sand bar which may cause dangerous water conditions when swells hit the beach. The beach is posted "Dangerous Swimming."

MOKULEIA BEACH ★ (Slaughterhouse)
On Highway 30, past D. T. Fleming Beach Park, look for cars parked along the roadside and the Mokuleia-Honolua Marine Reserve sign. Park your car and hike down one of the steep dirt and rock trails - they're not difficult. There are no facilities. The wide, white sand beach has a gentle slope to deep water and is bordered by two rocky points and is situated at the foot of steep cliffs. The left middle part of the beach is usually clear of coral and rocks even in winter when the beach is subject to erosion.

During the winter this is *THE* bodysurfing spot, especially when the surf is heavy, however, dangerous water conditions also exist. This area is only for the strong, experienced swimmer. The summer is generally much better for swimming and snorkeling. In the past couple of years, this has become a very popular beach. Snorkeling is fair to good, especially around the left rocky point where there is a reef. Okay in winter when the ocean is calm and visibility good. NOTE: The beach is known as Slaughterhouse because of the once existing slaughterhouse on the cliffs above the beach, not because of what the ocean can do to body surfers in the winter when the big ones are coming in! Remember this is part of the Honolua-Mokuleia Bay Marine Life Conservation District - look but don't disturb or take.

HONOLUA BAY ★

The next bay past Slaughterhouse is Honolua Bay. Watch for a dirt side road on the left. Park here and walk in along the road. There is no beach, just cobblestone with irregular patches of sand and an old concrete boat ramp in the middle. Excellent snorkeling in summer, spring, and fall especially in the morning, but in winter only on the calmest days. In summer on calm days the bay resembles a large glassy pond and in our opinion, this is the best snorkeling on Maui. Note: After a heavy rainfall, the water may be turbid for several days before it returns to its sparkling clear condition again. You can enter at the boat ramp or over the rocks and follow the reefs either left or right. Remember this is a Marine Life Conservation area, so look but don't disturb.

There is an interesting phenomenon affecting the bay. As fresh water runoff percolates into the bay, a shimmering boundary layer (usually about three feet below the surface) is created between the fresh and salt waters. Depending on the amount of runoff it may be very apparent or disappear entirely. It is less prevalent on the right side of the bay. Honolua Bay is also an internationally known winter surfing spot. Storm generated waves come thundering in around the right point creating perfect waves and tubes. A good vantage point to watch the action is the cliffs at the right point of the bay, accessible by car on a short dirt road off the main highway.

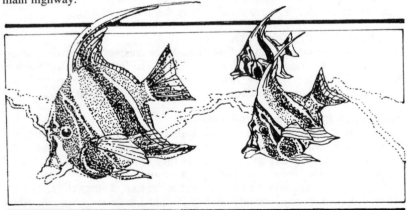

KIHIKIHI   JBayot

KIHEI BEACHES

The Kihei beaches aren't quite as beautiful as Wailea's. They don't have the nicely landscaped parking areas, or the large, beautiful resort complexes (this is condo country). They do offer increased facilities such as BBQs, picnic tables, drinking water, and grassy play areas. The Kamaole I, II and III beaches even have lifeguards. The beaches are listed in order from Maalaea Bay to Wailea.

MAALAEA BAY BEACH
This gently curving white sand beach stretches three miles from the Maalaea boat harbor to Kihei. For the most part, the beach is backed by low sand dunes and large generally wet, sand flats. Public access is from many areas along South Kihei Road. There are no facilities. Casual beach activities are best early in the morning before the strong, mid-morning, prevailing winds begin to sweep across the isthmus. Due to the length of the beach and the hard-packed sand near the water, this has become a popular place to jog. Windsurfing is popular in the afternoons.

The beach begins in front of the last three condominiums in Maalaea, the Kana'I A Nalu, Hono Kai and the Makani A Kai. Just past the Makani A Kai on Hauoli Street is a public park and beach access. There is a good section of beach here with a fairly gentle drop off. Also there are two small, sandy-bottomed pools, protected by the reef on either side of the small man-made rock jetty. These are good play areas for kids. The waves remain fairly calm, except at high tide or high surf conditions. The best snorkeling is out from the beach here, but the conditions are extremely variable, from fairly clear to fairly murky, depending on the time of year and prevailing conditions. Snorkeling is usually better in the winter months. The beach from this point to North Kihei is generally fronted by shelf rock or reef and is not good for swimming, but excellent for a lengthy beach walk! The beach becomes excellent for swimming and other beach activities in front of the North Kihei condos. Snorkeling is fair. A beach activity center is located on the beach at the Kealia Beach Center.

MAI POINA OE IAU BEACH PARK
On South Kihei Road, fronting Maui Lu Resort. Paved parking for 8 cars at the Pavilion (numerous other areas to park are along the road). 5 picnic tables, restrooms, showers. This is actually part of the previous beach. In-shore bottom generally sandy with patches of rock, fronted by shallow reef. Swimming and snorkeling are best in the morning before the early afternoon winds come up. Popular windsurfing area in the afternoon.

KAONOULULU BEACH PARK
Located across the street from the Kihei Bay Surf. Off-road parking for 20 cars, restrooms, drinking water, rinse-off showers, picnic tables, and four BBQ grills. Very small beach, well protected by close-in reef.

KAWILIKI POU PARK
Located at the end of Waipulani Street. Paved off-street parking for 30 cars, restrooms, large grassy area, and public tennis courts. Fronts Laule'a, Luana Kai

and the Maui Sunset Hotel. Tall graceful palms line the shoreline. Narrow sandy beach generally strewn with seaweed and coral rubble. (See GENERAL INFORMATION - Children, for frog hunting information)

KAWILILIPOA AND WAIMAHAIKAI AREAS
Any of the cross streets off South Kihei Road will take you down toward the beach where public right-of-ways are marked. Limited parking, usually on street. No facilities. The whole shoreline from Kalama Park to Waipulani Street (3 - 4 miles) is an area of interrupted beaches lined by residential housing and small condo complexes. Narrow sandy beaches with lots of coral rubble from the fronting reefs.

KALAMA BEACH PARK
Well-marked, 36-acre park with 12 pavilions, 3 restrooms, showers, picnic tables, BBQ grills, playground apparatus, soccer field, baseball field, tennis courts, volleyball and basketball courts. Lots of grassy area. There is no beach (in winter), only a large boulder breakwater. Good view of the cinder cone in Makena, Molokini, Kahoolawe, Lanai, and West Maui.

KAMAOLE I
Well-marked beach across from the Kamaole Beach Club. Off-street parking for 30 cars. Facilities include picnic tables, restrooms, rinse-off showers, rental equipment, children's swimming area, and lifeguard. Long, white, sandy beach offering good swimming, poor to fair snorkeling. NOTE: The small pocket of sand between rock outcroppings at the right end of the beach is known as Young's Beach. It is also accessible from Kaiau Street with parking for about 20 cars. Public right-of-way sign at end of Kaiau Street.

KAMAOLE II
Located across from the Kai Nani shopping and restaurant complex. On-street parking, restrooms, rinse-off showers, rental equipment, and lifeguard. White sand beach between two rocky points with sharp drop-off to overhead depths. Good swimming, poor to fair snorkeling.

KAMAOLE III ★
Well-marked beach across from the Kamaole Sands Condominiums. Off-street parking, picnic tables, BBQ's, restrooms, rinse-off showers, drinking water, playground equipment, a grassy play area, and a lifeguard. 200-yard long, narrow (in winter) white sand beach with some rocky areas along beach, and a few submerged rocks. Good swimming, fair snorkeling around rocks at south end of the beach. Kamaole II and III are very popular beaches with locals and tourists because of the nice beaches and easy access.

WAILEA BEACHES

This area generally has small, lovely, white sand beaches which have marked public access. Parking is off-street in well maintained parking areas, and restrooms as well as rinse-off showers are provided. You won't recognize this area from a few years ago. The new Grand Hyatt Wailea, Kea Lani and Four Seasons Resorts, along with the renovated Stouffer Wailea Beach and Maui Inter-Continental Resorts, have transformed this once under developed area into a world class resort destination riviling Kaanapali, and even surpassing Kaanapali in some ways.

KEAWAKAPU BEACH ★
There are two convenient public accesses to this very nice but generally under-used beach. There is paved parking for 50 cars across the street from the beach, about 2/10 mile south of Mana Kai Resort. Look for the beach access sign on the left as you travel south. There are two small crescent shaped, white sand beaches separated by a small rocky point. Good swimming, off-shore sandy bottom, fair snorkeling around rocks at far north end. There are rinse-off showers and a restaurant at the Mana Kai which is right on the beach. Access to southern end of beach - go straight at left turn-off to Wailea, road says "Dead End." Parking for about 30 cars. Rinse-off showers. Beautiful, very gently sloping white sand beach with good swimming. Snorkeling off rocks on left. Popular scuba diving spot. Four hundred yards off shore in 80 - 85 feet of water there is supposed to be an artificial reef of 150 car bodies.

MOKAPU BEACH ★
A public access sign (Ulua/Mokapu Beaches) is near the Stouffer Wailea Beach Resort. Small parking area, restrooms and showers. Rental equipment at nearby Wailea Resort Activities Center at Stouffer's. Beautiful white sand beach. Excellent swimming. Good snorkeling in mornings around the rocks which divide the two beaches. The best snorkeling is on the Ulua beach side.

ULUA BEACH ★
A public access sign (Ulua/Mokapu Beaches) is located near the Stouffer Wailea Beach Resort. Small paved parking area with a short walk to beach. Showers and rest rooms. Rental equipment is only a short walk away at the Wailea Ocean Activities Center. Beautiful white sand beach fronting the Elua Resort complex. Ulua and Mokapu Beaches are separated by a narrow point of rocks. The area around the beaches is beautifully landscaped because of the resorts. The beach is semi-protected and has a sandy offshore bottom. Good swimming, usually very good snorkeling in the mornings around the lava flow between the beaches. Come early to get a parking space!

WAILEA BEACH ★
One half mile south of the Inter-Continental Resort there is a public beach access sign and a paved road down to a landscaped parking area for about 40 cars. Restrooms and rinse-off showers. Rental sailboats and windsurfing boards are available. Beautiful wide crescent of gently sloping white sand. Gentle offshore slope. Good swimming. Snorkeling is only fair to the left (south) around the rocks (moderate currents and not much coral or many fish).

POLO BEACH

Just past the Kea Lani Resot turn right at the Wailea Golf Club-Fairway Restaurant sign and head down to the Polo Beach Resort condominiums. The public access sign is easy to spot. Parking for 40 cars in paved parking area. Showers and restrooms. The beaches are a short walk on a paved sidewalk and down a short flight of stairs. There are actually two beaches, 400 foot long north beach and 200 foot long south beach, separated by 150 feet of large rocks. The beaches slope begins gently, then continues more steeply off-shore and is not well protected. This combination can cause swift beach backwash which is particularly concentrated at two or three points and also a rough shore break, especially in the afternoons. The beach is dotted with large rocks. Fair swimming, generally poor snorkeling. Construction is underway adjacent to the Polo Beach condominiums, where the Wailea Suites resort is expected to be completed by 1991.

MAKENA BEACHES

This area includes the beaches south of Polo Beach, out to La Perouse Bay (past this point, you either hike or need to have a four-wheel drive). The Makena beaches are relatively undeveloped and relatively unspoiled, and not always easy to find. There are few signs, confusing roads, and some beaches are not visible from the road. Generally, no facilities and parking where you can find it. The nearest grocery is at the Wailea Shopping Center. We hope our directions will help you find these sometimes hard-to-find, but very lovely, nearly pristine beaches.

PALAUEA BEACH

As you leave Wailea, there is a four-corner intersection with a sign on the left for the Wailea Golf Club, and on the right for the Polo Beach Condos. 8/10 mile past here turn onto the second right turnoff at the small "Paipu Beach" sign. At roads end (about 1/10 mile), park under the trees. Poolenalena Beach lies in front of you. Walk several hundred feet back towards Polo Beach over a small hill (Haloa Point) and you will see Palauea Beach stretching out before you. A beautiful beach, largely unkown to tourists. The area above the beach at the south end has been developed with pricey residential homes.

If you drive down to the Polo Beach Condos instead, you can continue on Old Makena Road which will loop back to Makena Alanui Road after about a mile. Palauea Beach lays along this road, but is not visible through the trees. There is a break in the fence .35 miles from Polo Beach with a well worn path to the beach. Although this is all private and posted land, the path and the number of cars parked alongside the road seems to indicate that this beautiful white sand beach is getting much more public use than in the past. Good swimming. No facilities. Both Palauea and Poolenalena beaches have the same conditions as Polo Beach with shallow offshore slope then a steep dropoff which causes fairly strong backwash in places and tends to cause a strong shore break in the afternoon.

POOLENALENA BEACH

See directions for Palauea Beach. This is a lovely wide, white sand beach with gentle slope offering good swimming. This used to be a popular local camping spot, however no camping signs are now posted.

UPCOUNTRY ROAD
1.4 miles from Polo Beach. Currently closed in dispute over maintenance.

PAIPU BEACH (Chang's Beach)
Continue another 2/10 to 3/10 miles on Makena Alanui Rd., past Poolenalena and you will come to the Makena Surf Town Houses (about 1.2 miles from the Wailea Golf Club sign). This development surrounds Chang's Beach, however, there is a public beach access sign and paved parking for about 20 cars. It's a short walk down a concrete path to the beach. A rinse-off shower is provided. This small but sandy beach is used mostly by guests of the Makena Surf.

ULUPIKUNUI BEACH
Turn right just past the Makena Surf and immediately park off the road. Walk down to the beach at the left end of the complex. The beach is 75 to 100 feet of rock strewn sand and is not too attractive, but is well protected.

FIVE GRAVES
From the Makena Surf, continue down Old Makena Road another 2/10 mile to the entrance of Five Graves. There is ample parking. The 19th century graves are visible from Makena Rd. just a couple hundred feet past the entrance. There is no beach, but this is a good scuba and snorkeling site. Follow the trail down to the shore where you'll see a good entrance to the water.

MAKENA LANDING - PAPIPI BEACH
Continue another 2/10 mile on Old Makena Rd. to Makena Landing on the right. There is off-street parking for 22 cars. The beach is located at the entrance and is about 75 - 100 feet with gentle slope, sometimes rock strewn. Not very attractive and is used mostly for fishing, but snorkeling can be good if you enter at the beach and follow the shore to the right. Restrooms and showers available.

Instead of turning right onto Old Makena Road at the Makena Surf, continue straight and follow the signs to the Makena Golf Course. About 9/10 mile past the Makena Surf there is another turnoff onto Old Makena Rd. At the stop sign at the bottom of the hill, you can turn right and end up back at Makena Landing or turn left and head for Maluaka Beach. 2/10 mile past the stop sign you will see the old Keawalai Church U.C.C. and cemetery. Sunday services continue to be held here. Along the road is a pay phone.

MALUAKA BEACH ★ (Naupaka)
3/10 mile past the stop sign there is a turnaround and public entrance to this beach on the right. There are a few parking places near the entrance along the road, however, the main parking lot with restrooms and showers is located a short walk back up the road. The resort above the beach is the Maui Prince. This gorgeous 200-yard beach is set between a couple of rock promontories. The very fine white sand beach is wide with a gentle slope to deeper water. Snorkeling can be good in the morning until about noon when the wind picks up. There are interesting coral formations at the south end with unusual abstract shapes, and large coral heads of different sizes. Coral in shades of pink, blue, green, purple and lavender can be spotted. There are enough fish to make it interesting, but not an abundance. In the afternoon when the wind comes up, so do the swells, providing good boogieboarding and wave playing.

ONEULI BEACH (Black Sand Beach)

On Old Makena Hwy., past the Maui Prince Resort, just past the intersection of the old road is a dirt road turnoff. A 4-wheel drive or a high ground clearance vehicle is good idea for the very rutted 3/10 mile to the beach. The beach is coarse black sand and the entire length of the beach is lined by an exposed reef. No facilities.

ONELOA BEACH ★ (Makena Beach)

The entrance for the north end of the beach is at the second dirt road to the right off Old Makena Hwy. after the intersection of the old road. It is 3/10 mile from the turnoff to the beach and parking area with room for quite a few cars. The old, very rutted dirt road has been replaced by a graded and somewhat graveled road.

This very lovely white sand beach is long (3/4 mile) and wide and is the last major undeveloped beach on the leeward side of the island. Community effort is continuing in their attempt to prevent further development of this beach. The 360-foot cinder cone (Pu'u Olai) at the north end of the beach separates Oneloa from Puuolai Beach. The beach has a quick, sharp drop off and rough shore break particularly in the afternoon. Body surfing is sometimes good. Snorkeling around the rocky point at the cinder cone is only poor to fair with not much to see, and not for beginners due to the usually strong north to south current.

PUUOLAI BEACH (Little Makena)

Take the first Oneloa Beach entrance, and park at Oneloa Beach. From there, you hike over the cinder cone. There is a flat, white sand beach, with a shallow sandy bottom which is semi-protected by a shallow cove. The shore break is usually gentle and swimming is good. Bodysurfing sometimes. Snorkeling is only poor to fair around the point on left. Watch for strong currents. Although definitely illegal, beach activities here tend to be au naturel.

AHIHI-KINAU ★ (NATURAL RESERVE AREA)

About 3/4 mile past Makena Beach, a sign indicates the reserve. There is a small, 6-foot wide, sandy beach alongside the remnants of an old concrete boat ramp. Although it's located in a small cove and is well protected, the beach and cove are very shallow with many urchins. There is also very limited parking here. Up around the curve in the road is a large parking area. It's a short walk to the shore on a crushed lava rock trail. Another couple hundred feet to a very small (3 foot) and partially hidden sand and pebble beach that makes a better entrance to the water than over the rocks. There is excellent snorkeling directly off shore to the right and left. Remember, this is a marine reserve - look, but don't disturb. No facilities.

LA PEROUSE BAY

2 miles past Ahihi-Kinau, over a road carved through Maui's most recent lava flow, is the end of the road unless you have a 4-wheel drive. The "road" is extremely rough and we would recommend a hike rather than a ride. It's about 3 or 4 miles from road's end at La Perouse Bay to the Kanaio beaches. If you hike, wear good hiking shoes as you'll be walking over stretches of sharp lava rock. There are a series of small beaches, actually only pockets of sand of various compositions, with fairly deep offshore waters and strong currents.

WAILUKU - KAHULUI BEACHES

Beaches along this whole side of the island are usually poor for swimming and snorkeling. The weather is generally windy or cloudy in winter and very hot in summer. Due to the weather, type of beaches, and distance from the major tourist areas on the other side of the island, these beaches don't attract many tourists (except Hookipa, which is internationally known for wind surfing).

WAIHEE BEACH PARK
From Wailuku take Kahekili Highway about three miles to Waihee and turn right onto Halewaiu Road, then proceed about one-half mile to the Waihee Municipal Golf Course. From there, a park access road takes you into the park. Paved off-street parking, restrooms, showers, and picnic tables. This is a long, narrow, brown sand beach strewn with coral rubble from Waihee Reef. This is one of the longest and widest reefs on Maui and is about one thousand feet wide. The area between the beach and reef is moderately shallow with good areas for swimming and snorkeling when the ocean is calm. Winter surf or storm conditions can produce strong alongshore currents. Do not swim or snorkel at the left end of the beach as there is a large channel through the reef which usually produces a very strong rip current. This area is generally windy.

KANAHA BEACH PARK
Just before reaching the Kahului Airport, turn left, then right on reaching Ahahao Street. The far south area of the park has been landscaped and includes BBQs, picnic tables, restrooms, and showers. Paved off-street parking is provided. The beach is long (about one mile) and wide with a shallow offshore bottom composed of sand and rock. Plenty of thorny Kiawe trees in the area make footwear essential. The main attraction of the park is its peaceful setting and view, so picnicking and sunbathing are the primary activities. Swimming would appeal mainly to children. Surfing can be good here.

WINDSURFING

H. A. BALDWIN PARK
The park is located about 1.5 miles past Spreckelville on the Hana Highway. There is a large off-street parking area, a large pavilion with kitchen facilities, picnic tables, BBQs, and a tent camping area. There are also restrooms, showers, a baseball and a soccer field. The beach is long and wide with a steep slope to overhead depths. This is a very popular park because of the facilities. The very consistent, although usually small, shore break is good for bodysurfing. Swimming is poor. There are two areas where exposed beach rock provides a relatively calm place for children to play.

HOOKIPA BEACH PARK
Located about two miles past Lower Paia on the Hana Highway. Restrooms, showers, four pavilions with BBQ's and picnic tables, paved off-street parking, and a tent camping area is provided. Small, white sand beach fronted by a wide shelf of beach rock. The offshore bottom is a mixture of reef and patches of sand. Swimming is not advised. (The area is popular for the generally good and, at times (during winter), very good surfing). Hookipa is internationally known for its excellent wind surfing conditions. This is also a good place to come and watch both of these water sports.

HANA

WAIANAPANAPA STATE PARK
About four miles before you reach Hana on the Hana Highway is Waianapanapa State Park. There is a trail from the parking lot down to the ocean. The beach is not of sand, but of millions of small, smooth, black volcanic stones. Ocean activities are generally unsafe. There is a lava tunnel at the end of the beach that runs about 50 feet and opens into the ocean. Other well marked paths in the park lead to more caves and fresh water pools. An abundance of mosquitos breed in the grotto area and bug repellent is strongly advised.

HANA BEACH PARK
If you make it to Hana, you will have no difficulty finding this beach on the shoreline of Hana Bay. Facilities include a pavilion with picnic tables, restrooms and showers, and also Tutu's snack bar. About a 200-yard beach lies between old concrete pilings on the left and the wharf on the right. Gentle offshore slope and gentle shore break even during heavy outer surf. This is the safest swimming beach on this end of the island. Snorkeling is fair to good on calm days between the pier and the lighthouse. Staying inshore is a must, as beyond the lighthouse the currents are very strong and flow seaward.

KAIHALULU BEACH (Red Sand Beach)
This reddish sand beach is in a small cove on the other side of Kauiki Hill from Hana Bay and is accessible by trail. At the Hana Bay intersection follow the road up to the school. A dirt path leads past the school and disappears into the jungle, then almost vanishes as it goes through an old cemetery, then continues out onto a scenic promontory. The ground here is covered with marble-sized pine cones which make for slippery footing. As the trail leads to the left and over the edge of the cliff, it changes to a very crumbly rock/dirt mixture that is unstable at best.

You may wonder why you're doing this as the trail becomes two feet wide and slopes to the edge of a 60 foot cliff in one place. The trail down to the beach can be quite hazardous. Visitors and Hana residents alike have been injured seriously. It is definitely not for the squeamish, those with less than good agility or young-sters. And when carrying beach paraphernalia, extra caution is needed. The effort is rewarded as you descend into a lovely cove bordered by high cliffs and almost enclosed by a natural lava barrier seaward. The beach is formed primarily from red volcanic cinder, hence its name. Good swimming, but stay away from the opening at the left end because of rip currents. Although definitely illegal, beach activities here may be au naturel at times. The Hotel Hana Maui has plans to improve the access to this beach sometime in the future.

KOKI BEACH PARK
This beach is reached by traveling 1.5 miles past the Hasegawa Store toward Ohe'o Gulch. Look for Haneoo Road where the sign will read "Koki Park - Hamoa Beach - Hamoa Village." This beach is unsafe for swimming and the signs posted warn "Dangerous Current."

HAMOA BEACH ★
This gorgeous beach has been very attractively landscaped and developed by the Hotel Hana Maui in a way that adds to the surrounding lushness. The long white sand beach is in a very tropical setting and surrounded by a low sea cliff. To reach it, travel toward Ohe'o Gulch after passing through Hana. Look for the sign 1.5 miles past Hasegawa store that says "Koki Park - Hamoa Beach - Hamoa Village." There are two entrances down steps from the road. Parking is limited to along the roadside. The left side of the beach is calmer, and offers the best snorkeling. Because it is unprotected from the open ocean, there is good surfing and bodysurfing, but also strong alongshore and rip currents are created at times of heavy seas. The Hana Hotel maintains the grounds and offers restrooms, changing area, and beach paraphernalia for the guests. There is an outdoor rinse-off shower for non-hotel guests. Hay wagons bring the guests to the beach for the hotel's weekly luau.

RECREATION
AND TOURS

INTRODUCTION

Maui's ideal climate, diverse land environments, and benign leeward ocean has led to an astounding range of land, sea and air activities. With such a variety of things to do during your limited vacation time, we suggest browsing through this chapter and choosing those activities that sound most enjoyable. The following suggestions should get you started.

BEST BETS

To see and experience the real Maui, take a hike with guide Ken Schmitt.

For spectacular scenery and lots of fresh air, try the 38-mile coast down the world's largest dormant volcano on a bicycle, or one of several other Upcountry bicycle trips.

For great snorkeling try Honolua Bay, Namalu, Ahihi Kinau, or Olowalu.

Take a helicopter tour and get a super spectacular view of Maui.

Golf at one of Maui's excellent courses.

Sail to Lana'i and snorkel Hulopoe Beach with the Trilogy Cruise.

If the whales are in residence, take advantage of a whale watching excursion to view these beautiful mammals a bit more closely.

For an underwater thrill consider an introductory scuba adventure, no experience necessary.

For those who like to stay dry in the water, take a submarine or semi-submersible boat trip to view the underwater sights off Lahaina.

For a wet and wild water tour, plus snorkeling, try a raft trip.

If you're really adventurous, consider parasailing (during the summer when the whales have gone back north!), sea kayaking, or try the new scuba kayaking at Kapalua.

For great scenery at a great price, drive yourself to Hana and the O'heo Pools or to Upcountry and Haleakala.

271

OCEAN ACTIVITIES

SNORKELING

Maui offers exceptionally clear waters, warm ocean temperatures and abundant sea life with safe areas (no adverse water conditions) for snorkeling. If you are a complete novice, most of the resorts and excursion boats offer snorkeling lessons. Older folks can enjoy this sport that needs little experience and there is no need to dive to see all the splendors of the sea. If you are unsure of your abilities, the use of a floatation device may be of assistance. Be forewarned that the combination of tropical sun and the refreshing coolness of the ocean can deceive those paddling blissfully on the surface, and result in a badly burned backside. Water resistant sunscreens are available locally and are recommended.

Equipment is readily available at resorts and dive shops, and as you can see, much less expensive at the dive shops (even better are the weekly rates). For a listing of dive shops see Scuba Diving.

TYPICAL RENTAL PRICES -
MASK-FINS-SNORKEL FOR 24 HOURS:
Maui Dive Shop in Kihei - $7.50
Fun Rentals in Lahaina - $5.00
Frog Man - $7.50
Hyatt Regency Resort at Kaanapali - $20.00

Snorkel Bobs in Kihei and Napili has about the best weekly rates for mask, fin and snorkels at $15 per week. Silicon mask sets at $27 per week and prescription masks at $39.

Good snorkeling spots, if not right in front of your hotel or condo, are only a few minutes' drive away. The following are our favorites, each for a special reason.

WEST MAUI

Black Rock - At the Sheraton in the Kaanapali Resort. Park at the Whaler's Shopping Center and walk down the beach. Clear water and a variety of tame fish - these fish expect handouts!
Kapalua Bay - Public park with off street parking, restrooms and showers. A well protected bay and beautiful beach amid the grounds of the Kapalua Resort. Limited coral and some large coral heads, fair for fish watching. Arrive early as parking is very limited!
Namalu Bay - Park at Kapalua Bay, walk over from Kapalua Bay to the bay which fronts the grounds of the resort. Difficult entry, very good on calm days.
Honolua Bay - No facilities, park alongside the road and walk a 1/4 mile to the bay, but the best snorkeling on Maui, anytime but winter.
Olowalu - At mile marker 14, about 5 miles south of Lahaina. Generally calm and warmer waters with ample parking along the roadside. Very good snorkeling. If you find a pearl earring, let us know, we have the match!

EAST MAUI

Ulua-Mokapu Beach - Well-marked public beach park in Wailea with restrooms and showers. Good snorkeling on the Ulua side of the rocky point separating these two picturesque and beautiful beaches.

Maluaka Beach - Located in Makena, no facilities and along the road parking. Good coral formations and a fair amount of fish at the left end of the beach.

Ahihi Kinau Natural Reserve - Approximately five miles past Wailea. No facilities. This is not a very crowded spot and you may feel a little alone here, but the snorkeling is great with lots of coral and a good variety of fish.

Generally at all locations the best snorkeling is in the morning until about 1 p.m., when the wind picks up. For more information on each area and other locations, refer to the BEACHES chapter.

A good way to become acquainted with Maui's sea life is a guided snorkeling adventure with Ann Fielding, marine biologist and author of *Hawaiian Reefs and Tidepools and Underwater Guide to Hawai'i*. She takes small groups (minimum 2, maximum 6) to Honolua Bay in summer and Ahihi Kinau in winter. These morning (8:30 am - 12:30 pm) excursions begin with an introductory discussion on Hawaiian marine life, identification and ecology which is followed by snorkeling. Floatation devices, snorkel gear and refreshments are provided for the $40 fee. Phone 572-8437 for information.

You may feel the urge to rent an underwater camera to photograph some of the unusual and beautiful fish you've seen, and by all means try it, but remember, underwater fish photography is a real art. The new use once underwater cameras are a fun and inexpensive and available everywhere. There are two new video tapes of Maui's marine life available at the island bookstores if you want a permanent record of the fish you've seen.

REEF DWELLERS   J. BAYOT

There are two other great places to snorkel, however, you need a boat to reach them. Fortunately, a large variety of charter services will be happy to assist.

Molokini Crater - This small semicircular island is the remnant of a volcano. Located about 8 miles off Maalaea Harbor, it affords good snorkeling in the crater area. These waters are a marine reserve and the island is a bird sanctuary. Molokini is usually a 1/2 day excursion with a continental breakfast and lunch provided. Costs are $40 - $80 for adults, $25 - $42 for children under 12. (You may find rates even lower with current price wars among the heavy competition.)

Hulopoe Beach, Lana'i - This is our favorite. Located on the island of Lana'i, it's worth the trip for the beautiful beach and the abundant coral and fish. We saw a school of fish here that was so large that from the shore it appeared to be a huge moving reef. After swimming through the school and returning to shore we were informed that large predatory fish like to hang out around these schools! Lana'i is usually a full-day excursion with continental breakfast, BBQ lunch and a optional island tour. $90 - $110 for adults. Half-day trips may be available.

A variety of snorkel/sail/tour options are available for snorkeling along East and West Maui's coastline, Molokini, Moloka'i or Lana'i. Your first decision is choosing between a large or small group tour. Large groups go out in substantial monohull or catamaran motor yachts of 60 - 90 feet in length. They get you there comfortably and fast, but without the intimate sailing experience of a smaller, less crowded boat. There are also many sleek sailboats (monohull, catamaran or trimaran) that you can share with 4 to 8 people or privately charter. Another option for a Maui sea excursions is the Zodiac type rafts that use 20 - 23 foot inflatable rafts powered by two large outboards. These rides can be rough, wet and wild. All tours provide snorkel gear with floatation devices, if needed, and instruction. Food and refreshments are provided to varying degrees. For a list of outings, see the section on Sea Excursions.

MOLOKINI... again
Molokini is a 10,000 year old dormant volcano with only one crescent shaped portion of the crater rim now providing a sanctuary for marine and bird life. The crater on the inside of the island offers a water depth of 10 - 50 feet, a 76 degree temperature and visibility sometimes as much as 150 feet on the outer perimeter creating a fish bowl effect.

Molokini has been making a slow comeback. Our first trip to the crescent shaped crater was in the days when only two or three boats operated trips. It was truly picture perfect, resembling a huge fish bowl. However, for several years after the detonation of some submerged bombs by the Navy, the aquatic life was sparse. The many tour boats dropping anchors further damaged and destroyed the reef. While it hasn't been restored to the way it was during our first excursions a number of years ago, it is now returning to a much improved condition. Fortunately, concerned boat operators pushed for and were finally granted semi-permanent concrete mooring anchors, thereby preventing further reef damage. There is even talk that the number of boats may be somehow limited. Most trips are taken in the morning, some do offer afternoon trips, but expect rougher ocean conditions. On occasion even the morning trips are forced to snorkel at an alternative site, usually La Perouse.

We recommend **Blue Water Rafting** ★ for those die-hard snorkelers who would enjoy their early bird arrival to the crater with the opportunity to explore three different Molokini dive locations. They arrive at the crater first and snorkel the best spot before the big boats come in. Then it's a stop at the far crater wall for a second snorkeling opportunity. A third stop takes you to a spot over the underwater crater rim where the water on the crater side is shallow, but drops off out of sight dramatically on the other side. About $55. (808) 661-4743.

The **Prince Kuhio** is a 92' cruise boat, so if you are a little uncomfortable with a smaller boat, this may be an option for you. They only do cruises to Molokini, but are available for private charter. Their Molokini trip runs daily 7:15 - 11:15, adults $78, kids $41.60 (tax included) and they take about 150 passengers. Since it is a bigger boat, it takes only about half the time to get there. Lots of tables and benches for inside seating. The food is adequate, danish pastries, tea, coffee and juice enroute out and deli sandwiches for "lunch" (served at 9:30 a.m.) Also available was beer, wine, juice and sodas. They also serve champagne enroute back. (242-8777)

The **Four Winds** departs daily from Maalaea from Molokini. The half-day excursion is 7:30 - 12:30 and priced at $66 per person, max. 112. Unfortunately, at capacity the boat can be a little bit crowded. One of several boats operated by Classic Charters, this one has a few unique options. This boat is equipped with a slide! They offer a BBQ as compared to a very similar basic (buffet) deli lunch and the breakfast is a varied selection of fresh bagels and cream cheese with jellies. A nice change from the old Danish! Also fresh pineapple and orange slices. The BBQ lunch is cooked on board on three grills on the back of the boat...lunch selections include Mahi Mahi, Burger or chicken breast. All very good, and nice selections of condiments for the burgers. Beer, wine and soda included as well. Lay-out of the boat is nice, but it lacks seating except on the top deck. They also offer "Snuba," currently the only cruise offering it, as an optional activity for $39. The snuba activity takes six people at a time with air tanks carried on rafts which float at the surface. You can go down to a depth of twenty feet. The Four Winds also offers an afternoon snorkel cruise. (879-8188)

SCUBA DIVING

275

SCUBA DIVING

Maui, with nearby Molokini, Kahoʻolawe, Lanaʻi and Molokaʻi, offers many excellent diving locations. A large variety of dive operations offer scuba excursions, instruction, certification and rental equipment. If you are a novice, a great way to get hooked is an introductory dive. No experience is necessary. Instruction, equipment and dive, all for $34.95 - $95 with the average about $60. Dives are available from boats, or less expensive from the beach. A beginning beach dive may be advisable for the less confident aquatic explorer. For those who are certified but rusty, refresher dives are available.

The mainstay of Maui diving is the two-tank dive, two dive sites with one tank each. Prices depend on location and include all equipment. A trip runs about $90. If the bug bites and you wish to get certified, the typical course is five days, eight hours each day, at an average cost of $350 plus books. One dive shop suggested that visitors with limited time, do "PADI" dive preparation on the mainland and can then be certified on Maui in just two days. Classes are generally no more than 6 persons, or if you prefer private lessons, they run slightly more. Advanced open water courses are available in deep diving, search and recovery, underwater navigation and night diving (at a few shops). If you wish to rent equipment only, a complete scuba package including wet suit runs about $25 per day.

The larger resorts also offer instruction and some offer certification courses and arrange for excursions. Many of the dive operators utilize boats specifically designed for diving. Information, equipment, instruction and excursions can be obtained at the following dive shops and charter operators. As you can see by the number of listings, diving is very popular around Maui.

WEST MAUI

Aquatic Charters &
Underwater Video
879-0976

American Institute
of Diving
278 Wili Ko Pl. #18
Lahaina, 96761
667-5129

Beach Activities
Kaanapali, 661-5500

Captain Nemo's
150 Dickenson St.
Lahaina, 661-5555
1-800-367-8088

Kapalua Dive Co.
Kapalua Bay Hotel
669-4664

Dive Maui, Inc.
Lahaina, 667-2080

Extended Horizons
P.O. Box 10785
Lahaina, 667-0611

Frogman
(44' catamaran)
Kaanapali 661-3633

Hawaiian Reef Divers
129 Lahainaluna
Lahaina, 667-7647

Lahaina Divers
710 Front St.
Lahaina, 667-7496
1-800-657-7885

Maui Marriott
Ocean Activities
661-5388

EAST MAUI

Ed Robinson's
Diving Adventures
Kihei, 879-3584
1-800-635-1273

Maui Dive Shops
Kihei Town Center
Kihei, 879-1919

Makena Coast Charters
Kahului, 874-1273

Maui Dive Shops
Azeka Center, Kihei
879-3388

Maui Sun Divers
Kihei, 879-3631 or
879-3337

Mike Severns
Kihei, 879-6596

Ocean Activities
1325 S. Kihei Rd.
#212, Kihei
879-4485

Molokini Divers
1993 S. Kihei Rd
879-0055

The Dive Shop of
Kihei, 879-5172

Underwater Habitat
Groups of 6
Lana'i and Molokini
244-9739

Scuba Shack
Valley Isle Divers
Kihei, 879-3483

Kapalua Dive Company is featuring a Kayak Scuba Dive that was developed out of necessity in the summer of 1990. The Kapalua area coastline offers some of the finest diving on the West Coast of Maui, however, entry over lava rock was not feasible. "The Scrambler" offers the means to reach terrific dive spots while not creating the noise or potential anchor damage of a full size dive vessel. "The Scrambler" kayak was designed by Tim Niemier, Olympic Kayak coach. It weighs 35 lbs., is approximately 11 feet long, made of recyclable polyurethane and is described as a sit on top, self scupping kayak. The paddler is not tied, strapped or sealed inside the kayak, therefore, if it should roll the paddler is free to swim to the side, roll the kayak back upright and climb aboard. The term self scupping refers to the design which allows water to drain free of the topside without any procedures on the part of the paddler. This makes the kayak unsinkable. Departing from Kapalua Bay, each diver paddles his or her own kayak (although a double kayak is available for tight knit buddy teams) along the rugged and scenic Kapalua coastline for 15 to 20 minutes prior to reaching one of two different dive sites. Trips are limited to a maximum of four divers, price is $89 per person. Also available are Underwater Scooter Dives, Night Dives, snorkeling, sailing and windsurfing. Call direct to the Kapalua Activity Center at 669-4664.

Books of interest available at dive shops or area bookstores:
Comprehensive Guide to Scuba Diving in Hawaii, Phil Hoffman. 111 pgs., $6.95
The Diver's Guide to Maui by Chuck Thorne. $7.95
Skin Diver's Guide to Hawaii by Gordon Feund. 72 pages, $2.50.
Hawaii Diver's Manual, 162 pages, $3.00.
Underwater Videographer's Handbook, 128 pages, by Lynn Laymon $19.95

SNUBA

One of the newer water recreations available is Snuba which is a combination of snorkeling and scuba diving, allowing the freedom of underwater exploration without the heavy equipment of scuba diving. In brief, the snuba diver has a mask and an airhose that is connected to the surface. The only Snuba experience that we were able to track down was aboard the Four Winds. It is an extra fee option on their Molokini Cruise. See listing under Maui Classic Charters (879-8188).

SEA EXCURSIONS

Maui offers a bountiful choice for those desiring to spend some time in and on the ocean. Boats available for sea expeditions range from a three-masted schooner, to spacious trimarans and large motor yachts, to the zodiac type rafts for the more adventurous. Your choice is a large group trip or a more pampered small group excursion with a maximum of six people. Two of the most popular snorkeling excursions are to Molokini and Lana'i. Most sailboats motor to these islands and, depending on wind conditions, sail at least part of the return trip. All provide snorkel equipment. Food and beverage service varies and is reflected in the price. Many sailboats are available for hourly, full day or longer private charters.

Excursion boats seem to have a way of sailing off into the sunset. The number of new ones is as startling as the number of operations that have disappeared since our last edition. As mentioned previously, competition to Molokini has become fierce. Twenty to thirty boats a day now arrive to snorkel in this area. Many more boats now take trips to Lana'i as well. Currently there is only one company offering inter-island transportation to Moloka'i.

In the following list, phone numbers of the excursion companies are included in case personal booking is desired, however, most activity desks can also book your reservation. The best deal with an activity operator is *Tom's Cashback Tours* who can book most boats and offers a 10% refund. They are located in Lahaina and can be reached at 661-8889.

PRICES PER PERSON WILL RUN YOU ACCORDINGLY:
Full day trip to Lana'i $110 - $140
1/2 day trip to Molokini (3 - 6 hours) $35 - $99
1/2 day Maui coastline (3 - 4hrs.) $40- $65
Full day Maui coastline $80 - $90
Sunset sails (1 1/2 - 2 hrs.) $30 - $40
Whale watching (3 hrs./seasonal) $30- $40
Private charters $75 per hour and up, $400 per day and up
Dinner cruise $40 - $60

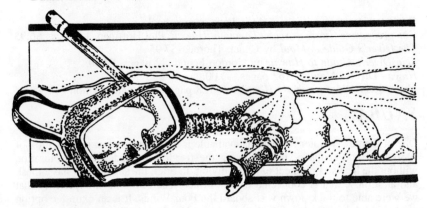

EXCURSION - CHARTER LISTING

ADVENTURE ONE - Powerboat - 25 people Molokini snorkel with food $49, whale watch seasonal. Departs Maalaea. 242-7683, 1-800-356-8989

ALIHILANI YACHT CHARTERS ★ - *First Class*, a 65' sailboat, takes 24 passengers on morning snorkel sails, departs Kaanapali beach or Lahaina Harbor, includes gourmet lunch as well as beer & wine. Departs 9 am returns 12:30. $65 adult, $50 child. Afternoon tradewind sail is a 1 1/2 hours of *true* sailing, beverages only served. Departs 2 pm, 3:30 pm and 5 pm. $35 adult, $25 child. Saturday Lana'i sail, all day. Includes breakfast, snacks, snorkeling, and lunch at Manele Bay. $125. 871-1156, 1-800-544-2520, FAX (808) 871-0682

Private charters and overnight charters can include catered meals. This cruise is a real find, but will appeal to a very specific kind of traveler. It's nothing like any of the other visitor boats, this is a yacht! It should appeal to people who REALLY like to sail, and for the more adventurous types. If you enjoy sailing, don't miss this one. A new trip, still in the planning stages, is a helicopter/boat tour of Maui, Lana'i and Moloka'i. It will include a helicopter tour one way, a stop at Manele Bay Hotel for a meal and then back by boat. Cost $280.

BLUE WATER RAFTING ★ - 3 1/2 hr. Molokini snorkel, 3 different sites in the crater, 2 hr. Molokini, snorkel 1 site, $35 - $99. Departs Kihei Launch ramp. Enjoy your ride on the latest concept in inflatable boats, the Novurania, a sleek Italian hybrid featuring a ridged fiberglass deep V hull for a smooth ride, and inflatable pontoons for stability and easy entry and exit for snorkeling. Max. 6 people. 879-7238. See review in "Snorkeling" and following excursion listings.

CAPT. NEMO'S - *Seasmoke*, 58' catamaran. Morning snorkel, sunset sail, seasonal whalewatch, introductory or certified dive to Lana'i. Departs Kaanapali Beach. 661-5555, 1-800-367-8088. $69 snorkel, $95 introductory scuba dive, certified dive $85.

CINDERELLA YACHT CHARTERS - *Cinderella*, 50' Columbia Sloop. 3/4 day sail/snorkel, max. 6 people. Departs Maalaea harbor, 242-2779.

CLUB LANAI - See description following excursion listings. Day trip to private beach on Lana'i. 871-1144

CORAL SEA/WINDJAMMER - *Coral Sea*, 65' glass bottom boat, whale watch and dinner cruises, departs Lahaina. *Spirit of Windjammer*, 65' 3-masted schooner. Full-day trip to Lana'i, 2-hour Maui coastline dinner cruise, takes large groups. Departs Lahaina. 667-8600, 1-800-843-8113

FRIENDLY CHARTERS - *Maalaea Kai II*, 44' trimaran, takes a max. of 36 people on Molokini snorkel/cruise and 2-4 hour snorkel/sail. Private charters available. Maalaea Harbor. 871-0985

GEMINI - 64' glass bottom catamaran. Departs Kaanapali Beach. Used by the Westin Hotel. Snorkel sail, Lana'i Adventure, dinner sail. 669-0508

HAWAIIAN RAFTING ADVENTURES (formerly Capt. Zodiac) - DESTINATION PACIFIC - 1223 Front St., Lahaina. 667-4348 26' diesel. Marine biologist, skipper-owner Ted Mickowski offers sportfishing, snorkeling, scuba for beginners or advanced, professional photography, underwater video. 6 people max., can launch from Kihei or Lahaina. Trips range from $79 for a 1 tank introductory dive, $89 for a 2 tank dive at Lana'i to PADI certification $350 or private charter $500. *Zodiac* - 23' zodiac rafts, max. 16. Seasonal whale watching $40 adult, $35 child. 1/2 snorkel/whale watch $55 adult, $45 child. Equipment, snacks and beverages included. Departs Mala Wharf. *Gina Marie* - 36' bayliner sportfisher. Full and partial day of sportfishing. Lahaina Harbor. 1/2 day with continental breakfast $90, full day with breakfast/ lunch $149 .

IDLE WILD CHARTERS - 35' Hawaiian sailing cat, max. 20 people. Snorkel/sail, whale watching, Molokini trips, private charter. Departs Maalaea. 572-8964

KAMEHAMEHA SAILS, INC. - *Kamehameha*, 40' catamaran. Snorkel/sail, sunset sail, whale watching, private charter, max. 15 people. Departs Lahaina harbor, 661-4522. Snorkel tours start at only $24!

KAPALUA KAI - Picnic, snorkel, sails daily 10 am - 2 pm, $65 adults, $35 kids. Evening sail - see "Dinner Cruises." Private charters available, 667-7777.

KAULANA - 65' power catamaran, departs Lahaina Harbor, 871-1144. Whale watching/sunset cocktail cruise, "guaranteed whale sightings or next cruise free."

KIELE V - 55' catamaran, 4 hr. snorkel/sail $65 adult, $35 kids. Afternoon sail $35 adults, $15 kids. Contact Hyatt Regency, Kaanapali (808) 661-1234 ext. 3104.

LAHAINA EXPEDITIONS ★ - Ferry service to Lana'i four times daily, five trips on Fridays. $50 round trip adult, $40 child. 661-3756. If you'd like to explore Lana'i on your own, you can take the early morning ferry boat over and return on the late afternoon trip. From the dock it is a moderate, but easy walk to Manele Bay and the adjacent Manele Bay Resort. There is a free shuttle that runs between the Manele Resort and the Koele Lodge located in central Lana'i. You could have lunch at either resort! They can also arrange for a rental car $50, or Jeep $100, for more in-depth explorations.

MAKENA BOAT PARTNERS - *Kai Kanani*, 46' catamaran, departs at Maui Prince Hotel for Molokini, 879-7218.

MAUI CLASSIC CHARTERS - *Teragram*, a 67' racing yacht designed by John Alden in 1929, takes 40 passenger on half day snorkel sail to Lana'i and whale watch in season. $56 adult, $39 child. *Lavengro*, a 60' gast rigged Schooner built in 1926, does Molokini sail, $56 adult, $39 child. *Four Winds*, a 53' double deck glass bottom catamaran, has BBQ grills, waterslide, daily learning snorkel, afternoon whale watch. Departs Maalaea harbor, 879-8177 , 879-8188.

MAUI DIVE SHOP - Books boating activities at Kihei Town Center 879-1919, Azeka's 879-3388, and Lahaina 661-5388.

MAUI-MOLOKAI SEA CRUISES - *Prince Kuhio*, 92' motor yacht. Whale watching, private charters, 1/2 day Molokini, departs Maalaea. 242-8777 or 1-800-468-1287. See review in "Snorkeling."

OCEAN ACTIVITIES - *No Ka Oi IV* and *No Ka Oi III*, 37' Tolleycraft. Scuba trips, 12 max., deep sea fishing, 6 max. *Wailea Kai*, 65' catamaran, snorkel, whale watch, dinner cruise. *Maka Kai*, 65' catamaran, whale watching, snorkeling, party boat fishing. *Manute'a*, 50' catamaran, Lana'i trip, dinner cruise, whale watching. All boats depart Maalaea except *Manute'a* which departs Lahaina Harbor. 879-4485 or 1-800-874-9303

OCEAN ENTERPRISES - 6 passenger cabin cruisers, snorkeling, scuba, sportfishing. 879-7067 or 874-9303

OCEAN RIDERS - "Adventure Rafting" on one of two rafts, 15 - 18 people max. 3 unusual destinations (depends on daily weather conditions). Reefs of Kaho'olawe, Moloka'i's cliffs or Lana'i. 661-3586

PACIFIC WHALE FOUNDATION CRUISES ★ - *Whale One*, 53' motor vessel, Maalaea. *Whale Two*, 50' sailing ketch, Lahaina. Whale watching, Molokini snorkel, sunset cruise. A portion of each ticket is donated to Pacific Whale Foundation. 879-8811

PRINCESS CRUISES - *Lahaina Princess* and *Maui Princess*. 661-8397 or 1-800-833-5800

SAIL HAWAII - *Fiesta* and *Mele Kai*, 37' and 40' sailing yachts. 6 people max. 5 hr. Molokini snorkel or sunset sail. Trip destinations flexible. Departs from Kihei Cove Park, 879-2201.

SEA ESCAPE - You-Drive zodiac boat rentals, 879-3721.

SEALINK OF HAWAII - *Maui Princess*, 150 passenger 118' excursion ferry. Service between Maui and Moloka'i daily. $25 adults one way. $50 round trip. Children half price. 1-800-833-5800, (808) 661-8397

LAHAINA HARBOR

SCOTCH MIST CHARTERS - *Scotch Mist II* and *Santa Cruz* 50' sailboats, take 23 people max on West Maui 1/2 day snorkel/sail, or champagne sunset sail, or private charters. Departs Lahaina harbor. 661-0386

SENTINEL YACHT CHARTERS - 42' sloop, max. 6 passengers for snorkeling, whale watching, overnight inter-island charters. 661-8110

SILENT LADY - Handsome 64' custom built whaling schooner. Previously only available as private charter, but now offer public five hour snorkel sail to Molokini, seasonal whale watching. 242-6499 or 661-1118

TRILOGY EXCURSIONS ★ - *Trilogy I*, 52' trimaran, *Trilogy II*, 55' catamaran, and *Trilogy III*, a 51' catamaran, do full-day snorkel/picnic/sightseeing tours to Lana'i. A definite best bet. *Trilogy IV,* a 44' trimaran, does 1/2-day sail/snorkel to Molokini. Departs Lahaina Harbor. $139 all day Lana'i, $75 half day to Molokini. 661-4743 or 1-800-874-2666. See review following excursion listings.

WHALE MIST - 36' monohull sailboat. Whale watch/sunset cruise, snorkeling trip goes to area off shore from Launiupoko Beach. Also operates a para-sail/snorkel combo for $68. 667-2833, 1-800-366-6478

WHITE WING CHARTERS - *White Wing*, 35' trimaran, does 6-hr. sail/-snorkel/fishing. Available for overnight and inter-island excursions, max. 6. Departs Maalaea Harbor. 242-9609

ZIP-PURR - 47' catamaran, departs Kaanapali Beach. Built by owner/captain Mike Turkington. Morning snorkel sail along Maui's coastline. Sunset sail, seasonal whale watch, private charters. 667-2299

BLUE WATER ADVENTURES!
While Molokini continues to be a much touted snorkeling spot, those seeking something a little different should check with *Blue Water Rafting* ★ about their East Maui trip. The area past Makena is geologically one of Maui's youngest. The coastline is only accessible by foot, however, a trip on the Novurania (a sleek Italian inflatable boat) will get you up close to see the beautiful and unusual scenic wonders of Mother Nature. Natural lava arches, pinnacles and caves are explored with the picturesque slopes of Haleakala providing a magnificent backdrop. Our chosen day for the expedition proved to be an exhilarating and wet one! The ocean conditions were somewhat rougher than desired, but our hearty group of six agreed to push forward. With spray from the ocean drenching us, one of the more witty members of our group donned his snorkel and mask. It performed admirably at keeping the water out of his eyes! The scenic vistas were fabulous and the boat was able to maneuver through one of the arches and up close to the cliffs which appeared to have been sculpted by a fine artisan. A brief stop for some mid-morning nourishment and a snorkel at La Perouse before returning to the Kihei Boat Ramp. This is a trip that can be best experienced only in this manner. To the best of our knowledge, only Blue Water Rafting is offering this trip. So, for an unusual and exciting Maui adventure, check this one out! Phone 879-7238.

A TRIP TO LANA'I

We hadn't done a trip aboard *Trilogy* ★ for a few years and wanted to see how things had changed over the course of time. It appears that the Coon family knows not to mess with a good thing. The morning boat trip over to Lana'i still starts earlier than most would like, but once underway with warm (yes, still homemade by the Coons) cinnamon rolls and a mug of hot chocolate or coffee, it seems all worth the effort. Don't forget to bring the camera! Two boats bring about 60 guests to the island each day for snorkeling, sun and fun at Manele Bay. With the additional number of people on the trip, they have now divided the snorkeling and Lana'i island tour in two. One boat load walks to the beach and snorkels, tours the island and eats. The beginning snorkelers are carefully instructed in a tide pool before entering the ocean. The other group tours the island, snorkels and then eats at a second "sitting." If you would prefer, you can also skip the tour of Lana'i City and snorkel even longer. The chicken is cooked on the grill by the ship's captain and served on china plates. Mrs. Coon still isn't giving out the secret ingredients for her salad dressing to anyone. Some work has been done to beautify the eating area with additional plants and an awning. Just about the only change seemed to be the way they cooked the noodles and they are even better! Leftovers from the meal are deposited nearby and you might catch a glimpse of the "wild" cats dining side by side with the "wild" turkeys! Unfortunately the Coon brothers don't get out of the office much any more to skipper the boats, but our Captain was energetic and really seemed to enjoy the trip as much as the rest of us, although the rest of the crew weren't as congenial as on a previous trip. This is a very special outing and well worth considering as a part of your island holiday. Phone (808) 661-4743 or 1-800-874-2666. $125 - $139 for this all day trip (7 a.m. to 4 p.m.) includes continental breakfast, lunch and snorkel gear.

The Coon family's Trilogy operation has now expanded to a half day Molokini snorkel aboard their new 44 foot trimaran cutter *Trilogy IV*. We haven't tried it, but if its even half as good as their Lana'i venture, it bears looking into. The trip features a continental breakfast, with those same good cinnamon rolls, snorkel lessons and equipment, and an all you can eat hot lunch. Departs Maalaea Harbor 6:30 a.m. from slip 99, behind the Coast Guard Station, returns at noon. Adults $75, Children $37.50. Same phone numbers as above.

SPINNER DOLPHINS

CLUB LANA'I

This is a one-of-a-kind operation on Maui and the closest thing the visitor will find to Gilligan's Island. It began operating in 1987, closed and then reopened in the spring of 1992. Things have changed little since they opened originally. The current going rate is $79 for a trip that departs the Lahaina Harbor at 8 a.m. and returns at 3 p.m. Enroute there is a continental breakfast of donuts and coffee and, once you arrive, it is a full day of choosing whatever you want to do. There is biking and kayaking and plenty of time to do nothing at all but enjoy a hammock. The craftmaking in the little huts is gone, apparently they have a more casual theme where they demonstrate coconut cutting or the like along the beach for guests to watch. Lunch is a very heavy meal which includes of mahi, beef and chicken, served with macaroni salad, coleslaw, green salad, bean salad and marinated vegetables. They serve iced tea and punch and they still serve their special Lana'i Tai's at the bar. Most of the guests take advantage of the coastline snorkeling, which leaves plenty of room for the remaining guests to pick out the perfect hammock. Keep an eye out for Mary Ann and the professor! (871-1144)

DINNER - SUNSET CRUISES

Dinner cruises are quite popular on Maui with their free flowing Mai Tai's, congenial passengers, tropical nights, and Hawaiian music which entertains while the boat cruises along the coastline. Dinner aboard most is definitely not haute cuisine, but usually quite satisfactory, especially after a few Mai Tai's. The live entertainment varies from amateur to very good to none at all. (We have a personal dislike for those cruises that get the slightly intoxicated guests up to don Hawaiian attire and perform the hula.) Cruises typically last about two hours and prices run about $40-60. Samples of dinners listed may vary. Most dinner cruises accommodate 20-100 people. While there are several new dinner cruises, all in all, don't expect the kind of food quality you'd experience at one of the islands land-locked restaurants.

The best value is *Frogman* with their current price of $39.95.

The *Lahaina Princess*, with its table seating and formally dressed crew, is probably what most would envision a dinner cruise to be.

Though very different, the *Windjammer* or the *Manutea* or the get the nods for the overall best of the bunch. The *Windjammer* was fun and good-touristy (as opposed to bad-touristy) and has everything the visitor would want, music, dancing, a good meal and friendly people. It's very Hawaiian, but also lively and fun. *Manutea* on the other hand would be one to do if you've been to Maui before, it's more like the Old Lahaina Luau of Dinner Cruises - more subtle, peaceful and relaxing, more romantic and the best dinner by far.

The *Gemini* wasn't operating a dinner cruise in time to review, but it is a very nice boat and since the Westin is preparing the fare, should be a good meal. As for sunset cruises, the *Kapalua Kai* is a classy option, but the true sailing enthusiast should investigate the *First Class*. *Sea Sails* was fun and the *Kaulana* pleasant and comfortable. It's a really tough choice, but there is a quality trip for any visitor.

First Class ★ - (Sunset cruise) Alihilani Yacht Charters offers an evening sailing cruise aboard the yacht *First Class*, operated by Ross Scott, Jr., of the Sunshine Helicopter family. This is a quality operation with a brand new, very sleek yacht. The boat is a 65' MacGregor with a beautiful, plush interior! An afternoon tradewind sail is a one and one half hours of *true* sailing. Beverages only served, mai tai's, soft drinks and beer. Departs 2 pm, 3:30 pm and 5 pm. $35 adult/$25 child. This cruise is a real find to a very specific kind of traveler. It's nothing like any of the other visitor boats, this is a yacht! It should appeal to people who REALLY like to sail and for the more adventurous types. The boat glides through the water making a very fast, but smooth ride! If you enjoy sailing, don't miss this one. 871-1156, FAX (808) 871-0682 or 1-800-544-2520

Frogman - (Dinner cruise) The least expensive dinner cruise option at $39.95 departs from Maalaea four nights a week. Only twenty-one passengers maximum, so you're definitely away from the crowds. Seating is along the sides or up front on the bow of the boat. The evening starts out with Mai Tais or beer, wine or soda, a green salad, teriyaki chicken or prime rib with mashed potatoes and roll. There is a bit of time between the salad and the rest of the meal, which might be because the meal is served on wooden "TV" trays which pretty much lock you into your seat, much like the pull-down tray does on an airline. They put up the sails as soon as possible before dinner, so while you actually do get to sail, you are a bit confined to your seat! Although other passengers didn't seem to object, it detracted from our experience. The food seemed vaguely familiar and, sure enough the catering service is the same as the Wailea Kai. Interesting that the food was a bit better, so don't know if this was a better night for the caterer or what. However, still not a memorable meal. The boat ride itself was lovely, especially the sail and the weather was perfect. In summary, a good value and the only boat that truly provided a dinner/sunset "sail." (667-7622)

Gemini - (Sunset Cruise & Dinner Cruise) This 64 ft. catamaran, used is by the Westin and departs from Kaanapali Beach. No dinner cruise during whale season, only an evening pre-sunset cruise. The dinner cruise was not operating as we prepare this text, but will run about $55-60 for adults. The food, prepared by the Westin, should be a cut above. The tradewinds cruise is $30 adults, $20 kids and hours are 4:30 - 6:30. This is a glass bottom catamaran with long tables and padded seats inside which are accessible for dining. The evening cruise is a BYOB, but they serve a raw veggie platter with dip, Maui chips and mixed nuts, sodas and iced tea. The wide passage areas all around, accessible steps and ample headroom make it a comfortable boat. There are viewports on each side (glass bottom windows) and big side windows. No music or entertainment, just a good chance to wind down on a pleasant sail. An amusing and true story - there was a newlywed couple on board that had been out the past three nights in a row. The boat didn't have enough guests to do a Friday night trip so they cancelled the cruise and the honeymooners were disappointed so they chartered the whole boat for themselves. The Gemini also does snorkel sails. (669-5701)

Kapalua Kai ★ - ("Sunset" cruise) The only boat departing from Kapalua. Technically not a sunset sail because they operate 4 - 6 p.m. all year. In the winter it is a sunset cruise, in the summer and spring they call it their "Ahiahi Sail." Price is $35 adults, $20 kids and includes non-alcoholic drinks (beer, etc., available for a small fee). They provide deli pupus which included a platter of turkey, ham, salami, cheddar and swiss accompanied by a basket of mini-rolls (french, sour dough and whole wheat.) A tray of relish items and pineapple slices as well. This is one of the nicest and newest boats on Maui, a 53' gold coast yacht catamaran with lots of open ledges for seating and tables inside. The trampolines have big mats for sitting or reclining upon. The quantity and quality of food make it a good value, but not too heavy in the event you've planned dinner out afterwards. A classy cruise and worthy of the Kapalua name, in fact the whole operation is well done. (669-4665)

Kaulana - (Sunset cruise) Departing from the Lahaina Harbor this vessel offers good seating areas on benches on top and on the sides. Musical entertainment included Hawaiian and contemporary music, and there was room to dance. Pupus included fresh vegetables and dip, cheese cubes served with crackers and bread sticks, fruit platter, chicken wings and drumsticks (spicy!) and onion rings with dip. Open bar. The cruise went up past Kaanapali. Daily 5 - 7 p.m. (times change with the seasons), except Sunday and Monday, $35 adults, $17.50 kids. An enjoyable, comfortable trip aboard this 65' power catamaran. Operated by the folks that run Club Lana'i. (871-1144)

King Kamehameha - (Sunset cruise) A small cat, max. 15 people, with limited padded seating around the wheel area and a big net out front. You may have recognized it by the big picture of King Kamehameha on the sail! Owner Tom Warren has been sailing on various charter boats since 1969 and purchased the *Kamehameha* in 1977. This is the most inexpensive of all the sunset cruises, only $24, and again is one of those BYOB. Snacks include Maui Chips. A good option if you're seeking a smaller boat. Unfortunately, we were not able to do a personal review of this one. (661-4522)

Lahaina Princess - (Dinner cruise) This boat is operated by the same company as the *Maui Princess*, which runs a Maui to Moloka'i shuttle. This cruise begins a little later than the others. The tables below are set up for dinner and this reviewer found it a bit confining. It can be compared with a dining car on a train, tables on both sides and nice big windows to look out. The live music below proved a bit too loud for the small area. On the top deck there was an open air cocktail lounge which was pleasant, but the space filled quickly and if you didn't arrive first, there was only standing room. Their aim seems to be to take the place of the Stardancer, but, on a much smaller boat this is extremely difficult to do. Elegance is attempted here with the crew in tuxedos, even the girls had tuxedo jackets and skirts. The burgundy of the crew's bow ties and cummerbunds matched the burgundy linen napkins on pink linen tablecloths. The food was served with silverware and china, although the drinks were in plastic cups. While guests were up above, salads were set out along with a tray of baked potato toppings. Dinner was a choice of prime rib or teriyaki chicken and both were very good. They were accompanied by a baked potato and carrots. Cheesecake with raspberry puree made for a tasty dessert. The dancing area could accommodate about three couples maximum. They certainly get an "E" for effort in elegance, but its pretty hard to compete with its predecessor. We can recommend it, but not very enthusiastically. Adults $59, children $35. Departs Lahaina Harbor. From O'ahu toll free 1-800-533-6899, from Mainland toll free 1-800-833-5800, local reservations and information 661-8397.

Manutea - (Dinner cruise) A 50' catamaran, which appears to be very casual and sporty, actually transforms into a rather romantic dining atmosphere. Dinner is served on wooden "table for two" trays which are brought out and placed on plastic bench-type seats. So each couple has a private table in-between. The boat cuts the engine to make for a very quiet and peaceful dining experience. The music is mellow/easy listening guitar and no dancing, polynesian revue or hula show here. The food was exceptionally good for a dinner cruise - catered by the Maui Marriott and served with china and linen napkins. Very like an airplane dinner in First Class - a cut above coach and passable in a good restaurant, but still a bit like "airline" (boat) food. A choice of entrees includes New York Strip with Madeira Sauce, boneless breast of chicken teriyaki, Mahi Mahi or a vegetarian Pasta Primavera. Accompanying the meal was rice pilaf, sauteed vegetables and dessert was cherry pie. Wine and champagne are included for dinner. Seating is a maximum of 30 which also adds to the romantic ambience. Price is $59 per person. Children are not encouraged as evidenced by the single price. Daily except Monday. (879-4485)

Scotch Mist - (Sunset Cruise) 23 passenger max. Trips daily. Beer, wine, soft drinks, no pupus, just chips. $35 adults, $25 for kids under age 12. Departs Lahaina Harbor. (661-0386)

Sea Sails - (Sunset Cruise) The catamaran *Anuenue* meets you in front of the Kaanapali Beach Hotel Shack with boarding from the beach. You'll be stepping into the water a few inches, so long pants will need to be rolled up. During whale season, they don't actually sail however. It's approximately a two hour trip, which changes seasonally with the time of sunset. The appetizers included fresh cut vegetables with dip and a tray of fried won tons with sauce. The two young crew members were lively and talked informally and comfortably with the guests. The $32 plus tax includes beer, wine, soda and pupus. Children under 12 are $22, Mon-Sat., max. 40 passengers. They also operate the Sea Horse. (661-5555)

Silent Lady - (Sunset cruise) 64' custom built whaling schooner available for sunset cruises only by private charter. A beautiful boat, but unfortunately we weren't able to review before press time. R. R. Box 379, Suite 410, Wailuku, HI 96793. (242-6499 or 661-1118)

Spirit of Windjammer - (Dinner cruise) A 70' three masted schooner with table seating, open bar (wine with dinner). Hawaiian entertainment with the waiter/waitresses doubling as dancers. Singer/Guitarist Ernie Paiva has been entertaining on the Windjammer for eleven years! The cruise, 5-7 p.m., was a well-paced, two plus hours. The live music was continuous during the first hour allowing for time to settle in, relax and talk. This was followed by dinner (green salad, beef burgundy and boneless breast of chicken teriyaki, baked potato, vegetables, dinner rolls and dessert). The meal was good, the apple pie was served warm and apparently the portions were ample as several guests took home doggie bags. Time for more music, and a Hawaiian show. The crew/dancers and guests spend the last few minutes dancing as the boat comes into port. On the whole a good cruise, fun and lively, with all the guests seeming to have a good time. (661-8600). Prices including tax is $56.25 adults, $28.12 kids.

Wailea Kai - (Dinner cruise) Departs Maalaea Harbor three nights a week 5 - 7 p.m. This 75 passenger, 65' catamaran which is nice, but seems better suited for an afternoon swimming/snorkeling excursion rather than a dinner cruise. Only one section is somewhat "inside" with a few seats and the buffet and bar along with the two musicians can be found there. There is a semblance of a very small dance floor. This cruise was a bit less expensive than the others. The buffet is an all you can eat, but the food was, at best, mediocre and served on sectional trays which didn't add to the enjoyment. This reviewer would have preferred quality over quantity. A hula dancer entertained and following dinner the same dancer preformed a Tahitian number. Then the guests decked out in hula finery to perform a dance number (they loose a few points from us for this!). A very basic, typical dinner cruise with nothing in particular to recommend. (879-4485) $50 adults and children.

Whale Mist - (Sunset cruise) 36' monohull sailboat, max. 18, whale watch/sunset cruise, $35 adults/$25 children. Sunset cruise. Depart Lahaina, slip #5. Combo trip includes sunset or three hour snorkel and a parasail for $68. (667-2833)

Whale II - (Sunset cruise) Operated by Pacific Whale Foundation the trip is two hours, 5 - 7 pm. No entertainment. Guests were provided with paper "trays" which worked pretty well for holding the pupus. There was one food platter with veggies and dip and another seafood platter with crackers. The seafood platter was very tasty, medium size prawns, imitation crab meat pieces, clams in the shell and fish cake slices. However, this particular evening there didn't seem to be enough food for the amount of people on board. As a defense, the whale season had just ended and this was the first sunset cruise of the season, so perhaps it was just a matter of getting things up and rolling. The drinks included coke, beer, wine or mai tais. Price is $30 adults, $24.50 children. Departs Lahaina Harbor. (879-8811)

Zip-purr - (Sunset Cruise) Owned by Julie and Mike "Turk" Turkington. He built this 47' sailboat and its captain. While it can carry a maximum of 49 passengers, they prefer to book no more than 35 - 40. They do their cruise Tuesday, Thursday and Saturday, and ALWAYS sail, even though it can be a bit rough, which should appeal to the sporty types. There is no entertainment and they don't currently have a liquor license, so it is a BYOB and runs $30. Their mini-buffet serves fresh fruit (mango, orange, pineapple and cantaloupe slices), ham, turkey and sliced cheeses accompanied by a basket of soft mini-rolls, carrots, cucumbers and celery with dip and Maui chips, pretzels lots of crackers, cheese balls, mixed nuts AND two kinds of brownies - chocolate and vanilla. A cooler of sodas, a jug of water and passion-orange juice rounded out the selection. A nice padded seating area inside and benches at various spots.

They pick up at three different areas, depending on the weather. At El Crab Catcher, the Sheraton and in front of the Maui Eldorado's Beach Club at Kaanapali Beach. They put out a line to troll and while on board a fish was hooked, which was exciting. Earlier in the day they had caught a large fish and cut it up right there and everyone sampled very fresh sashimi. The crew was pleasant, but didn't spend any time getting to know the guests. (667-2299)

SUBMARINES

A new category to the activities section of this guide! With the departure of the glass bottom Lin Wa, the 1990's has brought high tech to undersea viewing with three new companies.

The *Maui E-Ticket* was the first of the semi-submersibles to arrive on Maui. The boat departs from the Lahaina Harbor for a short excursion along the coastline to the reef of Puunoa. There is plenty of room on the top deck and access into the viewing lounges is fairly easy. The theater style seating allows everyone to have their own 5 foot viewing window. The lounges are air conditioned for comfort and spacious enough to avoid any closed in feeling. Since the vessel is a semi-submersible, there is always the option of going up on deck. Currently they are only offering day trips, but there was talk of doing an evening trip utilizing flood lights. Shortly after departure from the wharf, an informative narration which begins discussing the history and evolution of the islands and continues on to the aquatic life of the region. The reef explored offers some varied types of fish and the crew throwing bread overboard encourages them to come closer. A plastic card is attached to each seat for fish identification. Soft drinks in souvenir glasses were served when we took the excursion shortly after they initiated their operation. Something that may have been an early promotion and not continued. There is a concession on board, however. $39.95. 669-8000.

The *Atlantis Submarine* has a two hour tour that runs $74, children 36 inches to 12 years of age $48, a little expensive for some travel budgets. The *fully submersible submarine* is an 80 ton, 65 foot touring vessel that accommodates 46 passengers. Four dives daily at 10, 12, 1 and 2 begin at their Pioneer Inn shop, which also affords you plenty of time to shop for logo items from polo shirts, to visors, beach bottles, jelly beans or beach towels. For $10 you can get photographed holding an Atlantis-logoed lifesaver. There is a short boat ride to reach the submarine and quite surprisingly it suddenly emerges out of the middle of the depths of the Pacific. Then you step across from the tender and load onto the submarine. The seats are lined up on both sides in front of 1/2 a porthole. The submarine submerges about 150 feet. The area is a little close, but the temperature is kept

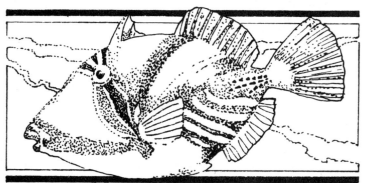

HUMUHUMUNUKUNUKUAPUA'A

cool and comfortable. There are plenty of fish, and fish cards at each station help you identify them. Rocks and coral formations resemble an environ that is somehow extra-terrestrial. Upon completion of the trip you are bestowed with the title "Atlantis Submariner" which includes a certificate that must be picked up back at the office. (One more chance to do a little shopping?) 667-2224.

Another semi-submersible on Maui is the **Nautilus**. This one only partially submerges, so at any time you can go up on deck for some fresh air, or if you feel a bit claustrophobic. It departs at least 5 times a day, times change seasonally. The bottom is six feet below the surface and they cruise around about 5 feet from the ocean floor off of Puamana. The total trip an hour, but once you are underway, you begin viewing, while the Atlantis does require some coordinating to get from the dock to the submarine. The Nautilus seats are more comfortable, allowing for a bit more room to walk around. The Nautilus also provides a complimentary monogrammed drinking glass with "POG" (a Hawaiian fruit punch) or water. One of the crew scuba dives out to hold up interesting items for the guests to view. $39.95 adults, $19.95 children 5 - 12 years, children 4 and under are free. 667-7647.

The *Atlantis* does have clearer viewing since they are down so deep and have infra-red lights. The *Nautilus* makes use of sunlight, which at times can be bright, other times cause the water to be hazy. In brief, the *Nautilus* and the *Maui E Ticket* are more like dry snorkeling and the *Atlantis* more like dry scuba diving. The *Atlantis* has a smoother, plane-like motion, while the *Nautilus* is more like a helicopter, bobbing and rocking as it maneuvers. The *Atlantis* does provide the submarine experience, but you pay the price. The *Nautilus* is $39.95 (check "This Week Maui" magazine for a $10 off coupon), quite a bit less expensive than the *Atlantis*. If you are a snorkeler, you won't see much on the *Nautilus* or the *Maui E Ticket* than you would if you were swimming. But if you are unable or unwilling to get wet, then one of these trips may be an option to consider.

WHALE WATCHING

Every year beginning in November and continuing until April, the humpback whales arrive in the warm waters off the Hawaiian Islands for breeding, and their own sort of vacation! The sighting of a whale can be an awesome and memorable experience with the humpbacks, small as whales go, measuring some 40 - 50 feet and weighing in at 30 tons.

The panoramic vistas as you drive over the Pali and down the beachfront road to Lahaina afford some excellent opportunities to catch sight of one of these splendid marine mammals. However, PLEASE pull off the road and enjoy the view. Many accidents are caused by distracted drivers.

For an even closer view, there are plenty of boat trips. Although most every boat operator does whale watching tours in season, you may want to check into the one sponsored by Pacific Whale Foundation 879-8811. As they are a research group, they are very well informed and knowledgeable about the whales. You can report your sightings by calling Whale Watch Hotline at 879-8860.

DEEP SEA FISHING

Deep sea fishing off Maui is among the finest in the world and no licenses are required for either trolling or bottom fishing. All gear is provided. Fish that might be lured to your bait include the Pacific Blue, Black or Striped Marlin (Au) weighing up to 2,000 lbs., Yellow Fin Tuna (Ahi) up to 300 lbs., Jack Crevalle (Ulua) to 100 lbs., Bonita-Skipjack (Aku) to 40 lbs., Dolphin Fish (Mahi) to 90 lbs., Waho (Ono) to 90 lbs., Mackerel (Opelu), Amerjack (Kahala), Grey Snapper (Uku), Red Snapper (Onaga), and Pink Snapper (Opakapaka).

Boats generally offer half or full-day fishing trips on a share or private basis with prices running from $65 - $75 shared or $300 - $350 private for a half day (4 hr.), and $100 -$110 shared or $450 -$550 private for a full day (8 hr). Some are willing to take non-fishing passengers along at half price. Most boats take 4 - 6 on a shared basis, however several can handle larger groups.

FINDING A CHARTER: Your local activity center may be able to direct you to a particular boat that they favor, or you could go down to the docks at the Lahaina or Maalaea Harbor in the afternoon and browse around. There are also a number of activity booths at both harbors that can be consulted. When reserving a spot, be aware that some boats will give full refunds only if 48-hour notice is given for cancellation. If you want to take children fishing, many have restrictions for those under age 12. If you are a serious fisherman, you might consider entering one of the numerous tournaments. Some charters offer tournament packages. Following are a list of just some of the charter fishing boats. While not a scientific study, Finest Kind and Exact (both operated by Finest Kind, Inc.) have managed to be consistently mentioned in the local newspaper for regular catches of very large fish.

A WORD OF ADVICE: The young man had a grin that reached from ear to ear as he stood on the pier in Maalaea, holding up his small ahi for a snapshot of his big catch. The surprise came when the deck hand returned it to the ice chest and continued on with his work. The family all stood, unsure what to do. It appeared that the fish was to remain on board, while the family had envisioned a nice fresh fish dinner. Finally one family member spoke up and a very unhappy crew member sliced a small filet, tossed it into a sack and handed it to the young man. Unlike sportsfishing charters in some parts of the country, the fish caught on board generally remain the property of the boat. The pay to captain and crew is minimal and it is the selling of the boat's catch that subsidizes their income. Many vacationers booking a fishing excursion are unaware of this fact. There seems to be no written law for how fishing charters in Hawaii handle this, at least everyone we talked to had different answers. Many of the brochures lead one to believe that you keep your fish, and they neglect to mention that it may be only a filet of fish. Occasionally you may find a head boat which operates under a different sort of guideline. In this situation, you pay for your bait, gear, and boat time and then keep the fish. In any case, be sure you check when you book your trip about just what and how much fish will be yours to keep. If the person at the activity desk assures you that you keep your catch, don't leave it there, also check with the captain when you board. Communication is the key word and have a mahi mahi day!

LAHAINA HARBOR

AERIAL SPORTSFISHING
CHARTERS
PO Box 831, Lahaina, 667-9089
Aeril I, II and III

FINEST KIND, INC.
Exact, 31' Bertram
Finest Kind, 37' Merritt
P.O. Box 10481, Lahaina
Maximum 6 people, 661-0338
Reel Hooker, 35' Bertram

HINATEA SPORTSFISHING
Hinatea, 41' Hatteras
PO Box 1238, Lahaina, 667-7548
Full day only, Slip #27

ISLANDER II SPORTSFISHING
36' Uniflite, 667-6625

LAHAINA CHARTERS
Broadbill, 36' Harcraft
Judy Ann II, 43' Delta (max 8)
Alohilani, 28' Topaz (max 6)
PO Box 12, Lahaina
maximum 6 people, 667-6672

MAALAEA HARBOR

CAROL ANN CHARTERS
33' Bertram, max. 6
877-2181 or 242-4575

OCEAN ACTIVITIES CENTER
Departs Maalaea, 879-4485

LAHAINA FISH COMPANY
Their 50'boat departs twice daily
from the Lahaina Harbor for a half
day of sportfishing for $75. 661-0929
or 669-4334.

LUCKEY STRIKE CHARTERS
Luckey Strike, 45' custom
Kanoa, 31' Uniflite, max. 6
Luckey Strike has a large cockpit
with full sunshade that can
accommodate up to 22 people.
Also does bottom fishing.
PO Box 1502, Lahaina, 661-4606

MANO KELA SPORTSFISHING
Mano Kela, 48' deluxe sportfisher
6 passenger, includes a/c, microwave,
TV, VHS. Exclusive full day $988,
half day $572. Charters available
(808) 661-3446

WESTIN MAUI - *Absolute*, 31 ft.
Bertram sportfisher. 8 hour charter,
$625. 667-2591

RASCAL
SPORTSFISHING CHARTERS
Rascal, Bertram 31', 874-8633
Slip #13

SMALL BOAT SAILING

Small boat sailing is available at a number of locations with rentals, usually the 14', sometimes 16' and 18', Hobie Cat. Lasers are also available. Typical rental prices are $35 - $40 per hour, and lessons are available. Most of the resorts have sailing centers with rental facilities on the beaches. There is also one at the Kealia Center in Kihei.

FOR MORE INFORMATION ON RENTALS CONTACT:
West Maui Sailing School. Also windsurfing, kayak and snorkel equipment. (667-5545)
Sea Sails - Located at the Kaanapali Beach Hotel Beach Shack. (661-5222)
Maui Sailing Center - Kealia Beach Plaza (879-5935)
Ocean Activities Center - Stouffer Wailea Beach Resort (879-9969)

WINDSURFING

Windsurfing is a sport that is increasing in popularity astronomically. Hookipa Beach Park on Maui is one of the best windsurfing sites in the world. This is due to the consistently ideal wind and surf conditions, however, this is definitely NOT the spot for beginners. For the novice, boardsailing beginner group lessons run $25 - 30 an hour, which generally involves instruction on a dry land simulator before you get wet with easy to use beginners equipment. Private less run about $67.50 per hour. Equipment and/or lessons are available from the following:

Hawaiian Island Windsurfing - Pro shop, sales, service, rentals and instruction. Three hour group beginner lessons or advanced water start $59. Private instruction $49 for 75 minutes. Toll free 1-800-231-6958 or locally 871-4981.

Hawaiian Sailboarding Techniques - 444 Hana Hwy., Kahului. Alan Cadiz and his staff of professional instructors offer a full range of small group and private lessons for beginner or expert. They specialize in one-on-one instruction tailored to each person's ability, budget and goals. 871-5423.

Hi-Tech Surfsports - In front of Whalers Village shops on Kaanapali Beach.

Kaanapali Windsurfing School - Hanakaoo Beach by Hyatt Regency. 2 hour and a half hour beginner group lessons $50/ Private beginner $40 per hour. 667-1964

Maui Magic Windsurfing School - Group & private lessons for all levels. Beginning group 2 1/2 hours $60; private 1 1/4 hours $75; three day less package $165. 520 Keolani Place, Kahului (877-4816), 1-800-872-0999 U.S. and Canada.

Maui Sailing Center - Free windsurfing demonstration is featured 9 am daily at Kealia Beach Plaza as does a two hour class, first on land and then on the water. Lesson reservations necessary. Rental equipment available. Kealia Beach Center (879-5935).

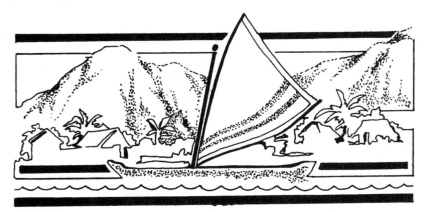

Maui Windsurf Co. - Retail and rental equipment featuring F2, Seatrend and rental only of Angulo custom boards. offers group instruction for novice or the experienced and rental equipment. 520 Keolani Place, Kahului (877-4816) 1-800-872-0999 U.S. and Canada.

Ocean Activities Center - At Stouffer Wailea Beach Resort (879-9969)

Sea Sails - Located at Kaanapali Beach Hotel Beach Shack. (661-5222)

Second Wind, has exclusive rights on Maui for sales of Anglo custom boards, clothing, and Angulo rentals. Proshop rental, used and new sales. Private lessons $45 per hour, $49 for two hour class. 1-800-852-SHOP in U.S., (808-877-SHOP).

Windsurfari - offers packages which include accommodations, rental car, windsurfing equipment and excursions with Alan Cadiz's Hawaiian Sailboarding. 1-800-736-6284 or (808-871-7766).

Windsurfing West Maui - Does lessons, also has travel packages 1-800-782-6105. Works together with Hawaiian Island Windsurfing listed above.

Some resorts offer their guests free clinics. Rental by the hour can get expensive at $15 - $20 per hour and $40 - $65 per four hours. A better rate is $35 for all day. If you are interested in renting equipment for longer periods or desire more advanced equipment try:

Hawaiian Island Windsurfing - (871-4981), 460 Dairy Road, Kahului, or *Sailboards Maui* - (871-7954) 210 Dairy Road, Kahului. Typical costs are $45 for full day, $250 for 7 days. Deposit may be required. Rental includes board, universal mast, boom, sail and soft car rack. No reservations and no refunds unless returned within one hour. You pay for broken, lost or stolen equipment.

SURFING

Honolua Bay is one of the best surfing spots in Hawaii, and undoubtedly the best on Maui, with waves up to 15 feet on a good winter day and perfect tubes. A spectacular vantage point is on the cliffs above the bay. In the summer this bay is calm and, as it is a Marine Reserve, offers excellent snorkeling.

Also in this area is Punalau Beach (just past Honolua) and Honokeana Bay off Ka'eleki'i Point (just north of the Alaeloa residential area). In the Lahaina area there are breaks north and south of the harbor and periodically good waves at Awalua Beach (mile marker 16). On the north shore Hookipa Beach Park, Kanaha Beach, and Baldwin all have good surfing at times. In the Hana area there is Hamoa Beach. There are a couple of good spots in Maalaea Bay and at Kalama Beach Park.

Conditions change daily, and even from morning to afternoon around the island. Check with local board rental outlets for current daily conditions.

Hawaiian Sailboarding Techniques - (871-5423) 444 Hana Hwy., Kahului. HST goes "surf-surfari" to wherever the best place for learning happens to be that particular day. Small groups and private instruction available for beginners wanting to cruise the waves their first time out, also intermediate and advanced lessons. Current rates for longboard surfing class is $60 each two hours, three people per class maximum, includes surfboard.

Indian Summer Surf Shop - Lahaina. Surfboard rentals. Can recommend instructors. Also have kayak rentals. 661-3053 and 661-3794.

Maui Surfing School - (877-0625) Andrea Thomas originated the "Learn to Surf in One Lesson" and is reported to have taught thousands of people between the ages of 3 and 70. She's been teaching on Maui since 1980 and offers private and group lessons specializing in the beginner and coward. Board rentals available. Lahaina Harbor.

Books of interest available at local bookstores: *Surfing Hawaii* by Bank Wright, 96 pages softcover $5.95. *Hawaii Surfing Map*, descriptions of 97 surfing spots.

BODY SURFING

Mokuleia (Slaughterhouse) Beach has the best body surfing especially in the winter. This is not a place for weak swimmers or the inexperienced when the surf is up, it can be downright dangerous. The high surf after a Kona storm brings fair body surfing conditions, better boogieboarding, to some beaches on leeward Maui. A book that might be interesing and is available at local bookstores is *How to Body Surf* by Nelson Dewey, 10 pages softcover, $1.00.

JET SKIIS

Thrillcraft activities, which include parasailing and jetskiing have been banned during whale season. Currently the "open season" for participating in jet skiing recreation is May 15th until December 15th. Currently the only jet ski operation, *Pacific Jet Ski Rental*, is at the south end of Kaanapali Beach at Hanakaoo Beach Park. They have two and three passenger wave runners. (667-2066)

PARASAILING

The parasail "season" on Maui is May 16 - December 14th due to the restrictions during whale season. For those that aren't familiar with this aquatic adventure, parasailing is a skyward adventure where you are hooked to parachute and attached to a tow line behind a boat and soon are floating high in the air with a bird's eye view of Maui. The flight lasts 8 to 10 minutes which may be either too long or too short for some! Price about $50. Some charge for an "observer" (friend) to go along, others allow them free.

West Maui Parasail - Lahaina Harbor, Slip #17. Uses "Skyrider," a three passenger aerial recliner. Dry take-off and landing. Boat departs every 30 minutes with six passengers. They use a 600 ft. line so passengers are 4 - 400 feet above the water. Call for reservations. (661-4060).

UFO Parasail - Observers can go free. Departs in front of Whaler Village. They use a new wrinkle, a self-contained "winch" boat. You get started standing on the boat and as your parachute fills, you are simply reeled out 200 - 400 feet. When it comes time to descend, you're simply reeled back in.

Parasail Kaanapali - Departs from the Mala Wharf. (669-6555).

Whale Mist - Operates a combo trip which includes a sunset or 3-hr. snorkel plus parasail for $68. (667-2833)

WATERSKIING

Kaanapali Water Ski - Departs Mala Wharf. $30 one person for 15 minutes. Half-hourly rate for one to three skiers $50. Hourly rate for 1 - 5 skiers $90. Can pick up along most Kaanapali hotel beaches. (661-3324)

KAYAKS

Maui Kayaks - The novice or experienced paddler can join a half or full day guided trip along the Kihei coast. Hourly rentals also available. Contact: Bill Pray, Maui Kayaks, 50 Waiohuli St., Kihei, Maui 96753. (874-3536)

Sea Sails - Location at Kaanapali Beach Hotel surf shack. Have wave ski rentals. (661-5222)

Maui Sailing School - has kayaks. Kealia Beach Center. (879-5935)

Indian Summer Surf Shop - Lahaina. Has kayak rentals. (661-3053 or 661-3794)

SEA KAYAKING

LAND ACTIVITIES

LAND TOURS

Land excursions on Maui are centered upon two major attractions, Hana and the O'heo Valley, and Haleakala Crater. Lesser attractions are trips to the Iao Valley or around West Maui. You can do all of this by car (refer to the WHERE TO STAY - WHAT TO SEE chapter), however, with a tour you can sit back and enjoy the scenery while a professional guide discourses on the history, flora, fauna and geography of the area. The single most important item on any tour is a good guide/driver and, unfortunately, the luck of the draw prevails here.

Another, somewhat expensive option, is a personalized custom tour. A local resident will join you in your car for a tour of whatever or wherever you choose. You can do the driving or sign on your guide with your rental car company to do the driving. This may allow you the opportunity to linger at those places you enjoy the most, without following the pace of a group. Your guide may also be able to take you to locations the tour vans don't include.

Driving to Hana and back requires a full day and can be very grueling, so this is one trip we recommend you consider taking a tour. A Haleakala Crater tour spans 5-6 hours and can be enjoyed at sunrise (3 am departure), mid day or sunset. The West Maui and Iao Valley trips are half-day ventures. Only vans travel the road to Hana, however, large buses as well as vans are available for other trips. (Be aware that some vans are not air conditioned.) Prices are competitive and those listed here are correct at time of publication. Some trips include the cost of meals, others do not.

Also available are one day tours to the outer islands. The day begins with an early morning departure to the Big Island, O'ahu or Kaua'i. Some excursions provide a guided ground tour, others offer a rental car to explore the island on your own.

Akamai - Overnight trips to all islands. (871-9551, 1-800-922-6485 from U.S. mainland)

Aloha Nui Loa Tours - Hana ($84 plus tax). They also provide a special horse-back tour. A drive to Hana is followed by a ride over the ranchlands of the Hotel Hana, then a lunch at a quiet beachfront. Pick up from all Maui locationmns. Personal Tours. Breakfast included. (879-7044)

Arthur's Limo Service - They provide tours to Haleakala and Hana in their luxury limousine or their new super stretch van. $60 per hour plus tax and tip. (871-5555 or 1-800-345-4667 inter-island or from Mainland.

Ekahi Tours - Herbie Watson and his crew provide tours of Hana ($75 adult, $55 child) Other areas charter for $65 per hour. (877-9775)

RECREATION AND TOURS
Land Tours

Grayline - Provides a variety of large bus and small van tours to Halekala and Hana. $70 includes lunch at Hana Ranch. Various prices depending on pick up and length of trip. (877-5507)

Guides of Maui - Discover Maui in your car with an island resident as your guide. Explore the destinations of your choice. $174 for two people (plus gas). (877-4042) (1-800-228-6284).

Maui Art Tours - See listing under Art Tours

No Ka Oi Scenic Tours - Takes you to Hana ($72 includes lunch at Hana Ranch), Iao Valley and Haleakala ($42). (871-9008)

Polynesian Adventure - Haleakala ($50/children $35), Hana ($62/children $50), as well as one day trips to the other islands (from $140 each island). (877-4242 or 1-800-622-3011 from Mainland U.S.)

Roberts-Hawaii Tours - Offers land tours in their big air conditioned buses or vans. They depart to all scenic areas from Kahului, Kihei, Wailea, and the West Maui Hotels. (871-6226 or 1-800-767-7551 U.S. Mainland)

Sugar Cane Train - The Sugar Cane Train makes six round trips daily with one way fares for adults $7.50, two way is $11. Children 3-12 years are $3.75 one way, $5.50 round trip. Their main depot is located just outside of Lahaina, turn at the Pizza Hut sign. The Kaanapali Station is located across the highway from the resort area. The free Kaanapali trolley picks up at the Whaler's Shopping Center and drops off at this station. The Puukolii boarding platform and parking lot is located on the Kapalua side of Kaanapali.

They offer several package options which includes a self-guided tour of historic landmarks and admission into the Baldwin House, the Chinese Museum and the Carthaginian II for $12.50 adults and $5.50 children or combine the train ride with the Omni Experience Theater $14 adults $7.75 children. If you plan on a full day round trip excursion, buy your return tickets early as they often sell out quickly. (661-0089)

Temptation Tours ★ - If you'd really like to pamper yourself, then enjoy the luxury of a tour by these folks. Working in conjunction with Sunshine Helicopter they provide a unique option to either Hana or Upcountry Maui. The "Hana Skytrek" is their ultimate package that begins with a helicopter trip to Hana, a tour of the town and Waianapanapa in a luxury van, an elegant lunch and then drive back to Kahului. (Or the reverse where you drive to Hana and fly back.) $199. The Hana picnic is a round trip in their 6-8 passenger limo van for $110, or have substitute lunch at the Hotel Hana Maui for $139.

Their newest tour begins with an ascent up Haleakala in their luxury limo-van, to the eucalyptus forests an pastureland of the Thompson Ranch. An hour and a half to enjoy the view on horseback is followed by elegant lunch at the Silver Cloud Ranch. There is also time to enjoy the jacuzzi with a view. Price is $149 for the all day excursion. (877-8888)

Trans Hawaiian - A day trip to Hana ($74 adult, $69 senior, $55.50 children under 12) departs 7 am and returns about 5:30, lunch at Hana Ranch included. Haleakala sunrise or morning tour ($52 adult, $46 senior, $36.25 child under 12). Also available are day trips to Hawai'i, Kaua'i, and O'ahu via jet. Guided tours on the outer islands or a car can be included for self-guided exploration. (877-7308 or 871-7940, U.S. Mainland 1-800-533-8765)

ART TOURS

Maui Art Tours offers visitors an opportunity to visit the homes and studios of three or four of Maui's fine artists, meet them and watch them work. This unique day-long adventure is provided in a luxury air-conditioned car and includes a gourmet lunch. Cost is $200 per person. P.O. Box 1058, Makawao, Maui 96768. (808-572-3453)

THEATER

The Children's general information section covers information on the *Maui Youth Theater* which has some excellent productions. There are frequently plays at the Iao Theater in Wailuku. Check the local paper for listings. The newest entry into theater on Maui is *Theatre, Theatre Maui*. The production company performs at Dickenson Square, 180 Dickenson, Lahaina. Tickets run about $10 and are available at Lahaina Coolers Restaurant or call 875-4449. Lahaina Coolers is planning to work in conjunction with the plays, working some "theme" menu items into their menu to coincide with the production.

BIKE TOURS

The Hawaiian Islands offer an endless array of spectacular air, sea and land tours, but only on Maui is there an experience quite like the bicycle ride down from the 10,000 foot summit of the world's largest dormant volcano. Bob Kiger, better known as Cruiser Bob, was the originator of the Haleakala downhill. (Cruiser Bob is reported to have made 96 individual bike runs himself to thoroughly test all aspects of the route before the first paying customers attempted the trip).

Each tour company differs slightly in its adaptation of the trip, but the principal is the same, to provide the ultimate in biking experiences. For the very early riser (3 am) you can see the sunrise from the crater before biking down. Later morning expeditions are available as well. Your day will begin with a van pickup at your hotel for a narrated trip to the Haleakala summit along with safety information for the trip down. The temperature at the summit can be as much as 30 degrees cooler than sea level, so appropriate wear would include a sweater or sweatshirt. General requirements are for riders to wear closed-toe rubber soled shoes, sun glasses or prescription lenses (not all helmets have visors), a height requirement of 5 feet is requested by some and no pregnant women are allowed on the trip. Bikers must also sign an acknowledgement of risk and safety consideration form. For the descent, riders are equipped with windbreaker jackets, gloves, helmets and specially designed bicycles with heavy duty brakes.

A leader will escort you down the mountain curves with the van providing a rear escort. Somewhere along the way will be a meal break. Some tours provide picnics, others include a sit-down meal at the lodge in Kula or elsewhere. Actual biking time will run about 3 hours for the 38-mile downhill trip. The additional time, about 5 hours, is spent commuting to the summit, meals, and the trip from the volcano's base back to your hotel. Prices for the various tours are competitive and reservations should be made well in advance.

We biked down with Maui Downhill and opted for the "late" 7 am trip. We found them to be very careful, courteous and professional. Unfortunately they don't have control over the weather and the day we chose was clear on the drive up, fogged in and misty at the summit and a torrential downpour for more than half of the 38 miles down. Due to the weather, we couldn't enjoy much of the scenery going down, but probably wouldn't have had much time to gander as it is important to keep your eyes on the road! The leader set a fairly slow pace, not much of a thrill for the biking speedster, but safe and comfortable for most. At any time we were invited to hop in the van, but ours was a hearty group and after a stop to gear up in rain slickers, we all continued on. Our leader also advised that if the weather posed any kind of risk, he would load us on the van. The weather broke long enough for us to enjoy sandwiches or salads at the Sunrise Market and to bask in the sun's momentary warmth. In radio contact with the group just ahead of us we were advised that the rain promised to await us just a little farther down the volcanic slope. As predicted, the drizzle continued as we biked down through the cowboy town of Makawao. We arrived in Paia only a little wetter for the experience.

Chris's Bike Adventures - (871-BIKE) This is the newest of the island bike expeditions and offers some interesting options. However, these bike rides take riders around upcountry, not just down it. They use 21 speed mountain bikes and provide helmets, gloves and weather gear.

The Haleakala Wine Trek travels to the Tedeschi Winery and beyond to the remote lava fields above La Perouse. Includes crater viewing and short hike, a continental breakfast and picnic lunch. Sunrise, full day and half day trips available. $84 full day, $60 half day.

The Wilder Side of Haleakala is the above trip plus some biking along the wilder, remote backside of Haleakala. Forty miles, all day $95.

The Coastal Challenge is a trip along the remote northwest coastal (Kahakuloa) side of Maui. Includes off-road biking, half $55 or full day $79.

Or combine a boat trip with a bike exploration of either Lana'i or Moloka'i $148 - $160 for the full day adventures.

Cruiser Bob's - (667-7717) (1-800-654-7717 U.S. Mainland or inter-island.) This is the original Haleakala downhill trip. You can choose between an early (3 am) sunrise trek or the regular excursion for $104 includes tax. Both include continental breakfast and sit down lunch at Kula Lodge.

Maui Downhill - (871-2155 or 1-800-535-BIKE in U.S.) Transportation from your hotel/condo. The sunrise trek includes a brunch after the ride. The day trip begins with a continental breakfast at the base yard before departure up the mountain and a picnic lunch at the Sunrise Market (and protea gardens) on the way down. Sunrise is $105 including tax, continental breakfast/brunch at Sandalwood in Kula.

Maui Mountain Cruisers - (572-0195 or 1-800-232-MAUI in U.S.) Pickup provided from Kaanapali, Lahaina, Kahului and Kihei. Sunrise cruise includes a continental breakfast and brunch at Sandalwood Restaurant in Kula. Midday trip includes continental breakfast and gourmet picnic lunch at Sunrise Market or Sandalwood Restaurant. $95.20 plus 4% tax.

BIKE RENTALS

Bikes and mopeds are an ambitious and fun way to get around the resort areas, although you can rent a car for less than a moped. Available by the hour, day or week, they can be rented at several convenient locations.

A & B Rentals - 3481 Honoapiilani Hwy. at the ABC store. They have mopeds, bicycles, beach equipment, surfing and boggie boards, snorkel gear, fishing poles and underwater cameras. Mopeds run $25 for 24 hours, bikes $10 day or $50 week. (669-0027)

Fun Bike Rentals - 193 Lahainaluna Rd., Lahaina. In addition to bikes they have boogie boards, beach chairs and even baby strollers! (661-3053)

BUNGEE JUMPING

Now here is a delimma. Is it an *air,* or a *land* activity when you begin on *land,* ascend to a height of 150' on a crane, and then jump off into the *air.* Well, that about summarizes *Bungee Jump Maui.* An activity that this editor has absolutely no desire to perform -- so don't await any reviews from here!

Michael Sobel began the operation this past summer in Kihei and reportedly has a total state of the art operation. Special computer programs verify weight information of the jumper and double check hookups through a bar code type of mechanism before allowing the gate to be unlocked at the top of the tower. There is also a rigorous training procedure to become a "jump master" which, we're told, is similar to that of a certified dive instructor. A video of your jump is available for an additional fee. $79 for one jump. It may or may not be reassuring to note on their advertisement that they carry a million dollars worth of insurance. Kihei Industrial Park. Hours 8:30 - 5:30 daily. P.O. Box 10893, Lahaina, HI 96761 (669-LEAP).

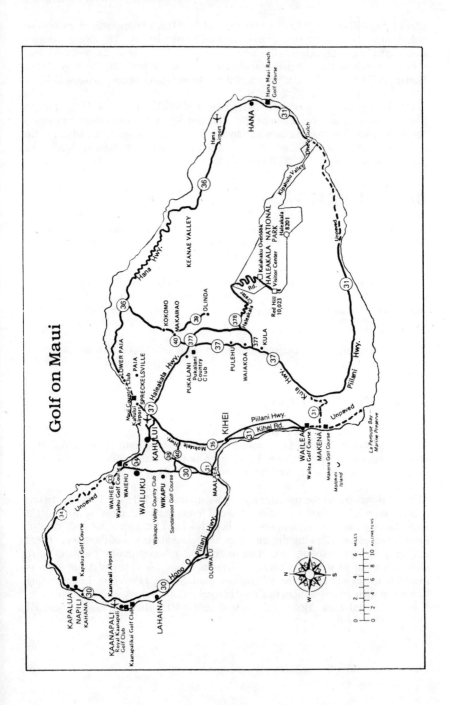

Golf on Maui

GOLF

Maui's golf courses have set for themselves a high standard of excellence. Not only do they provide some very challenging play, but they also offer distractingly beautiful scenery. Most of the major resorts offer golf packages and for the avid player, this may be an economical plan.

Sunseeker Golf Schools at Kaanapali offers golf instruction for the beginner or the advanced. Each Wednesday and Saturday at 10 am they conduct a free golf clinic. They offer private lessons ($35 for 45 minutes), playing lessons (one person $100, couple $150) and special one day classes ($175) classes. Phone 667-7111.

KAANAPALI
The Kaanapali Resort offers two championship courses. Green fees are $100 for 18 holes, cart included. Twilight rate $65. Residents $50. Located at the Southern entrance to the Kaanapali resort area is the Royal Kaanapali driving range. (661-3691). Discounts during low season May 1 - November 30.

The North Course has been attracting celebrities since its inaugural when Bing Crosby played in the opening of the first nine holes. Designed by Robert Trent Jones, this 6,305 yard course places heavy emphasis on putting skills. At par 72, it is rated 70 for men and 71.4 for women.

The South Course first opened in 1970 as an executive course and was reopened in 1977 as a regular championship course after revisions by golf architect Arthur Snyder. At 6,205 yards and par 72 it requires accuracy as opposed to distance, with narrower fairways and more small, hilly greens than the North Course. As an added distraction, the Sugar Cane Train passes by along the 4th hole.

KAPALUA

The Kapalua Resort features the Bay Course and the Village Course. Green fee $110 includes cart; resort guest $70; Maui resident $45; Twilight play 2 p.m. - 6 p.m. $60. Guests may reserve tee-off times up to 7 days in advance. Non-guest reservations 2 days in advance. (669-8044)

The Bay Course, under the design of Arnold Palmer, opened October 13, 1975 and sprawls from sea level to the mountain's edge. This beautiful and scenic par 72, 6,850 yard course has a distinctly Hawaiian flavor. Imagine a 530-yard par four that travels downhill doglegging past the ancient stones of a pre-missionary fishing village to a green positioned on a black lava peninsula surrounded by white sand beaches. Or how about a 158-yard par 3 where the tee shot has to loop over a small bay. No wonder this course demands a controlled and knowledgeable game.

The Village Course opened in 1981 and sweeps inland along the pineapple fields and statuesque pine trees. At par 71 and 6,858 yards designer Arnold Palmer and course architect Ed Seay are reported to have given this course a European flavor. Resembling the mountainous countryside of Scotland, this course is reputed to be the most difficult and demanding in Hawaii and one of the most challenging in the world.

The Plantation Course opened in 1991, designed by Coore and Crenshaw of Austin, Texas. The 18-hole championship is situated on 240 acres north of the Village Course. The 7,263 yard course has a par 73. This course is the new home of the Kapalua International Championship of Golf held each November. In 1992 the event will be sponsored by Lincoln-Mercury and ABC sports will televise the event. The course features expansive greens, deep valleys and expansive fairways. The Plantation Course opened May 1991 and was named by Golf Digest as runner-up as the country's Best New Resort Course for 1991.

KIHEI

The Silversword Golf Course, a non-resort course, offers a 6,800 yard par 71, 18-hole course located off Piilani Highway near Lipoa Street. Green fees are currently $65 includes shared cart. Rental clubs and shows available. Driving range open 8 a.m. to 9 p.m. daily, except Sundays. A bucket of balls (approx. 50) is $3. Maui residents receive a discounted green fee. (874-0777)

MAKENA

Offers two courses, the Molokini and the Haleakala course. One 18-hole course opened at the same time as the Maui Prince resort, the second 18 holes, by Robert Trent Jones II International, is nearing completion. Resort guests $55; twilight $40. All others $100; twilight $60. Fees include cart. (879-3344) Another golf course above Ahihi Bay in Makena is being proposed.

The Makena Course is a Trent Jones designed 6,800 yard par 71, 18-hole course which opened in 1981. It winds among the hillsides and down along the coastline, where remnants of early Hawaiian rock boundary walls have been preserved. The large cactus which abound in this area were imported to feed the cattle which were once ranched in this area.

WAILEA

The Wailea resort offers the challenging Orange and Blue Courses. Greens fees for the Blue course is $125; resort guests $75; and $115 for the orange course, resort guests $65. Carts included. Maui residents receive guest rates. (879-2966)

The Orange Course is a par 72, 6,810 yard championship course designed by Arthur Jack Snyder. It opened in 1978. With trees, ancient stone walls, narrow fairways and dog legs at half the holes, it is a considerable challenge.

The Blue Course is par 72 and 6,700 yards from the championship tees. It opened in 1972. Four lakes and 72 bunkers provide added hazards along with the exceptional scenery. The 16th hole is especially lovely with numerous people stopping to snap a picture from this magnificent vantage point.

The Gold Course, currently under development, is considered by designer Robert Trent Jones, Jr. as a "pure golf course." This means that there will be no housing surrounding the course, just golf! A new clubhouse will serve both the Gold and Orange course and will overlook the Pacific with a panoramic view. The course is expected to take three and a half years to complete.

WAIKAPU

The *Waikapu Valley Country Club* is a par 72, private course that will eventually become a membership course. In the meantime it is being used exclusively by guests of the Four Seasons and Grand Hyatt resorts. *The Waikapu Sandalwood Golf Course* is a public course 6,433 yards, par 72. Tee-off hours 7 a.m. - 1 p.m. The $65 green fee includes a cart. Both courses were designed by Robins Nelson of the Honolulu firm of Nelson and Wright and are located along the isthmus of the island at the base of the west Maui range. One of the most unusual course features is a two acre lake containing irrigation water from the Waihee ditch. Silica sand imported from California fills sandtraps and the greens utilize non-seeding hybrids. The clubhouses, however, may well prove to be the most incredible feature of the courses. Currently still under construction, the Country Club facility is an original design of Frank Lloyd Wright and had been designed for a Mexican official, but was never completed. Arthur Miller and famous wife Marilyn Monroe at one time considered purchasing the plan as well. The 70,000 square foot floor plan will certainly be a center piece for the course and Maui as well. The second clubhouse is designed by a Maui firm utilizing a style of C.W. Dickey. Phone number for both courses: 242-7090.

PAIA

The Maui Country Club is a private course which invites visitors to play on Mondays. Call on Sunday after 9 am to schedule Monday tee times.It originally opened in 1925. The front 9 holes have a par 37 as do the back nine. Greens fees are $45 cart included for 9 or 18 holes. (877-0616)

PUKALANI

Pukalani Country Club and Golf Course is nestled along the slopes of Haleakala and affords a tremendous panoramic view of Central Maui and the ocean from every hole. Designed by Bob Baldock, the first 9 holes opened in 1980. Nine additional holes have been added making a par 72, 6,692 yard course. Greens fees are $60 for 18 holes, $32 for nine holes, cart included. (572-1314)

WAILUKU
The Waiehu Municipal Course, which is north of Wailuku, opened with nine holes in 1929 and an additional 9 holes were added later. This a par 72 course. Greens fees are $25 weekdays and weekends and holidays. A cart is optional at $14 for 18 holes, $7 for 9 holes, pull cart $2. Phone (243-7400 or pro shop 244-5934)

TENNIS

Tennis facilities abound on Maui. Many condos and major hotels offer tennis facilities, also, there are quite a few very well kept public courts. They are, of course, most popular during early morning and early evening hours.

PUBLIC COURTS
Hana - Hana Ball Park, one lighted court.
Kahului - Maui Community Cntr. (Kaahumanu and Wakea Ave.) has 2 unlighted courts. Kahului Community Center (Onehu and Uhu St.) has two lighted courts.
Kihei - Kalama Park has two lighted courts. Six unlighted courts in park fronting Maui Sunset condos.
Lahaina - Lahaina Civic Center has two lighted courts and there are four lighted courts at Malu-ulu-olele Park.
Makawao - Eddie Tam Memorial Center has two lighted courts.
Pukalani - Pukalani Community Center has two lighted courts, located across from the Pukalani Shopping Center.
Wailuku - Maui Community College has four lighted courts available after school hours. (244-9181)

PRIVATE COURTS WITH FACILITIES OPEN TO PUBLIC
Hyatt Regency, Kaanapali. Six courts. FEE CHARGED for guests and non-guests. (661-1234 ext. 3174). Guests $12 and $15. Non-guests $20.
Kapalua Bay Hotel, Kapalua. Offers the Tennis Garden with 10 courts. Tennis attire required at all times. Guests $10, non-guest $12. (669-5677)
Makena Tennis Club, 5415 Makena Alanui, Makena. Six courts. Resort guests $5, non-guests $8. (879-8777)
Maui Marriott Resort, Kaanapali. Guests and non-guests can play on five courts, three are lighted. (667-1200)
Napili Kai Beach Club, Napili. Currently due to costruction, no courts. Will have some in the future. (669-6271)
Royal Lahaina Hotel, Kaanapali. Has the 2nd largest facility on the island with 11 courts, 6 lighted and 1 stadium court. Guests $6, non-guest $9. (661-3611)
Sheraton Maui Hotel, Kaanapali. Has 3 lighted courts. Fee $12 all. (661-0031)
Wailea Tennis Center, Wailea. Has fourteen courts, 3 lighted, 3 grass. Grass $40 - $60 guests, $50 - $80 non-guests. Resort guests $10 and non-guests $15 for regular courts. (879-1958)

RESORT COURTS RESTRICTED TO GUESTS
Hale Kamaole, Hotel Hana Maui, Kaanapali Alii, Kaanapali Plantation, Kaanapali Shores, Kaanapali Royal, Kahana Villa, Kamaole Sands, Kihei Akahi, Kihei Alii Kai, Kihei Bay Surf, Kuleana, Maalaea Surf, Mahana, Makena Surf, Maui Hill, Maui Islander, Maui Lu Resort, Maui Vista, Papakea, Puamana, Royal Kahana, Sands of Kahana, Shores of Maui, The Whaler.

HORSEBACK RIDING

Historically, the first six horses arrived on the islands in 1803 from Baja California. These wild mustangs were named "Lio" by the Hawaiians, which means "open eyes wide in terror." They roamed and multiplied along the volcanic slopes of Maui and the Big Island until they numbered 11,000. They adjusted quickly to the rough terrain and had a reputation for terrific stamina. Today these ponies, also known as Kanaka ponies or Mauna Loa ponies, are all but extinct with fewer than a dozen purebreds still in existence.

Lush waterfalls, pineapple fields stretching up the mountain's flanks, cane fields, kukui nut forests and Haleakala's huge crater are all environments that can be enjoyed on horseback. Beginner, intermediate or experienced rides lasting from 1-2 hours or up to three days. Most stables have age restrictions.

Adventures on Horseback - A 5 hour waterfall ride outside Haiku is $150 per person and includes lunch and gear. Enjoy the cliffs of North Maui, the slopes of Haleakala, the old Hana Hwy, rainforest streams and secluded waterfalls. breakfast, picnic lunch, and swimming. Maximum 6 riders. (242-7445)

Aloha Nui Loa Tours - Drive to Hana for a tour of the town, lunch on a quiet beach, and a ride across the scenic pastureland of the Hotel Hana Ranch with a personal guide. Children over age 7 with experience can ride alone. Pick up from all Maui locations. $120 plus tax. (879-7044).

Charley's Trailride and Pack Trips - Features overnight trips to Haleakala with guide arranging cabin and supplies. Rates for 4 - 6 people are $150 per person, food provided; $125 per person if you bring your own. Rates for 2 - 3 people are $200 each with food provided. $75 non-refundable deposit unless rain cancels trip. Write Charles Aki, c/o Kaupo Store, Hana, Maui, HI 96713. (248-8209)

Hotel Hana Maui - Guided trail rides around the 4,500 acre working cattle ranch on open range, shoreline, rain forest and mountains. $55 for guest, private 2 hr. ride. $27.50 for one hour guest ride. Non guests $65 for two hour ride. (248-8211)

Holo Lio Stables - Located near the Makena Beach. Shoreline, sunset or moon-light rides $20 - $35. All day trips $65. (879-1085)

Makena Stables - 7299 South Makena Rd., rides are along the King's Hwy. and La Perouse Bay. Guided tours $85 for three hour, $125 for six hour. (879-0244)

Pony Express Tours - Has trips into Haleakala Crater, weather permitting, Mon. - Fri. The Kapalaoa Cabin Tour is 12 miles and 8 hours starting at the craters rim for $130 plus tax per person and includes lunch. Half day trips $110. One hour rides $30, two hour $50. (667-2202 and 667-2200)

The Rainbow Ranch - Follow Honoapiilani Hwy. 11 miles north of Lahaina, entrance near exit for Napili. They tour the mountain area. Trips are available for beginning, intermediate or advanced riders in either English or Western style. 1-hour mountain trip $30, 1 1/2 hr. $45, 2 1/2 hr. $50, 3 1/2 hr. $85, 2- hr. sunset trip $50, 3 hr. picnic ride $60. (669-4991)

Thompson Riding Stables - Located on Thompson Rd. in Kula, the Thompson Ranch was established in 1902. Located at the 3,700 foot elevation they offer trail and crater tours, day and overnight camping, or sunset and picnic rides. 1 1/2 hr. $35. Child can ride with adult. 2 hr. picnic $45, 2 hr. sunset without food $40, with food $45. (879-1910 or 244-7412.)

HIKING

Maui offers many excellent hiking opportunities for the experienced hiker, or for a family outing. Comprehensive hiking information is available from several excellent references (see ORDERING INFORMATION). Craig Chisholm and his wife Eila were the pioneers in the field of Hawaiian hiking information with the 1975 release of *Hawaiian Hiking Trails*, and it has been contiually updated. They recently began work on separate island hiking guides. *Kaua'i Hiking Trails* is now available, but *Maui Hiking Trails* and *Big Island Hiking Trails* not yet complete. The Chisholm's books are attractively done with beautiful color illustrations in the frontpiece, and easy to follow U.S. Geological maps for each of the hikes. Throughout the text are black and white photos. These books are thoroughly researched by the authors and very accurate. The *Hawaiian Hiking Trails* book has six trails described for Maui.

The first edition of Robert Smith's *Hiking Maui* was published in September 1977. He continues to update his book every couple of years. He also has books for the other islands. The books are compact in size with a color cover and a scattering of black and white photographs. The Maui edition covers 27 trails.

Kathy Morey writes *Maui Trails* which is published by Wilderness Press. There are over 50 trails listed in the hiking table of contents, however, some are really more walks than hikes. It has plenty of easy-to-use maps.

We're not going to even attempt to cover the many hiking trails available on Maui, but would like to share with you several guided hiking experiences which we have enjoyed.

Among the most incredible adventures to be experienced on Maui is one, or more, of the fifty hikes your personal guide *Ken Schmitt* has available. These hikes, for 2 - 6 people only, can encompass waterfalls and pools, ridges with panoramic views, rock formations, spectacular redwood forests (yes, there are!), the incomparable Haleakala Crater or ancient structures found in East Maui.

Arriving on Maui in 1979, Ken has spent much of that time living, exploring and subsisting out-of-doors and experiencing the "Natural Energy" of this island. This soft spoken man offers a wealth of detailed knowledge on the legends, flora, fauna and geography of Maui's many diverse areas. Ken has traversed the island nearly 400 times and established his fifty day hikes after considerable exploration. His favorites are the 8 and 12 mile crater hikes which he says offer a unique, incredible beauty and magic, unlike anywhere else in the world. The early Hawaiians considered Haleakala to be the vortex of one of the strongest natural power points on earth.

The hikes are tailored to the desires and capabilities of the individual or group and run 1/2 or full day (5 - 12 hours). They range from very easy for the inexperienced to fairly rugged. Included in the $60 - $90 fee (children are less) are waterproof day packs, picnic lunch, specially designed Japanese fishing slippers, wild fruit and, of course, the incredible knowledge of Ken. Also available are overnight or longer hikes by special arrangement. Ken can be reached at 879-5270, or by writing *Ken Schmitt*, P.O. Box 330969, Kahului, Maui, HI 96733.

WEST MAUI

Escape! Just a few miles beyond Kapalua is a world far removed from the tourist haunts. With naturalist *Ken Schmitt*, some unique sights are in store for the hiking enthusiast. The hike overall is a fairly easy one that most people could enjoy. However, there are a few places requiring the footing of a mountain goat and a moderate climb up a rather steep slope.

This West Maui hike leads first to an unusual Hawaiian archeological site. While visitors are familiar with Haleakala and the role it played as the islands most sacred spot, the circle of stones in West Maui is unknown to most and is an area veiled with mystery and filled with beauty. The first portion of the hike is less than a mile over private land (which Ken has permission to cross). A dirt path used by cattle twists and turns with low hanging bows of Australian pine (false ironwood) trees. Emerging on a grassy bluff with the crystal blue Pacific below and the warm sunny skies above is a delightful surprise. Except for an overly friendly horse, there is no sign of civilization for as far as the eye can see. The circle of stones, with a large central stone, dominates Kanounou Point. Resembling the Indian medicine wheels of Colorado and Wyoming, this area is still revered by the Hawaiians as a source of power. Evidence of this was apparent with the small, beautiful purple crystals that had been left as an offering in the center alter stone. Ken explains that there is a fairly straight ley line through the islands that emits a subtle force field. On each of the islands that cross this path you will find a similar Hawaiian structure. As Ken speaks, a Great Frigatebird (which land only to nest) soars overhead. This is truly is a place full of beauty and peace.

As with each hike, Ken introduces the group to the tropical flora of the area. At this location we discover the beautiful, low growing, multi-blossomed Lantana, the Beach Naupaka, the half blossom with a legend of lost love.

The second portion of the hike also covers about a mile in distance. While we begin our trek less than a mile from the first site, the environs are dramatically different. Descending a natural path along the side of the cliff we enter into what appears to be an area more lunar than terran. When the lava of West Maui's volcano, Mauna Kahalawai, spewed forth this area was covered by water. The lava erupted from a localized vent during the third series (and probably the last, occuring approximately 5,000 - 10,000 years ago) of West Maui eruptions and poured into the ocean where it was rapidly cooled, creating unusual and intriguing formations, caverns and blow holes.

The highlight of this portion of the sojourn was standing next to one of the island's most spectacular blow holes and being sprinkled (or drenched depending on the tide and wave activity) with salty spray. Many a visitor view this powerful natural phenomena from afar, but few experience the excitement so close at hand. This half day hike ends with the return back up the bluff to a picnic lunch of sandwiches and fresh fruit on the summit with a panoramic view of the deep blue Pacific. This hike can be conveniently combined with a snorkeling trip to Honoloa Bay (in summer) where Ken explains the reef and marine life.

A NOTE: On February 4, 1992, Colin Cameron announced the granting of a permanent conservation easement for the native forest lands of Pu'u Kukui. The preservation of a spectacular forest region and an important watershed is an very important step for the environment of West Maui. The Pacific Region of the Nature Conservancy accepted this grant which forms the largest private nature preserve in the state. There are many endangered flora and fauna that make their home in this region. It was a wonderful gesture for today and the future. Sadly, Colin Cameron passed away in early summer of 1992.

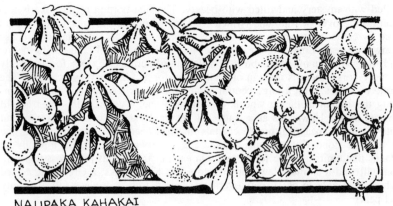

NAUPAKA KAHAKAI

CENTRAL MAUI

A wonderful hike for the family is to the ***Twin Falls*** area on Maui's windward side. This easy trail passes through cattle pastures and then woodlands to three beautiful and tantalizingly cool fresh water pools formed by cascading falls. It is a popular hike enjoyed by many visitors and island residents over an easy to follow trail described in many hiking books. However, it is Ken that makes the trip special. The average hiker would pass right over the fallen kukui nuts while Ken stops, opens several and passes them around for a taste test, warning that they have a strong laxative quality! A small purple blossom, an herbal blood purifier, is sampled, a juicy guava and liliokoi are tasted and the base of one of the pandanus blossoms with a caramel-like flavor can be chewed on. Passing over a canal, Ken explains the history of the early cane industry when this series of amazing water channels was built one day short of a two year deadline.

UPCOUNTRY MAUI

Poli Poli is ideally situated on the leeward slopes of Haleakala. Cool crisp mountain air provides a temperate climate for hiking and the trails are suitable for the entire family. Since the weather can be cool, warm attire and rain apparel should be included in your day or night pack, however, the clouds often clear and treat visitors to a sunny and very mild afternoon. To get to the turn off, go just past the Kula Botanical Gardens and turn on Waipoli Rd., or go 3/10 mile past the junction of Hwy 37 and Hwy 277. Follow the paved, steep and windy road approximately 3.9 miles (about 26 minutes), then continue another 5.8 miles or about 20 minutes on gravel road. The last 1/4 mile is downhill and especially rutted and can be very muddy and too slippery for anything but a four wheel drive when wet. *WARNING: Rental car agencies are not responsible for damage done to cars that travel this road.* We have found it passable in a car with high clearance if the road has been recently graded and is dry. Once you reach the park there is a graveled parking area and a grassy camping area. Two BBQ's and the luxury of a flush toilet in a small outhouse. Drinking water is available. Trail options include a .8 mile trek to the Redwood Forest, a 6 mile Haleakala Trail, 4.8 mile loop trail, 1.0 mile to the cave shelter and 1.5 miles to the Plum trail.

The 4.8 mile loop is a very easy trail and with frequent snack stops, even our three year old was able to make it the entire distance. There is an array of lush foliage and plums may be ripe if you arrive during June and July. The clouds can roll quickly in, causing it to be pleasant and warm one minute and cool the next, as well as creating some interesting lighting effects amongst the trees. The cave shelter, is a bit of a disappointment. It is a shallow cavern and reaching it meant a descent down a steep incline of loose gravel that was too difficult for our young ones. The Eucalyptus was especially fragrant as the fallen leaves crunched underneath our tennis shoes. An area along the trail that had been freshly rutted by wild boars demonstrated the incredible power of these animals. On one trip we heard a rustling in the bushes nearby followed by grunting sounds. We have been told that while you definitely want to avoid the wild boars, they are accustomed to being hunted and will also choose to avoid you. Apparently we were down wind of them and since they have poor eyesight we passed by quietly without them noticing us and without seeing them.

HALEAKALA

A hike, once again with Ken Schmitt, is a thrill for all the senses. Not only does he pack a great lunch and yummy snacks, but the hike provides beauty for the eyes, cool, fresh air for the lungs, tantalizing scents for the nose, peace and serenity for the ears, and an opportunity to touch and get in touch with Maui's natural beauty. We chose a trip to Haleakala to see the awesome crater up close. The trip was an 8-mile hike down Switchback (Halemauu) Trail to the Holua cabin and back. The first mile of the trek was over somewhat rocky, but fairly level, terrain. The next mile seemed like three as we descended seemingly endless hairpin twists down the side of the crater with changing panoramic vistas at each turn. Sometimes fog would eerily sweep in, hovering around and obscuring the view completely, only to soon move away. The vegetation (following a period of heavy rains) was exceptionally lush. All the greenery seemed quite out of place in the usually rather desolate crater.

We continued along the crater floor and past the Holua cabin to reach the Holua lava tube. The small opening was not marked and could be easily overlooked. A small sign advised the use of lights inside the cave. We prepared our flashlights and bundled up for the cooler temperatures to be encountered below. A ladder set by the park service provides access. Once at the base of the ladder, the cavern was large, cool and dark. While there were several directions that lead quickly to dead ends, Ken took us further down the main tube. The cavern was so large that seldom did we have to do more than occasionally duck. Once inside we turned out the lights to enjoy a few moments of the quiet darkness. The tube travels about 100 yards with a gradual ascent to daylight. As daylight peeks down through the dark shaft, it appears the end is in sight. Another turn in the tunnel reveals not the end, but a natural altar-like flat rock piled with assorted stones. Light cascading through a hole in the ceiling casts an almost supernatural glow to eyes now accustomed to the darkness. The effect is to create a luminescence on the stones making them appear to be statues set in a natural cathedral. A very awesome experience. Returning to the cabin, we picnicked on the grounds while very friendly nene geese begged for handouts. Ken advised against feeding them as the park rangers would prefer the geese not become dependent on human handouts. After a rest in the warm sun, we retraced our path back up Switchback Trail to the van and continued on to enjoy the summit before heading back to town.

Other more strenuous and lengthy crater ventures include the Sliding Sands Trail and one that traverses down the side of the volcano through the Kaupo Gap.

Available through Paradise Publications are two excellent photo-filled books from K.C. Publications. *Haleakala* and *Hawai'i Volcanos*. Order information is available at the end of the book.

The public is invited to join the guided hikes of the **Maui Chapter of the Sierra Club**. This is a wonderful and affordable way to enjoy Maui with a knowledgeable group of people. There are weekend outings twice a month, donations are accepted. At the Sierra Club contact Mary Evanson (572-9724).

The Hawaii Nature Center, 875 Iao Valley Road, Wailuku, Maui, HI 96793. (244-6500) This is a new field site of the Honolulu Center that offers a limited number of hikes. Cost is $3.

The Waikamoi Preserve, Box 1716, Makawao, Maui, HI 96768. (572-7849) On the second Saturday of every month hikes are conducted on this 5,230 acre Nature Conservancy preserve. A $15 donation is requested for non-Conservancy members, $5 is charged for members. Reservations are required. On Moloka'i the Nature Conservancy also runs monthly tours at the Kamakoau Preserve (a rain forest preserve). The Moloka'i address is PO Box 220, Kualapuu, Moloka'i, HI 96757. (553-5236)

Haleakala National Park offers guided hikes on Monday and Thursday mornings free of charge. Call to verify days and times with the range office at 5722-9306.

Hiking off established trails without a knowledgeable guide is *definitely* not advised, however, the following sources will help you find and enjoy the many established hikes. *Hawaiian Hiking Trails* by Craig Chisholm, 128 pages, $12.95, has nearly 50 hiking trails throughout the islands, seven of these are on Maui. Look for their upcomming *Maui Hiking Trails*. Robert Smith's book *Hiking Maui* 160 pages, $8.95, will guide you on 27 fairly accessible trails throughout Maui. Both of these publications are available from Paradise Publications, see ordering information at the back of the book. A good trail companion book might be *Trailside Plants of Hawaii's National Parks* by Charles Lamoureux, 77 pages with great pictures for $4.95. Available at Maui bookstores.

CAMPING

MAUI COUNTY PARKS

County permits for the two county parks, H.A. Baldwin and Rainbow Park, can be obtained by writing the Dept. of Parks and Recreation, County of Maui, 1580 Kaahumanu Ave., Wailuku, Maui, HI 96793. (243-7389). Maximum length of stay is three consecutive nights per campsite. Fee per night is currently $3 per adult and 50 cents per child below age 18.

H.A. Baldwin Beach Park - This county park is a grassy fenced area near the roadside. It is located near Lower Paia on the Hana Hwy. and has tent camping space, restrooms and outdoor showers.

Rainbow Park - Located in Paia. Facilities: Restrooms.

STATE PARKS

There are only two State Parks on Maui and one on Moloka'i where camping is allowed. A permit is required from the Division of State Parks at 54 South High Street, Wailuku, HI 96793. (243-4345) There is currently no charge for tent camping, but a permit is required. The two campsites on Maui are Polipoli and Wainapanapa and on Moloka'i camping is permitted at Palaau. Permits are issued between 8 am and 4:15 pm on weekdays only. The maximum length of stay is five consecutive nights and they do have a limit on the number of campers per campsite. You will need to provide names and ID numbers of those camping. ID numbers consist of Social Security Number, Driver's License, State ID or Passport.

PoliPoli Springs Recreational Area - Located in Upcountry, this state park has one cabin and offers tent camping. This is a wooded, two-acre area at the 6,200 foot elevation on Haleakala's west slope and requires four wheel drives to reach. Extensive hiking trails offer sweeping views of Maui and the other islands in clear weather. Seasonal bird and pig hunting. Nights are cold, in winter below freezing. No showers. Toliets, picnic tables. The single cabin sleeps 10 and has bunk beds, water, cold shower, kitchenware. Sheets and towels can be picked up along with the key. See additional description in the hiking section which follows.

Wainapanapa State Park - Located near Hana. Tent camping, 12 cabins. More information on this location can be found under WHERE TO STAY - HANA. Restrooms, picnic tables, outdoor showers. This is a remote volcanic coastline covering 120 acres. Shore fishing, hiking, marine study, forests, caves, blow holes, black sand beach and heiau. The park covers 7.8 acres. BRING MOSQUITO REPELLENT!

Other day use state park camps, see beaches.

NATIONAL PARKS

The most recent information we have received states that a permit is not currently required to camp at either Hosmer's Grove or O'heo. A maximum stay of three nights is allowed. For information on camping within the Haleakala Crater, contact them at PO Box 369, Makawao, HI 96768 or phone (808) 572-9306 for the latest data. For information on use of one of the three cabins located in the Haleakala Crater, please refer to the Upcountry accommodations section of this book.

Hosmer Grove - Haleakala National Park. Tent camping. No permit required. Located at the 7,000 foot elevation on the slope of Haleakala. Cooking area with grill, pit toilets, water, picnic tables.

Ohe'o Gulch - Haleakala National Park, just outside of Hana. Tent camping. No permit required. Chemical toilets, picnic tables, BBQ grills, bring your own water.

OTHER PARKS

The following parks had previously been listed as allowing tent camping, but recent information no longer shows them as available facilities. Check with the county and state to verify current status on these properties.

Honomanu Bay - This county park is in the Hana

Hookipa Beach Park - A county park, has restrooms and outdoor showers.

Kaumahina State Wayside - Located in the rain forest area 28 miles from Kahului Airport on the Hana Highway. Restrooms, picnic tables, outdoor BBQ, no drinking water.

Currently there are no rental companies offering camping vehicles. There have been a few companies in recent years, but they have come and gone quickly. Car rental agencies generally prohibit use of cars or vans for camping. Camping equipment is available for rent at Silversword Stoves in Makawao. (572-4569)

Camping, hiking and activity package tours are offered from *Pacific Quest Outdoor Adventures* on Kaua'i, The Big Island and Maui. Eight to thirteen day trips are offered year round and include inns, meals, local air and ground transportation, natural and cultural history tours. Trips begin at $1,400. 59-496 Pupukea Rd. (638-8338 or 1-800 776-2518 from U.S. and Canada)

Robert Smith, author of a series of Hiking books for the islands, also offers group hiking excursions to Maui and the neighbor islands. Contact: *Hawaiian Outdoor Adventures*, PO Box 869, Huntington Beach, CA 92648. (714) 960-0369.

See listing under Hiking for information on Ken Schmitt who might be available for overnight excursions on Maui.

Charley's Trail Rides offers guided overnight horseback trail excursions from Kaupo up the Haleakala slopes to the crater. Parties of 4 - 6 persons $150 each includes meals, cabin or campsite equipment, parties of 2 - 3 are $200 each. Advance notice and deposit required. Write c/o Kaupo Store, Kaupo, HI 96713. (248-8209)

HUNTING

Contact *Hunting Adventures of Maui, Inc.*, 645B Kapakalua Rd., Haiku, Maui, HI 96708 (808-572-8214). Year round hunting season. Game includes (Kao) Spanish Goat and (Pua'a) Wild Boar. Hunting on 100,000 acres of privately owned ranches with all equipment provided. Rates $400 first person, $150 each additional person, 3 max. (non-hunters free) includes sunrise-sunset hunt, food, beverages, four wheel drive transportation, clothing, boots, packs, meat storage and packing for home shipment, hotel or airport pick up. Rifle rentals and taxidermy available. Also available are sightseeing safaris and overnight lodgings for small groups.

WILD BOAR

ARCHERY

Valley Isle Archers holds weekly meetings in Kahului at the National Guard Armory each Wednesday, visitors are welcome. An annual competitive shoot is held each year in June on Kamehameha Day.

RUNNING

Maui is a scenic delight for runners. *Valley Isle Road Runners* can provide you with up-to-date information on island running events. They can be reached at 242-6042. Also available at area bookstores is *HAWAII: A Running Guide* by Noel Murchie and Paul Ryan, softcover. $6.95.

FITNESS CENTERS AND HEALTH RETREATS

If you are interested in keeping in shape while you are on Maui and you have no fitness center at your resort, there are several fitness centers that welcome trop in Guests. Several fitness retreats are listed below.ith the following facilities which welcome drop in guests.

Nautilus World Fitness Center, Dickenson Square, Lahaina (667-6100)
Nautilus World Fitness Center, 1325 Lower Main St., Wailuku (244-3244)
Valley Isle Fitness Center, Wailuku Industrial Park, (242-6851)
Valley Isle Fitness Center, Lipoa Shopping Center in Kihei (874-2844)
World Gym Lahaina, Inc. at Lahaina Shopping Center, 845 Waqinee (667-0422)
Powerhouse Gym, Kihei Commercial Center, 300 Ohukai Rd., C-112 in Kihei (879-1326)
Lahaina Health Club, 286 Lahainaluna Rd. (667-6684)

Grand Hyatt Wailea invites non-guests to their luxurious spa. Price is $75 per day with various added fees for massage and extras. (875-1234)

The Hotel Hana Maui offers a *Wellness Center*. The hotel is offering a seven day Hana Health and Fitness Retreat at the beginning of each month conducted by Director Jacque Waters. The retreat is limited to twelve guests and includes hiking, exercises, and a 1,200 calorie daily menu. Arrangements are made through the hotel number 248-8211 and the charge is $2,00 and up which includes room and meals.

The Strong, Stretched and Centered Fitness Body/Mind Institute is offered by Gloria Keeling. The six week health and fitness retreats are designed for personal wellness as well as fitness instruction certification. Gloria explains that this is a program where people learn completely new lifestyles and learn how to teach those lifestyles to others. The $4,000 cost includes meals, land transportation, accommodations in the Kihei area and classes. P.O. Box 758, Paia, HI 96779. (808) 575-2178.

AIR TOURS

SMALL PLANE FLIGHTSEEING

Flightseeing trips are available via helicopter or small plane and include Hana and Haleakala as well as island flights to Mauna Loa on the Big Island, O'ahu, Kaho'olawe, Lana'i or Moloka'i. Small plane trips are less expensive, but you won't get as close to the scenery. Prices are from $39 for half-hour flights to $125 for full-day trips combined with ground tours.

Akamai Tours - Overnight trips to other islands. (871-9551) 1-800-922-6485

Heavenly Hana Tours - For some of us who have experienced the drive along the road to Hana, the only way to visit Hana is to fly... with Heavenly Hana Tours you'll flight-see from Kahului to Hana and arrive relaxed, refreshed and ready to sight-see a mere 40 minutes later. A continental breakfast is provided before you even leave Kapalua and it goes on the plane with you for a mid-morning "nosh" while touring Hana by van. You'll see all the famous Hana sights with no muss, no fuss and most important, no white-knuckling your rental car steering wheel over the long and winding road. You'll see Hana Bay, Hana Town, Wailua Falls and the Seven Sacred Pools (which are neither seven nor sacred and should properly be referred to as Ohe'o Gulch). You'll see red - the red sand of Koki Beach - be in the black - on the black sand beach of Waianapanapa Park - and enjoy a colorful buffet lunch at Hana Ranch Restaurant. Heavenly Hana Tours is operated by Maui residents Richard and Jayne Armijo, Donald Fry and Kim Carroll. So... to see Hana, the heavenly way, call 661-9955. The Hana tour is a fly one way and drive one way $88.

Paragon Air - Charter service to all islands, five passenger, prices vary. P.O. Box 628m, Haiku, HI 96708. (244-3356)

BIPLANE

Biplane Barnstormers - open-cockpit rides for one or two people in their bright red reproduction of a 1935 Waco biplane. It's just as you'd imagine - you soar high above the island, but not so high you can't tip your wing or wave a friendly "shaka" (Hang Loose!) to the beachgoers, picnickers or snorkelers below. There you are ... "Flying Down to Ohe'o" ... the wind in your face, goggles pressed against your nose, leather helmet jauntily strapped under your chin - all you need is a long flowing scarf trailing behind the plane! Per person prices range from $75 for a 30 minute introduction to $225 for a 90 minute circumnavigation around the island. Another option is an Aerobatics ride that takes passengers through loops, spins, rolls - even hammerhead stalls! Owners Steve and Vicki Coan are new to Maui, but not new to flying, expecially glider flying. Steve recently won his fourth consecutive title at the National Glider Aerobatic Championships and helped the U.S. team place third (their highest finish ever) at the World Championship held recently in Poland. Whether adventurous, nostalgic or just curious, you can say "Hello, Good Biplane," by calling Vicki at 878-2860.

HELICOPTER TOURS

The price of an hour helicopter excursion may make you think twice. After all it could be a week's worth of groceries at home. We had visited Maui for 7 years before we finally decided to see what everyone else was raving about. It proved to be the ultimate island excursion. When choosing a special activity for your Maui holiday, we'd suggest putting a helicopter flight at the top of the list. (When you get home you can eat beans for a week!) Adjectives cannot describe the thrill of a helicopter flight above majestic Maui. The most popular tour is the Haleakala Crater/Hana trip which contrasts the desolate volcanic crater with the lush vegetation of the Hana area. Maui's innermost secrets unfold as the camera's shutter works frantically to capture the memories (one roll is simply not enough). and pilots narrate as you pass by waterfalls cascading into cool mountain pools. Truly an outstanding experience. Keeping up with the prices is impossible. Listed are standard fares, and we hope you'll be delighted to learn of some special discount rates when you call for reservations. Currently all helicopters depart from the Kahului heliport.

Alexair - Four passenger. Hughes 500. Hana/Haleakala 45 minute special $110. Other flights range from 20 minute West Maui for $49 to circle of Maui with grand stop for $220. (871-0792) (1-800-462-2281)

Blue Hawaiian - Six passenger A Star. (871-8844 or 1-800-247-5444) West Maui (30 minutes, $90) Hana/Haleakala (45 minutes, $115), Hana/Haleakala Deluxe (60 minute $149), Complete island $195 (1 hour 45 minutes), Sunset $175.

Cardinal Helicopters - (877-2400) 45 minute flight $99, 60 minute flight with two hour Hana land tour $169.

Hawaii Helicopters Inc. - (877-3900) Three, 6-passenger ASTAR jet turbine helicopters. Trips include 30 minutes rainforest and Hookipa beach flight, sunset or sunrise trips, West Maui/Moloka'i or a 2 1/2 hour air and ground excrusion which includes a champagne picnic at Wainapapa Park in Hana.

Kenai Helicopters - (871-6463 or 1-800-622-3144) Departs from Kahului. Maui No Ka Oi Deluxe for $206/person, West Maui and Kalaupapa on Moloka'i ($185), Hana/Haleakala ($145).

Papillon - (669-4884 or 1-800-367-7095)

Sunshine Helicopters Inc. ★ - (871-0722) (1-800-544-2420) Their fine ground and flight crews, will make sure that your experience in one of their four passenger Bell 206 Jet Rangers is one of your most memorable. The West Maui trip is filled with cascading waterfalls, but given the choice, our favorite is still the Hana/Haleakala flight! Also a free video tape of your trip, and they have bilingual pilots! New options include a flight with a touchdown at one of several sites on Maui, and charter trips to Lana'i. $59 for 20 minute West Maui (a great way to get a taste of a helicopter ride), 45 minute Haleakala/Hana flight $119, $1,200 for an all day trip to a secluded beach drop off on Lana'i! We've flown with them a number of times and they are excellent! Be sure to give Anna a special Aloha from us!

THE ISLAND
OF LANA'I - COUNTY OF MAUI

INTRODUCTION

The meaning of Lana'i seems to be steeped in mystery, at least this was our experience. Several guidebooks report that the name means "swelling" or "hump." In discussions with local residents we were told it meant the obvious interpretation of "porch" or "balcony." Perhaps because Lana'i is, in a rather nebulous fashion, the balcony of Maui. So, with no definitive answer we will continue the search, but, in the meantime, come enjoy this little piece of Paradise.

Just before and just following the turn of the century, Lana'i was a bustling sheep and cattle ranch. Beginning in the 1920s Dole transformed Lana'i into the largest single pineapple plantation in the world. The 1990s has brought Lana'i into the tourist industry with the opening of two new elegant and classy resorts, the country-style Lodge at Koele in Lana'i City and the seashore resort at Manele Bay. Under the helm of David Murdock, the metamorphosis has been a positive one with young people returning to the island to work in the new tourism industry. Cattle are again dotting the landscape and a new piggery has been developed as the silver-blue fields of pineapple rapidly fade into extinction.

The rich and famous may soon be anteing up to purchase a vacation home on Lana'i with the recent passage of preliminary approval for construction of luxury homes in the Koele district on 68 acres.

As with each Hawaiian Island, Lana'i is unique. The price for a stay at the two resorts may be steep, but if you want to really indulge, read on! A truly luxurious and relaxing island get-away that is only eight miles, but in many ways, 30 years removed from Maui. Lana'i will simply enchant you.

GEOGRAPHY AND CLIMATE

Lana'i is 140 square miles, making it the sixth largest of the eight major Hawaiian islands. It is situated eight miles to the west of Maui and seven miles south of Moloka'i.

It is likely that millions of years ago, when the glaciers were larger and the seas much lower, that Maui, Lana'i, Moloka'i and Kaho'olawe comprised one enormous island. This is further substantiated by the fact that the channels between the islands are more shallow and the slopes of the islands visibly more gradual than on the outer coastlines of the islands.

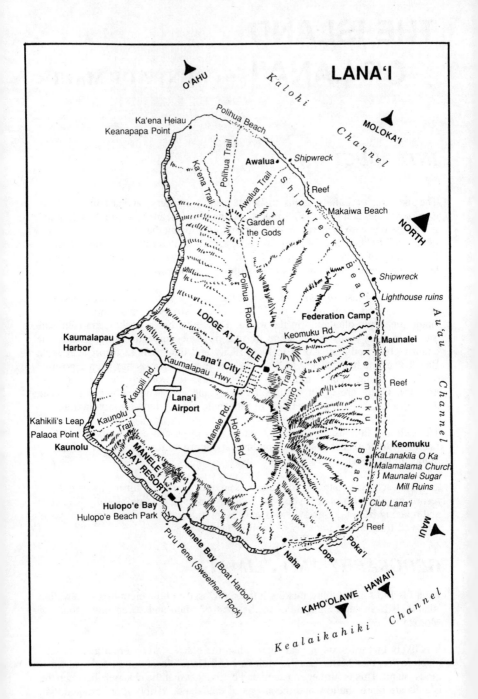

LANA'I

O'AHU

Kalohi

MOLOKA'I

Channel

Ka'ena Heiau
Keanapapa Point

Polihua Beach

Awalua • Shipwreck

Reef

Ka'ena Trail

Polihua Trail

Awalua Trail

Makaiwa Beach

NORTH

Garden of
the Gods

Shipwreck Beach

Polihua Road

Shipwreck

Lighthouse ruins

Au'au

LODGE AT KO'ELE

Federation Camp

Keomuku Rd.

Maunalei

Kaumalapau
Harbor

Lana'i City

Kaumalapau Hwy.

Munro Trail

Keomuku Beach

Channel

Kaupili Rd.

Lana'i
Airport

Manele Rd.

Ho'ike Rd.

Reef

Kahikili's Leap
Palaoa Point
Kaunolu

Kaunolu
Trail

Keomuku
KaLanakila O Ka
Malamalama Church
Maunalei Sugar
Mill Ruins

MANELE BAY RESORT

Club Lana'i

Hulopo'e Bay
Hulopo'e Beach Park

Reef

MAUI

Manele Bay (Boat Harbor)

Naha

Lopa

Poka'i

Pu'u Pene (Sweetheart Rock)

KAHO'OLAWE

HAWAI'I

Kealaikahiki

Channel

The island of Lana'i was formed by a single shield volcano. A ridge runs along the eastern half of the island and forms its most notable feature. This large, raised hump is dotted with majestic Norfolk pines. The summit of the island is Lanaihale located at an elevation of 3,370 feet. A rather strenuous hike along the Monro Trail provides access to this summit where you will be treated to the only location in Hawai'i where you can view (on a clear day) five other Hawaiian islands. Maunalei and Hauola are Lana'i's two deepest gulches. Today the Maunalei Gulch continues to supply the island with its water. The center of the island, once a caldera, is now the Palawai Basin and has been used as both farm and ranch land.

Lana'i has one city, cleverly dubbed Lana'i City. Located at an elevation of about 1,700 feet, it can be much cooler, and wetter, than the coastline. It is the hub of the island, or what hub there is, and visitors will soon learn that all roads lead to Lana'i City. The island population in 1992 was about 3,000, with almost everyone a resident of Lana'i City. The houses are generally small, mostly roofed with tin and the yards are abloom with fruits and flowers.

Rainfall along the coastline is limited, 4 or 5 inches a year. The heart of the island and Lana'i City may have rainfall of 20 inches or more, and the higher slopes receive 45 to 60 inches annually. The weather in Lana'i City might range from 80 degree days in September with lows in the mid-sixties, to cooler January temperatures in the low 70s, dropping an additional 10 degrees at night. The coastline can be warmer by 10 degrees or more.

Pineapples and pines, not palms, have been the predominant vegetation on the island, but that is rapidly changing. At its peak in the 1970s, there were 15,000 acres of pineapple in cultivation. Very quickly the acreage is being reduced and will ultimately fall to 100 - 120 acres, only enough for local consumption. The pineapple fields are now turning to production of hay and alfalfa, and some fields are already spotted with black angus cattle as Castle & Cook begin their diversification program. Other acreage has been converted to an organic garden for use by the Manele and Koele restaurants. A piggery and a chicken house have also been established with an aim of making Lana'i more self sufficient.

The island flower is very unusual. The Kaunaoa is more a vine in appearance than a flower and there are two varieties. One grows in the uplands and the other near the ocean. The ocean species have a softer vine with more vivid hues of yellow and orange than the mountainous counterparts. Strands of the vine are twisted and adorned with local greens and flowers to make beautiful and unusual leis. The mountain vines make a stiffer lei and, we were told, are used for leis for decorating animals. One of the best places to spot this plant is along the drive down to Keomuku and Shipwreck Beach or along the shoreline.

Driving around Lana'i you will note that it is a very arid island. Water supply has always been a problem and most of the greenery is supplied by the Norfolk pines which dot the island.

HISTORY OF LANA'I

The historical tales of the island of Lana'i are intriguing, filled with darkness and evil. As legend has it, in ancient times the island of Lana'i was uninhabited except for evil spirits. It is said that in the olden days, those who went to Lana'i never returned and that the island was tabu. Hawaiians banished wrong-doers to Lana'i as punishment for their crimes. The story continues that around the 16th century on West Maui there was a chief named Kaka'alanaeo. He had a son named Kaulula'au who was willful and spoiled. The people became furious with his many misdeeds and finally rebelled and demanded that Kaulula'au be put on trial by the ancient laws. The verdict was guilty and, according to the ancient laws, his punishment was death. His father begged for his life and it was agreed that Kaulula'au would be banished to the island of Lana'i. He was set ashore near the Maunalei Gulch, the only source of potable water on the island. His father promised him that if he could banish the evil spirits from Lana'i, he could then set a bonfire as a signal and his father and the warriors would return for him. And, as luck would have it, Kaulula'au managed to trick the evil spirits and send them over to Kaho'olawe. He signaled his father and returned to Maui, heralded now as a hero. (Be sure you take time to view the beautiful, large murals on either side of the entrance at the Manele Bay Resort. One depicts the fallen son being taken by canoe to Lana'i. The other shows Kaulula'au, head held high in victory, standing over his signal bonfire.) At this point in time Maui was reaching its population zenith and many of the people relocated to Lana'i with settlements near Keomuku and inland as well.

The first archeological studies were done in 1921 by Kenneth Emory from the anthropology department of the Bishop Museum. His work was originally published in 1923. (Hardcover reprints of the book are available at Walden bookstores on Maui.) Kenneth Emory found many ancient villages and artifacts which had been, for the most part, undisturbed for hundreds of years. He found the area of Kaunolu to be Lana'i's richest archaeological region filled with house sites and remnants of a successful fishing village. He also ventured to the eastern coastline and explored Naha and Keomuku. He noted eleven heiaus, found relics including old stone game boards and discovered a network of trails and petroglyphs. Before the construction on the two new resorts began, the first archeological team since 1921 arrived. Villages were studied and ashes from old fires were analyzed. The findings showed that the ashes dated from 900 A.D., much later than the other islands which were inhabited as early as 40 or 50 B.C. One of the earliest heiaus is in the Kaunolu area, and it is thought that this region may have been one of the earliest Hawaiian settlements.

While the Hawaiian population increased throughout the archipelago, Lana'i was left largely uninhabited until the 1500s. Two of Captain Cook's ships, the Discovery and The Resolution, reported a visit to Lana'i. They found the Hawaiians friendly along the windward coastal area where they replenished their supplies of food and water. In talking with the islanders they estimated that the population was approximately 10,000. They observed and noted that the island was a dry dustbowl and that the people fished and grew some taro. About this same time, chiefs of Maui became worried that the people on Lana'i might become too powerful. So they divided Lana'i into 13 ohanas (ohana means family, but this refers more to regions) and put a konahiki in charge of each -- this way insuring that no one chief would be too powerful. These district names are still used today. They are Kaa Paomai, Mahana, Maunalei, Kamoku, Kaunolu, Kalulu, Kealiakapu, Kealiaaupuni, Palawai, Kamao, Pawili and Kaohai.

Six months after the island was visited by Cook's vessels a tragic event happened that would change life on Lana'i forever. Inter island battles among the island chiefs were not uncommon, but until this time Lana'i had remained unaffected. In 1778 Kalaniopu'u, the chief on the Big Island, launched an unsuccessful attack on Lahaina, Maui. He retreated, then turned and attacked central Maui. Here again his warriors were overcome. As they returned to the Big Island in great anger he passed the island of Kaho'olawe, which was loyal to the Maui chieftains. In retaliation Kalaniopu'u's warriors massacred the entire population on Kaho'olawe. Bolstered by his victory, Kalaniopu'u turned once again to assault Lahaina and again was defeated. Now enraged, Kalaniopu'u and his warriors chose to strike the leeward coastal villages of Lana'i. Lana'i's warriors were unprepared and retreated to the Ho'okia Ridge to have a better location from which to launch their counterattack. However, without access to food and water, the Lana'i warriors soon weakened and Kalanaiopu'u moved quickly to crush them. The Big Island warriors continued around Lana'i and systematically destroyed all the villages. Kalaniopu'u returned to the Big Island of Hawai'i and there, seven months later, he died and his lieutenant, Kamehameha came to rule. Today less than 100 Lana'ians are part or full blooded Hawaiian.

During the rule of Kamehameha the population increased. The king and his warriors would visit Kaunolu Bay on Lana'i's southwestern coastline. Here Kahekili is said to have leaped from a cliff above the sea into the Pacific waters, proving his loyalty to the king. Other warriors were then challenged to follow his example and the area continues to be referred to as Kahekili's Leap.

The elders from the Church of Jesus Christ of Latter Day Saints acquired land on Lana'i from one of the chiefs in 1855. In 1860 Walter Murray Gibson came to Lana'i with the intent of establishing a Mormon colony called the City of Joseph in the Palawai Basin. Gibson had been instrumental in assisting Kamehameha. He served on his cabinet and was among the advisors for the construction of the Iolani Palace. He purchased 20,000 acres of land on Lana'i and obtained leases on more. By 1863 there were about 600 Mormons living on Lana'i. In 1864 when the church elders arrived to visit, they discovered that Walter had purchased additional lands with the church money but had listed ownership under his own name, and he wasn't willing to release them. He was quickly expelled from the church and the Mormons went on to develop their church on O'ahu. As owner of 26,000 acres Gibson first established the Lana'i Sheep Ranch which later became the Lana'i Ranch. In 1867 the population was 394 people (the 600 Mormons had departed earlier), 18,000 goats and 10,000 sheep. In 1870 Gibson attempted a cooperative farm, but this operation soon proved unsuccessful. By 1875 Gibson was controlling 90 percent of the island for ranch or farming operations. In 1874, Gibson's daughter Talula married Frederick Harrison Hayselden, formerly of England and Australia, and by the early 1880s Frederick was managing the ranch. Walter Gibson died in San Francisco in 1888 and ownership of the land transferred to his daughter, Talula Hayselden, and his son-in-law Frederick.

By 1894 the Lana'i Ranch now ran 40,000 sheep, 200 horses, 600 head of cattle in addition to large herds of goats, hogs and wild turkeys. However, by 1898 the ranch was in debt, but the sugar industry looked promising. The Hayselden's established the Maunalei Sugar Company on the island's windward coast. They begin by building three wells and a wharf at Kahalepalaoa for shipment of the cane to Olowalu on Maui for grinding. A railroad was also built between the wharf and Keomuku along with a two-story building, a store, boarding house, camp houses and barracks.

In 1802 a Chinese entrepreneur spent only one season attempting sugar cultivation in Naha from wild sugar cane. The Maunalei Sugar Company in nearby Keomuku did little better, lasting only a little more than two years. The Hayselden's constructed a six mile train track for transporting their sugar cane, however, they failed to heed the respect for the local culture and custom. Stones from an ancient heiau (temple) were used to build part of the railroad bed and then the disasters began. Their Japanese workers fell sick and many died. The ever important supply of drinking water went brackish and rain did not fall. Company records show the closure was due to lack of labor and water. The local population knew otherwise. Fred and Talula Hayselden soon left Lana'i.

On Lana'i we heard a report that the Maunalei Plantation House was transported to Maui and became Pioneer Inn, but this was not accurate. Apparently some years ago the Honolulu Star-Bulletin printed an article to this effect. G. Alan Freeland, son of Pioneer Inn's founder George Freeland, spoke with Lawrence Gay, the owner of most of Lana'i at the turn of the century, and was told that when the construction of the Pioneer Hotel was completed, the similar-designed building on the island of Lana'i was still standing.

In 1902 Charles Gay (a member of the Robinson family from Ni'ihau) and George Monro visited the island of Lana'i and Gay acquired the island at public auction for $108,000. He enlarged his holdings further through various land leases. Gay began making major improvements and bringing cattle from Kaua'i and Ni'ihau to his new ranch on Lana'i. In 1903 Gay purchased the remaining holdings from the Hayseldens and through land leases and other avenues, became the sole owner of the entire island. By 1909 financial difficulties forced Charles Gay to loose all but 600 acres of his farmland. On the remaining acres he planted pineapples and operated a piggery while moving his family from Koele to Keomuku.

In 1909 a group of businessmen that included Robert Shingle, Cecil Brown, Frank Thompson and others, purchased most of the island from Charles Gay for $375,000 and formed the Lana'i Ranch Company. At that time there were 22,500 sheep, 250 head of cattle, and 150 horses. They changed the emphasis from sheep to cattle and spent 200,000 dollars on ranch improvements. However, because the large herds were allowed to graze the entire island, destroying what vegetation was available, the cattle industry was soon floundering. The island population had dwindled to only 102 at the turn of the twentieth century with fifty people living in Koele (means farming) and the rest along the windward coastline in Keomuku. There were only thirteen men to work the entire cattle ranch, which was an insufficient number to manage the 40,000 head of beef on land that was over-grazed by the cattle, pigs and goats that roamed freely.

George Monro, a New Zealander by birth and who had visited the island in 1902, was asked to return by the new owners to manage the ranch. Soon after arrival he began instituting much needed changes. He ordered sections of the range fenced and restricted the cattle to certain areas while allowing other areas to regrow. He also ordered the wild pigs and goats to be rounded up and destroyed. In 1911 the large three million gallon storm water reservoir, now the beautiful reflecting pond, was built. In 1912 an effort to destroy the goat population began in earnest. The first year 5,000 goats were killed and an additional 3,300 more were destroyed by 1916. (It wasn't until the 1940s that the last pigs and goats were captured.) Sheep dogs were introduced to assist the cowboys. Water continued to be a major concern. An amateur naturalist, Monro noted that the Cook Island pine tree outside his home seemed to capture the mist that traveled past the island. Today, as in the days of Monro, there is only one Cook Island pine tree on the island. The tree planted in 1875 by Frederick Hayselden is the same one that stood outside of Monro's home and has become a noted Lana'i landmark. It remains a stately sight right outside the Koele Lodge. From that pine an idea was born, and Monro ordered the paniolos (Hawaiian cowboys) to carry a bag of Norfolk Pine seeds. They poked a small hole in the sack and, as they traveled the island on horseback, they left a trail of pines. The result is an island of more pine than palm. In 1914 the automobile age arrived on Lana'i in the form of a single 1910 Model T owned by George Monro.

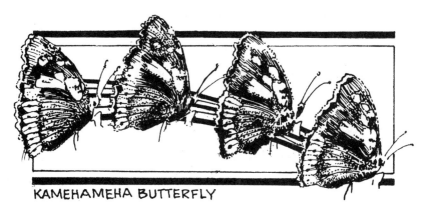

KAMEHAMEHA BUTTERFLY

By 1917 there were 4,000 head of cattle and 2,600 sheep, but profits were slim and the Lana'i Ranch Company sold its land to the Baldwin family for $588,000 and George Munro remained as foreman. The ranch slowly became more profitable. In 1920 axis deer were introduced on Lana'i from Moloka'i and a pipeline was constructed from Maunalei Gulch to provide additional sources of fresh water.

In 1920 James Dole came to Lana'i, liked what he saw, and purchased the island in 1922 for $1.1 million from Alexander & Baldwin. George Munro was retained as manager. Castle & Cooke acquired one third ownership in the Hawaiian Pineapple Company soon after. The Kaumalapua harbor was dredged and a breakwater constructed in preparation for shipment of pineapple to O'ahu for processing. Lana'i developed into the single largest pineapple plantation in the world, which produced 90% of the United States total pineapples. The company was called Hawaiian Pineapple Company until 1960 when the name was changed to Dole Corporation. In 1986 David Murdock became the major stockholder of Castle and Cooke and the chairman of the board. Today the company is called Dole Company Foods.

Also in the 1920s the community of Lana'i City began. The houses were very small, only large enough for the workers as families were discouraged. The workers arrived from Japan, Korea and the Philippines. The last residents left the Palawai Valley and moved to Lana'i City between 1917 and 1929. The population of Lana'i soared to 3,000 by 1930. In the 1950s larger homes, located below Fraser Ave., were built to accommodate the workers and their families and in the 1950s employees were given the option of purchasing their homes fee simple.

In 1923 Dole realized the need to provide a center for entertaining island guests and had "The Clubhouse" constructed. Today it is known as Hotel Lana'i. The dining room provided meals for guests as well as the nurses and patients from the plantation hospital. Also constructed in the center of town was Dole Park. The building in the middle was once a bowling alley, pool hall and restaurant until the late 1970s when it was made into a meeting hall. As a part of the development of Lana'i, David Murdock had a large new community center built, complete with swimming pool. It's located a block away from the park.

The word Manele means low area. The Manele boat harbor was once a small black sand beach and a fishing shrine found here indicates it was used by the early Hawaiians. You can spot the old pepe (cattle) ramp that Charles Gay used for loading his steers onto freighters. In the 1970s E.E. Black was contracted to build the breakwater. It is tradition for any new project in Hawai'i to be blessed at the onset, but E.E. Black chose to forgo the blessing. After only 20 feet of breakwater were constructed, the huge crane fell in the ocean and the people then refused to work. After great effort, another crane was brought over to lift the first from the ocean, but by the time it was recovered, the saltwater had taken its toll and it was worthless. Before resuming construction E.E. Black held a blessing ceremony, the people returned to work, and the breakwater was completed without further incident.

GETTING THERE

To reach Lana'i you may travel by air or sea. The Lana'i airport is serviced by Aloha Airlines, Aloha IslandAir, Hawaiian Air, Air Molokai and a newcomer Trans Air. There is no jet service. Airfare is about $60 one way from Lana'i to O'ahu. By boat you can travel a cool and comfortable 45-minutes from the Lahaina harbor aboard the Expedition. For a $25 one-way ticket, children $20, you can have a scenic tour, spotting dolphins, flying fish, and whales during the winter season. It is a pleasant way to travel, and much more affordable for a family than air transportation. The boat travels round trip (three times daily Mon - Wed. and four times Thurs - Sun.) to Manele Harbor where a shuttle van will pick you up for transport to the Manele Lodge and from there up to Koele Lodge. Reservations are advised as space is limited. Phone: 661-3756.

GETTING AROUND

A complimentary shuttle runs every hour between the Lodge at Koele and Manele Bay resort. Beginning on Friday afternoon at 3 p.m. the schedule increases to every half hour until Sunday afternoon. Depending on how busy they are, they run mini-vans or larger size school type buses. We found no trouble in asking for a van to run us into Lana'i City from the Lodge at Koele. Bikes are available at Koele for guests to use or enjoy a brisk 15 - 20 minute walk to downtown Lana'i City. For further independent exploration there are several rental car companies. Since many of the island's roads are unimproved and even a small rainshower can render dirt roads impassable, most guests are advised to rent one of the 4-wheel drive Trackers. They run about $100 per day and arrangements can be made through the concierge.

ACCOMMODATIONS - RESTAURANTS

There are currently three choices for hotel accommodations. Lana'i's original Hotel Lana'i and the two new luxury hotels, Manele Bay Resort and the Lodge at Koele. More on these three accommodations in the following sections.

CAMPING

Tent camping is available at Hulopoe Bay. Permits are issued by Castle and Cooke, at PO Box L, Lana'i City, Lana'i, HI 96762. Phone (808) 565-6661.

HOMES

Lana'i Realty can assist with furnished home rentals. They currently manage two properties. A 2 bedroom at $110 and a 2 1/2 bedroom at $125 per night. Deposit required and no credit cards. Contact Kathy Oshiro, Lana'i Realty, Box 67, Lana'i City, HI 96762, phone 565-6597. Office hours weekdays 8:30 until noon and 1:30 to 5:30 (Hawaiian time).

BED & BREAKFAST

Lucille Graham operates the island's only registered bed and breakfast facility, Lana'i Bed & Breakfast. She rents out two rooms of her three bedroom plantation style home. One room offers a queen size bed and the other a double plus a single bed. The two guest rooms share a half bath, although she tells us that seldom are both rooms rented at the same time. The shower room is also shared. Room rates are $45 for a single person, $50 for double occupancy, 3 adults are $75, and discounts are available for a family of three. Prices do not include the 9% room tax. Lucille might start your day off with her popular buttermilk oatmeal pancakes and then set you on your way with beach towels, snorkeling equipment and a jug of water. Contact Lana'i Bed & Breakfast, Box 956, Lana'i City, HI 96763. Phone (808) 565-6378. Her residence is at 312 Mahana Place in Lana'i City.

Another couple, Michael and Susan Hunter operate "Dreams Come True" offering three rooms in their home/art studio at 547 - 12th St. They also have a separate fully furnished home (2 bedroom plus separate cottage) with outside tubs and showers, enclosed fenced yard, for $175 for six. The second home can be rented as a bed and breakfast for a larger group. Continental breakfast provided, as well as airport pick up and drop off. A truck and a jeepster are available for rent. PO Box 525, Lana'i City, HI 96762. Phone (808) 565-6961.

For other information you might wish to contact the local visitor information center and speak with the very friendly and helpful Jeannie Mitchell. Destination Lana'i, PO Box 700, Lana'i City, 96763 (808) 565-7600.

HOTELS

HOTEL LANA'I
Hotel Lana'i, built in 1923, is also run by Castle and Cook. Before the opening of the new resorts, this ten room hotel had the only accommodations on the island. You'll still find it a quiet and comfortable accommodation with very basic rooms. The room prices surprised a number of people as in early 1992 they nearly doubled. Single or double occupancy $95, $10 per night additional person, tax not included. Children ages eight and under are free in room with parents. You'll want to book as far in advance as possible. For information or reservations write: Hotel Lana'i, PO Box A-199, Lana'i, HI 96763. (808) 565-7211 or toll free 1-800-624-8849.

The restaurant at the Hotel Lana'i is a popular place for island residents and it offers the only bar in town. Hours are 7:30 a.m. - 9 a.m. for breakfast, lunch is served 11:30 a.m. - 1:30 p.m. and dinner 6:30 p.m. - 8:30 p.m. Sunday they serve breakfast only 7:30 a.m. until noon and then dinner from 6:30 p.m. - 8:30 p.m.. The bar closes at 9 p.m. Dinners are a simple but varied assortment. "Peel & eat shrimp" appetizers or soup & salad bar $5 - $7 prime rib, stir fry chicken or shrimp, fresh fish and daily pasta specials $15 - $20. Meals include salad bar, white or brown rice, or potato of the day. Lunch offerings are burgers, sandwiches and daily specials $4.50 - $6. Breakfast $3 - $6. The food was simple and good, but not extraordinary, the service fast and friendly.

THE MANELE BAY RESORT

The resort is spread across the cliffside of Hulopoʻe Beach like an enormous Mediterranean Villa. It is a strikingly beautiful building with a pale blue tile roof. There are four buildings in the East wing and five in the West wing, and each is slightly different. The rooms are lined along sprawling walkways which meander through five lush courtyard gardens, each with a unique theme. The gardens include The Hawaiian, the Bromelaid, The Chinese, the Japanese and the Kaamaina Gardens. The original resort plan called for a 450 room hotel directly on the beach, but was revised to the current structure with 250 rooms on the cliff alongside the beach. Behind the resort a new 138 acre, 18 hole golf course is under construction. There was discussion of expanding the area and development of some condominiums, but for now that idea is on hold.

The Hulopoʻe Court is the more casual dining room serving breakfast, lunch and dinner, with a children's menu available. Breakfasts include fresh juices or fruits $4.25 - $8.25, continental breakfasts $9 - $10. Lunch selections offer unusual salads and soups like chilled papaya bisque with cinnamon croutons or avocado, tomato and artichoke salad $6.25 - $8.50. Main lunch courses feature grilled swordfish with red pepper, whole wheat noodles with roma tomatoes, artichokes, baby leeks and pecorio cheese $12.75 - $15.75. Dinner appetizers are a large selection of interesting taste treats running $6.50 - $10.50, pasta dishes in small or large plates $7.75 - $25, fresh hawaiian fish $26 - $28, or more traditional fare such as grilled veal chop with an osso bucco sauce, tiger prawns cooked in lemon olive oil $24. - $28.

The Ihalani, when it opens, will be the formal dining room at the Manele Bay Resort. The opening date has been delayed several times.

Hale Aheahe, which means House of Gentle Breezes, is located off the upper main lobby. There is an indoor lounge and outdoor veranda from which to enjoy nightly entertainment. Afternoon and evening entertainment is also provided in the Kailani Terrace, the lower lobby area. The Pool Grill opens at 11 a.m. and serves sandwiches and salads and a children's menu is also available here.

MANELE BAY RESORT

In many of the areas the ceilings have been given very special attention. In the main dining room are huge floral paintings, in the Hale Aheahe lounge you'll see fish and starfish. The resort took advantage of the undiscovered talent of the island residents and much of the artwork was done by local residents.

If you're thinking that maybe too much laying in the sun and fine food will affect your waistline, then hurry into the fitness studio. Open 6 a.m. - 6 p.m. there is plenty of equipment, then treat yourself to a steam room, massage, pedicure or facial.

This place is truly an island get-away. If our stay was any indication, then celebrities have quickly found Lana'i to be a convenient and luxurious retreat. Both Kevin Costner and Billy Crystal were guests during our brief stay.

We enjoyed the proximity to the beachfront, but the pool seemed the place to be and lounges were filled by mid-afternoon. It seems here on Lana'i, there is no reason to hurry. The pool water is slightly warm, yet delightfully refreshing and, if the Hawaiian sun becomes to hot, pool staff are on hand to provide chilled towels or atomizers of spring water facial spritzers. Attendants from the adjoining restaurant circulate taking drink and sandwich orders. The poolside restaurant was a little pricey, but the portions large and even the fish sandwich featured the fresh catch. We noted with appreciation that they provided a more economical children's menu here as well as in their main dining rooms.

The rooms are spacious, a bit larger than the standard rooms at Koele and each wing differs slightly in decorating style. Our wing had bright, bold yellow wall coverings and bedspreads accented with very traditional furniture. The bathroom amenities thoughtfully included suntan lotion and moisturizer in a little net bag to take along to the pool or beach. Rooms have a private butler mini-refrigerator.

Room rates begin at $325 for oceanview, oceanfront and mini suites run upwards of $500 and their presidential suite runs $1200. (That is per day.) Full American Plan (Breakfast, lunch and dinner) or Modified American Pflan (Breakfast Dinner) are available. Prices through the end of 1993 for FAP are $115 adult, $30 child 8 years and under. MAP $90 adults, $25 child 8 and under.

Reservation information is available from Rock Resorts, Inc., PO Box 774, Lana'i City, HI 96763. Phone 565-7300.

LODGE AT KOELE
The Lodge at Koele is not what a visitor might expect to find in Hawai'i. Guests arrive via a stately drive lined with Norfolk pine to this Victorian era resort that typifies turn of the century elegance. The inscription on the ceiling of the entry was painted by artist John Wullbrandt and translates "In the center of the Pacific is Hawai'i. In the center of Hawai'i is Lana'i, In the heart of Lana'i is Koele" and Lana'i may quickly find its way into your heart as well.

The rug in the entry is circa 1880, made of Tibetan wool. The Great Hall features enormous natural stone fireplaces that hint at the cooler evening temperatures here in upcountry Lana'i. The twin fireplaces on either side of the lobby are the largest in the state of Hawaii and the Lodge itself sets the record for being Hawai'i's biggest wooden structure. The high beamed ceilings give the room a spacious character, yet the atmosphere is welcoming and the comfortable furnishings invite you to sit and linger. Designer Joszi Meskan of San Francisco spent more than two years securing the many beautiful artifacts from around the world. A descriptive list is available from the concierge. The Great Hall's rug was handmade in Thailand for the resort and utilizes 75 different colors. Some of the furniture are replicas, but many pieces are antiques, including the huge altar desk where steaming morning coffee awaits the guests. Be sure to notice the two exotic chandeliers, with playful carved monkeys amid the leaves, designed for the great hall by Joszi Meskan. The large portrait on one end of the Great Hall is of Madame Yerken, painted by Belgian artist Jan Van Boern in 1852. An intricately stenciled border runs around the perimeter of the ceiling with antelope, deer and wild turkeys. Another more subtle stenciling is done around the floors. The skylights are beautiful, etched glass. The furnishings are covered in lush brocade tapestries and suede upholstery in hues of burgundy, blues and greens. The room is accented with fresh flowers, many of them orchids grown in the greenhouse located beyond the reflecting pool. The woodwork is finely carved, with pineapples often featured. At the end of an exhausting day of vacationing, there is nothing like curling up in the big overstuffed armchair next to a crackling fire with an after dinner drink to enjoy the evening entertainment, play a game of checkers or visit with local women as they demonstrate Hawaiian quilting. Green is the color theme throughout the resort with the bellman, concierge and front desk staff crisply attired in pine green suits.

Surrounding the main building is a wonderful veranda with comfortable rattan furniture and accented by Hawaiian quilted pillows. (Similar pillows, by the way, are for sale through the concierge, $100 each.) Huge trees hug the building and the view of the horses and fields beyond has a tranquilizing effect. The setting is truly picture perfect.

Several public rooms surround the Great Hall. The library overlooks spacious lawns and offers newspapers from around the world as well as books, backgammon and chess. A large screen television shows movies in the evenings with popcorn. The trophy room also has an assortment of board games and an interesting, but very uncomfortable, English horn chair. Both of these rooms have

KOELE LODGE

fireplaces which can be lit at the request of the guests. A music room and tea room on the other side of the lobby host afternoon tea served daily between 3 - 5 p.m. and pupus (appetizers) from 5 - 7 p.m. A slide show depicting the history of Lana'i is offered several times a week.

Adjoining the Great Hall is the Terrace Dining Room, open for breakfast, lunch and dinner. The food is excellent and the service outstanding. In fact, the restaurants at the Lodge at Koele could very possibly be the best in all of Hawai'i. We were also very pleased that they provided a children's menu which offered a varied dinner selection priced $5 - $6. The formal dining room, open for dinner only, is tucked away in the corner of the resort and requires a jacket and tie for the gentlemen. Restaurant chef, Darin Schulz makes excellent use of the five acre organic farm to ensure the freshest ingredients in his meal preparations. Herbs, white eggplant, purple turnips, yellow teardrop tomatoes are among the many varied crops. Simple foods with unusual ingredients and elegant presentations are the key here.

Breakfast at the Terrace Dining Room might include Lana'i axis deer sausage, waffles with a lilikoi coconut chutney, or breakfast bread pudding with cinnamon berry sauce. Available are full breakfasts $8 - $12.75 or a la carte items. Lunch is another dining experience extraordinaire. Sample a toasted sandwich of lobster, avocado and gruyere cheese $12.50, peppered breast of chicken club sandwich with Koala bacon $10.50 or seared ahi on a salad of field greens $15. Dinner entrees offer a mixed grill of lobster, prawn sausage and herb skewered scallops with a stew of country ham, white beans and winter greens $30, or fricassee of rabbit with fresh noodles and foie gras carrot dauphinoise and macadamia spaetzel $29. Any of the many varied choices will not disappoint your pallet!

This was once the site of the farming community known as Koele and the pine lined driveway was planted in the 1920s and led to the 20 or 30 homes in this area. Only two remain on the property and are owned by the Richardson family, descendants of the early Lana'i paniolos. The church was moved to the front grounds of the Lodge and a small schoolhouse is being restored and converted into a museum.

The grounds of this country manor are sprawling and exquisitely landscaped. More than a mile of lush garden pathways and an orchid house can be enjoyed while strolling the grounds. The large reflecting pond was once the reservoir for the town of Koele. There are plenty of activities to be enjoyed from strolling the grounds to swimming or just relaxing in the jacuzzi's. (See WHAT TO DO for more information.) In fact, it is so relaxing and so lovely, that we didn't even miss the beach. But if you're hankering for some sand and sun, it is only a 25 minute shuttle trip to the shore.

Maids in starched black & white add to the elegance and the uniformed staff are very friendly and courteous. We were impressed with the quality of service at the Lodge. It is also pleasing to know that the development of the tourist industry on Lana'i has meant a return of many of the island's young people.

There are 102 guests rooms at the Lodge and they are artistically decorated in three different fresh, bright color schemes. The artwork that lines the corridors was done by some of the many talented Lana'i residents and each floor has a different theme. The beds feature a pineapple motif and were custom made in Italy then handpainted by Lana'i artisans. The floral pictures on each door were painted by the postmaster's wife! The bathrooms have Italian tile floors and vivid blue marble counter tops. Room amenities are thoughtfully packaged and include an array of fine toiletries. There are in-room televisions with video recorders and a couple of beautifully carved walking sticks in the closet tempt the guest to enjoy one of those leisurely walks around the grounds.

The Garden Rooms ($275) are located on the ground floor and are slightly less expensive than the Koele Rooms ($295), which are the same size, but on the second floor. The Plantation Rooms ($350) are slightly larger. The Plantation Suites ($700) have a wrap around lanai and a separate living and sleeping area with a murphy bed in the living room. The Plantation Room and Plantation Suite can be combined into one large living area. The Banyan Suites ($425 - $700) provide separate living room and sleeping areas, an oversized lanai plus the added luxury of private butler service. These rooms are located along the balcony above the Great Hall and are the only guest rooms that are air conditioned. They are slightly larger than the regular rooms and just as beautifully decorated. Whether your luggage needs packing, a bath needs to be drawn, a dinner reservation is required or a suit needs pressing, the butler is ready to assist. The butlers are schooled for a year and must pass rigorous testing before being licensed. Full American Plan (Breakfast, lunch and dinner) or Modified American Plan (Breakfast - Dinner) are available. Prices through the end of 1993 for FAP are $115 adult, $30 child 8 years and under. MAP $90 adults, $25 child 8 and under. Reservation information is available from Rock Resorts, Inc., PO Box 774, Lana'i City, HI 96763. Phone 565-7300.

As much as we enjoyed the Manele Bay Resort, we found something very appealing about this Lodge in upcountry. Perhaps it was because the service was so superb, perhaps it was because the air was so fresh, perhaps it was the comfortable and homey quality of the great hall, or perhaps it was because we truly were in the heart of Lana'i. This resort had a special quality, and both kids and adults in our group were enchanted. Our visit will long be a fond memory... that is until we visit once again!

KOELE LODGE GROUNDS

SHOPPING - LOCAL EATING

There are two grocery stores from which to choose. *Richard's*, which has the honor of being on Lana'i since 1946, and the small *Pine Isle Market*. Since everything must be brought in by barge, prices are steep. Don't be surprised if they are closed for noontime siesta and shut for the day by 6 p.m. You won't find any fresh pineapple in the stores here. After working long hours in the field, the residents have little craving for this fruit. Visitors, however, can arrange through the concierge to order pineapples by the dozen to take home. The *Dis & Dat* shop is Lana'i's version of a souvenir shop. It does have a few T-shirts, some coffee mugs, and beach towels. Across the park is an art gallery called *Island Collections* operated by artist Steve Lance. This is the beginning of Lana'i's cultural center. Work by Lana'i artists and other island artists are on display. Just another building down is the workshop where island residents can come to pursue their artistic abilities. The building called S.T. Properties had us under the impression that inside would be a real estate office. We were pleasantly surprised to discover this was one of two local fast food restaurants and is locally known as *Tanegawa's*. Open for breakfast and lunch and closed for the day at 12:30, you can select a sandwich or burger $1.50 - $3, plate lunches $4 - $5 and breakfasts $4 - $5. The fare is filling and the atmosphere charmingly rustic. Next door is the only other casual dining spot in Lana'i City. The *Blue Ginger* serves up the best, freshly made pastries in town. (They also happen to be the only bakery!) Open at 5:30 a.m. for breakfasts which are surprisingly diverse for such an early hour! Eggs, pancakes and even waffles with blueberries, strawberries or macadamia nuts. Lunch includes sandwiches, local style plate lunches and saimin, dinners include steak, seafood and pizza. Prices are moderate. With the recent opening of the Blue Ginger, there are now two restaurants open for three meals a day, and Blue Ginger serves in-between meal hours too! HOURS: 5:30 a.m. - 9 p.m. Phone: (808) 565-6363.

The Hotel Lana'i has a restaurant, see description listed under the Hotel Lana'i section. The Lodge at Koele and the Manele Bay both have small sundry gift shops. There are also shopping excursions available to Lahaina. Leaving the Manele Harbor aboard the Expedition, you can arrange for a day of shopping in Lahaina town. Cost is $25 per person one way.

RECREATION

GOLF
There are several selections for the golfer on Lana'i. At Koele there is one 18-hole course, another 9-hole course and one stupendous 18-hole putting course. An additional 18-hole course is being developed at Manele.

The *Challenge of Manele*, which has yet to be completed, was designed by Jack Nicklaus and Greg Norman and will be a championship 18 hole course.

The 18-hole *Experience at Koele* was designed by Greg Norman and Ted Robinson. From a golfer's standpoint, Greg Norman assures the golfing guest that this course will require both skill and strategy and adds that it is the only course in Hawaii with Bent grass greens. The beauty of the course, he continues, with its lush natural terrain -- marked by thick stands of Norfolk pines -- and panoramic views will make concentrating on the game difficult for even the most expert golfer. The signature 8th hole of the Experience at Koele has a truly inspired setting. This is a 390 yard par 4 with a dramatic 200 foot drop in elevation from tee to green. The course is laid out on a multi-tiered plan. The upper seven holes meet the lower eleven at this sublime tee. From the top of the bluff at the eighth tee is a view so stunning that our first thought was that this could be right out of Shangrila. The mist floats by this enchanted valley, filled with lush vegetation and with a lovely lagoon. The lagoon at one time had served as a back up reservoir for the old cattle ranch. Now, while we are not golf aficionados, this single hole was enough to at least consider taking up the sport! Charges for either the Experience at Koele or the Challenge of Manele is $75 for resort guests, $130 for non-resort guests.

The Cavendish, a 9 hole, 36 par, 3071 yard course, (complimentary for guests of either resort) is located at the front of the Koele Lodge, was the island's first.

Golfers and non-golfers of all ages will delight in the executive 18-hole putting green at Koele. A beautifully manicured course with assorted sand traps and pools lined with tropical flowers and sculptures. Putt-putt will never be the same again! No charge.

TENNIS
There are plexipave courts at both Koele and Manele Bay. These are complimentary for use by hotel guests. Lessons are available at an extra charge. There is also a public course at Lana'i School in Lana'i City.

HORSEBACK RIDING
The Lodge at Koele has an impressive new stable. One hour beginners rides are $25 for ages 9 and older. The two hour plantation ride is $50. There are weight limits.

The horse drawn hay wagon was out of commission during our visit, but the Lodge at Koele hopes to reinstate this activity, so check with the concierge.

HIKING

Walking sticks are provided in all the rooms at the Lodge at Koele for guest usage. It's almost impossible to resist strolling around the pastoral grounds. Near the Koele Lodge are two small houses. These were originally located where the orchid house is now. The Richardson families live here, their ancestors were among the early Lana'i paniolos. You can stroll around the front grounds to view the enormous Cook Island pine or enjoy watching guests try their hand at lawn bowling, crochet or miniature golf. Walk down to the horse stables or peak inside the old church. The stables are new, but the church was relocated due to the construction of the Lodge. A small school was also moved and it is being currently being restored and perhaps will one day house Lana'i's first museum.

The Munro Trail is a 20 mile loop trek along the ridge of Lana'i. The view from the 3,370 ft. summit of Lanaihale can be spectacular on a clear day. This route can be tackled by four-wheel drive vehicles, but only during very dry conditions. For the adventurous, there is also the High Pasture Loop, the Old Cowboy Trail, Eucalyptus ladder or Beyond the Blue Screen. A light to moderate weight raincoat might be a good idea to take along if you're planning on hiking. The concierge can provide you with a map showing the various routes. Picnics can be provided by the hotel.

MISCELLANEOUS

Lawn bowling and both English and American croquet fields surround the Lodge at Koele. Guests can also borrow a mountain bike and ride into town, around the resort paths, or in the early morning or early evening they are allowed to ride along the golf course paths. One evening we followed one of the garden paths behind the putting green that led to a very steep golf cart track from the lower nine holes to the upper nine. It was so steep, in fact, that it proved quite a challenge to just walk the bikes up. After the journey up, we were delighted to find an ample supply of water and cups that reappeared every couple of holes on the golf course. Once on top we traveled around a few holes of the golf course which were fairly level. We were pleasantly surprised to find ourselves at the tee off for the 8th hole of the golf course, and as previously described, it was an inspired location. We then attempted to ride down from the tee to the green. The path down was so steep that it required brakes on full force to go slow enough to maintain control! Beyond is another picturesque lagoon and more golf cart trails to follow, again, on flat ground. The walk into town takes about 15 minutes at a fairly brisk pace, but only about 5 minutes by bike. Biking is a good option for seeing Lana'i City or if you want to sample some of Lana'i's local eateries.

Both resorts have wonderful swimming pools. The Koele pool, flanked by two bubbling jacuzzi's was seldom busy. The Manele pool is slightly larger and, at a lower elevation than Koele, became quite hot during the afternoon. The adjacent poolside restaurant provided refreshing drinks and light food fare, while pool attendants would circulate with chilled towels and spring water spritzer for a quick facial spray. Guests at the resorts have pool privileges at both facilities.

Scuba diving, fishing expeditions, raft trips and other ocean excursions can be arranged through the concierge at either resort. Half day raft trips (2 1/2 hr.) run $40 - $60. Half day (3 1/2 hr.) sailing and snorkeling trips depart three times daily and run about $80.

At both resorts, a sheet describing the activities for the next day are left in the room with the evening maid service.

LODGE AT KOELE -- There may be a pineapple cutting and tasting demonstration, a display of ancient Hawaiian weapons or an evening opportunity to visit with local women as they sew Hawaiian quilts. Each morning guests are invited to enjoy a complimentary hot beverage and just sit in the Great Hall and relax. High tea is served in the tea room each afternoon and in the evening there are complimentary pupus, also available in the tea room. The music room has an array of interesting musical instruments lining the wall. The grand piano here is for the use of guests. In the trophy rooms are board games, the library has books and evening movies and popcorn. Complimentary video tapes are available at the concierge for guests to view in their rooms. At night there is varied musical entertainment in the Great Hall. The twin fireplaces are ablaze and the overstuffed chairs invite you to just slow down. The fireplaces are lit, upon request, in the library, music or trophy room.

TOURS

Both Manele and Koele offer complimentary tours daily of their resorts. Just sign up at the concierge. The tour of Koele is especially informative and discusses the many unique pieces of art gracing the lobby. A worthwhile 30 minutes.

There is also a 1 1/2 - 2 hour guided island tour. It leaves from the Lodge at Koele and there is a $10 charge. Guests board a mini-van for a mini-tour of the island. Our guide was Joe, who had worked in the pineapple industry for many years before joining the resort staff. You'll learn a great deal about the island's history and see its more scenic points.

You can also take a historical tour without leaving the comfort of the Koele's music room. Several times a week guests are invited to a slide presentation depicting the early history of Lana'i.

WILIWILI

WHAT TO SEE

There are only three paved roads on Lana'i outside of Lana'i City, no stop lights, and very few street signs once you leave town. After driving around on even a dry day, we assure you that they aren't kidding when they recommend four wheel drive. On rainy days, you can be fairly certain you'll get stuck in the mud and muck! You can fairly well see all of Lana'i in a long day, but if you want to slow down, do some hiking, or simply sit in the sun on a quiet beach, there is plenty to occupy you for days. Either of the resorts can provide you with a map and advice. We were pleased that Pete Agliamo forfeited a day of fishing to act as a tour guide. Born in the Philippines, he has lived for 43 years on the island and worked for Dole driving pineapple trucks. Besides being an active fisherman he has hunted around the island for years and was a most knowledgeable guide. Leaving the driving to him was a delight as we cruised along the dirt roads and "talked story." Along the road to the Garden of the Gods we asked him if he was taking a short cut. Judging by the fact that we were zooming between pastures with cattle and abandoned pineapple fields with no street signs at all, we were certain we'd taken the back way, but he assured us we were on the main road. It seemed to us that it wouldn't be all that hard to get lost on Lana'i! Since there are no local quick marts, be sure you pack plenty of water and bring along a picnic, because we're sure you'll find the perfect spot to enjoy it.

We headed east and were pleasantly surprised to find the road to the **Garden of the Gods** was smooth, packed dirt that was free of ruts. We had been told that David Murdock had been on the island recently and taken guests down to Polihua Beach, so the road had been graded before his arrival. A 20 minute ride took us through a stand of ironwoods before we reached the large carved stone announcing our arrival in the Garden of the Gods. (And by the way, the stone had been carved by Pete's daughter!) We arrived during mid-day, but the best time to see this lunar-like and rather mystical place is early morning or late evening. In the early morning, on a clear day, you can see the faint outline of Honolulu's skyscrapers and a sharp eye can observe axis deer out foraging. The rays of the sun in the early evening cast strange shadows on the amber baked earth and huge monolithic rocks and your imagination can do the rest. Interestingly enough, here, in what

GARDEN OF THE GODS

seems to be the middle of nowhere, with no one in sight, and a peaceful stillness, (except for the occasional call of a bird or the wind brushing against your cheek) are street signs! One indicates Awailua Rd. which is a very rugged and steep dirt path down to the ocean. Most of these roads are used by the local residents for fishing or hunting. Be advised, if you attempt to start down, there may be no place to turn around should you change your mind. Follow Polihua Road and you'll arrive at a stretch of white sandy beach with rolling sand dunes. According to Lawrence Kainoahou Gay, in his account entitled "True Stories of the Island of Lana'i," the word Polihua means Poli (cover or bay) and hua (eggs). He reports that in this area turtles would visit to lay their eggs above the high water mark. He had seen turtles, in days gone by, that were large enough to carry three people! This beach is not recommended for safe swimming or other water activities. The Kaena Road winds down to a very isolated area called Kaena Iki Point, which is the site of one of Lana'i's largest Heiaus.

Shipwreck Beach, or Kaiolohia, on Lana'i's northeast coast, is about a half hour drive along a paved road from the Lodge at Koele. Enroute down you'll note that there are many little rock piles. At first glance they appear to be of some relic of the distant past, however, we were told that this idea began with the boyscouts that would come yearly to Lana'i yearly in the 1960's. The road is lined with scrub brush, and as you begin the descent to the shoreline you catch a glimpse of the World War II liberty ship. Be sure to keep an eye out for pheasant, deer, turkeys and the small Franklin partridges. At the bottom of the road you can choose to go left to Shipwreck Beach or continue straight and follow the coastline on the unpaved, dusty and very rugged Awalua Road to Club Lana'i. Club Lana'i is a day resort that shuttles visitors from Lahaina, Maui to the leeward shores of Lana'i for a day of relaxation and recreation sort of a Hawaiian version of Gilligan's Island. It's a bit of a drive and slow going. Four wheel drive vehicles are advised. It is about five miles down the road to Keomuku. There are still remnants of the failed Maunalei Sugar Company near Keomuku, and a Japanese cemetery, also a memento of the failed sugar company. The beaches are wonderful for sunbathing or picnicking, but not advisable for swimming, Beyond are Naha and Lopa, two uninhabited old villages. The old Kalanakila a ka Malamalama church is located near Keomuku, was recently renovated.There are also some ancient Hawaiian trails at Naha. The road ends at Naha and you will have to retrace your drive back the same route.

If you're headed for Shipwreck Beach, go left where the sign says "Federation Camp." This is Lapahiki Road, and while dry and bumpy during our drive, we understand a little precipitation can make it impassible except in a 4-wheel drive. The dirt road is lined by Kiawe trees and deserted little houses. This is a getaway spot for the local residents, although there is no fresh water. The reef along Kaiolohia Beach is very wide, but the surf can be high and treacherous. During a storm, waves come crashing down over the liberty ship that now sits on the reef. This was one of three Navy L.C.M.'s ships that were not shipwrecked, but purposely grounded in 1941-1942. The other two have disappeared after losing their battle to the ocean. Barges are also towed over, anchored and left to rot as well. The channel between here and Moloka'i is called Kolohi, which means mischievous and unpredictable. The channel between Lana'i and Maui is the 'Au'au channel which means to bathe. There were several ships that were wrecked here or on other parts of the island. In the 1820s the British ship *Alderman Wood* went aground; in 1826 the American ship *London* was wrecked off Lana'i. In 1931 George A. Crozier's *Charlotte C.* foundered somewhere along the beach. The 34 foot yawl called *Tradewind* was wrecked off the mouth of the Maunalei Valley on August 6, 1834 while cruising from Honolulu to Lahaina. There is a remnant of an old lighthouse and also some old petroglyph sites nearby. The concierge desk can give you a list of petrogylphs around the island. Please respect these sights. The beach is unsafe for swimming, but you might see some people shorefishing. Sometimes after storms, interesting shells, old bottles and assorted artifacts are washed up along the shoreline.

One area you probably won't visit is Pohaku "O" which roughly translates to mean rock. This is in the Mahana region of Lana'i on the island's leeward side. The rocks here resemble tombstones and were avoided by the early Hawaiians as a place of evil. In the evenings, and sometimes during the day if the breezes are favorable, the wind blowing by the rock creates an "O" sound that changes with the wind, which is the reason this rock received its evil connotations.

For another adventure, leave Lana'i City and follow Kaumalapau Hwy. past the small airport and continue on another five minutes toward Kaumalapau Harbor. It's paved all the way! The harbor isn't much to see, but the drive down to the water shows the dramatically different landscape of Lana'i's windward coastline. Here you can see the sharply cut rocky shoreline that drops steeply into the ocean, in some places more than 1,500 feet. The Kaunolu Bay can be accessed from the Kaumalapau Hwy. along a very, very rugged road. Follow the road just a bit further and you'll reach the harbor. The bulk of the island's materials come in by barge and barges were the route used to take the thousands of tons of pineapples to O'ahu for processing. Each pineapple crate weighed seven tons and a barge could haul 170 crates at a time. Today, pineapple production has become too expensive on Lana'i. Hawai'i is finding it hard to compete with countries such as the Philippines, where people are willing to work at a much lower daily wage and the fruit can be grown and processed for much less. In the past, freight was brought to Lana'i aboard the barges returning from Honolulu after delivering the pineapple. Today the Young Brothers have the contract for freight delivery.

Hulopo'e Beach is a splendid marine reserve along a crescent of white sandy beach is Hulopo'e Beach which fronts Manele Resort. It is also Lanai's best swimming beach. As with all beaches, be aware of surf conditions. There are attendants at the beach kiosk that can provide beach safety information. Although netting and spearfishing is not allowed, shorefishing is permitted. The best snorkeling is in the mornings before the surf picks up. Across the bay from the Manele Resort are a series of tidal pools. When the tide drifts down, sea creatures emerge making this a great spot for exploration. Reef shoes are available at the hotel's beach kiosk for resort guests, a recommended protection when prowling around the rocky shoreline. A climb up the bluff and you will be rewarded with a great view of Maui and Kaho'olawe. A large monolithic rock sits off the bluff. This is Pu'upehe (often referred to as Sweetheart Rock) that carries a poignant local legend.

As with most oral history, legends tend to take on the special character of the storyteller. Such is the story of Pu'upehe. We asked three people about the legend and heard three different versions. One made the hero into a jealous lover, the other a thoughtful one. So here is our interpretation. There was a strong handsome young Hawaiian man whose true love was a beautiful Hawaiian woman. They made a sea cave near Pu'upehe rock their lover's retreat. One day the man journeyed inland to replenish their supplies, leaving his love in the sea cave. He had gone some distance when he sensed an impending storm. He hurriedly returned to the sea cave, but the storm preceded him and his love had drowned in the cave. He was devastated. Using superhuman strength he carried her to the top of the monolithic rock called Pu'upehe and buried her there before jumping to his death. Whether there is truth to this legend is uncertain, but some years back a scientist did scale the top of the peak, which was no easy task, to investigate. No bones or other evidence was found, however, we were told that in ancient times, the bones were removed and hidden separately away. And so ends this sad tale of lost love.

Manele is a quaint boat port which offers excellent snorkeling just beyond the breakwater. When the surf at Hulopo'e is too strong, Lana'i tour boats often anchor here for snorkeling.

WILDLIFE

You'll notice very quickly that there are many, many birds on Lana'i. A far greater number than on Maui. Fortunately for the birds, Lana'i does not have mongoose as predators. Wild turkeys, the last non-native animal to be introduced to Lana'i, are hunted in early November for about two weeks. They are easily spotted, but we understand as soon as November 1st appears (the turkeys must have calendars) they disappear until promptly after Thanksgiving. These wild birds look very lean and don't appear to make a very succulent Thanksgiving dinner. The easiest place to spot them is down near the Manele boat harbor where a group of turkeys and a pack of wild cats together enjoy the leftovers from the Trilogy boat's daily picnics. Pheasant are also hunted seasonally. Wild pigs and goats were rounded up and captured years ago, so the only island pigs are now in the piggery where they are raised for island consumption. Pronghorn antelope, introduced in 1959, have now been hunted to extinction. Twelve axis deer were introduced by George Monro and have adapted well to Lana'i. It is estimated that there are some 3,000 - 6,000 animals and, given the fact that they produce offspring twice yearly, the numbers are ever growing. In fact deer far outnumber Lana'i's human population. The deer run a mere 110 - 160 pounds and are hunted almost year round. It is easiest to spot these lean, quick deer in the early mornings or late evenings bounding across fields, but during the day they seek sheltered, shaded areas. There are still a few remaining mouflon sheep, a crossbreed between a goat and deer, which have distinctive and beautiful curved horns. You'll note many of the houses in Lana'i City are decorated with arrays of horns and antlers across their porch or on a garage wall.

BEACHES IN BRIEF

Along Lana'i's Northern Shore is Polihua. There is an interesting stretch of long sand dunes. This coast is often very windy, and some days the blowing sand is intense. The surf conditions are dangerous and swimming should not be attempted, ever. Also along the Northern Shore is the area from Awalua to Naha. The beaches are narrow and the offshore waters are shallow with a wide reef, however, the water is often murky. Swimming and snorkeling are not recommended. Surf conditions can be dangerous. Lopa on the Eastern shore is a narrow white sand beach that can be enjoyed for picnicking and sunbathing.

Along the Western coastline is Kaunola, a rocky shore with no sandy beach and no safe entry or exit. Conditions can be dangerous. Swimming is not advised at any time. Also on the Western shore is Kaumalapau Harbor, the deep water harbor used for shipping. Water activities are not recommended at any time.

The southern coastline affords the safest ocean conditions. Manele Bay is the small boat harbor, however, water activity is not recommended due to heavy boat traffic. Hulopoe Bay is the island's best and most beautiful white sand beach. It is located in front of the Manele Bay Resort. It is popular for swimming, surfing, boogie-boarding and snorkeling. The tidepools make for fun exploration and although a marine preserve, shore fishing is permitted. On summer weekends the camping area is often filled with local residents. However, large swells, high surf conditions can exist. During times of high surf, undertows become very strong. Entry is hazardous during these conditions. During these times it is not safe to stand or play even in the shore break, as severe injury can occur. Be aware of water safety signs. There are no lifeguards on duty. However, there are attendants at the resort's beach kiosk who might be able to answer questions you have. Never swim alone and always exercise good water safety judgement.

MANELE - Manele also has varied daily activities. A tour of the resort is available and there is afternoon and evening entertainment in the lower lobby and the bar. Complimentary video tapes are available for guest use in their rooms and complimentary morning coffee is a pleasurable experience in orchid & coral lounges.

CHILDCARE

The Manele Bay has daytime childcare which can be used by Lodge guests as well. At the time of our visit it was complimentary and not in much demand. It may be that they will charge for it in the future. The 9 a.m. - 3 p.m. program is run by the pool staff and is a very casual affair where the children can play games or swim in the pool. Private babysitting is also available through the concierge for about $10 an hour.

RECOMMENDED READING

An excellent account of the history of the island is *"True Stories of the Island of Lana'i"* by Lawrence Kainoahou Gay, the son of Charles Gay. First published in 1965 and reprinted in 1981 it is available for $12 at the resort gift shops on Lana'i and probably could be obtained through bookstores on the neighbor islands as well.

RECOMMENDED READING

Ashdown, Inez. *Ke Alaloa O Maui. Authentic History and Legends of the Valley Isle.* Hawaii: Kama'aina Historians. 1971.

Ashdown, Inez. *Stories of Old Lahaina.* Honolulu: Hawaiian Service. 1976.

Barrow, Terence. *Incredible Hawaii.* Vermont: Charles Tuttle Co. 1974.

Begley, Bryan. *Taro in Hawaii.* Honolulu: The Oriental Publishing Co. 1979.

Bird, Isabella. *Six Months in the Sandwich Islands.* Tokyo: Tuttle. 1988

Boom, Bob and Christensen, Chris. *Important Hawaiian Place Names.* Hawaii: Bob Boom Books. 1978.

Chisholm, Craig. *Hawaiian Hiking Trails.* Oregon: Fernglen Press. 1989.

Christensen, Jack Shields. *Instant Hawaiian.* Hawaii: The Robert Boom Co. 1971.

Clark, John. *Beaches of Maui County.* Honolulu: University Press of Hawaii. 1980.

Daws, Gavan. *The Illustrated Atlas of Hawaii.* Australia: Island Heritage. 1980.

Echos of Our Song. Honolulu: University of Hawaii Press.

Fielding, Ann. *Hawaiian Reefs and Tidepools.* Hawaii: Oriental Pub. Co.

Haraguchi, Paul. *Weather in Hawaiian Waters.* 1983.

Hawaii Island Paradise. California: Wide World Publishing. 1987.

Hazama, Dorothy. *The Ancient Hawaiians.* Honolulu: Hogarth Press.

Judd, Gerrit. *Hawaii, an Informal History.* New York: Collier Books. 1961.

Kaye, Glen. *Hawaiian Volcanos.* Nevada: K.C. Publications, 1987.

Kepler, Angela. *Maui's Hana Highway.* Honolulu: Mutual Publishing. 1987

Kepler, Cameron B. and Angela Kay. *Haleakala, A Guide to the Mountain.* Honolulu: Mutual Publishing. 1988.

Kyselka, Will and Lanterman, Ray. *Maui, How it Came to Be.* Honolulu: The University Press of Hawaii. 1980.

Lahaina Historical Guide. Tokyo: Maui Historical Society. 1971.

Lahaina Restoration Foundation, *Story of Lahaina.* Lahaina: 1980.

London, Jack. *Stories of Hawaii.* Honolulu: Mutual Publishing. 1965.

Mack, Jim. *Haleakala and The Story Behind the Scenery*. Nevada: K.C. Publications, 1984.

Mrantz, Maxine. *Whaling Days in Old Hawaii*. Honolulu: Aloha Graphics. 1976.

Na Mele O Hawai'i Nei. Honolulu: University of Hawaii Press. 1970

Nickerson, Roy. *Lahaina, Royal Capital of Hawaii*. Hawaii: Hawaiian Service. 1980.

On The Hana Coast. Hong Kong: Emphasis Int'l Ltd. and Carl Lundquist. 1987.

Pukui, Mary K. et al. *The Pocket Hawaiian Dictionary*. Honolulu: The University of Hawaii Press. 1975.

Randall, John. *Underwater Guide to Hawaiian Reef Fishes*. Hawaii: Treasures of Time. 1981.

Smith, Robert. *Hiking Maui*. California. 1990.

Stevenson, Robert Louis. *Travels in Hawaii*. Honolulu: University of Hawaii Press. 1973.

Tabrah, Ruth. *Maui The Romantic Island*. Nevada: KC Publications. 1985.

Thorne, Chuck. *50 Locations for Scuba & Snorkeling*. 1983.

Titcomb, M. *Native Use of Fish in Hawaii*. Honolulu: University of Hawaii Press. 1952.

Twain, Mark. *Letters from Mark Twain*. Hawaii: University of Hawaii Press. 1966.

Twain, Mark. *Mark Twain in Hawaii*. Colorado: Outdoor Books. 1986.

Wallin, Doug. *Exotic Fishes and Coral of Hawaii and the Pacific*. 1974.

Westervelt, H. *Myths and Legends of Hawaii*. Honolulu: Mutual Publishing. 1987.

Wisniewski, Richard A.. *The Rise and Fall of the Hawaiian Kingdom*. Honolulu: Pacific Basin Enterprises. 1979.

"One cannot determine in advance to love a particular woman,

nor can one so determine to love Hawaii.

One sees, and one loves or does not love.

With Hawaii it seems always to be love at first sight.

Those for whom the islands were made,

or who were made for the islands,

are swept off their feet in the first moments of meeting,

embrace and are embraced."

Jack London

'OHI'A LEHUA

INDEX

HELICONIA, BIRD OF PARADISE   JANORA BAYOT

READER RESPONSE
ORDERING INFORMATION

Dear Reader:

We hope you have had a wonderful visit to Maui. Since this book expresses primarily our own opinions on accommodations, restaurants, and recreation, we would sincerely appreciate hearing of your experiences. Any updates or changes would also be welcomed. Please address all correspondence to Paradise Publications.

FREE! A complimentary copy of Paradise Publication's quarterly newsletter, *THE MAUI UPDATE*, is available (at no charge) by writing Paradise Publications (Attention: Newsletter Dept.) 8110 S.W. Wareham, Portland, OR 97223, and enclosing a self-addressed, stamped, #10 size envelope. Subscription is $10 annually.

MAUI, A PARADISE FAMILY GUIDE (Including the Island of Lana'i), by Greg & Christie Stilson. The island of Maui is one of Hawai'i's most popular. This guide is packed with information on over 150 condos & hotels, 200 restaurants, 50 great beaches, sights to see and travel tips for the valley island. All new! The island of Lana'i, as a part of the County of Maui, has been added to this popular guide. Lana'i recently joined the tourist industry with the opening of two fabulous new resorts. There is fine dining, local eateries, remote beaches, wonderful hikes and an enchantment unlike any other island. *"A down-to-earth, nuts-and-bolts companion with answers to most any question."* L.A Times. 320 pages, multi-indexed, maps, illustrations, $12.95. Fifth edition.

KAUA'I, A PARADISE FAMILY GUIDE, by Don & Bea Donohugh. Island accommodations, restaurants, secluded beaches, recreation and tour options, remote historical sites, an unusual and unique island tour, this guide covers it all. "If you need a 'how to do it' book to guide your next to Kaua'i, here's the one."..."*this guide may be the best available for the island. It has that personal touch of authors who have spent many happy hours digging up facts.*" Hawaii Gateway to the Pacific Magazine. 290 pages, multi-indexed, maps, illustrations, $12.95. Fourth edition.

HAWAI'I: THE BIG ISLAND, A PARADISE FAMILY GUIDE, by John Penisten. Outstanding for its completeness, this well-organized guide provides useful information for people of every budget and lifestyle. Each chapter features the author's personal recommendations and "best bets." Comprehensive information on more than 70 island accommodations and 150 restaurants. Sights to see, recreational activities, beaches, and helpful travel tips. 280 pages. Multiple indexes, maps and illustrations. 300 pages. $12.95. Third edition.

UPDATE NEWSLETTERS! *THE MAUI UPDATE, THE KAUA'I UPDATE,* and *HAWAI'I: THE BIG ISLAND UPDATE* are quarterly newsletters published by Paradise Publications that highlight the most current island events. Each features late breaking tips on the newest restaurants, island activities or special, not-to-be missed events. Each newsletter is available at the single issue price of $2.50 or a yearly subscription (four issues) rate of $10. Orders to Canada are $3 each or $12 per year.

Also available from Paradise Publications are books and videos to enhance your travel library and assist with your travel plans!

For a full listing of current titles send request to Paradise Publications. Prices are subject to change without notice.

BOOKS

MAUI, THE ROMANTIC ISLAND, and *KAUA'I, THE UNCONQUERABLE* by K.C. Publications. These two books present full color photographs depicting the most magnificent sights on each island. Brief descriptive text adds perspective. Highly recommended. 9 x 12, 48 pages, $5.95 each, paperback.

HALEAKALA and *HAWAII VOLCANOES* by K.C. Publications. Each fascinating and informative book is filled with vivid photographs depicting these natural volcanic wonders. A great gift or memento. 9 x 12, $5.95 each.

WHALES, DOLPHINS, PORPOISES OF THE PACIFIC by K.C. Publications. Enjoy the antics of these beautiful aquatic mammals through full color photographs and descriptive text. A great book for children!! 9 x 12, paperback, $5.95

SHARKS! by K.C. Publications. Loaded with incredible photography, this book describes the many varied predators of the deep. 9 x 12, paperback, $5.95.

HAWAIIAN HIKING TRAILS by Craig Chisholm. This very attractive and accurate guide details 49 of Hawaii's best hiking trails. Includes photography, topographical maps, and detailed directions. An excellent book for the outdoorsperson! 6 x 9, paperback, 152 pgs., $14.95. 1991.

KAUAI HIKING TRAILS by Craig Chisholm. New from Fernglen Press this 160 page book features color photographs, topographical maps and detailed directions to Kaua'i's best hiking trails. A quality publication. $12.95. 1991.

HIKING MAUI by Robert Smith. Discover 27 hiking areas all around Maui. 5 x 8 paperback, 160 pages. $8.95. Also by Robert Smith. *HIKING KAUA'I*, over 40 hiking trails throughout Kaua'i. 116 pages, $8.95. *HIKING HAWAII (The Big Island)*, 157 pages, $8.95, and *HAWAI'I'S BEST HIKING TRAILS*, 250 pages, $12.95, all six islands are included with a total of 42 trails. Black & white photographs and maps.

COOKING WITH ALOHA by Elvira Monroe and Irish Margah. Discover the flavors and smells of the Hawaiian islands in your own kitchen with this beautiful illustrated and easy-to-follow cookbook. Delicacies range from exotic pickled Japanese seaweed or taro cakes to flavorful papaya sherbet or chicken 'ono niu. Drinks, appetizers, main courses and desserts are covered. 9 x 12, paperback, 184 pages, $7.95.

VIDEOS   (All Videos are VHS format)

FOREVER HAWAII
This 60 minute, video portrait features all six major Hawaiian islands. (Note: Does not include coverage of the new resorts on Lana'i.) It includes breathtaking views from the snowcapped peaks of Mauna Kea to the bustling city of Waikiki, from the magnificent Waimea Canyon to the spectacular Halakeala Crater. A lasting memento. $29.95

FOREVER MAUI
An in-depth visit to Maui with scenic shots and interesting stories about the Valley Isle. An excellent video for the first time, or even the returning Maui visitor. 30 minutes. $24.95

FLIGHT OF THE CANYON BIRD
An inspired view of the Garden Island of Kaua'i from a bird's eye perspective; an outstanding 30 minute piece of cineamatagraphy. This short feature presentation explores the lush tropical rainforests surrounding Waialeale (the wettest spot on earth), the awesome Waimea Canyon and the Napili Coastline. The narration explores the geologic beginnings of the island and its historical beginnings as well. An outstanding presentation and a valuable tool for vacation preparation, a lasting memento or a gift! $19.95.

EXPLORE HAWAII: A TRAVEL GUIDE
The scenes are similar to that of Forever Hawai'i, but this is a very fast paced 30-minute tour of all six islands. One helpful feature of this tape is the way place names of the areas being viewed are displayed on the screen. A great way to learn correct Hawaiian pronunciations! $19.95.

*KUMU HULUA: KEEPERS OF A CULTURE
This 85-minute tape was funded by the Hawaii State Foundation on Culture and Arts. If you enjoy the hula and culture of Hawai'i, then this is the tape for you. The tape includes hulas from various troupes on various islands, attired in their brilliantly colored costumes. It explores the unique qualities of hula as well as explaining the history. A documentary style production with many wonderfully performed dances. $29.95.

*TARGET: PEARL HARBOR
This historical documentary includes eyewitness accounts of survivors of the December 7, 1941 attack. Featuring a dramatic narrative with actual footage and modern reenactment. This tape was released to commemorate the 50th anniversary of the Pearl Harbor Attack. $29.95

*WHALE SONG
The majestic humpback whales have chosen Hawai'i as their winter paradise. Join Lloyd Bridges as he narrates this excellent video which explores the world of cetaceans. Dolphins and whales are intelligent mammals that are portrayed in their undersea home with rare footage. 40 minutes. $24.95.

*HULA - LESSONS ONE AND TWO
"Lovely Hula Hands" and "Little Brown Gal" are the two featured hulas taught by Carol "Kalola" Lorenzo. She explains the basic steps of the hula. Kalola, born on the island of Maui, has been singing and dancing since she was six. A fun and interesting video for the whole family. 30 minutes. $19.95.

SHIPPING

In the Continental U.S.-- Please add $4 for 1 to 4 items (books or videos). Each additional item over 4, please add $1. Orders shipped promptly by UPS (United Parcel Service). Addresses which are Post Office boxes will be shipped U.S. Mail, first class. If you'd prefer items shipped bookrate mail, we'll be happy to quote you shipping costs.

Hawai'i and Alaska -- Please add $4 for the first book/tape, $1 each additional book/tape when shipped to the same address. Orders shipped U.S. first class mail.

Canadian Orders -- Please add $4 for the first book and $1 each additional book/tape. Orders shipped U.S. airmail.

NOTE: UPS overnight or two-day airmail service is available. Call for quotes. For larger orders, we can ship by other means. Call for shipping quotes. Generally all books/tapes will be sent out within 24 hours. Those which are a special order item (indicated by an "*") may require additional shipping time; 4 -6 weeks in some cases.

A GIFT? We'd be happy to forward books as a gift. Simply supply us with the name and address. If you'd like to enclose a personal note, please do so, or we can provide one for you.

Please include your check or money order with your order. We can accept Visa or Mastercard orders also.

PARADISE PUBLICATIONS
8110 S.W. Wareham, Suite 202
Portland, Oregon 97223
Phone or FAX (503) 246-1555